Polyculturalism and Discourse

At the Interface

Series Editors
Dr Robert Fisher

Advisory Board

Professor Margaret Chatterjee
Dr Wayne Cristaudo
Dr Mira Crouch
Dr Phil Fitzsimmons
Dr Jones Irwin
Professor Asa Kasher

Dr Martin McGoldrick
Revd Stephen Morris
Professor John Parry
Professor Peter L. Twohig
Professor S Ram Vemuri
Revd Dr Kenneth Wilson, O.B.E

Volume 39

A volume in the *At the Interface* project
'Diversity and Recognition'

Probing the Boundaries

Polyculturalism and Discourse

Edited by

Anja Schwarz
and
Russell West-Pavlov

Amsterdam - New York, NY 2007

The paper on which this book is printed meets the requirements of "ISO 9706:1994, Information and documentation - Paper for documents - Requirements for permanence".

ISBN: 978-90-420-2307-9
©Editions Rodopi B.V., Amsterdam - New York, NY 2007
Printed in the Netherlands

Contents

Introduction ix
Russell West-Pavlov and Anja Schwarz

Coming to Terms with Genocidal Pasts in
Comparative Perspective:
Germany and Australia 1
A. Dirk Moses

„Ein komplexes und wechselhaftes Spiel":
Sprachliche Resignifikation in
Kanak Sprak und Aboriginal English 31
Steffi Hobuß

Strategic Uses of Multiculturalism in
Germany and Australia 67
Anja Schwarz

Privileged Discourses of Hate in Australia
and Germany: the Holocaust and the
Stolen Generation 91
Katharine Gelber

Discourses of Uprooting, Discourses of
Re-Routing. Autobiographical Discourse
and Cultural Nomadism in
Foucault, Castro and Flusser 121
Russell West-Pavlov

Towards another Modernity? Multicultural
Discourse in German and Australian Film
from the 1970s to the 1990s 161
Tim Mehigan

"We will decide who comes to this country":
Inclusion, Exclusion and the National
Imaginary   177

Fiona Allon

Von der Expansion zur
Lokalisierung der Wissenschaften in
multikulturellen Gesellschaften:
Australische und Europäische Erfahrungen   203

Ulrich Lölke

Negotiating Nationhood in Multi-Ethnic
Germany: an Australian Perspective   225

Nicholas K. White

The Pacific Solution meets Fortress Europe:
Emerging Parallels in
Transnational Refugee Regimes   247

Justine Lloyd and Anja Schwarz

Index   271

Notes on Contributors   277

Welcome to *At the Interface/Probing the Boundaries*

By sharing insights and perspectives that are both inter-disciplinary and multi-disciplinary, *ATI/PTB* publications are designed to be both exploratory examinations of particular areas and issues, and rigorous inquiries into specific subjects. Books published in the series are enabling resources which will encourage sustained and creative dialogue, and become the future resource for further inquiries and research.

Polyculturalism and Discourse is a volume which inaugurates a research project of the same title. The theoretical strand which unifies the project is the role of discourse as a social instance which structures knowledge and action of social actors, but which can also be appropriated by them and reworked in their own interests. The individual sub-projects thus pay particular attention to questions of the control, circulation, ownership and contestation of discourses within these two societies. The research group will be collaborating on a number of publications and is committed to exploring the issues of discourse, multi- and polyculturalism in the Australian German contexts understood as discursive interventions in the public sphere.

Dr Robert Fisher
Inter-Disciplinary.Net
www.inter-disciplinary.net

Introduction

In the wake of the murder of the Dutch filmmaker Theo van Gogh and a series of arson attacks on churches and mosques in the Netherlands in November 2004, a debate about the 'integration of foreigners' resurged in Germany. Politicians from across the party spectrum called upon 'foreigners' to display their (ostensibly inadequate) allegiance to 'mainstream German cultural values', to abandon their putative 'parallel societies', and to learn German (a demand addressed, in strictly logical terms, to those who would not understand it, and thus a sort of negative self-fulfilling prophecy which created the refractory constituency it targeted.). Angela Merkel, then chairperson of the conservative Christian Democratic Union, and the country's current chancellor, declared on 24 November 2004, "Die multikulturelle Gesellschaft ist grandios gescheitert" – "Multicultural society has failed magnificently". In the face of what is clearly a multi-ethnic everyday reality such 'talk' is not 'descriptive'. One is therefore obliged to ask, To what end are such statements uttered? What is their intention? To whom might such comments be addressed? How are they received? What reactions or responses do they elicit? Who explains, comments, glosses, interprets such words, and in which contexts?

Such 'talk' about migration, cultural diversity and national identity in the German context is clearly situated within mainstream political discourse, a mainstream both reflective and productive of a broad consensus within German society on these issues. It remains to a large extent hegemonic, and has until now ensured that the German state continues in its reluctance to accept multiple cultural affiliations on the part of its citizens, while at the same time belonging to a Europe which is increasingly dismantling national borders, and a world where polylingualism and polyculturalism are the rule rather than the exception. But this sort of 'talk' is also subject to vehement and ongoing contestation and happens in other places, not just within the political arena. By being repeated, replicated, inflected, contested across the spectrum of social topographies, it remains open to modification and transformation. The range of 'talking places' in society is too great and complex for the hegemony of a particular form of 'talk' or discursive strand ever to be absolute.

We take this example because it formed the immediate context in which this project was conceived. Any number of other examples – say the debate which broke out in Australia at roughly the same time, following a further indigenous 'death in police custody', subsequent riots and lynchings of indigenous youth in rural Queensland – might afford material for the questions about the structure and functioning of political and public discourse posed above. More importantly, such discourses in the public realm, in their very immediacy, form the ambient context in which this volume of essays intends (to the extent that such a mode of communication is capable of this) to intervene.

Foucault once said that discourse represented a "violence done to things", a way of working in the world.[1] It is the interlocking disparity between the 'non-discursive realm' and discursive events, but also the manner in which the latter can mould and inflect the former, which interests us here. How does 'talk' in its regularity and materiality as event, whether verbal or printed or mediatic, work upon other forms of 'talk' or upon the world of actions? More specifically, how does discourse on polyculturalism in contemporary society influence the manner in which people from diverse cultural and ethnic backgrounds think and talk about their everyday lives?

We are convinced that most of what is done in the world of politics and social interaction is governed by regimes of discourse. These regimes are made up by the regular and regulated patterns of speech acts in the public realm which make certain policies and actions conceivable and legitimise or contest them – from the protocols that guide the structures and routines of action, to the ways in which that action is commented, judged, and perhaps subsequently modified in the light of reactions and responses to it. Whether Foucault's theory of discursive events and of the discursive archive in the 1960s and 1970s, or Butler's recent work in the 1990s on discursive performativity and reiteration, discourse theory has been marked by a double conviction: first, that discourse does not just describe the world from outside, but models and moulds the social practices which it pervades, as well as the bodies it interpellates, bestowing them with social existence; and secondly, that because discourse is not outside worldly practices, but threaded through them and providing the fabric of their meaning, it is not merely an archive or a set of rigid scripts or programmes, but open, in its very 'iterativeness', to modification between one temporal instance of a discursive structure and another. It might, as Butler argues in *Excitable Speech*, even come to 'inaugurate in language' speakers using the hegemonic terms in ways that counter the intention of the initial speech act.[2] Discourse takes effect on social actors and their world, but they can also take effect on discourse, not as 'sovereign subjects' but as actors whose agency reflects the way they are constituted in language; these actors operate within an unstable linguistic field of constraints from the very outset. The chapters in this volume explore the implications of that double notion with reference to for what we call 'polyculturalism'.

This term itself exemplifies that principle. We have opted to eschew using the more obvious term 'multiculturalism' because, as Anja Schwarz demonstrates in her article in this volume, that word is unstable, possessing quite different significations depending upon its usage in varying cultural and political contexts and at various points in their specific national contexts. Multiculturalism is a term which is constantly being 'reiterated', that is, picked up in a given discursive context and re-inflected by the discursive practices of warring discourse-users. With this in mind, we coined what we assumed to be a new term, 'polyculturalism' in the hope of being able to relaunch this necessary and important debate on terrain less congested by an aggregate of conflicting prior discursive usages. The desire for such new terms is a recurrent feature of this discursive field: an area of public debate massively overdetermined by utterances from a range of speakers striving once and for all to settle the 'true meaning' of multiculturalism. Thus distinctions are often made between 'de facto'- or 'small-m' multiculturalism which is said to address the multicultural reality of contemporary societies and 'capital M' Multiculturalism, denoting political agendas addressing this reality.

We do not intend to fill 'polyculturalism' with any such meanings. Indeed, we wished to preserve a certain degree of 'play' in the term chosen. At the same time however, we did not coin it with the intention of 'stepping out of the ring', in the ingenuous belief that there is some 'objective' site of academic discourse which would not be tainted by the corrosive influence of 'power-knowledge'. And, in fact, a simple keyword search in the internet demonstrated this impossibility in a telling manner. The search revealed that members of a neo-conservative US-American internet forum had indeed been using the term for some time and were debating its viability as a discursive tool in countering what they perceived to be a left-wing multiculturalist agenda (in the US, similarly to Germany, multiculturalism has never been sanctioned through government policy on the federal level, thus making the term more vulnerable to such attacks than in the Australian context).

Conversely, the term 'policulturalism' has been employed by scholars working within the South African post-Apartheid context to refer to a field of discursive debate in which a myriad of new histories have been released into the public domain. The demise of pre-1994 censorship has allowed the emergence of many once-repressed forms and genres of histories, all too often reified and commodified under the neo-liberalism which swiftly followed in the wake of political liberalization. 'The prefix marks two things: plurality and its politicization.'[3] A 'policultural' field of disparate discourses would be characterized neither by the reduction of difference to trademarking in a discursive realm in which heritage and ethnicity are immediately recuperated by a commodifying market, nor to the artificial foreclosure or fallacious resolution of dissonance through a rhetoric of legal settlement evinced, for instance, in the Truth and Reconciliation Committee. 'Policulturalism' in this context indexes a stubbornly uncompromising and open-ended engagement between the many ethnic fractions and their irreducibly specific histories: "A form of cultural dissensus and alterity", to appropriate Bhabha's formulation, "where non-consensual terms of affiliation may be established on the grounds of historical trauma".[4] It refers to a debate which resists the erasure of discursive difference precisely because this is the very factor that furnishes the grounds for genuine discursive interaction.[5]

Precisely this is the manner in which we have intended in our choice of such a neologism. Our employment of the term 'polyculturalism' for this publication, instead of attempting to ascribe to it a specific meaning, is therefore intended to destabilise any notions of a seemingly 'given' meaning. Rather, our usage aims to re-open a space in which the workings of discourse, both as archive or practice, and as intervention, can be considered in greater depth. The inter-cultural perspective shared by all essays in this volume contributes to this goal: whereas the majority of discourse analytical work addresses the diversity of speaking positions, as well as the arbitrariness of ascribed meanings, within a historical framework delimited by national boundaries, the texts collected here transgress this perspective in working comparatively between Australia and Germany. While not eschewing the historical dimension championed by Foucault and others, they show that the aspirations of discourse analytical work can equally be achieved by comparing similar discursive fields in different countries.

The jocose question of 'How to do things with words' (the title of Austin's famous 1962 treatise on speech acts) admirably points to the way in which discourses influence all levels of social practice down to the most microscopic details of our intimate bodily habitus. We believe that for this reason, academic discourse has a participatory role to play in entering the fray and getting its hands dirty. What sort of impact academic discourse may make upon other discourses is a moot point. Whether academic discourse *has* an impact is beyond dispute. The question lies elsewhere. The real issue regarding academic talk and writing is that of the degree to which productive interactions and translations come about. The question is one of the why and wherefore, determined by the sorts of other discourses academic speech acts connect and interact with, the ways in which those meetings happen, and the discursive and non-discursive results which emerge from these meetings. The nexus of interdiscursive encounters between the academic and the extra-academic field is far too complex to be dismissed with tired gestures towards the ivory tower.

This volume gathers ten scholars whose transdisciplinary work consistently evinces a dual focus. The core group of researchers in the 'Polyculturalism & Discourse' consortium are based in German and Australian universities and thus their common context forms the focus of this first volume in the series. Their contributions, which will be summarised briefly below, reflect a wide range of disciplinary affiliations at the same time as evincing, on the one hand, a shared commitment to pursuing a politically informed discourse analysis, and on the other hand, an interest in comparative modes of analysis performatively embodying a 'polycultural' methodology. All the contributions to this volume are of comparative nature, combining perspectives upon the Australian and German contexts of polycultural discursive practices. Later volumes will broaden the focus of the analysis, so as to make the consortium a genuinely transnational community with fluid boundaries and a nomadic gaze upon diverse 'polycultural realities'.

A. Dirk Moses undertakes a comparison of the process of confronting genocide in Australia and Germany in the contemporary period. He contends that half a century of 'working through' the Nazi era and the Holocaust in Germany can offer fruitful perspectives for the much more recent Australian debate on 'genocide' perpetrated against the indigenous population in the two centuries since the white settlement and/or invasion of Australia in 1788. Moses argues that these debates are so heated – both on the right and on the left – because the affect the myths of origin of both the German and the Australian nations and their respective collective self-images. The chapter analyzes the various discourses at work at both ends of the political spectrum in the two national contexts, concluding that the similarities between them are significant enough to permit helpful comparisons. Neither national debate can be seen as conclusive, however, so long as demands for reparation and compensation on the part of the victims remain partially unanswered – as is the case both in Australia and Germany.

Steffi Hobuß's essay performs a comparison of contemporary intercultural language development. Her essay searches for the 'implicit philosophies of language' in 'Kanak Sprak' in Germany and Aboriginal English in Australia. In each of these linguistic contexts she finds the practice of 'resignification' at work. The chapter uses Foucault's and Butler's theories of discourse to outline a theory of active 'resignification' which is then explored with reference to 'Kanak Sprak' and the work of Mudrooroo and Phillip Gwynne. Hobuß's chapter demonstrates that 'fictionality' allows a significant realm of linguistic creativity and 'intervention' within the space of hegemonic discourse – but at the same time that such discursive contestation also reaches back into the realm of real political practice, with real implications for all social actors, whether privileged 'white' or 'marginalized'.

Anja Schwarz's chapter undertakes an analysis of German and Australian discourse on these two nations' de facto cultural diversity by highlighting the different ways in which both societies have made sense over the past decades of socio-political terms such as assimilation, integration and, more importantly, multiculturalism. Her comparative study, situated on the level of political vocabulary, shows how the meaning taken on by these terms does not simply derive from the political reality they are said to address. Rather, their denotations depend on the political convictions and tactics of the respective speakers, as well as their positioning within in the discursive field they engage in. Employing a chronology of the Australian employment of the expressions 'assimilation', 'integration' and 'multiculturalism' as analytical backdrop, she offers a comparative perspective on the German use of the term multiculturalism. This approach can – at least partly – explain the expression's highly controversial role in the context of Germany's debate on a proposed immigration law between Spring 2001 and June 2004. It demonstrates that a comparative approach to discourse analysis might help to render more transparent the particularities of national debates, opening them up to productive questions.

Kath Gelber reads two contemporary texts which embody 'discourses of hate' in Australia and Germany. Both issued from the pens of prominent politicians, Herron and Hohmann, and concern representations of the two nations' unpalatable pasts: the 'stolen generations' issue in Australia, and the Holocaust in Germany. Gelber analyses the two texts as discursive attempts to achieve a particular kind of reconstruction of the past, one which denies the link between the past and contemporary practices of discrimination, harm and violence. She claims that as politicians, both speakers/writers can issue their statements from a position of relative power, thus exploiting a privileged position within networks of the distribution of discourse, and in a manner which denies the contestability of the claims. Herron's submission on the 'stolen generations' mobilizes a range of 'scientificist' discourses which attempt to discredit the nature of the evidence gathered and the discursive conditions under which it was gathered, in particular that of Australian indigenous society. Similarly, Hohmann's speech questions notions of collective responsibility in the present by making a comparison with the Jewish people. The burden of his argument is to suggest that would be just as logical to describe Jews as a perpetrator-people as it is to describe Germans in the same manner. He too bases his argument on a range of statistical figures, thus combining a spurious 'objectivity' and party-political authority. In both cases, Gelber examines the broader social and discursive contexts in which these texts were written and spoken, showing that their reconstructions of the past in the interests of an exculpation of the nation in the present do indeed have very concrete repercussions, be it the hindrance of compensation to the victims or their families, or the encouragement of ongoing discrimination against marginalized communities within Australian and German society. To that extent, such texts reaffirm the very harms whose past and present meaning they seek to reconstruct.

Russell West-Pavlov interprets cross-cultural autobiographies as interventions into an all-pervasive discursive practice in Western societies which implicitly assumes an isomorphism between the discrete individual subject and the monocultural nation. Narratives of selfhood which posit the closure and unicity of individual subjectivity frequently serve the rhetorical purposes of the nation as an ostensibly monocultural entity with closed boundaries. West-Pavlov reads Brian Casto's collection of autobiographical pieces *Looking for Estrellita* and Vílem Flusser's 'philosophical' autobiography *Bodenlos* as iconoclastic discursive interventions into the space of hegemonic autobiographical practice. Both works speak of migrant subjectivities whose narratives are tales of border crossing – both in the geographical sense of emigration and re-settlement, and in the more radical sense of an intersubjective communication between cultural 'selfhood' and 'otherness'.

Tim Mehigan offers a comparative view of the discourse on cultural plurality in films of the 1970s to the 1990s in German and Australia. Mehigan places his examination of discourses of pluralism within a tension between cultural tradition and liberal rationalism, a tension, he suggests, which goes back to the historical tensions between Romanticism and its Enlightenment predecessor, with their respective emphases upon specific and universal values. Concentrating on Rainer Werner Fassbinder's *Angst essen Seele auf* (Fear Eats the Soul, 1974) and Werner Herzog's *Where the Green Ants Dream* (1984) in Germany, and Baz Luhrmann's *Strictly Ballroom* (1992) and Steve Thomas's documentary *The Hillmen* (1996) in Australia, Mehigan outlines possible stances taken on cultural specificity taken by these filmmakers. Both Fassbinder and Herzog remain sceptical about the possibilities of recognition of cultural plurality in 1970s 'Gastarbeiter' Germany and 1980s indigenous Australia. In contrast, Thomas' and Luhrmann's films, while staging similar conflicts between mainstream Anglo-Australian and peripheral ethnic-Australian cultures, are less dubious regarding the reciprocal interactions between cultural communities. In the 1990s,

Australian film as a prominent public discourse appears to entertain the possibility of infiltration of the mainstream by non-Anglo ethnicity as a welcome opportunity for a transformation of the hegemonic culture and its discourses.

Fiona Allon examines recent discourses of exclusion and selection in immigrant policy in Australia. Her analysis is placed in the framework of the crisis of multiculturalism in its Australian manifestation, where it has served to celebrate and contain cultural difference simultaneously. In a broader context of accelerating globalization, discourses of national allegiance become increasingly obsolete, and in the face of rapid change, increasingly shrill. Allon explores the psychogeography associated with Australia's insular place on the margins of South-East Asia, a position which has, paradoxically, produced both a deep conviction of an ability to filter contact with other nations and a sense of vulnerability to invasion – a simultaneous belief in the capacity and the need to control entries from the outside world. Since Federation in 1901, Australia's own sense of itself as a nation has been intimately tied up with immigration restriction and was thus from the outset inherently racialized. Even the period in which the Australian government officially espoused a policy of multiculturalism has been recently interpreted as further moment of containment of difference, and thus evincing continuities with the more restrictive discursive and policy trends since the election of the Howard government in 1996. Allon draws comparisons with similar discursive strategies of exclusion evident in the German debates of the 1990s over integration, 'ghetto culture', 'parallel societies' and *Leitkultur* (hegemonic, mainstream culture), and detects comparable 'spatial anxieties' at work in both the Australian and German contexts. Allon detects an increasing disjunction between the exponential increase in the transnational border-crossing phenomena engendered by real processes of globalization, and reactionary discourses of racialized restriction and delimitation according to national boundaries. More concerningly, a similar, but better concealed disjunction is also evinced in liberal discourses of multiculturalism. Allon illustrates this by examining several visual icons from the German and Australian contexts. Both celebrate, ostensibly, an open, plural, multicultural society by using the image, in the one case of Germany as a 'family', and in the other, by placing people of visibly ethnic identity in an Australian landscape. Both images, Allon suggest, elide the very real strategies of exclusion still at work in both societies, and at the same time reveal the workings of multiculturalism in its tendency to 'tolerate' differences which are coded as 'discrete' and 'essential'. To this extent, these images are symptomatic of the manner in which multiculturalism leaves the nation-state and its boundaries intact, as well as retaining the dominance of a core 'national' identity ignoring the real diversity of these communities.

Ulrich Lölke's chapter addresses the question of the reciprocal relationships and influences which have existed and continue to exist between polyculturalism and science. Lölke is particularly interested in the cultural plurality which results today from the European expansion which came about in the wake of colonialism, and the impact this plurality may have upon conceptualizations of science. He contrasts universalistic and specific, localized models of science, suggesting that contemporary reflection upon the epistemologies of scientific knowledge-production will gain much by scrutinizing the specific epistemological economies at work in various cultural contexts. Lölke focuses on the one hand upon the German context, asking about the manner in which European science developed on the basis of early German voyages of discovery. In von Humboldt's and Forster's travel accounts there is still in evidence a 'dialectical tension' between the universalist aspirations of the scientist-explorers and the rising consciousness – brought about by the journey itself and the 'places' it traversed – of the obstacles to such a project. On the other hand, Lölke examines the contemporary power constellations of competing knowledge systems which become visible when various epistemic traditions collide with one another. His example is taken from the Australian indigenous context, in which European scientific and indigenous knowledge meet in school syllabi. In such epistemological 'contact zones', scientific discourse could possibly relinquish its policing function and instead become one of several equal discursive instances in dialogical interaction.

Nicholas White's article in this volume is an 'on the ground' study of the manner in which discourse on nationhood actually functions across a cultural boundary – specifically, that constituted by the interaction of an Australian observer in a German High School in Osnabrück. White's article explores the contradictory terms in which Australians and Germans understand themselves as members of nation-states on the basis of different histories. Different national traditions give a very different sense of 'ingrained nationhood', and this in turn impacts upon the discursive strategies which underlie it. The author examines in detail the resonances of various discursive categories which his teacher colleagues use to label their own self-description and the normative expectations they impose upon others. Essentialist understandings of culture model much of the discursive patterning of national self-image, but such understanding must be taken seriously for it underlies the de facto manner in which such discourses do have a hold on consciousness – even among those who may dispute the tenacity of a ideas of fixed, bounded national identity. Ironically, White shows, even those of his interlocutors who contested essentialist notions of national identity were bound to work within the parameters set by those terms in order to recast new versions of the old terminology. Discourses of the nation, White's study shows, can be modified, but only after acknowledging the purchase they continue to have on hearts and minds.

Justine Lloyd's and Anja Schwarz's contribution surveys a current trend in nations such as Germany and Australia, to 'push out their borders' and thereby transnationalise the once clearly-delineated boundaries between nation states and their others. The authors analyse this phenomenon by focusing on the figure of the refugee in Australian and German debates on immigration. Refugees, previously marginal to these discussions, have increasingly taken centre stage in public discourse while, at the same time, their status vis-à-vis the nation has become highly ambiguous: as 'inside' outsiders they are, on the one hand, guests within the sovereign nation, while at the same time subject to contingent geo-politics of admission and residency which aim to keep them from reaching this insider status. Lloyd's and Schwarz' analysis links this emergence of the refugee at the centre of national debates to current fortifications of national space. They posit that rather than a simple closure of borders in response to the incursion of 'illegal' and 'dangerous' people into the nation, the new border regimes produce a new, asymmetrical mobility order: they result in in-between places such as the 'buffer zones' produced by 'safe third countries' or 'international zones' within the nation. In these zone which may be outside the state's borders but still within its realm of sovereign control or, conversely, within the nation's boundaries but without access to its welfare and legislative system relationships between stable, national selves and mobile, foreign others, between legitimate border-crossers and unruly, undocumented, improper subjects are constructed.

The collection inaugurates an ongoing series of interventions launched by the members of an international research consortium working under the title 'Polyculturalism & Discourse'. The consortium gathers together scholars concerned to make an impact in the public sphere in the area of inter-, trans-, and cross-cultural interaction and global migration by thinking and writing about the ways in which these areas of social and political life are 'talked about'. The aim of the consortium is to focus upon a range of issues located in the vicinity of the nexus of discursive practice (whether hegemonic or contestatory) and polycultural social identity and existence. We hope that this pilot-project, the first in an ongoing series of specific thematic interventions under the heading of 'Polyculturalism & Discourse', may provide useful perspectives for agents contesting given patterns of discursive practice in a diverse range of social fields.

Russell West-Pavlov and Anja Schwarz

Notes

1. Foucault 1971, 55.
2. Butler 1997.
3. Comaroff 2005, 131.
4. Bhabha 1990, 12.
5. See Comaroff 2005, 142.

References

Bhabha, Homi K. 1990. *The Location of Culture.* London: Routledge, 1997.
Butler, Judith. *Excitable Speech.* London and New York: Routledge, 1997.
Comaroff, Jean. "The End of History, Again? Pursuing the Past in the Postcolony." In. *Postcolonial Sudies and Beyond*, edited by Ania Loomba, Suvir Kaul, Matti Bunzl, Antoinette Burton and Jed Esty, 125-144. Durham: Duke University Press, 2005.
Foucault, Michel. *L'Ordre du discours.* Paris: Gallimard, 1971.

An earlier version of A. Dirk Moses' chapter in this collection appeared in *Aboriginal History* 25 (2001), and is reprinted here by kind permission of the editors and editorial board of that journal.

Coming to Terms with Genocidal Pasts in Comparative Perspective: Germany and Australia

A. Dirk Moses

1.   Introduction

The question of how countries deal with the material and symbolic legacies of totalitarian rule, genocide, and civil war in their immediate pasts is spawning a growing body of research on recent national and regional cases - post-apartheid South Africa, post-communist central and eastern Europe, and post-dictatorial South America - as well as on the 'classic' instances of postwar Japan and Germany.[1] Closely related is the voluminous literature on collective memory, much of which studies the impact of trauma on cultural and political group identity.[2] Nowhere is the connection between genocidal pasts and collective memory more evident than in the Federal Republic of Germany, which is widely recognised as the paradigmatic case of what there is called a successful *Vergangenheitsbewältigung* or *Aufarbeitung der Vergangenheit* - the 'mastering,' 'working through,' or 'coming to terms with' a national history dripping with the blood of civil war and genocide. In this instance, in an appropriate symmetry, it is the paradigmatic case of genocide - the systematic murder of millions of Jews, Roma, homosexuals, mentally disabled, and other groups. In Germany, 'coming to terms with the Nazi past' is a key element in the development of its democratic and liberal political culture after 1945.[3]

The question is not of mere academic interest: it goes to the heart of the self-understanding of countries where genocide taints their histories. What of such a discourse in Australia? Since the publication over the past quarter century of substantial research on nineteenth century frontier violence, and in 1997 of the *Bringing them Home* report on the forcible removal of Aboriginal children from their families, talk of genocide is in the air.[4] Yet many Australians object that it is not a term relevant to the history of their country, and they hold a post-genocidal reckoning to be unnecessary, even mischievous and divisive.[5] Moreover, the conservative and right-wing opponents of the genocide concept contend that it is a weapon deployed by a "new class" of left-liberal intellectuals to establish (or reinforce) its supposed cultural hegemony. The debate has now reached a stalemate with rival factions of the intelligentsia now disputing the very facts of Australian history.[6]

This chapter argues that the process of 'coming to terms with the past' in Australian can be productively stimulated by considering the

German experience with which it has important similarities as well as differences. But before analysing each case in turn, it is necessary to consider the relevant literature in anthropology and the sociology of knowledge to clarify the issues underlying the public-intellectual struggles that constitute Australia's 'culture wars.'

2. National Origins, Symbolic Capital, and the Perpetrator Trauma

The issue at stake is the nation-building project, which requires mythic origins (cosmogenies). Such origins are necessary for nation-building because they permit the "narration of the nation" by conjuring the illusion of a "continuous narrative of national progress" that renders natural the construction of "a people" by obscuring the contingent and artificial nature of that construction.[7] As Etienne Balibar points out "[t]he myth of origins and national continuity...is...an effective ideological form, in which the imaginary singularity of national formations is constructed daily by moving back from the present into the past." Moreover, cosmogenies are used to repair the social fabric.[8] Thus in relation to traditional societies, Mircea Eliade identified their function in providing models of exemplary conduct that could be reiterated to "create the world anew" when group decline was perceived or social healing was required. Despite obvious differences between such societies and the modern world, Eliade's observation contains a telling insight. Members of nation-states inscribed by its rituals and myths may not invest them with supernatural powers, but the nation's origins are sacred nonetheless because "in one way or another one 'lives' myth, in the sense that one is seized by the sacred, exalting power of the events recollected or re-enacted."[9] 'Coming to terms with the past' disables this integrative power by linking the nation's origins to catastrophes, like genocide and civil war, in its recent past.

How is this discourse mobilised? Conservatives claim that the 'privileged,' left-liberal elite in the universities and media purvey guilt and shame about the past to its own advantage. Is this true? Sociologists like Alvin Gouldner used the term "new class" to refer to both the technocrats that administer modern capitalism and to the humanistically-oriented cosmopolitan intelligentsia that tries to establish its influence by setting the moral and symbolic agenda of the nation's collective consciousness.[10] Similarly, Pierre Bourdieu argues that the leftist intelligentsia comprises the dominated faction of a dominant class in which bourgeois elites hold sway.[11] In terms of his elaborate theory of capital (economic, social, cultural, symbolic) and social class, he maintains plausibly that both sectors of the dominant class engage in struggles with one another for symbolic capital to define, and thereby make, social reality.[12]

But the motivation and actual role of the subordinate intelligentsia in power struggles remains unclear.[13] In fact, because symbolic capital is the means by which direct forms of domination by other capitals are obscured, and is therefore a derivative rather than an autonomous power in its own right, Bourdieu discounts the analysis of ideologies in themselves.[14] To be sure, while the respective positions of rival factions of the intelligentsia in the intellectual field are obviously relevant considerations, any satisfactory sociology of intellectuals needs to account for the powerful emotions and commitments that drive them.

In order to understand the ideological heat in debates about national origins, it is necessary to turn to the concept of 'perpetrator trauma' developed by Cathy Caruth, Richard Bernstein, and Jan Assmann with reference to Freud's *Moses and Monotheism*. After the Israelites murdered Moses, Freud points out, they reverted initially to their old polytheistic religion, only later turning to Moses's monotheism. The trauma was experienced by the descendents of the perpetrators when they realised the crime their ancestors had committed. Caruth uses this idea to suggest that perpetrator trauma is delayed or latent, because at the moment of the deed the subject does not realise what it is doing. Subsequently, the perpetrator-collective suffers 'traumatic recall' as the deed, which is only constituted as such in public memory, enters the consciousness of the population.[15] The perpetrator trauma continues to haunt the perpetrator-collective until it changes sufficiently to narrate it into a new legitimating story as a constitutive part of its self-understanding.

In this chapter, I argue that the perpetrator trauma is at once the source of indignation experienced by many intellectuals at the suffering inflicted by the collective to which they belong, and the mechanism by which they liberate themselves from domination by the technocratic bourgeoisie and national-conservative intellectuals. I argue, further, that the critical public discussion this liberation unleashes about national origins is instrumental in the *political humanisation* of the polity, which hitherto has been in thrall to the legitimating myths of the national-conservative intellectuals.[16]

But it is too simply to heroise the left-liberal wing of the intelligentsia. The moral sensitivity that drives it can mean that it develops alternative legitimating myths. It is necessary to distinguish the senses in which 'coming to terms with the past' is used. On the one hand, it is referred to as a process of honest and critical reckoning with a tainted national past. On the other, it is often used as a partial and moralistic discourse by oppositional intelligentsia in its struggle for symbolic capital in the intellectual field. Usually, leftist intellectuals will link the two senses of the term by claiming to be agents of the overarching process, thereby equating political humanisation with their domination of symbolic politics and influence in policy making. The West German case, however, shows that political-moral progress is a by-product of a public sphere in which critical reason functions, which means that neither faction of the intelligentsia is able to dominate the other.

3. The Creation of a German 'Self Critical Community'

The Federal Republic had two myths of origin: the moral legitimacy of the republican foundation in 1949, and the viability of German national identity itself. The former was more important for liberals, the latter for conservatives. Although many conservatives were not enamoured of the new Federal Republic's parliamentary liberalism in 1949, the intensity of the cold war meant that liberals and conservatives shared an anti-communist orientation that affected their 'answer' to the Nazi past. Both limited their reckoning with the past to legal and constitutional matters, prosecuting war criminals, paying reparations to Israel, and banning extremist parties on the left and right. Although liberals were by no means aggressive nationalists, even they did not want to abandon a sense of positive continuities with the German past. After all, they represented the liberal parliamentary traditions that could be traced to the first half of the nineteenth century. Conservatives, for their part, did their utmost to disentangle Nazism from German traditions by blaming the left and mass democracy for the plebeian Hitler who was, they insisted, a socialist of sorts. They did not deny the Nazi crimes, but laid the blame for their commission at the feet of 'modernity' rather than their cherished nationalist tradition. The answer to the Nazi past was to maintain pride in positive German national traditions and its latest garb, the anti-communist Federal Republic.

Leftist critics attacked both these myths of origin. First, they argued that, because the course of German history had culminated in Nazism and organised mass murder, most national traditions were irredeemably tainted. Consequently, they urged radical economic and political change along democratic socialist lines. Second, when these hopes were dashed by foundation of the Federal Republic in 1949, they indicted it as a 'restorationist' regime whose continuities with the Nazi system were as, if not more, significant as the differences.[17] It was no coincidence, they averred, that many erstwhile Nazis had found a comfortable home in West Germany.[18]

Typologically, such critics were oppositional, cosmopolitans intellectuals who were moved by shame and indignation for what their countrymen and -women had done. They were the agents of traumatic recall in the Federal Republic, sentinels of Holocaust memory and solidarity with the countless victims of Germans.[19] Ever suspicious of perceived fascist continuities, they began the 'culture of vigilance' - critics called it "alarmism" - against perceived backsliding into "bad old German ways" in culture and politics.

Their project also entailed remaking German subjectivity. Heavily influenced by Alexander and Margarethe Mitscherliches' socially-applied psychoanalysis, as well as by theories of mass culture and fascism of the recently returned Frankfurt School, the oppositional intelligentsia eventually developed an emphatic post-national, even anti-national, subjectivity. For the problem was not only capitalism, but the specifically German cultural pathologies of the 'authoritarian personality' and underdeveloped, weak ego that sought compensation in strong leadership and the collective security (the *Wir-Gefühl*: 'we feeling') of group identity.[20] The main thesis of the Mitscherliches' famous book, *The Inability to Mourn* (1967), was that West Germans were caught in a debilitating melancholia, as they were unable to mourn for the narcissistic collective love objects of Hitler and the German nation. Melancholia, or depression, was the poisoned fruit of a blocked mourning process, which, if successfully negotiated, released the subject from its libidinal fixation on the love object and permitted a new investment to be made. In the postwar context, the Mitscherliches were appalled by the continuing national orientation of West Germans that they thought was preventing them from engaging in antifascist politics and democratic socialist reconstruction. *The inability to mourn* became the prime explanatory device by which the German left proclaimed its post-national credentials and with which it sought to reconfigure the subjectivities of other West Germans.

The fascinating feature of the West German confrontation with the Nazi past is not only how this minority position became institutionalised in public memory and inscribed in personality structures by the 1990s, but also its twisted path and the attenuated manner in which it occurred. For unlike recent explanations that stress the victory of the dissident wing of the intelligentsia,[21] a kind of compromise between the warring factions in fact has been reached. This process becomes explicable by examining two aspects of this institutionalisation. The first is generational change. The postnational subjectivity became the norm for the majority of the most celebrated postwar political generation, the sixty-eighters, born in the 1940s and therefore in lesser need of the integrating power of founding myths of Federal Republic than their 'nazified' parents.[22] Because they regarded Nazism as archetypically German, their loyalty moved to universal values, which Jürgen Habermas, the most significant theorist of this orientation, celebrates as the fruit of a post-conventional (i.e., post-national) identity.[23] In their profound alienation from the national culture and institutions of West Germany, they exhibited the main symptoms of the perpetrator trauma. Their sympathies lay not with their compromised parents and their national tradition, but with the victims of National Socialism.

This transfer of loyalties, however, did not signal a balanced or healthy towards the past. For in the 1970s, these victims were not necessarily Jews. In fact, the sixty-eighters' (and by extension, the German left's) militant anti-Zionism and anti-Americanism ("USA=SA SS") meant that they saw communists and workers as the Nazi regime's prime targets.[24] And by facilely identifying themselves with these victims to avoid the moral pollution bequeathed to them by their parents, some sixty-eighters joined the terrorist 'armed struggle' against the 'fascist' West German state, committing dozens of murders along the way, while many others of their generational cohort sympathised with the cause.[25] Their sour reaction to the collapse of the East Germany in 1989/1990 showed that many sixty-eighers still hoped that the German Democratic Republic could have moved in a democratic socialist direction rather than join the west. As some commentators wryly noted, it was now the turn of the sixty-eighters to mourn for the love object of a united socialist Germany.[26] The destruction of the national-conservatives myths of origin by the perpetrator trauma does not mean that the bearers of the trauma necessarily have the 'answer' to the riddles of history.

Because of such excesses in the 1970s, many liberals who had been reformers in the previous decade entered into an alliance with conservative professors and intellectuals, decrying the 'new elite' that had entered the universities, schools and media and had supposedly taken control of the country.[27] Until the 1980s, Holocaust memory remained undetermined as the leftist intelligentsia rethought the meaning of the past and posture towards Israel, while liberals and conservatives waged trench warfare against them on university committees. In the context of the cold war, however, the left's main weapon remained the claim of the uniqueness of the Holocaust, because it entailed the bankruptcy of the national ideal and implied the country's negative myth of origin. Debates about the Holocaust are always also debates about the viability of a German national identity as the well-known historical controversies of the 1980s and 1990s show: the Historians' Debate of 1986, the Goldhagen Debate of 1996/1997, the discussion on the travelling exhibition on the war crimes of the German Army and on the Berlin Holocaust Memorial in the late 1990s.[28]

Consequently, when Helmut Kohl's conservative Christian

Democrats returned to power federally in 1982, they proclaimed a "spiritual-moral change" (*geistige-moralische Wende*) to make good the damage the 'the intellectuals', as they were called, had inflicted on the national fabric. Instead of 'emancipation' they preached 'identity,' and conservative historians made the same moves by challenging the new language of the uniqueness of the Holocaust that the cosmopolitan intelligentsia was beginning to institutionalise in the public sphere through prominent left-liberal newspapers.[29]

Yet the neo-nationalist campaign ultimately failed, most notably in the 'Historians' Dispute' [Historikerstreik] and Bitburg affair of the mid-1980s, because liberal intellectuals sided with leftists like Jürgen Habermas. In their view, the neo-conservative instrumentalisation of the past for contemporary nationalist cultural politics was immoral and threatened to revive illiberal mentalities by its discursive affinities with far-right ideologues and movements. They attacked this defence of national myths of origin as "relativising the Holocaust," "normalising the past," and "apologetic."[30] As a result of this left-liberal alliance, the Holocaust has since become anchored in the Federal Republic as a negative myth of origin, its new source of historical legitimacy. Two hundred and fifty sites of Holocaust mourning now exist there, and a football field sized memorial to murdered European Jewry has been constructed next to the Reichstag and Pariser Platz in Berlin. As Jan Assmann observed, "As a perpetrator trauma, Auschwitz is a latent experience. After the 'material reality' of the facts became known immediately after the war, the 'historical truth' needed decades to sink into general consciousness and find appropriate forms of remembrance."[31]

Does this mean that the humanistic intelligentsia has prevailed? Have Germans now engaged in the *Trauerarbeit* - the work of mourning urged by the Mitscherliches - and detached themselves from their collective narcissism? Superficially, it appears as if they have. The leftwing of the political class remains committed to universal values and is suspicious of 'national interests,' and its collective pride rests on the perception of having successfully expedited the generational mission to remake of German subjectivity and institutionalise a kind of tempered antifascism.[32]

To be sure, the perpetrator trauma is essential to rupture the continuity of national traditions by pointing out the criminality or ambivalence of the country's origins. But this is only part of the story. The discourse of 'mastering the past' is a necessary but insufficient condition for political humanisation. Because political and moral communities are necessarily concrete and possess a diachronic consciousness, the abstract universalism of the German left and the radical historical rupture it entreats could never command a minimum consensus in the public sphere. The other key factor, then, is the alliance between leftist and liberal intellectuals against the conservative-nationalist intelligentsia, because it permits the combination of the moral energy of the perpetrator trauma with the commitment to the country's historical institutions that the liberals represent. Relevant here is the fact that liberals tend to employ the language of shame to refer to German crimes, while the left uses the language of guilt.[33] The former implies the continuity of the German cultural nation, while the latter, in an analogy with the psychoanalytic procedure of working through, is indentured to a protocol of redemption that issues in a radical new identity. The liberal language of shame and regret secures this continuity. Michael Walzer calls such a liberal universalism "reiterated" rather than abstract, because it is located within the national narrative that has been purged of its potential criminality by the mediation of critical reflection. Cosmopolitanism becomes anchored in the subjectivities and structures of the society, and its citizens become rooted cosmopolitans, or "cosmopolitan patriots," as Anthony Appiah has recently advocated.[34]

If one side cannot impose itself, how does the public sphere function? By referring current problems to the perceived pathologies of the nation's history, it is the space in which inherited traditions and discourses, as well as political, economic, and social structures, are scrutinised in light of universal principles. Since the war, Germans have thrashed out the *contested lessons* of their past. A minimum consensus about the past, and therefore the present and future nature of German democracy, started to develop when both sides relativised their absolute positions. In the 1980s and 1990s, the left slowly gave up its dreams of a 'third way' between socialism and capitalism and began to desist from using the Holocaust to attack the foundation of the 1949 republic, so liberals and conservatives could accept the commemoration of the Holocaust as the legitimating origin of the polity, which is henceforth constituted as an anti-genocidal moral community and inheritor of positive German traditions. A "self-critical community" (Homi Bhabha) emerges in which the open debate about the meaning of the past provides the orientation in the present and a guide for the future.[35]

No one perspective on the past, then, whether nationalist or anti-fascist, affords a privileged perspective, conclusive answer, or knockdown argument. Rather than the narrative closure implicit in absolute claims to 'master' or even conclusively 'come to terms with the past,' the comportment to history I claim to see in the German case is a continuous process of considering the various meanings of a genocidal past and what should be done about it. This is democracy based not on an uncritical national continuity, nor on abstract norms that entail a temporal rupture and refoundation of the polity, but on the operationalisation of what the 'Sydney School' of political and legal philosophy calls "critical public reason" and the "jurisprudence of regret."[36] What is noteworthy about such regret is its recognition that this process is an open-ended, critically hermeneutical relationship to national traditions. As the American legal philosopher, Gerald Postema, notes, "This is *prophetic* memory, forcing the nation to take an honest, inclusive look at its past, forcing it to face its hypocrisy. The power of this criticism comes precisely from this fact that the principles it appeals to are historically grounded in the nation."[37]

4. Australia's 'History Wars'

Not for nothing have Australia's 'history wars' been called a "foundational dispute."[38] Comparison with Germany reveals significant similarities and differences between the two cases. Let us begin with the former.

A. The Similarities

1) The Australian leftist intelligentsia also articulates the perpetrator trauma by consistently highlighting the dark aspects of the country's past. No less a figure than Manning Clark observed in the bicentennial year that "Our history is in danger of degenerating into yet another variation of oversimplification - a division of humanity into 'goodies' and 'baddies'," although he clearly welcomed this "radical literature" to counter the prevailing conformist and triumphalist nationalist teleology.[39] Clark's intervention, as one observer noted recently, "was a piece over which the Liberal Party are still smarting," because it called on Australians to "gain wisdom" by recognising the evil that lay at the heart of their country's foundation, namely, the evil visited upon the Aborigines, the convicts, and the environment.[40] Although Clark did not criminalise the entire Australian past *per se*, the balance of his case was very much at the critical end of the spectrum, ridiculing mercilessly as he did the cherished ideals of Australian conservatism. For the "myth about the beneficial role of British civilisation" needed to be ruptured, he pleaded, so Australians could "choose what we like from the baggage train of our past, and take what we want into the future."[41] The country's origin, far from heroic, was poisoned. Clark's was a call, in effect, to start again, to refound the country.

2) As in Germany, the left gained a presence in the institutions of cultural transmission, especially the universities. More so than Germany, however, such advances in the intellectual field were conferred with official legitimacy. The then Labor Party Prime Minister, Paul Keating,

and his speech-writer, the historian Don Watson, were highly sensitive to race issues, and in 1992 Keating delivered his so-called 'Redfern Speech' in which he publicly avowed "our" (i.e., European-Australian) responsibility for the lethal practices and policies towards Aborigines in the past.[42] The contemporaneous Mabo High Court judgement reinforced the new public language with the much-quoted words that the dispossession of the Aborigines was "the darkest aspect" of Australian history that had bequeathed a legacy of "unutterable shame." Mabo represented a fundamental challenge to the nationalist-conservative myth of white settlement.[43]

3) The response of conservative intellectuals was also reminiscent of their German counterparts. In terms very much like Helmut Kohl when he came to power in 1982, John Howard and right-wing intellectuals sought to repair the damage they perceived to have been done by the cosmopolitan intellectuals and the Labor Party after the Coalition won the federal election in 1996.[44] And, as in Germany, a victory for the conservatives was accompanied by mobilisation further to the right in the form of Pauline Hanson and her 'One Nation' Party.

In order to understand the conservatives' reaction, it is necessary to appreciate their sense of impotence in the public sphere, a syndrome analysed acutely by Ghassan Hage, who calls their political language a "discourse of decline" that reflects a real loss of symbolic power.[45] As in the controversy over Asian immigration in the 1980s, the historian Geoffrey Blainey has provided the coalition parties with the analysis and metaphors it uses to challenge the left's definition of public language regarding Aboriginal issues in the 1990s. He does not deny the reality of frontier massacres and dispossession but seeks to disable the left from blaming the British in a criminal way by setting the conflict in a world-historical context. In a similar way, Ernst Nolte hoped to take the sting out the leftist claim about the Holocaust's uniqueness. Where for Nolte it was the forces of revolution and counter-revolution unleashed in 1789 in the wake of whose maelstrom Germany was a hapless agent, for Blainey it was the "unique confrontation in recorded history" of British modernity and its system of land use, and the Aborigines with their incompatible culture. It was not a matter, then, of evil, avaricious Britons vanquishing the innocent, peaceful, and ecologically responsible natives, but an unavoidable, even tragic chapter of world history.[46]

Because Blainey is too clever and sensitive to deny – although he does play down – the suffering inflicted by whites, it needs to be balanced by white suffering and redeemed by a greater good.[47] This theodicy is Australian civilisation itself. In a century of totalitarian genocide and mass killing, Australia was one of the few countries to retain its democratic system of government; its brutally harsh environment was rendered viable and prosperous by the Europeans, and its farms fed millions beyond its shores. It is "one of the world's success stories." Consequently, Australians can be "proud" (rather than ashamed) of their national identity.[48] This is the argument with which modern conservatism reformulates the myth of origin to see off the critical scholarship of the last generation. "I do not feel it is accurate or fair to portray Australia's history since 1788 as little more than a disgraceful record of imperialism, exploitation, and racism," John Howard wrote with indignation. "Such a portrayal is a gross distortion, and deliberately neglects the overall story of great Australian achievement that is there in our history to be told."[49]

Rescuing this theodicy has meant that the conservative government colludes with conservative intellectuals, just as Kohl's government did in the 1980s. Most recently, it takes the form of the intriguingly named 'Bennelong Society', formed in 2000 by figures around the *Quadrant* magazine and senior government and former ministers to influence public opinion and policy debates. Part of their manifesto is to ensure that "decent respect be shown to individuals, religious bodies and governments in Australia who have tried to share with Aborigines what they thought were the best things in their way of life."[50]

4) The genocide issue has become the functional equivalent of the uniqueness of the Holocaust in Germany: the blemish that soils the myth of origin by preventing it from doing the magic work of social integration and healing. Just when it appeared that conservatives thought they had regained control of the historical and national agenda, their complacency was shattered by a spectacular instance of traumatic recall, the *Bringing them Home* report on the stolen generations in 1997, which also received considerable international attention, including screaming headlines in Germany of "Australia's Holocaust."[51] The return of the repressed came not in the form of records of frontier violence, but in the largely twentieth century phenomena of eugenicist and assimilationist programmes that forcibly removed thousands of 'mixed blood' Aboriginal children from their families. What is more, the report argued that even the postwar assimilation policies were genocidal in terms of the United Nations Convention on the genocide.

Conservative commentators were quick to identify the meaning of this accusation. Ron Brunton of the *Institute of Public Affairs* (IPA) averred that "the genocide 'finding' has been greeted with joyous acclaim by those people in the universities, churches, and other usually suspect institutions who know in the depth of their bowels that Australia is bad."[52] In other words, it threatened to cede symbolic power back to the rival intelligentsia and undermine, once again, the national myth of origins, especially since the removal policies were expedited in the name of Australian civilisation.[53] Brunton himself made the link between genocide and national viability explicit: "if Australia is to maintain its dignity as a nation, it cannot afford to have a second 'genocide' finding made against it."[54] Another IPA contributor, Patrick Morgan, articulated the same fear: "The adversary view of Australia undermines belief in our nation and deprives us of a *raison d' etre*. It causes internal collapse from pointless guilt and remorse."[55] The *Bringing them Home* report, a newspaper columnist complained, was a piece of "cultural defamation".[56] Keith Windschuttle, a publicist favoured by the conservative federal government, was upset by the "charge that the British colonisation of this country was a process comparable to the Nazi destruction of the Jews in Europe".[57] Earlier, he had expressed his concern about the "movement on the left" that threatens "the most far-reaching proposals for the reorganisation and even the eventual break-up of the Australian nation."[58] *Quadrant* editor Padraic McGuinness also objected strongly to "hysterical claims of genocide," "the bemoaning of the past," and to the intellectuals whom he derides as "inner-urban ferals."[59] "The essence of the message is that there has been much exaggeration," he continued, "the invention of charges like genocide and holocaust has been a matter to impose a kind of moral ascendancy intended to stifle policy debate."[60]

The intractability of the 'culture wars' in Australia lies in the fact that McGuinness is both right and wrong: the genocide charge, at least for certain episodes of Australian history, *is* true, and it *does* cede leftist and liberal intellectuals symbolic capital. Such shifts, however, cannot account for the existential fears that such conservatives express. The Mitscherlich account of the relationship between individual and collective identity explains why nationalised subjects experience a dramatic loss in self-esteem when the national ego ideal is damaged. In the Australian case, the extremism of statements by Brunton, Morgan and Windschuttle suggests that this analysis should be extended by asking whether such figures experience castration anxiety, that is, a fantasised danger to their genitals symbolised by the national ideal that makes them feel powerful and good about themselves.

5) In yet another similarity with the German experience, when such evidence of genocide, or at least genocidal rhetoric, is uncovered, as in the eugenicist policy announcements of the 1930s, it is placed at the feet of the rival intellectual tradition. "It is true that some of the policy makers and administrators were in past years motivated by notions of eugenics and Darwinian ranking of races," McGuinness conceded. But with a historical magic wand he determined that "this was the orthodoxy

of the left and the progressive social engineers, not of conservative governments."[61] The point is not, however, whether conservative or progressive governments instituted such policies, but that they were formulated in the service of a nationalist project of Australian civilisation. It is this continuity for which contemporary conservatism stands and that is now at issue. But McGuinness is impervious to such logic. Any ill that now threatens the nation-building project is automatically split off from his own intellectual commitments and emotional investments. Accordingly, the problems of Aborigines today are not the poisoned fruit of two centuries of racism, but of the separatist, anti-assimilationist polices of 'do-gooder' intellectuals and public servants like H. C. Coombs. And so we end up with surely the most bizarre inversion of the historical scales when McGuinness claims that the "continual desire to argue that they [Aborigines] have been subjected to genocide and are deserving of infinite and eternal compensation" is the "sophisticated racism" of the white elite.[62]

6) We know that in Germany the consensus about the uniqueness of the Holocaust was only won with the consent of liberals during the 1980s. In a telling parallel, the intellectuals doing the running on the genocide issue in Australia since 1997 have been liberals and left-liberals, in particular the political scientists Robert Manne and Colin Tatz and the philosopher Raimond Gaita.[63] As editor of *Quadrant*, Manne turned the hitherto truculent anticommunist monthly into a lively forum of ideas until he resigned in 1997 after a campaign to oust him by a group of indignant conservatives who accused him of "selling out" to "the left".[64] Indeed, Manne had given Gaita and others space to reflect on the moral implications of the Mabo decision. Until then, as in Germany in the 1970s, such liberals (or left-liberals, as Gaita regards himself) often sided with conservatives and remained suspicious of the left and its moral weapon, so-called "political correctness."[65] In 1993, for example, Manne was concerned that "the power of that intellectual movement, which aspires to enforce a dreary political conformity on all matters touching upon race and gender, is growing."[66] He even voted for the Coalition in 1996, and Gaita excoriated "large parts of the left" for "foolishness, complacency and intolerance."[67]

Like the German liberals in the 1980s, though, they became less disturbed by leftist academics than the incoming conservative government's counter-politics of memory, in the Australian case, the Coalition's refusal to accept the "moral basis" of Mabo and reconciliation (as Manne put it), and then with its curt dismissal of the *Bringing them Home* report. Its indulgent tolerance of Hanson's racist populism offended their sense that liberal societies are held together by moral restraint. The danger to Australian political culture no longer came from the left and political correctness, Manne concluded, but from the conservatives and their unofficial, covert alliance with the far right. Reviewing Hanson's manifesto, *The Truth*, Manne entreated it to members of the government as a mirror in which to behold their ugly reflection: "Many will find their own ideas - on the new class, political correctness, Mabo, multiculturalism, Asian migration, the High Court - absorbed, simplified, systematised, and radicalised."[68]

This change of direction, however, did not mean that Manne had joined 'the left,' as his right-wing critics charge. Again, like their German counterparts, such liberals do not criminalise the national past; in fact, Manne emphasised how much of it was admirable.[69] Nor do they engage in the politics of guilt. As early as 1993, Gaita distinguished carefully between the meaning and significance of guilt and shame, advocating the latter as the appropriate response to aspects of Australia's past.[70] Accordingly, their posture to the *Bringing them Home* report was qualified, rejecting "morbid self-abasement," encouraging further reflection and research (currently undertaken, among others, by Manne), while urging fellow Australians to bear witness to the suffering that had been inflicted on the victims of the removal policies.[71] Finally, they reject the post-colonial answers the Australian left proffers to the Australian past, more sanguine as they are about the possibility of reconciliation, and sceptical about the existence of an identifiable indigenous agency.[72] "The Left in Australia now offers enthusiastic support for the ideas of Aboriginal self-determination and land rights," Manne declared, "but has tended to close its eyes to the depth of social breakdown within the traditional world."[73]

B. The Differences

Despite these structural similarities, there are three striking differences between the two cases.

1) Unlike Germany, Australia is a settler society, and its genocidal moments are the result of a colonisation process. Strange as it may seem, this fact makes the viability of Australian nationality more precarious than the German one, which long preceded the Holocaust. For in the Australian case, the very existence of the nation state and the nationalised subject is predicated on the dispossession, expulsion, and where necessary, extermination of the Indigenous peoples.[74] This means that the customary conservative ploy of acknowledging the 'dark sides' of an otherwise salutary project is incoherent because the 'dark sides' were intrinsic to the process and cannot be split off.[75] The survival and eventual prosperity of European settlement depended on the large-scale destruction

of Aboriginal societies, because the racism of the settlers nearly always precluded local negotiations with Indigenous groups and because such groups usually put up stiff resistance when they were not decimated by imported disease. The settlers were at once intrepid farmers *and* ethnic cleansers, even genocidal killers. They had to be to.[76] The positive myth of origin is at once the negative one.

2) Because Aborigines survived the gamut of policies to assimilate, expel and exterminate them, and because so many Aboriginal individuals and communities live in desperate circumstances, they remain an object of white Australian policy reflection. No comparable issue confronts Germany in relation to Jews, who were a highly integrated and successful minority before National Socialism, and whose population is rapidly growing today due to immigration from Russia.

The current Australian debate is framed rather starkly in terms of integration/ assimilation versus self-determination/ separate development/ treaty. There is no space here to consider these arguments in detail. The task is to determine their significance for the question of 'coming to terms with the past' for the Australian myth of origin. The underlying issue is the prospect of the rival nationalism of pan-Aboriginalism, which is necessarily inconsistent with the universalistic pretensions of white Australian citizenship. All conservative arguments are mustered to render illegitimate such a project, such as claiming Aborigines are incapable of running sophisticated organisations, that they entertain the vain hope of recreating pre-industrial, tribal society, and that their own welfare would be best served by adopting European cultural mores.[77]

The link between the leftist intelligentsia and Aboriginal nationalism in this debate is certainly clear in the minds of right wing commentators. The problem, they complain, is the unholy alliance between Aboriginal leaders and leftist intellectuals, supposedly in thrall to a Rousseauean hatred of western civilisation and ridden with 'middle class guilt,' who rejoice in the supposed unspoiled harmony of 'primitive cultures' while hypocritically enjoying the accoutrements of urban comfort. Black Armband scholarship "has produced a small class of Aboriginal leaders who have been remarkably successful in demanding their own institutions. Their next objective is a treaty that will give them separate political status."[78] "They have abandoned scholarship for politics," Windschuttle complains, "in a misguided attempt to support Aboriginal demands by defaming the British colonisation of this country."[79] The anxiety about the sullied national origins is evident in the conservatives' intemperate rhetorical caricatures of their opponents' argument: "The only alternative [to assimilation] is the creation of ghettos and zoos, which is what so many of the well-meaning ideologues of multiculturalism and the preservation of 'aboriginality' seem to want." Reconciliation "pretends that the problem is psychological and moral: rejig the public mind, ask leading political figures to adopt a contrite demeanour and apologies for the sins of history, and all will be well."[80]

In fact, no-one argues that changes in symbolic politics will solve the pressing problems faced by Aboriginal communities. But it is a necessary conditions for a solution. Left-liberals like Gaita think that historical responsibility and shame entail listening to Aboriginal voices and openness to alternative political arrangements. Conservatives retort that such voices (i.e., ATSIC) are unrepresentative, self-servingly elitist and do not reflect the actual integration of Aborigines in the towns and cities.[81] Gaita responds by saying that it is not up to white Australians to lecture Aborigines about what they should do.[82] Since there is no one Aboriginal voice to which to listen, the question appears to be whether non-Indigenous Australians should support Aboriginal leaders in their efforts to develop pan-Aboriginal consciousness. And as nation-building is driven by elites, a process as much alive in Australia today as in the past, the next question is: which nation-building project should have priority, the European-colonial or the pan-Aboriginal one? The alternative slogans 'assimilation' and 'Aboriginal sovereignty' are shorthands for these rival nation-building projects.

A quick glance at the literature on the emancipation of German Jews shows this to be a false dichotomy, because it does not capture the complexity of German Jews' integration in Germany in the nineteenth century. For the hybridised identity they created issued from a process of acculturation in which Jews developed a distinct sub-culture that retained an emphatic sense of Jewishness as well as of Germanness.[83] Similarly, in Australia, we are dealing not with the anachronistic retention of premodern 'Aboriginality,' as many conservatives suggest (McGuinness's "zoos and ghettos"), but with the acculturation of Indigenous peoples in which they develop a hybrid culture of their own.

Moreover, the hobgoblin of a 'break-up of Australia' does not appear to be on the agenda of Indigenous leaders like Geoff Clark. In calling for a treaty, he declares that he is not "talking of two nations." He saw such a document, and the process by which it is generated, as making good the "unfinished business" of the country's foundation, namely, the absence of symmetrical negotiations in 1788 in which "they [the British] should have sought the informed consent of the Indigenous peoples to inhabit this country."[84] This is not a case, then, of a separate Aboriginal state, but of renegotiating the terms of the original settlement. This process sounds very much like the open-ended hermeneutical comportment to national traditions after the rupture of the national myth of origin by the perpetrator trauma.

3) Unlike Germany, however, progressive philosophies of history that redeem suffering - theodicies - have not been discredited. As Blainey articulated clearly in 1993, conservatives must hold fast to a theodicy to redeem the undeniable suffering caused by the march of the progress in which they set so much store. With endearing candour, they recognise that Aboriginal societies had to give way before the superior British alternative. Were Aborigines to survive at all, so the argument runs, they had to adopt the white man's ways, thereby conceding the illiberal and potentially exterminatory potential at the heart of western civilisation.[85] In a notably unguarded statement, the former anthropology lecturer Roger Sandall goes so far as to admit that "Western Culture" advances by "creatively destroying" (his words) obsolete traditions, and he advocates the same work of destruction for Aboriginal culture today.[86]

Australian liberals and leftists will have none of this, because, like contemporary Germans, their comportment to history has been transformed by the Holocaust. After all, Australian intellectuals do not debate issues of race and nationalism in a historical vacuum. The Holocaust exerts its presences here in the form of large survivor communities, Jewish organisations, intellectuals of Jewish descent, and its seepage into popular cultural memory since the 1970s through films, books, and war crimes trials. Discourse about the Holocaust provides a range of mobilisable terms like "the banality of evil" and genocide "denial."[87] Then there is the Holocaust's relationship to the concept of genocide. For our purpose, the significant issue is that it has become the secular symbol of evil in the western world, a status that has had a signal bearing on the genocide debate. For, from one perspective, the uniqueness of the Holocaust can mean that events that do not resemble it are not genocidal at all.[88] The federal government's denial of the stolen generations and Inga Clendinnen's attack on Manne's *In Denial* were driven by such an understanding.[89] Others, though, find another message in the Holocaust, recently articulated in elegant terms by Martin Jay:

> Historicising the Holocaust need not mean reducing it to the level of the 'normal' massacres of the innocents that punctuate all of recorded history, but rather remembering those quickly forgotten and implicitly forgiven events with the same intransigent refusal to normalise that is the only justifiable response to the Holocaust itself.[90]

Behind this careful balancing of the particular and universal in the Holocaust stands the historical philosophy of the German critic Walter Benjamin. To arguments that western culture advances by creative destruction, Benjamin pointed out that such historicism and theodicies view the past through the eyes of the victors and retrospectively justifies their actions and morality. He urged anamnestic solidarity with the victims today as a way of interrupting the supposed ineluctable and necessary process of civilisation. "There is no document of civilisation which is not at the same time a document of barbarism."[91] Benjamin articulates the perpetrator trauma, and he exemplifies the suspicion many intellectuals now have of theodicies. In this mode, the Holocaust is neither sacralised, nor banalised - the twin dangers highlighted recently by Tzvetan Todorov[92] - and assumes the status of a moral source with which to combat all forms of racism.

This was the interpretation adopted by Manne in the Demidenko debate in 1996, which was essentially about whether the Holocaust would be inscribed into Australian public culture as such a source. "Are we not too part of that common civilisation which experienced the shock of Auschwitz and which internalised its meaning?", he asked.[93] In his review of Manne's book on the debate, the conservative commentator Frank Devine effectively denied that we were, or indeed that we should be.[94] Fellow columnist, Michael Duffy, agrees, concerned as he is at the "growing influence of people, Jewish and non-Jewish, with a particular interest in the Nazi Holocaust." To be sure, he acknowledges that because many Jews have fresh memories of "victimisation and suffering" they "may be able to view the situation of Aborigines with greater clarify and compassion" than other Australians. Yet the dangers of this Holocaust paradigm is the point of his article, tellingly entitled "Keep the H Word out of our History."[95] Manne's Holocaust-inflected Jewish "preconceptions," Duffy insinuates, are "damaging the truth."[96] It is no coincidence that the intellectual camps at war over the Demidenko book are by and large the same as those in the genocide debate. There is no consensus on Holocaust consciousness in Australia, and it is readily apparent in the differing attitudes towards pan-Aboriginal political consciousness.

5. Conclusion

The German case shows that political humanisation issues from an open-ended discussion in a public sphere where the taboos of national myths of origin have been shattered by a consensus among leftist and liberal intellectuals about the need to thematise the barbarism inherent in those origins. At the same time, no faction of the intelligentsia, particularly the left- and right-wing factions with their absolute answers to 'the past', are able to impose themselves. Such a public sphere is the basis of a 'self-critical community' and it permits the problems highlighted by the perpetrator trauma to be addressed against an open horizon about the meanings of the past.

So does Australia have anything to learn from the German experience? The answer to this question depends on whether the similarities between the two cases are more significant than the differences. There are good reasons to suppose that they are. Australia shares the basic problem of national myths of origin and the consequent perpetrator trauma and process of political humanisation it inaugurates. Australia certainly needs to become a 'self-critical community'. The differences are significant only for the specific problems that such a process must address. In the Germany, the perpetrator trauma continues until the grounds for indignation about the past are addressed: compensating the victims of Nazism, ending racist violence against non-Europeans, liberalising the naturalisation laws. In Australia, it will also haunt future generations until Indigenous Australians can flourish here as well as any non-Indigenous Australian. We do not know what such a future society will look like: the point of political humanisation is to include relevant social stakeholders in the public conversation. A good start will have been made when Aborigines are not discussed as objects of white policy.

Notes

1. Adam 2001; Barkan 2000; Buruma 1994; McAdams 1997; Minow 1998; Schwan 2001; Villa-Vicencio and Verwoerd 2000.
2. Hirsch 1995; Olick and Robbins 1998; Olick 1998; Klein 2000.
3. Olick and Levy 1997. The authors also stress the importance of this process for West Germany's international credibility.
4. Gaita 2000a; Manne 1998; van Krieken 1999; Moses 2003a. A genocide debate has been gaining momentum since the 1980s when Bernard Smith, in his Boyer Lectures, said that Australians had been "caught out as it were red-handed playing the genocide game': Smith 1980, 52; Tony Barta's 1987 intervention is the first systematic treatment of the issue in the scholarly literature: Barta 1987. The most recent contribution is Reynolds 2001 and Moses 2004.
5. Clendinnen 2001, 6-7, 26; Windschuttle 2002.
6. A response to the rightwing attack on Aboriginal history, see Manne 2003, MacIntrye and Clark 2003 and Moses 2003b.
7. Bhabha 1990, 1; Attwood 2000, 15.

8. Balibar 1991, 87; Bain Attwood has made a similar argument: Attwood 1996.
9. Eliade 1963, 19.
10. Gouldner 1979.
11. Bourdieu 1984, 120; cf. Milner 2000.
12. Bourdieu 1987, 13-14.
13. Bourdieu's argument even becomes circular and appeals positivistically to 'reality' as a limit to the classificatory ambitions of intellectual groups: "In the struggle to make a vision of the world universally known and recognised, the balance of power depends on the symbolic capital accumulated by those who aim at imposing the various visions in contention, and on the extent to which these visions are themselves grounded in reality." Ibid 15.
14. Bourdieu 1998, 47; idem 1977, 188. Mark Davis's perceptive study of Australian cultural elites, *Ganglands*, makes a similar argument to Bourdieu, contending that intellectual rivalry can be explained along generational lines: Davis 1999.
15. Bernstein 1998; Assmann 1997; Caruth 1995. For a discussion of history and trauma in general, see LaCapra 2001.
16. Although narratives of such progress are unfashionable, indeed, inexplicable for many intellectuals, when seen in light of Germany's moral collapse in the Nazi years, the Federal Republic's political humanisation is readily apparent. Foucault is often cited as authority for the proposition that regimes of truth replace one another without moral progress, yet his own "What is Enlightenment" shows that in fact he did believe in the hypergood (Charles Taylor) of human autonomy and that he saw important gains for this ideal in postwar Europe. Foucault 1984, 46-47.
17. Wipperman 1976.
18. Barta 1989; Habermas 1996.
19. Geyer 1996.
20. Mitscherlich 1975. I discuss the theory in Moses 1999.
21. Geyer 1996; Albrecht et. al., 1999.
22. Marcuse 2001. Marcuse's book is an indispensable analysis and survey of post-war West German reckoning with the Nazi past.
23. Habermas 1990; Bernard Giesen calls it a "Holocaust identity": Geisen 1998.
24. Diner 1993, 117ff.; Marcuse 13. The German Democratic Republic claimed to have made a clean break with the nationalist past, and having smashed the capitalist substructure of fascism, it did not have any Nazi continuities with which to reckon. For this reason, it could,

with a good antifascist conscience, help train Palestinian terrorists and condemn the Federal Republic as an irredentist state. See Herf 1997.
25. Moses 1998a.
26. Lewis 1995.
27. Wippermann 1976; Schelsky 1975; Sontheimer 1976.
28. Maier 1988; Moses 1998b; Heer and Naumann 2000.
29. Maier 1988.
30. Olick 1998.
31. Assmann 1999, 48.
32. Naumann 2000.
33. Schaap 2000.
34. Appiah 1997.
35. Bhaba 1998.
36. Ivison 2000; Webber 1995; Patton 1995.
37. Postema 1991, 1180. For the 'politics of regret,' Olick and Coughlin 2003.
38. Beilharz 2001, 68.
39. Clark 1988, 13.
40. McKenna 1997, 18.
41. Clark 1988, 12, 15.
42. Keating 1995; Watson 2000.
43. Attwood 1996.
44. Howard 1996.
45. Hage 1998.
46. Blainey 1993; Maier 1988; Moses 2000a, 38.
47. On mythologies of white victimhood, see Curthoys, A.1999.
48. Blainey 1993, 15.
49. Howard 2000, 13.
50. Partington 2000.
51. Schmid 2000, 78; Decoust 2000; Romeo 2000, 15-16; Kiernan 2000.
52. Brunton 1998, 20.
53. van Krieken 1999.
54. Brunton 1998, 24.
55. Morgan 1999, 12.
56. Sheehan 2001, 22.
57. Windschuttle 2000b, 21.
58. Windschuttle 2000a, 8.
59. McGuiness 2000a, 2-4.
60. McGuiness 2000b, 18; Phillip Knightley made this implausible equation, but he is the only one I know of: Knightley 2000, 107.
61. McGuinness 2000a, 2.

62. McGuinness 1998, 139. I discuss issues of revisionism and denial in Moses 2003b.
63. Tatz 1999.
64. Manne 1997a, 2-3.
65. Manne 1982; idem 1994.
66. Manne 1993a, 2-3.; idem 1993b, 17.
67. Manne, 1996c 3; Gaita 1997, 47.
68. Manne 1997b, 85-86.
69. Manne 2000, 14.
70. Gaita 1993a; idem, 1993b. Manne has referred consistently to these writings and this distinction: Manne 1996b, 11.
71. Gaita 2000b, 171; In a careful, philosophical reflection on the relevant concepts, Gaita cast doubt on the efficacy of applying genocide to postwar Australia, and he took pains to distinguish between cultural genocide, genocide (according to the UN definition) and the Holocaust: Gaita 1995.
72. On the leftist view, see Povinelli 1998.
73. Manne 2001a, 22.
74. Barta 1987.
75. Howard 2000.
76. Moses 2000b.
77. Arndt 2001, 11; Duffy 2001a, R14; Johns 2001, 9-18; Howson 1999, 10-14; Howson 2000, 20-24; Sandall 2001, 2-3; Samuels 2000, 13; Windschuttle 2000a.
78. Duffy 2001a.
79. Windschuttle 2000c.
80. McGuinness 2000a, 3; Sandall 2001.
81. Brunton 1997; Windschuttle 2001, 5; Sandall 2001.
82. Gaita 2000.
83. Sorkin 1987.
84. Clark 2001, 11.
85. Samuels 2000.
86. Sandall 2001. The Bennelong Society writes of "the destruction of the old": Partington 2000.
87. Levey 2001; Curthoys, N. 2001; Tatz 1997.
88. The interpretation of the Holocaust is the target of Novick 1999.
89. Howard was prepared to "express his sorrow and distress at the appalling tragedy which overcame the Jewish people", but no more than "regret" at what previous Australian governments had done to Aborigines: Grattan, Kerr and Metherell 2000; Clendinnen 2001. This is also the editorial position of the *Courier Mail* (Brisbane): Editorial:

7 April 2001. Cf. Gaita 2000, 110.
90. Jay 1998, 204; cf. Gaita 1995.
91. Benjamin 1969, 256.
92. Todorov 1996.
93. Manne 1996a; Manne 1996d.
94. Devine 1996.
95. Duffy 2000, 10.
96. Duffy 2001b; Manne talks of his youth as the child of refugee central European Jewish parents in his Deakin Lecture: Manne 2001b.

References

Adam, Heribert. "Divided Memories: Confronting the Crimes of Previous Regimes." *Telos* (2001): 87-108.

Appiah, Kwame. "Cosmopolitan Patriots." *Critical Inquiry*, 23 (1997): 617-39.

Arndt, Bettina. "A Culture of Denial." *Sydney Morning Herald*, 26 April 2001.

Assmann, Jan. *Moses the Egyptian: the Memory of Egypt in Western Monotheism.* Cambridge, Mass.: Harvard University Press, 1997.

Assmann, Jan. "Tagtraumdeutung." *Frankfurter Allgemeine Zeitung*, 1 July 1999.

Attwood, Bain. "Mabo, Australia and the End of History." In *In the Age of Mabo*, edited by Bain Attwood, 100-116. Sydney: Allen and Unwin, 1996.

Attwood, Bain. "All Australians Would Gain From a Treaty." *The Australian*, 8 June 2000.

Balibar, Etienne. "The Nation Form: History and Ideology." In *Race, Nation, Class: Ambiguous Identities*, edited by Etienne Balibar and Immanuel Wallerstein: 86-106. London: Verso, 1991.

Barkan, Elazar. *The Guilt of Nations: Restitution and Negotiating Historical Injustices.* New York: Norton, 2000.

Barta, Tony "Relations of Genocide: Land and Lives in the Colonization of Australia." In *Genocide and the Modern Age: Etiology and Case Studies of Mass Death*, edited by Isidor Walliman and Michael N. Dobkowski: 237-251. Westport, Conn.: Greenwood Press. 1987.

Barta, Tony. "Anti-Fascism and Democracy in Dachau, 1945." In *Radical Perspectives on the Rise of Fascism in Germany, 1919-1945*, edited by Isidor Walliman and Michael N.Dobkowski: 289-318. New York: Monthly Review Press, 1989.

Beilharz, Peter. "Australian Civilization and its Discontents." *Thesis Eleven* 64, (2001): 65-76.

Benjamin, Walter. "Theses on the Philosophy of History." In Walter Benjamin, *Illuminations*, edited by Hannah Arendt: 253-264. New York: Schocken Books, 1969.

Bernstein, Richard. *Freud and the Legacy of Moses.* Cambridge and New York: Cambridge University Press, 1998.

Bhabha, Homi K. "Introduction: Narrating the Nation." In *Nation and Narration*, edited by Homi K. Bhabha: 1-7. London and New York: Routledge, 1990.

Bhabha, Homi K. "Foreword: Joking Aside: The Idea of a Self-Critical Community." In *Modernity, Culture, and 'the Jew'*, edited by Bryan Cheyette and Laura Marcus: xv-xx. Cambridge: Polity Press, 1998.

Blainey, Geoffrey. "Drawing Up a Balance Sheet of our History." *Quadrant* (July-August 1993): 10-15.

Bourdieu, Pierre. *Outline of a Theory of Practice.* Cambridge: Cambridge University Press, 1977.

Bourdieu, Pierre. *Distinction: a Social Critique of the Judgement of Taste.* Cambridge, Mass.: Harvard University Press, 1984.

Bourdieu, Pierre "What Makes a Social Class?" *Berkeley Journal of Sociology* 32 (1987): 1-17.

Bourdieu, Pierre. *Practical Reason.* Cambridge: Polity Press, 1998.

Brunton, Ron. "Shame about Aborigines." *Quadrant* (May 1997): 36-39.

Brunton, Ron. "Genocide, the 'Stolen Generations', and the 'Unconceived Generations.'" *Quadrant* (May 1998): 19-24.

Buruma, Ian. *The Wages of Guilt. Memories of War in Germany and Japan.* New York: Farrar Strauss Giroux, 1994.

Caruth, Cathy. Ed. *Trauma: Explorations in Memory.* Baltimore and London: Johns Hopkins University Press, 1995.

Clark, Geoff. "A Treaty would Unite, not Divide." *Australian*, 19 June 2001.

Clark, Manning. "The Beginning of Wisdom." *Time Australia*, 25 January 1988.

Clendinnen, Inga. "First Contact." *Australian's Review of Books* (May 2001).

Courier Mail. "Time to Stop the Real Genocide. Editorial." *Courier Mail*, 7 April 2001.

Curthoys, Ann. "Expulsion, Exodus and Exile in White Australian Historical Mythology." *Journal of Australian Studies* 61 (1999): 1-19.

Curthoys, Ned. "The Politics of Holocaust Representation: The Worldly Typologies of Hannah Arendt." *Arena Journal*, 16 (2001): 49-74. <www.arena.org.au/Archives/Journal%20Archive/Journal%2016/articles_16.html> (2002).

Davis, Mark. *Gangland: Cultural Elites and the New Generationalism.*

Sydney: Allen and Unwin, 1999.
Decoust, Michele. "Die verlorenen Kinder der Aborigines." *Die Tageszeitung*, 13 October 2000.
Devine, Frank. "Review of Robert Manne. *The Culture of Forgetting.*" *Quadrant* (July-August 1996): 94-96.
Diner, Dan. *Verkehrte Welten. Antiamerikanismus in Deutschland.* Frankfurt am Main: Eichborn, 1993.
Duffy, Michael. "Keep the H Word out of our History." *Daily Telegraph*, 5 January 2000.
Duffy, Michael. "Black and White Conceits." *Weekend Australian*, 26-27 May 2001a.
Duffy, Michael. "Who's Sorry Now?" *Courier Mail*, 7 June 2001b.
Eliade, Mircea. *Myth and Reality*. New York: Harper and Row, 1963.
Foucault, Michel. "What is Enlightenment?" In *The Foucault Reader*, edited by Paul Rabinow: 32-50. New York: Pantheon Books, 1984.
Gaita, Raimond. "Mabo (Part One)." *Quadrant* (September 1993a): 36-39.
Gaita, Raimond. "Mabo (Part Two)." *Quadrant* (October 1993b): 44-48.
Gaita, Raimond. "Remembering the Holocaust: Absolute Value and the Nature of Evil." *Quadrant* (December 1995): 7-15.
Gaita, Raimond. "Not Right." *Quadrant* (January-February 1997): 46-52.
Gaita, Raimond. *A Common Humanity: Thinking About Love and Truth and Justice.* London: Routledge, 2000a.
Gaita, Raimond. "Who Speaks, About What, To Whom, On Whose Behalf, With What Right?" In *Best Australian Essays*, edited by Peter Craven, 25-31. Sydney: Black Inc., 2000b.
Geisen, Bernard. *Intellectuals and the German Nation.* Cambridge: Cambridge University Press, 1998.
Geyer, Michael. "Politics of Memory in Contemporary Germany." In *Radical Evil*, edited by Joan Copjec: 169-200. London: Verso, 1996.
Geyer, Michael, Clemens Albrecht, Günter Behrmann and Michael Bock. *Die intellektuelle Gründung der Bundesrepublik. Eine Wirkungsgeschichte der Frankfurter Schule.* Frankfurt and New York: Campus, 1999.
Gouldner, Alvin. *The Future of Intellectuals and the Rise of the New Class.* London: MacMillan, 1979.
Grattan, Michelle, Joseph Kerr and Mark Metherell. "PM Offers Memorial for Blacks." *Sydney Morning Herald*, 23 May 2000.
Habermas, Jürgen. *Moral Consciousness and Communicative Action.* Cambridge, Mass.: MIT Press, 1990.
Habermas, Jürgen. "On How Postwar Germany has Faced its Recent Past." *Common Knowledge* 2 (1996): 1-3.
Hage, Ghassan. *White Nation: Fantasies of White Supremacy in a Multicultural Society.* Sydney: Pluto Press, 1998.

Heer, Hannes and Klaus Naumann. *War of Extermination: The German Military in World War II 1941-1944.* New York: Berghahn Books, 2000.

Herf, Jeffrey. *Divided Memory: The Nazi Past in the Two Germanys.* Cambridge and New York: Cambridge University Press, 1997.

Hirsch, Herbert. *Genocide and the Politics of Memory: Studying Death to Preserve Life.* Chapel Hill, N.C.: University of North Carolina Press, 1995.

Howard, John. "Confront our Past, Yes, But Let's Not be Consumed by it." *The Australian*, 19 November 1996.

Howard, John. "Towards a Common Destiny." *Sydney Morning Herald*, 12 May 2000.

Howson, Peter. "Rescued from the Rabbit Burrow: Understanding the 'Stolen Generation.'" *Quadrant* (July 1999): 10-14.

Howson, Peter. "Reality and Fantasy: The Abject Failure of Aboriginal Policy." *Quadrant* (April 2000): 20-24.

Ivison, Duncan. "Political Community and Historical Injustice." *Australasian Journal of Philosophy*, 3 (2000): 360-376.

Jay, Martin. *Cultural Semantics: Keywords for our Time.* Amherst: University of Massachusets Press, 1998.

Johns, Gary. "The Failure of Aboriginal Separatism." *Quadrant* (May 2001): 9-18.

Keating, Paul. *Advancing Australia: The Speeches of Paul Keating, Prime Minister*, edited by Mark Ryan. Sydney: Big Picture Publications, 1995.

Kiernan, Ben. "Australia's Aboriginal Genocide." *Bangkok Post*, 10 September 2000.

Klein, Kerwin Lee. "On the Emergence of Memory in Historical Discourse." *Representations*, 69 (2000): 127-50.

Knightley, Phillip. *Australia: a Biography of a Nation.* London: Jonathon Cape, 2000.

LaCapra, Dominick. *Writing History, Writing Trauma.* Ithaca and New York: Cornell University Press, 2001.

Levey, Geoffrey Brahm. "Reconciliation and 'the Banality of Evil.'" *Australian Financial Review*, 6 July 2001.

Lewis, Alison. "Analyzing the Trauma of German Unification." *New German Critique*, 64 (1995): 135-160.

MacIntrye, Stuart and Anna Clark. *The History Wars.* Melbourne: Melbourne University Press, 2003.

Maier, Charles S. *The Unmasterable Past: History, Holocaust and German National Identity.* Cambridge, Mass.: Harvard University Press, 1988.

Manne, Robert. *The New Conservatism in Australia.* Melbourne: Oxford University Press, 1982.

Manne, Robert. "On Political Correctness." *Quadrant* (January-February 1993a): 2-3.

Manne, Robert. "The Hidden Face of Freedom of Speech." *Sydney Morning Herald*, 9 August 1993b.

Manne, Robert. *The Shadow of 1917: The Cold War Conflict in Australia.* Melbourne: Text Publishers, 1994.

Manne, Robert. "The Demidenko Affair: Free Speech and Political Correctness." *Quadrant* (June 1996a): 8-15.

Manne, Robert. "Forget the Guilt, Remember the Shame." *The Australian*, 8 July 1996b.

Manne, Robert. "Editorial: The Coalition and the Aborigines." *Quadrant*, September (1996c): 3-4.

Manne, Robert. *The Culture of Forgetting: Helen Demidenko and the Holocaust.* Melbourne: Text, 1996d.

Manne, Robert. "Editorial: Why I have Resigned." *Quadrant* (December 1997a): 2-3.

Manne, Robert. "Paranoid Party Manifesto. Review of Pauline Hanson: The Truth." *Quadrant* (June 1997b): 85-86.

Manne, Robert. *The Way We Live Now: The Controversies of the Nineties.* Melbourne: Text Publishers, 1998.

Manne, Robert. "Honesty is the Best Federation Policy." *Sydney Morning Herald*, 20 November 2000.

Manne, Robert. "Charting a New Course for Black Survival." *Sydney Morning Herald*, 16 July 2001a.

Manne, Robert. "My Country – A Personal Journey. Deakin Lecture." Unpublished. Melbourne, 20 May (2001b).

Manne, Robert. Ed. *Whitewash: On Keith Windschuttle's Fabrication of Aboriginal History.* Melbourne: Black Inc., 2003.

Marcuse, Harold. *Legacies of Dachau: The Uses and Abuses of a Concentration Camp, 1933-2001.* Cambridge: Cambridge University Press, 2001.

McAdams, A. James. Ed. *Transitional Justice and the Rule of Law in New Democracies.* Notre Dame, Indiana: University of Notre Dame Press, 1997.

McGuinness, Padraic P. "The Political Elites' Contribution to Hansonism." In *Two Nations*, edited by Tony Abbott. Melbourne: Bookmann, 1998.

McGuinness, Padraic P. "Assimilation, Christians, and the Vicar of Bray." *Quadrant*, June (2000a).

McGuinness, Padraic P. "Aboriginal History: Black and White Views Won't Do." *The Australian*, 16 November 2000b.

McKenna, Mark. "The Black-Armbandwagon. *Eureka Street*, 7 (1997).

Milner, Andrew. "Class and Cultural Production." *Arena Journal*, 15 (2000): 117-137.

Minow, Martha. *Between Vengeance and Forgiveness: Facing History after Genocide and Mass Violence.* Boston: Beacon Press, 1998.

Mitscherlich, Alexander and Margarethe. *The Inability to Mourn: Principles of Collective Behavior.* New York: Grove Press, 1975.

Morgan, Patrick. "The End of Fortress Australia." *The Adelaide Review*, September 1999.

Moses, A. Dirk. "The State and the Student Movement, 1967-1977." In *Student Protest: The Sixties and After*, edited by Gerard de Groot: 139-149. London: Longman, 1998a.

Moses, A. Dirk. "Structure and Agency in the Holocaust: Daniel J. Goldhagen and his Critics." *History and Theory* 2 (1998b): 194-219.

Moses, A. Dirk. "The Forty-Fivers: a Generation between Fascism and Democracy." *German Politics and Society* 1 (1999): 94-126.

Moses, A. Dirk. "Right's Historical Wrongs." *The Australian*, 19 July 2000a.

Moses, A. Dirk. "An Antipodean Genocide? The Origin of the Genocidal Moment in the Colonization of Australia." *Journal of Genocide Research* 2 (2000b): 89-107.

Moses, A. Dirk. "Genocide and Holocaust Consciousness in Australia." *History Compass* 1: AU 28, 1-11 2003a <www.history-compass.com> (2003).

Moses, Dirk A. "Revisionism and Denial." In *Whitewash: On Keith Windschuttle's Fabrication of Aboriginal History*, edited by Robert Manne, 337-370. Melbourne: Black Inc., 2003b.

Moses, Dirk A. Ed. *Genocide and Settler Society.* New York: Berghahn Books, 2004.

Naumann, Michael. "Remembrance and Political Reality: Historical Consciousness in Germany after the Genocide." *New German Critique* 80 (2000): 17-28.

Novick, Peter. *The Holocaust in American Life.* Boston: Houghton Mifflin, 1999.

Olick, Jeffrey K. and Daniel Levy. "The Holocaust: Collective Memory and Cultural Constraint." *American Sociological Review* 6 (1997): 921-936.

Olick, Jeffrey K. "What Does it Mean to Normalize the Past? Official Memory in German Politics since 1989." *Social Sciences History* 22, (1998): 547-571.

Olick, Jeffrey K. and Joyce Robbins. "Social Memory Studies: from 'Collective Memory' to the Historical Sociology of Mnemonic Practices." *American Review of Sociology* 24 (1998): 105-140.

Olick, Jeffrey K. and Brenda Coughlin. "The Politics of Regret: Analytical Frames". In *The Politics of the Past: Repairing Historical Injustices*, edited by John B. Torpey: 37-62. New York: Rowman and Littlefield, 2003.

Partington, Geoff. "The Origins of the Bennelong Society: An Evaluation of A Workshop: Aboriginal Policy Failure, Reappraisal and Reform." 2000. <www.bennelong.com.au/papers/Articles/origins> (2000).

Patton, Paul. "Mabo, Freedom and the Politics of Difference." *Australian Journal of Political Science* (1995): 108-119.

Postema, Gerald. "On the Moral Presence of Our Past." *McGill Law Journal* 4 (1991): 1153-1180.

Povinelli, Elizabeth A. "The State of Shame: Australian Multiculturalism and the Crisis of Indigenous Citizenship." *Critical Inquiry* 24 (1998): 575-610.

Reynolds, Henry. *An Indelible Stain? The Question of Genocide in Australia's History.* Sydney: Viking, 2001.

Romeo, Antonella. "Die geraubte Generation." *Die Zeit*, 13 May 2000.

Samuels, Gordon. "One Past, One Future for us All." *The Australian*, 15 November 2000.

Sandall, Roger. "Romancing the Stone Age." *Sydney Morning Herald (Spectrum Supplement)*, 12/3 May 2001.

Schaap, Andrew. "Guilty Subjects and Political Responsibility: Arendt, Jaspers and the Resonance of the 'German Question' in Politics of Reconciliation." *Political Studies* 49 (2001): 749–66.

Schelsky, Helmut. *'Die Arbeit tun die Anderen': Klassenkampft und Priesterherrschaft der Intellektuellen.* Opladen: Westdeutscher Verlag, 1975.

Schmid, Thomas. "Australiens Holocaust." *Die Zeit*, 13 May 2000.

Schwan, Gesine. *Politics and Guilt: the Destructive Power of Silence.* Lincoln, Neb.: University of Nebraska Press, 2001.

Sheehan, Paul. "Saved, not Stolen: Laying the Genocide Myth to Rest." *Sydney Morning Herald*, 4 July 2001.

Smith, Bernard. *The Spectre of Truganini.* Sydney: Australian Broadcasting Commission, 1980.

Sontheimer, Kurt. *Das Elend unserer Intellektuellen.* Hamburg: Hoffmann und Campe, 1976.

Sorkin, David. *The Transformation of German Jewry, 1780-1840.* Oxford: Oxford University Press, 1987.

Tatz, Colin. "Genocide and the Politics of Memory." *Genocide Perspective* I (1997): 308-358.

Tatz, Colin. "Genocide in Australia." *Journal of Genocide Research* 1 (1999): 315-352.

Todorov, Tzvetan. "The Abuses of Memory." *Common Knowledge* 1 (1996): 6-26.

van Krieken, Robert. "The Barbarism of Civilization: Cultural Genocide and the 'Stolen Generations.'" *British Journal of Sociology* (1999): 295-318.

Villa-Vicencio, Charles and Wilhelm Verwoerd. eds. *Looking Back, Reaching Forward: Reflections on the Truth and Reconciliation Commission of South Africa.* London: Zed Books, 2000.

Watson, Don. *The Politics of History (or the History of Politics).* Sydney: History Council of NSW, 2000.

Webber, Jeremy. "The Jurisprudence of Regret: The Search for Standards of Justice in Mabo." *Sydney Law Review* 17 (1995): 5-28.

Windschuttle, Keith. "The Breakup of Australia." *Quadrant* (September 2000a): 8-18.

Windschuttle, Keith. "The Myths of Frontier Massacres in Australian History (Part I)." *Quadrant* (October 2000b).

Windschuttle, Keith. "The Myths of Frontier Massacres (Part II)." *Quadrant* (November 2000c): 17-25.

Windschuttle, Keith. "Selected Readings I." *The Australian Review of Books*, April (2001).

Windschuttle, Keith. *The Fabrication of Aboriginal History.* Sydney: Macleay Press, 2002.

Wippermann, Wolfgang. "The Post-War German Left and Fascism." *Journal of Contemporary History* 11 (1976): 185-219.

„Ein komplexes und wechselhaftes Spiel":
Sprachliche Resignifikation in Kanak Sprak und Aboriginal English

Steffi Hobuß

My essay performs a comparison of contemporary intercultural language development. It searches for the 'implicit philosophies of language' in 'Kanak Sprak' in Germany and Aboriginal English in Australia. In each of these linguistic contexts I find the practice of 'resignification' at work. The chapter uses Foucault's and Butler's theories of discourse to outline a theory of active 'resignification' which is then explored with reference to 'Kanak Sprak' and the work of Mudrooroo and Phillip Gwynne. It demonstrates that 'fictionality' allows a significant realm of linguistic creativity and 'intervention' within the space of hegemonic discourse – but at the same time that such discursive contestation also reaches back into the realm of real political practice, with real implications for all social actors, whether privileged 'white' or 'marginalized'.

Im Aufsatz wird ein Vergleich zwischen aktuellen interkulturellen Sprachentwicklungen vorgenommen: Der impliziten Sprachphilosophie in ‚Kanak Sprak' in Deutschland einerseits und Praktiken und Ausdrücken aus dem Feld des Aboriginal English im Kontext von Mudrooroos Werk und im Jugendroman Deadly, Unna? von Phillip Gwynne andererseits. Die Verwendung von im mehrkulturellen Feld diskriminierenden Ausdrücken wird daraufhin untersucht, unter welchen Bedingungen eine Wiederaneigung der jeweiligen Begriffe in resignifizierender Weise möglich ist.

Im ersten Teil ‚Von der Diskursanalyse zur Resignifikation' wird der Begriff der Resignifikation mit Foucault und Butler vor allem im Hinblick auf seine sprachpolitischen Implikationen erläutert. Schon bei Foucault findet sich der Anfang einer Theorie der Resignifikation. In seinem Denken über diskursive Praktiken und den Machtbegriff gibt es eine Kontinuität, die es erlaubt, den Vorzug der Diskursanalyse in ihrer spezifischen Perspektive auf diskursive Machtausübung zu sehen. Das Unternehmen der Resignifikation sprachlicher Diskriminierungen erweist sich als „komplexes und wechselhaftes Spiel" subversiver und politischer Wiederaneignungsmöglichkeiten, aber auch mit Beschränkungen und Risiken. Der zweite und der dritte Teil rekonstruieren einige Elemente solcher komplizierten Verteilungen, wobei die Diskursanalyse vor allem als erkenntnistheoretische Perspektive auf soziale Praktiken der Diskriminierung und deren Zurückweisung, Subversion und resignifizierenden Umkehrung dient.

Der Abschnitt über ‚Kanak Sprak' beleuchtet die sprachlichen Besonderheiten und Machtverteilungen, die sich in der Frage formulieren lassen: „Wieso dürfen Sie Kanake zu sich sagen und ich nicht?" Das Ergebnis zeigt: Das Opfer einer sprachlichen Verletzung kann zwar das Trauma nicht rückgängig machen, aber nur es selbst kann die Bezeichnung in einer entgegengesetzten Strategie als Selbstbezeichnung verwenden. Das rührt daher, dass man durch die sprachliche Verletzung seiner Selbstkontrolle beraubt wird. Jede neuerliche Anrufung würde den Kontextverlust reaktivieren (und darüber hinaus wie jede Anrufung auf den grundsätzlich imaginären Charakter dieser Selbstkontrolle verweisen).

Der dritte Teil betrachtet die Situation in Australien und zeigt im Vergleich Gemeinsamkeiten und Unterschiede: Zum literarischen und politischen Projekt der ‚Kanak Sprak' gibt es keine direkte australische Entsprechung, und die gesellschaftliche Situation der erst diskriminierten und dann resignifizierenden Menschen ist im Falle von Aboriginal English und dem Umgang mit diskriminierenden Bezeichnungen für die Aborigines eine andere. Denn ‚Aborigine' ist ein schillernderer Ausdruck als ‚Kanake', der in bestimmten Phasen eindeutig diskriminierend und nun aggressiv-selbstbewusst resignifizierend verwendet wurde, während jener eine scheinbar ‚neutrale', ‚bloß-klassifikatorische' Bedeutung beansprucht, in der die Diskriminierung auf der Ebene der Sprache verdeckt bleibt. Dadurch sind die Möglichkeiten der resignifizierenden Verwendung durch die Diskriminierten eingeschränkt: Eine Resignifikation erfordert eine erkenn- und umkehrbare diskursive Strategie.

Allen untersuchten Beispielen ist aber gemeinsam, dass die Fiktionalität eine wichtige Rolle spielt: ‚Kanak Sprak' ist ein teilfiktionales Unternehmen, das auf die Szene derer, die sich Kanaken nennen, bestätigend zurückgewirkt hat; Mudrooroos Reskription seiner Identität und seines ersten Buches ist ein Projekt, in dem die fiktionalen und die nichtfiktionalen Anteile nur schwer auseinanderzutrennen wären, was demonstriert, in welchem Ausmaß Subjekte als Effekte von Diskursen betrachtet werden können; Gwynnes Jugendroman erzählt eine fiktionale Geschichte mit deutlichen Anspielungen auf autobiographische Erfahrungen und real geschehene Verbrechen und demonstriert dabei die Bedeutung der Anrufungen für die Subjektkonstitution aller Angehörigen der dargestellten mehrkulturellen Gesellschaft, wobei sich die Angehörigen der hegemonialen Kultur nicht aus den verletzenden Geschehnissen heraushalten können. Betrachtet man den in den Texten vorhandenen expliziten und impliziten Bezug auf Begriffe wie Identität und Authentizität, könnte es so aussehen, als ob diejenigen, die Resignifikationen vornehmen, sich manchmal auf Modelle des Authentischen, Vordiskursiven berufen. Aber dagegen spricht deutlich Mudrooroos Ablehnung von Identitätszuschreibungen nach Maßgabe des Blutes oder der Rasse, wenn er sich auf seine geschichtliche Lebenserfahrung beruft, d.h. die Anrufungen, denen er ausgesetzt war, die er angenommen und die er vorgenommen hat. Die Ablehnung solch unhistorischer Identitätszuschreibungen ist ein gemeinsames Element aller untersuchten Strategien der Resignifikation als eines diskursiven Prozesses: Auch Zaimoglu verwahrt sich gegen die Festlegung auf ein ‚Erbe', die die Logik der Repression und der Zensur wieder in Geltung bringen möchte, und Gwynnes jugendliche Hauptfigur erlebt, wie gerade die festlegenden Zuschreibungen tödlich sein können und entschließt sich vor dem Hintergrund der erkannten diskursiven Anrufungen zu einem verantwortlichen Handeln. Darin liegt eine Chance für das mehrkulturelle Zusammenleben in beiden betrachteten Gesellschaften, zusammen mit der Hoffnung auf gelingende Resignifikationen, die durch Praktiken der Zensur nicht zu verhindern sind, weil die Zensur nur Ausdruck der Angst vor jenen Positionen ist, die für die Gesetzeslogik der Repression bedrohlich sein könnten.

1.   Von der Diskursanalyse zur Resignifikation

Im ersten Band seiner geplanten *Geschichte der Sexualität* mit dem Titel *Der Wille zum Wissen* findet sich bei Foucault der Anfang dessen, was man als Theorie der Resignifikation bezeichnen könnte, ohne dass er diesen Begriff hier selbst benutzte. Die entscheidende Passage steht im Kontext von Foucaults doppelter Abgrenzung von der Konzeption einer repressiven Macht einerseits sowie andererseits von der Annahme einer Gesetz-Begehrens-Struktur mit einem Gesetz, das einen Mangel und dadurch das Begehren erst erzeugt, weil beide Auffassungen ein zu stark juridisch-souveränes Verständnis der Macht hätten.[1] Im Kontrast dazu entfaltet er in Form einer Aufzählung, was er unter ‚Macht' versteht:

> die Vielfältigkeit von Kraftverhältnissen, die ein Gebiet bevölkern und organisieren; das Spiel, das in unaufhörlichen Kämpfen und Auseinandersetzungen diese Kraftverhältnisse verwandelt, verstärkt, verkehrt; die Stützen, die diese Kraftverhältnisse aneinander finden, indem sie sich zu Systemen verketten – oder die Verschiebungen und Widersprüche, die sie gegeneinander isolieren; und schließlich die Strategien,

in denen sie zur Wirkung gelangen und deren große Linien und institutionelle Kristallisierungen sich in den Staatsapparaten, in der Gesetzgebung und in den gesellschaftlichen Hegemonien verkörpern.[2]

Hier gibt Foucault keine Definition, sondern eine Aufzählung sehr verschiedenartiger Elemente in vier Gruppen, die dazu beitragen, dass sich in menschlichen Gesellschaften so etwas wie Macht ausmachen lässt: Er nennt (1) vielfältige „Kraftverhältnisse", (2) „das Spiel" von Auseinandersetzungen, in dem sie sich befinden und sich ständig ändern, (3) das bestärkende oder einschränkende Verhältnis solcher Kräfte zueinander und (4) die Strategien ihrer gesellschaftlichen Auswirkung und Verkörperung. So etwas wie ein Wesen der Macht ist Foucault gerade nicht bereit anzugeben, und er bezeichnet seine Auffassung insofern als „nominalistische": „Die Macht ist der Name, den man einer komplexen strategischen Situation in einer Gesellschaft gibt."[3] Macht sei stets etwas, das sich in einer Verteilung befinde, nicht etwas zum Haben oder Verlieren, sie „kommt von unten".[4] Daher rückt Foucault im folgenden Text zwar vom Sprechen über den Begriff ‚Macht' nicht vollständig ab, schreibt aber doch häufiger von „Machtbeziehungen". Machtbeziehungen seien allen anderen Typen von Verhältnissen nicht äußerlich, sondern ihnen immanent, und sie seien „gleichzeitig intentional und nicht-subjektiv".[5] Wie passt das zusammen, könnte man fragen, wie können Machtbeziehungen, die nicht derart funktionieren sollen, dass einzelne Subjekte repressiv auf andere einwirken, trotzdem als intentional gedacht werden? Diese Intentionalität möchte Foucault an dieser Stelle für die Erkennbarkeit der Machtbeziehungen in Anspruch nehmen: Er spricht von einem „Kalkül", von „Absichten und Zielsetzungen", die die Machtbeziehungen überhaupt sichtbar und erkennbar sein lassen, ohne dass sie als Wirkung auf eine Wahl oder Entscheidung eines individuellen Subjekts erklärend zurückgeführt werden könnten. Als Antwort gibt er die Auskunft, die Intentionalität oder Rationalität, die hier am Werk sei, lasse sich als die „Rationalität von Taktiken"[6] verstehen; es ließen sich eine Logik oder Absichten auch dann rekonstruieren, wenn niemand einzelnes sie souverän entworfen habe. Das von ihm so genannte „nominalistische" Denken des Machtbegriffs führt Foucault also zur Aufmerksamkeit auf die Machtbeziehungen, deren spezifische Rationalität er als die Rationalität von Taktiken begreift, und das wiederum führt ihn auf die Frage nach der Rolle des Widerstands: Widerstand lasse sich nicht mehr als etwas begreifen, das der Macht äußerlich und entgegengesetzt sei, Widerstand liege „niemals außerhalb der Macht"[7], es gebe auch nicht einen grundsätzlichen Ort des Widerstands im Sinne eines Orts „der Großen

Weigerung"[8]; und wieder gibt Foucault seine positive Bestimmung dessen, was man unter Widerstand verstehen könnte, nicht in Form einer Definition an, sondern folgendermaßen:

> es gibt einzelne Widerstände: mögliche, notwendige, unwahrscheinliche, spontane, wilde, einsame, abgestimmte, kriecherische, gewalttätige, unversöhnliche, kompromißbereite, interessierte oder opferbereite Widerstände, die nur im strategischen Feld der Machtbeziehungen existieren können.[9]

An die Stelle der Bestimmung eines grundlegenden theoretischen Ortes, von dem aus jeder Widerstand immer und situationsunabhängig zu denken sei, treten hier Widerstände im Plural, die als Praktiken in ihrer Vielfalt und Vielzahl jeweils immer schon im Feld von Machtbeziehungen stattfinden. Als Konsequenz dieser Argumentationskette vom Machtbegriff über den der Machtbeziehungen zum Widerstand formuliert Foucault vier Regeln, die bei der Untersuchung von Diskursen zu berücksichtigen seien, und erweitert seine früheren Überlegungen, vor allem aus der *Archäologie des Wissens*[10] und aus *Die Ordnung der Dinge*[11], um ein neues Element.[12] Erstens sei die „Regel der Immanenz"[13] zu beachten, dass nämlich jedes untersuchte Machtwissen stets in jeweils lokaler Form innerhalb gesellschaftlicher Praktiken auftrete und dort erkennbar sei, zweitens die „Regel der stetigen Variationen"[14] der Verteilung der Kräfteverhältnisse, die direkt aus Foucaults oben zitierter Beschreibung seines Machtverständnisses folgt, drittens die „Regel des zweiseitigen Bedingungsverhältnisses"[15] einer Gesamtstrategie und ihrer Taktiken, und viertens die „Regel der taktischen Polyvalenz der Diskurse"[16] – mit der uns Foucault auffordert, die Vielfalt diskursiver Elemente mit ihren mannigfaltigen Rollen innerhalb verschiedenartiger Strategien nicht vorschnell zu vereinheitlichen. Und nun folgt die entscheidende Formulierung des Ziels seiner Diskursanalyse:

> Diese Verteilung [...] mit den Varianten und unterschiedlichen Wirkungen je nach dem, wer spricht, seiner Machtposition und seinem institutionellen Kontext, *mit all ihren Verschiebungen und Wiederbenutzungen identischer Formeln zu entgegengesetzten Zwecken* – diese Verteilung gilt es zu rekonstruieren. [...] Es handelt sich um ein komplexes und wechselhaftes Spiel, in dem der Diskurs gleichzeitig Machtinstrument und -effekt sein kann, aber auch

Hindernis, Gegenlager, Widerstandspunkt und Ausgangspunkt für eine entgegengesetzte Strategie.[17]

Und im unmittelbar folgenden Text führt Foucault als Beispiel an, dass der starke Vormarsch der sozialen Kontrollen über die Homosexualität in der Psychiatrie, Jurisprudenz und Literatur des 19. Jahrhunderts auch erst „die Konstitution eines Gegen-Diskurses ermöglicht" habe: „die Homosexualität hat begonnen, von sich selbst zu sprechen [...] – und dies häufig in dem Vokabular und in den Kategorien, mit denen sie medizinisch disqualifiziert wurde."[18] Diese Passage enthält in komprimierter Weise sowohl Foucaults Verständnis der Untersuchung von Diskursen als Rekonstruktion der vielfältigen Varianten und Wirkungen diskursiver Elemente, wie er es in seinen vorherigen Werken entfaltet hatte, als auch den neuen Hinweis darauf, dass eine solche Rekonstruktion sichtbar machen könne, wie einzelne „Formeln" im Sinne individuierbarer diskursiver Elemente Verschiebungen unterliegen, Verschiebungen, die (mit der Wiederholung eines und desselben diskursiven Elements) sogar entgegengesetzten Zwecken dienen können. Foucault spricht hier davon, dass „der Diskurs gleichzeitig Machtinstrument und -effekt sein kann", was in diesem Kontext bedeutet, dass einzelne diskursive Elemente und ganze Diskurse *zur gleichen Zeit und mit identischen Mitteln* sowohl Macht ausüben als auch sich als Resultat der Machtausübung begreifen lassen. In diesem Sinne zeigt das Beispiel des Homosexualitätsdiskurses für Foucault, dass dasjenige Vokabular und diejenigen medizinischen Kategorien, mit denen Homosexuelle diskriminiert und disqualifiziert worden waren, dazu dienten, die Anerkennung der Rechtmäßigkeit oder sogar so etwas wie der Natürlichkeit der Homosexualität zu fordern. Hier sei erstens mit bestimmten diskursiven Einteilungen Macht ausgeübt worden, und zwar in diskriminierender Weise, zweitens habe dadurch „die Homosexualität" sich als Resultat dieses Diskurses konfigurieren können, um schließlich die Kategorien der einstigen Disqualifizierung zum Sprechen von sich selbst und zur Einforderung von Rechten zu nutzen, also als „Widerstandspunkt und Ausgangspunkt für eine entgegengesetzte Strategie". In diesem Verständnis von Gegen-Diskursen liegt auch der Ausgangspunkt für eine Theorie der Resignifikation; daran werden die Überlegungen Butlers systematisch anschließen.

In Foucaults genannten früheren Arbeiten, in denen es um den Begriff des Diskurses geht, finden sich die Voraussetzungen für dieses neue Denken des Widerstandes durch die Wiederholung einer „Formel" zu Zwecken, die den alten geradezu entgegengesetzt sein können, und damit Voraussetzungen dafür, die Diskursanalyse auch als Rekonstruktion solcher wiederholender Praktiken zu begreifen. In der *Archäologie des*

Wissens beschäftigt sich Foucault im Abschnitt über die Aussagefunktion mit der Frage, ob und ggf. in welchem Umfang man die Aussage durch ihren materiellen Status definieren kann. Dabei tritt das Problem auf, ob und wie man durch die „vielfältigen Vorkommnisse, durch diese Wiederholungen, diese Transkriptionen hindurch die Identität der Aussage feststellen"[19] kann. Weil Foucault hier auf Formationsregeln des Diskurses hinaus möchte, genügt es ihm nicht, Aussagen als Äußerungen zu verstehen; diese versteht er als „Ereignis, das sich nicht wiederholt".[20] Er möchte also Aussagen nicht als bloße einzelne Ereignisse behandeln, was es aber schwierig werden lässt, der Aussage eine „wiederholbare Materialität"[21] zuzusprechen. Hier befindet er sich in der Zwickmühle, dass er zum einen die materielle Existenzweise der Aussage beschreiben möchte und zum anderen aber die sich anbietende Definition im Sinne der Äußerung ablehnt. Dadurch wird ihm die Aussage zu einem „paradoxen Objekt"[22], und er schreibt:

> Das System der Materialität, dem die Aussagen notwendig gehorchen, gehört also mehr der Institution zu als als der räumlich-zeitlichen Lokalisierung; es definiert *Möglichkeiten der Re-Inskription und der Transkription* [...] mehr als begrenzte und vergängliche Individualitäten.[23]

Die spezifische Art der Materialität, die der Aussage zukommen soll, ist zunächst keine der räumlich-zeitlichen Lokalisierung, u.a. weil eine Aussage in verschiedenen materiellen Vorkommensweisen dieselbe sein kann (etwa auf einem Notizpapier, in einem Buch, in mündlicher Form). Individuierbare Einzelereignisse würde Foucault ja als Äußerungen bezeichnen. Da Aussagen aber reinskribiert und transkribiert werden können sollen, soll ihnen trotzdem eine eigene Materialität zukommen, die sie etwa von einer Proposition unterscheidet. Foucault hat sich hier die schwierige Aufgabe gestellt, sowohl der Tatsache gerecht zu werden, dass Aussagen in Form sprachlicher Formulierungen als Ereignisse auftreten, als auch eine Dimension haben, die darüber hinausgeht, insofern Aussagen noch etwas anderes sind als „die Abfolge von Anzeichen auf einer Substanz".[24] Möglicherweise trennt Foucault hier in zu starker und künstlicher Weise zwischen Instanzen der „Wiederholung ohne Veränderung ihrer Identität"[25], die er ausschließlich auf der Äußerungsebene ansiedeln möchte, und der Ebene der Aussagefunktion. Diese Dichotomie wird zwar vermeidbar, wenn man die Struktur von Sprechakten betrachtet und sie derart bestimmt, wie Butler das im Sinne von Derridas Begriff der Iterabilität vornimmt: dass es nämlich in der

Struktur des Zeichens selbst als Markierung (marque) liegt, dass es immer zugleich Wiederholung eines Alten und Bruch mit dessen Kontext und etwas Neues ist. Aber dann muss man aufpassen, die machttheoretische Perspektive nicht wiederum aus dem Blick zu verlieren, die die Möglichkeit der Resignifikation nicht allein innerhalb der Sprachstruktur ansiedelt, was ja gerade den Vorteil der Diskurstheorie ausmacht.[26] Mit Jürgen Link und Ursula Link-Herr[27] hebt Jäger[28] durchaus im Sinne dieser Problematik vier Aspekte der Foucaultschen Diskurstheorie besonders hervor: Erstens sei unter ‚Diskurs' nur die sprachliche Seite einer umfassenderen diskursiven Praxis zu verstehen, die ihrerseits aus dem gesamten Ensemble der jeweiligen Wissensproduktion besteht; zweitens analysiere Foucault das Verhältnis zwischen Diskursen als spezifischen Aussageformationen und ihren Gegenständen, aber nicht in der Weise der „optik-analogen"[29] erkenntnistheoretischen Modelle der Widerspiegelung, ohne dass damit wiederum ein linguistischer Idealismus verbunden sei, denn für Foucault gebe es diskursive neben nichtdiskursiven Praktiken; drittens habe man unter Diskursen im Foucaultschen Sinne „Streuungen"[30] von Aussagen zu verstehen (im Gegensatz zur relativen Geschlossenheit von Texten, die gleichwohl mehrere Themen enthalten können; Jäger spricht daher von „Diskurssträngen", die sich aus „Diskursfragmenten" zusammensetzen) – nach deren generierendem Prinzip Foucault in der *Archäologie des Wissens* sucht, jedoch ohne eines explizit angeben zu können[31]; viertens treten Diskurse immer als spezifische „diskursive Formationen" auf, deren relative Stabilität, Zerfallsereignisse und Neuformationen dasjenige seien, was sich untersuchen lasse. Mit dem zweiten Punkt könnte man sich so etwas angesprochen denken wie die Frage nach dem „Verhältnis von Diskurs und Wirklichkeit".[32] Jäger betont, dass es sich bei Foucault natürlich nicht um eine Widerspiegelungstheorie handelt; vielmehr führten die Diskurse ein „Eigenleben" und stellten „Materialitäten sui generis" dar.[33] Diese Beschreibung ist insofern missverständlich, dass sie den Eindruck erwecken könnte, es gebe neben dem Reich der normalen Gegenstände noch das Reich der Diskurse mit deren eigener Materialität. Jäger schließt dieses mögliche Missverständnis erst später aus, wenn er deutlicher formuliert, diskursive Praktiken seien „keine besonderen Tätigkeiten im Unterschied etwa zu ‚praktischen Tätigkeiten'".[34] Diskursive Praktiken *sind* praktische Tätigkeiten unter zahlreichen anderen und mit diesen in wiederum vielfältigen Weisen verknüpft. Damit kommt die Bestimmung diskursiver Praktiken demjenigen sehr nahe, was Ludwig Wittgenstein als „Sprachspiel" bezeichnet hat: „Ich werde auch das Ganze: der Sprache und der Tätigkeiten, mit denen sie verwoben ist, das ‚Sprachspiel' nennen."[35] Das Sprachspiel ist auch hier das Gesamte, es besteht aus der

Sprache, die ihrerseits aus praktischen Tätigkeiten besteht, und aus anderen Tätigkeiten, mit denen sie verwoben ist. Sprechen ist selbst Handeln und es kann doch eine Unterscheidung zwischen Sprechen und Handeln getroffen werden, deren Grenzlinie freilich vom Einzelfall, der Perspektive und der Neigung abhängt. Auch für Butlers Untersuchung der *Politik des Performativen* ist die Unterscheidung wichtig, da, wie Butler kritisiert, einige Fälle diskriminierenden Sprechens von der geltenden Rechtsprechung als „nur sprachlich" bewertet und damit der Kritik entzogen werden, andere Fälle resignifizierenden Gebrauchs aber als Handlung kritisiert und dann verboten werden; beides im repressiven Sinne. Butler stellt in ihren Büchern dar, auf welche Weisen erst durch die dauernde Zitation des zirkulierenden Wissens darüber, was Geschlecht ist, darüber was ein Körper ist, darüber, was ein Subjekt ist usw., diese erst als Gegebenheiten entstehen. So wird ihr zufolge z.B. „eine bestimmte gesellschaftliche Existenz des Körpers erst dadurch möglich, daß er sprachlich angerufen wird".[36] Und auch das Subjekt gelangt erst insofern zur Existenz, als es fundamental von der Anrede des Anderen abhängig ist, was auch bedeutet, dass jede einzelne neue Anrede prinzipiell Angst erzeugt, weil sie immer auch die anderen, vorausgegangenen, prägenden Anreden erinnert und reinszeniert, die wiederum erst dadurch die Kraft hatten und haben, die Existenz zu verleihen.[37] Es besteht also ein zirkulärer Zusammenhang zwischen der Anrufung und dem Subjekt. Auch das, was als zu Sagendes verboten oder zensiert wird, hat an diesem Bedingungsverhältnis teil, indem es nicht nur verbietend, sondern auch produktiv oder formativ verstanden werden kann; die „Subjektproduktion", wie Butler sich ausdrückt, geschieht auch durch die Regulierung des Sprechens des betreffenden Menschen sowie vor allem dadurch, dass reguliert wird, was in den gesellschaftlichen Bereich des sagbaren Diskurses fällt: „Die Frage ist nicht, was ich sagen kann, sondern was den Bereich des Sagbaren konstituiert, in dem sich mein Sprechen von Anfang an bewegt."[38] Jäger fasst sein Verständnis vom Verhältnis zwischen Subjekt und Diskurs bei Foucault in sehr ähnlicher Weise zusammen: „Das Individuum macht den Diskurs nicht, das Umgekehrte ist der Fall."[39] Der Diskurs „ist sozusagen Resultante all der vielen Bemühungen der Menschen, in einer Gesellschaft tätig zu sein. Was dabei herauskommt, ist etwas, das *so* keiner gewollt hat, an dem aber alle in den verschiedensten Formen und Lebensbereichen [...] mitgestrickt haben."[40] Dieses Verständnis des Verhältnisses von „Subjekt und Diskurs" oder „Anrufung/Anrede und Subjektproduktion" erlaubt es laut Butler zu sehen, auf welche Weise sprachliche Diskriminierung und sprachliche Verletzungen passieren, und zwar auch im mehrkulturellen Feld. Butler fragt, was man eigentlich behauptet, wenn man von sprachlichen

Verletzungen spricht, und weist darauf hin, dass man der Sprache eine starke Handlungsmacht zuschreibt; und wenn man von der verletzenden Kraft gewisser Äußerungen mit dem Ziel spricht, auf sprachliche Verletzungen anklagend hinzuweisen, tut man das wiederum in sprachlicher Weise und versucht damit also, dem einen sprachlichen Geschehen ein anderes ebenfalls sprachliches Geschehen entgegensetzen. Doch auch die Entgegensetzung macht von der Kraft der Sprache Gebrauch: „Wir sind gefangen in einer Bindung, die keine Zensur zu lösen vermag".[41] Denn auch eine Zensur wäre ein sprachliches Geschehen. Und schon auf der allerersten Seite von Haß spricht nennt Butler ihre These, dass unsere Verletzbarkeit durch die Sprache darauf beruht, dass wir nicht aus ihr hinauskönnen, weil es sprachliche Bedingungen sind, die uns konstituieren. Das gilt zunächst ganz grundsätzlich für jede Benennung als verletzende Handlung, weil jede Anrede die genannte Abhängigkeit von der Anrede des Anderen reaktiviert, aber in manchmal besonders auffälligem Maße für beleidigendes, diskriminierendes Sprechen.

Aber das verletzende Sprechen ist für Butler auch der Ansatzpunkt für das Denken möglicher Resignifikation: Ausgehend vom Beispiel der Verwendung des ursprünglich verletzenden Wortes ‚Nigger' im Rap zu Zwecken der Selbstdefinition[42] führt sie zunächst zwei Thesen an, die ihrer Meinung nach beide „der Resignifizierung der anstößigen Äußerung"[43] nicht Rechnung tragen können. Einerseits könnte man meinen, die verletzende Kraft der Wörter hänge vollständig vom Verwendungskontext ab, so dass eine Veränderung dieses Kontexts auch die Wirkung vergrößern, verringern oder aufheben könne. Diese Auffassung könne jedoch nicht erklären, auf welche Weise solche Wörter, wenn sie wirksam sind, ihre Macht ausüben. Die Gegenthese würde lauten, dass bestimmte Äußerungen kontextunabhängig verletzend seien, könne aber gerade die manchmal mögliche Umdeutung und Neuinszenierung nicht erklären. Butler selbst vertritt dagegen die Auffassung,

> daß die veränderliche Macht solcher Ausdrücke eine Art diskursiver Performativität markiert, die nicht aus diskreten Reihen von Sprechakten, sondern aus einer rituellen Kette von Resignifizierungen besteht.[44]

Butlers „diskursive Performativität" macht hier Gebrauch von Foucaults Diskurstheorie und von Aspekten seiner Bestimmung der Aussage, wenn es darum geht, dass anrufende, diskriminierende und verletzende Sprechakte nicht als Kette einzelner diskreter Sprechereignisse angemessen verstanden werden können. Sondern Butler denkt solche

Sprechakte als Kette miteinander verbundener Glieder, deren Verbindung eine der *rituellen* Wiederholung ist, in ihrem *Aufführungscharakter* also durch die Gleichzeitigkeit von Wiederholung und Neuaufführung gekennzeichnet ist. Die Unterscheidung zwischen Sprechen und Handeln erlaubt es zudem, zumindest einzelfallweise zwischen illokutionären und perlokutionären Wirkungen des Sprechens zu unterscheiden. Die „Kluft, die den Sprechakt von seinen künftigen Effekten trennt" hat dabei auch günstige Konsequenzen: „Sie eröffnet nämlich eine Theorie der sprachlichen Handlungsmacht, die eine Alternative zu der endlosen Suche nach rechtlichen Gegenmitteln darstellt."[45] Eine physische Verletzung dagegen bietet keinen Platz für eine solche Unterscheidung: Sie ist das Resultat physischer Gewalt, für die es keine Resignifikationsmöglichkeit gibt. Hier schließt Butlers Auffassung der sprachlichen Handlungsmacht über Austins Theorie der Performativität hinaus an ihre früheren Arbeiten über Geschlecht und Körper an, in denen sie dargelegt hatte, wie Handlungsmöglichkeiten mit Wiederholungen und Variationen zusammenhängen. Ihr Buch *Körper von Gewicht* verortet das Handlungsvermögen des Subjekts, das sich Normen widersetzt, gerade darin, dass es von solchen Normen erst befähigt, wenn nicht hervorgebracht wurde, die es „in einer ständig wiederholenden oder reartikulierenden Praxis" gelten lässt[46]; schon in *Das Unbehagen der Geschlechter* war für sie „die ‚Handlungsmöglichkeit' in der Möglichkeit anzusiedeln, diese Wiederholung zu variieren".[47] Ein enormes Gewicht lastet nun aber auf dem Charakter der Variation der Wiederholung – wodurch ist eine bestimmte Wiederholung nicht nur als eine variierende sondern als eine Widerstand leistende qualifiziert? Butler schreibt: „Brüche mit früheren Kontexten oder mit gewöhnlichen Anwendungen sind tatsächlich entscheidend für den politischen Vorgang der performativen Äußerung"[48] – aber wenn die Wiederholung ohnehin notwendig dafür ist, dass etwas Bedeutung hat, welche leistet dann den Bruch mit dem, was im Gegensatz zum Bruch der „gewöhnliche Kontext" wäre? In *Das Unbehagen der Geschlechter* beleuchtet Butler die paradigmatische Bedeutung der Parodie – in der Imitation hegemonialer Praktiken durch die Parodie werde der hegemonialen Kultur ihr Anspruch weggenommen, es gebe natürliche, wesenhafte Identitäten[49], aber auch hier schreibt Butler „Die Parodie an sich ist nicht subversiv".[50] Was macht also eine Wiederholung oder einen Akt der Parodie zu einem subversiven oder politisch widerständigen? Die Antwort lässt sich an einer Textpassage entfalten, deren Wichtigkeit leicht unterschätzt wird:

> Dennoch ist dieses Scheitern [parodistischer Inszenierungen, S.H.], ‚real' zu werden und das

> ‚Natürliche' zu verkörpern, meiner Ansicht nach eine konstitutive Verfehlung aller Inszenierungen der Geschlechtsidentität, weil diese ontologischen Orte grundsätzlich unbewohnbar sind. Von daher das subversive Gelächter im Pastiche-Effekt jener parodistischen Verfahren, die das Original, das Authentische und das Reale selbst als Effekt darstellen.[51]

Die Passage stammt aus einem Kontext, in dem es darum geht, dass alle Inszenierungen als natürlich gedachter Geschlechtsidentitäten für Butler daran scheitern müssen, dass sie einen natürlichen, substanzartig seienden Ort postulieren, dessen Ausdruck sie scheinbar sind, den es aber gar nicht gibt. An der Struktur des parodistischen Aktes selbst ist es nicht abzulesen, ob er eine resignifizierende, gegenstrategische Kraft entfalten kann. Butler schreibt hier aber vom subversiven „Pastiche-*Effekt* jener parodistischen Verfahren [Hervorhebung von mir, S.H.]", die nicht nur ihr eigenes Scheitern ausstellen, sondern auch die Naturalisierung von Effekten sichtbar machen. Welche das sein können, wird u.a. vom gesellschaftlichen Kontext des Resignifikationsaktes ahängen. Dafür wären höchstens notwendige, aber keine hinreichenden Merkmale angebbar. Die Parodie wird für Butler trotzdem nicht zu einem willkürlichen Verfahren, weil die Betrachter-Perspektive entscheidend dafür ist, ob der Pastiche-Effekt erzielt werden kann, der das subversive Gelächter ermöglicht. Eine Einschränkung, ein Risiko gibt es dabei: es ist niemals eine neutrale, unschuldige Wiederholung möglich:

> Niemand hat jemals eine Verletzung durchgearbeitet, ohne sie zu wiederholen: Ihre Wiederholung ist sowohl die Verlängerung des Traumas als auch das, was noch in der traumatischen Struktur als Distanz zu sich selbst erscheint, die konstitutive Möglichkeit, anders zu sein. Es gibt keine Möglichkeit, *nicht* zu wiederholen.[52]

Das Unternehmen der Resignifikation ist ein „komplexes und wechselhaftes Spiel": subversiver und politischer Wiederaneignungsmöglichkeiten, aber auch mit Beschränkungen und Risiken. Wenn Foucault oben von einer „Strategie" schrieb, die zwar intentional, aber nicht souverän zu denken sei, sind solche resignifizierenden Versuche gute Beispiele. Und der Begriff der Resignifikation schillert zwischen einer Sache der Sprachstruktur oder der Materialität des Zeichens einerseits (was Butler von Derridas

Iterabilitätsbegriff übernimmt) und andererseits dem Zugang über die Frage der Handlungsmacht, der bei Foucault stärker ausgeprägt ist, wenn er betont, es komme auf mehr an als die Äußerung.

Im Folgenden wird der Versuch unternommen, einige Elemente solcher komplizierten Verteilungen im Foucaultschen Sinne zu rekonstruieren, ohne dass dabei die Diskursanalyse als operationalisierbare Methode im technischen Sinne für die Entwicklung eines Instrumentariums zur quantitativen und qualitativen Textuntersuchung benutzt wird[53], sondern darüber hinaus und vor allem als erkenntnistheoretische Perspektive auf soziale Praktiken der Diskriminierung und deren Zurückweisung, Subversion und resignifizierenden Umkehrung. Foucault sagt:

> Was ich geschrieben habe, sind keine Rezepte, weder für mich noch für sonst jemand. Es sind bestenfalls Werkzeuge – und Träume.[54]

Auch wenn seine Äußerung es nicht ausschließt, solche Rezepte zu entwickeln, haben Foucaults Überlegungen im Folgenden eher die Rolle der Werkzeuge, mit deren Hilfe versucht werden soll, die machttheoretischen Dimensionen mitsamt den resignifikativen Möglichkeiten der Beispiele aus Deutschland und Australien zu erkunden. Diese Erkundung wird hier als das Spezifikum der Diskursanalyse gegenüber hermeneutischen und inhaltsanalytischen Verfahren betrachtet.[55] Für Bublitz et al. stehen die höchst ambivalenten Strukturen dessen, was Foucault unter Diskursen versteht, damit im Zentrum der Diskursanalyse als einer machttheoretischen Perspektive:

> Sie [die Diskurse, S.H.] sind in ihrer – potentiell grenzenlosen - Funktion als Produzenten von Wissen und Wahrheit und damit von sozialer Wirklichkeit derart ‚unberechenbar', dass die mühsam hergestellte Regelhaftigkeit von Wissen und gesellschaftlicher Praxis ständig aufs Neue gefährdet ist.[56]

Die ambivalente Struktur wird hier daran sichtbar, dass die Diskurse zugleich Regeln herstellende, bewahrende und verändernde Strukturen sind. Im Zitat ist von der ständigen Gefährdetheit der diskursiv „mühsam" hergestellten Regelmäßigkeiten die Rede; dadurch liegt der Akzent auf dem Schwanken und der Unsicherheit der sozialen Praktiken, und man könnte auf die Idee kommen, es fehle eine ‚Basis', auf der gesellschaftliche Regeln aufruhten und auf deren Grundlage sie definiert werden könnten. Dass in Foucaults Ansatz eine solche Basis fehlt, ist auch zutreffend, nur betont er weniger die bedrohlichen und unsicheren Konsequenzen, sondern die freiheitlichen Möglichkeiten, die sich daraus ergeben:

> Alle meine Untersuchungen richten sich gegen den Gedanken universeller Notwendigkeiten im menschlichen Denken. Sie helfen entdecken, wie willkürlich Institutionen sind, welche Freiheit wir immer noch haben und wieviel Wandel immer noch möglich ist.[57]

Dass die diskursiven Regelmäßigkeiten ständig aufs Neue gefährdet sind, liegt daran, dass sie nur in der Wiederholung von Praktiken existieren und immer wieder neu (und damit potentiell abweichend) aufgeführt werden müssen und können. Diese Möglichkeit der Freiheit ist für Foucault wie für Butler ohne die Gefährdung und ohne die ständige Wiederholung nicht zu haben.

2. Kanak Sprak

Was ist ein Kanak(e)? Der Ausdruck hat schon auffällig viele Bedeutungsverschiebungen durchgemacht. Die Einwohner des südpazifischen Neukaledonien, das 1853 zu französischem Kolonialbesitz erklärt worden war, nannten sich selbst Kanaken, wobei ‚Kanak' (wie in vielen solchen Fällen der Selbstbezeichnung) mit ‚Mensch' zu übersetzen ist. Im Jahr 1931 wurde einer Gruppe von Neukaledoniern eine Reise nach Paris angeboten[58], wo sie angeblich als „Delegation der Kanaken" zur Internationalen Kolonialausstellung eingeladen werden sollten, einer Feier der französischen Kolonialpolitik. Doch dort wurden sie im Zoo ausgestellt; sie sollten „sich die Gesichter bemalen, bedrohlich Waffen schwingen, Zähne fletschen und wildes Gebrüll ausstoßen, obwohl sie perfekt Französisch sprachen".[59] In der Berichterstattung von 1998 (anlässlich der Thematisierung des Vorfalls durch historische Dokumentationen, der Behandlung als Romanstoff und auch anlässlich des Sieges der „multikulturellen" französischen Mannschaft bei der Fußballweltmeisterschaft der Männer 1998[60]) bezieht sich der Begriff ‚Kanaken' auf die Einwohner der französischen Kolonie Neukaledonien, die in den selben Texten sowohl als „Kanaken" als auch als „Ureinwohner" und „Neukaledonier" bezeichnet werden. Damit wird das diskursive Wechselspiel in seiner historischen Abfolge zugleich aufgerufen und verdeckt, das aus den folgenden Etappen besteht: Erstens der Selbstbezeichnung der Neukaledonier als ‚Kanaken'; zweitens ihrer

Ausstellung in Käfigen im Zoo, an denen die Bezeichnung ‚Kanaken' auf einem Schild angebracht war – hier setzt die erste Diskriminierung ein, indem die Selbstbezeichnung verdinglichend aufgegriffen wird; drittens der beleidigenden Beschimpfung von Migranten als ‚Kanaken', u.a. türkischer Arbeitsmigranten in Deutschland; viertens der selbstbewusst-aggressiven Resignifikation, die unten genauer untersucht werden soll.

Besonders aufschlussreich ist die Verwendung der Ausdrücke im Text „Karembeus Urgroßväter wurden im Zoo ausgestellt" von Andrea Schlotterbeck, der ursprünglich am 15. Dezember 1998 als Artikel in der *Berliner Zeitung* erschien[61]; Anlass war ein nicht näher genanntes Interview des französischen Fußballers Karembeu: Der gesamte Artikel zählt 551 Wörter, davon entfallen drei auf ‚Kanaken', acht auf ‚Ureinwohner' und vier auf ‚aus Neukaledonien/neukaledonisch' (in Verbindung mit ‚Ureinwohner'). Das sind insgesamt 15 Vorkommnisse; in einem Text von 551 Wörtern heißt das, von allen 36,7 Wörtern ist eines eine solche Bezeichnung. Das ist eine vergleichsweise starke Präsenz dieser Bezeichnungen selbst in einem Text, in dem die französische Kolonialgeschichte thematisch ist. Auffällig ist die Häufung des Ausdrucks ‚die Ureinwohner', der eine gewisse hilflose Distanznahme ausdrückt in Zeiten, wo solche Ausdrücke normalerweise nicht mehr unproblematisch verwendet werden, weil ‚Ureinwohner' eine Nähe zu ‚Wilde' oder ‚Primitive' aufruft. Am interessantesten ist jedoch die Verwendung von ‚Kanaken'. Im ersten Vorkommnis steht es in Anführungszeichen und wird ergänzt durch „wie sich die Ureinwohner selbst nennen" – hier wird die Verwendung legitimiert durch den Verweis auf die Selbstbezeichnung. An den beiden folgenden Stellen werden jedoch ohne Anführungszeichen und ohne Anspielung auf die Selbstbezeichnung prädikative Aussagen über „die meisten Kanaken" (aus dem obigen Zitat) bzw. über „die Kanaken" getroffen. Hier verwendet die Verfasserin des Artikels im Dezember 1998 diese Bezeichnung ungeachtet der diskriminierenden Geschichte des Ausdrucks und macht den Versuch, unter Rückgriff auf die Tatsache der Selbstbezeichnung der benannten Gruppe das Wort sozusagen ‚unschuldig' oder ‚neutral' zu gebrauchen. Dabei wird aber, wie Butler gesehen hat, das Trauma der Diskriminierung und Unterdrückung wieder aufgerufen; der Versuch, die Bezeichnung neutral zu verwenden, scheitert damit. Das Ergebnis lautet also: Der Ausdruck ‚Kanake' kann seine kolonialisierende Bedeutung auf diese Weise nicht abschütteln. Seine Verwendung kann nicht völlig frei werden von der Verletzung, die mit ihm zugefügt wurde. Das führt zur Frage, unter welchen Bedingungen überhaupt eine Resignifikation eines solchen Ausdrucks glücken kann.

Dabei ist entscheidend, von wem und in welchem Kontext die

Worte aufgegriffen werden. Nur die Personengruppe, die vorher Opfer der diskriminierenden Rede war, besitzt offensichtlich die Kraft und die Berechtigung, die Worte gegen den alten verletzenden Kontext zu verwenden. Wie der eben betrachtete Artikel zeigt, kann jemand von außerhalb der betroffenen Gruppe nur das Trauma der beleidigenden Anrufung wiederholen; es liegt nicht in ihrer/seiner Macht, der Bezeichnung einen schmerzfreien Sinn zu geben. Das Opfer der sprachlichen Verletzung kann zwar das Trauma auch nicht rückgängig machen, aber nur es selbst kann die Bezeichnung überhaupt in einer entgegengesetzten Strategie als Selbstbezeichnung verwenden. Das rührt daher, dass man durch die sprachliche Verletzung seinen Kontext verliert, man weiß nicht mehr, wo man ist, man wird seiner Selbstkontrolle beraubt.[62] Niemand außer dem Betroffenen selbst kann die Resignifikation vornehmen: Jede neuerliche Anrufung, wie gut gemeint auch immer, würde die akute Wegnahme der Selbstkontrolle wiederholen und reaktivieren (und darüber hinaus wie jede Anrufung auf den grundsätzlich imaginären Charakter dieser Selbstkontrolle verweisen).

Ein Beispiel für die resignifikative Aneignung der ursprünglich verletzenden Anrufung mit dem Wort ‚Kanake' bietet die ‚Kanak Sprak'. Bekannt geworden ist dieser Kunstausdruck durch das erste Buch von Feridun Zaimoglu.[63] Es handelt sich dabei um die „Nachdichtung"[64] von 24 Gesprächen, die Zaimoglu mit türkischen Immigranten der dritten Generation geführt hat, die sich selbst selbstbewusst-aggressiv als „Kanaken" bezeichnen, nachdem sie früher diskriminierend mit diesem Ausdruck belegt worden waren; „ein Etikett, das nach mehr als 30 Jahren Immigrationsgeschichte von Türken nicht nur Schimpfwort ist, sondern auch ein Name, den ‚Gastarbeiterkinder' der zweiten und vor allem der dritten Generation mit stolzem Trotz führen".[65] Die sich selbst als Kanaken bezeichnen, wenden das negative Bild, das ihnen entgegengebracht wurde, zur positiven Selbstdefinition. Untereinander sprechen sie eine Mischsprache aus Deutsch und Türkisch, die gerade keine Lernersprache mit grammatischen und lexikalischen Unsicherheiten ist, sondern eine Gruppensprache als „ethnolektale Varietät".[66] Ihre deutschsprachigen Anteile haben besondere grammatische, lexikalische, prosodische und phonetische Eigenschaften; so fallen z.B. die meisten Präpositionen und Artikel weg, das neutrale grammatische Geschlecht wird auf fast alle Substantive ausgedehnt, der Sprechrhythmus ist durch bestimmte Hebungen und Senkungen gekennzeichnet, usw. In türkische Satzteile und Konstruktionen werden deutsche Phrasen eingebaut und umgekehrt. Nicht nur die Bezeichnung ‚Kanake' allein hat hier resignifikative Kraft, sondern diese sprachliche Vielfalt (eingeschlossen dialektales und/oder Standarddeutsch und dialektales und/oder Türkisch) ist ein Symbol für eine eigene sozio-kulturelle Identität: sie ermöglicht

> ein sehr ausdifferenziertes Kommunikationsverhalten, das vom häufigen Wechsel zwischen Sprachen und Varietäten gekennzeichnet ist. Dafür sind verschiedene kontextuelle Faktoren ausschlaggebend: der situative Anlass und die Gesprächspartner, das Gesprächsthema und die Art seiner Durchführung (z.B. witzig oder ernst), die Gesprächsdynamik und das vorausgesetzte kulturelle Wissen. In jedem Fall aber transportiert der Wechsel immer soziale und kontextuelle Bedeutung.[67]

Die Mischsprache scheint ein Symbol dafür zu sein, dass sich die SprecherInnen weder zur türkischen noch zur deutschen Gruppe zugehörig fühlen.[68] Ihr Alltag entspricht nicht dem „Integrationsgebot"[69], das vorsieht, dass sich Migranten in eine bestehende deutsche Kulturlandschaft einzugliedern haben. „Aber eine Idee von Heimat, die von den vielfältigen globalisierten Beziehungen absieht, ist eine Fiktion".[70] Es gibt schon immer sehr unterschiedliche Identitätsmodelle bei MigrantInnen in Deutschland; paradigmatische Fälle wären die Assimilation, die alten ‚Gastarbeiter', die in ihre Herkunftsländer zurückgekehrt sind, sowie diejenigen, die sich mit ihrem Verhalten der alten Nationalitätslogik verweigern wie die, die sich selbst als ‚Kanaken' bezeichnen und z.B. Assimilierte als „Assimil-Kümmel"[71] beschimpfen. All diesen unterschiedlichen Identitätsmodellen mit ihren zahlreichen Abstufungen einen Begriff der Heimat mit entsprechenden Verhaltensweisen vorschreiben zu wollen, kommt einer schlechten Entdifferenzierung gleich. Kanak Sprak ist inzwischen zu einer Mode geworden; auch deutsche Kinder übernehmen Sätze und Merkmale, nicht zuletzt durch die Kommerzialisierung in den Medien. Im Falle von Zaimoglus Buch *Kanak Sprak*, das mit zu dieser Mode beigetragen hat, handelt es sich um eine Repräsentation von Kanak Sprak in literrarisch stilisierter Form, „in fiktionale Kontexte gesetzt und mit vorkalkulierten Effekten verwendet".[72] Zaimoglu hat anderthalb Jahre hindurch „Protokolle" von Gesprächen mit Männern im „öffentlichen Leben in den Szenen der Kanaken-Ghettos"[73] geführt. Für die „Übersetzung"[74] oder „Nachdichtung"[75] ins Deutsche hat Zaimoglu die türkischen Anteile an der Lexik übersetzt und dabei, um der „Folklore-Falle"[76] zu entgehen, den stark symbolischen Jargon, der als „blumige Orientalensprache"[77] missverstanden werden könnte, reduziert; so schreibt er zum Beispiel „Bruder", wo eine wörtliche Übersetzung „mein Augenlicht" lautete. Herausgekommen ist ein Sprachbild mit einem weiten Spektrum:

> vom Müllabfuhr-Kanaken bis zum Kümmel-Transsexuellen, vom hehlenden Klein-Ganeff, dessen Geschenke ich nur mühsam zurückweisen konnte, bis zum goldbehängten Mädchenhändler, vom posenreichen Halbstarken bis zum mittelschweren Islamisten.[78]

Auch in der teilfiktionalen Form wird hier nicht nur der einzelne Ausdruck ‚Kanake' resignifiziert, sondern komplette Klischees werden aufgegriffen und gegen die ursprüngliche Strategie gewendet. Zaimoglu selbst interpretiert sein Verfahren folgendermaßen:

> In diesen Klischees offenbart sich der Hang der Deutschen, die Türken als Statisten in der Klammer der Moralkodizes zu sehen und ihnen jeden frei gewählten Zugang zur deutschen Gesellschaft abzusprechen. [...] Es sind die Zeiten eingeläutet, in denen jede Abstammung an den persönlichen Lebensentwürfen zerschellt. Jenseits der Zuschreibungsmodelle der Ausländerbetreuungsindustrie, die für sich immer noch das Meinungsmonopol beansprucht, sind die Deutschländer, die eingewanderten und die hier geborenen Türken, nicht nur längst in der bundesdeutschen Gesellschaft angekommen. Sie kämpfen um eigene Spielräume und verweigern den professionellen Ausländerbetreuern die Stereotypen mit Wiedererkennungswert.[79]

In dieser Selbstinterpretation spricht Zaimoglu vom „frei gewählten Zugang", von eigenen Spielräumen und „persönlichen Lebensentwürfen". Das klingt zunächst wie die Forderung nach einer souveränen Sprecherposition und damit nach einem sprachlichen Verhalten, das die komplizierten diskursiven Machtverteilungen im gesellschaftlichen Gefüge verkennt. Aber im Kontext des gesamten Zitats fällt auf, dass die drei Ausdrücke jeweils nur die eine Hälfte charakteristischer Oppositionen sind, die diese Textpassage organisieren. Der „frei gewählte Zugang" fungiert als Gegenbegriff zur „Klammer der Moralkodizes", mit denen die Deutschen die Immigranten festlegten; „eigene Spielräume" steht in Opposition zu den „Stereotypen", mit denen sie die „professionellen Ausländerbetreuer[...]" wiederzuerkennen strebten; die „persönlichen Lebensentwürfe" schließlich sind der feste Grund, auf dem die sonst so vordiskursiv gedachte „Abstammung" buchstäblich zerschellt wie etwas Fragiles, das zu Boden fällt. Durch die Oppositionen betont der Text die

Lage der ImmigrantInnen, die sich in Deutschland als Opfer diskriminierender Akte wiederfinden, und sich durch die Aneignung solcher Praktiken Handlungsmacht zurückholen. Freilich enthält das Zitat als Interpretation der Kanak Sprak eine implizite Sprachphilosophie und eine Theorie mehrkultureller Identität im heutigen Deutschland, die auch mit der Vorstellung einer Repression verknüpft ist. Ähnlich funktioniert ein Beispiel aus dem *Kanak Sprak*-Kapitel „Den Fremdländer kannst du nimmer aus der Fresse wischen":

> du willst es wissen, ich geb dir das verschissene wissen: wir sind hier allesamt nigger, wir haben unser ghetto, wir schleppen's überall hin, wir dampfen fremdländisch, unser schweiß ist nigger, unser leben ist nigger, die goldketten sind nigger, unsere zinken und unsere fressen und unser eigner stil ist so verdammt nigger, daß wir wie blöde an unsrer haut kratzen, und dabei kapieren wir, daß zum nigger nicht die olle pechhaut gehört, aber zum nigger gehört ne ganze menge anderssein und andres leben. Die haben schon unsre heimat prächtig erfunden: kanake da, kanake dort, wo du auch hingerätst, kanake blinkt dir in oberfetten lettern sogar im traum, wenn du pennst und denkst: joker, jetzt bist du in deiner eigenen sendung.[80]

Die aggressive Selbstbezeichnung als nigger beansprucht die in der Erfindung durch die anderen weggenommene Definitionsmacht und Handlungsmacht zurück. Und sie enthält eine Provokation im Vorwurf an die Urheber der Veranderung, die die Diskriminierung an den Absender zurückschickt. Dass die Provokation funktioniert, wurde an einem ‚Ausfall' der sozialdemokratischen Politikerin Heide Simonis in der Talk-Show III nach neun im Mai 1998 sichtbar[81], die neben Feridun Zaimoglu und anderen zu den eingeladenen Gästen gehörte. Der historisch-politische Kontext war die Diskussion um ein deutsches Einwanderungsgesetz, und Zaimoglus *Kanak Sprak* war drei Jahre zuvor erschienen.

Simonis kann, so der Einleitungstext zur schriftlich dokumentierten Sendung, in der Situation nicht damit umgehen, dass „,Ausländer' [...] ihnen, den Deutschen, sogar die Definitionsmacht über rassistische Verbalinjurien (‚Kanake') streitig machen. Da hat man sich's jahrelang verkniffen – und dann war alles umsonst".[82] In der Talkshow entzündete sich ein teils heftiger Wortwechsel an der Tatsache, dass Zaimoglu über die Selbstbezeichnung „Als Kankster, als Kanakyoungster und als Kanake"[83] sprach und zunächst im Gespräch mit der Moderatorin der Sendung deutlich machte, dass es Außenstehenden nicht zukomme, ihn so zu bezeichnen. Dabei betonte er, auch er (stellvertretend für diejenigen, die sich so nennen) habe „nicht die Definitionsallmacht, aber auch nicht das Monopol an Erklärungsmustern"[84]; er könne nicht über die kursierende Bezeichnung derart verfügen, dass er es z.B. Außenstehenden souverän gestatten könne, ihn ‚Kanake' zu nennen. In der Folge, nach einer szenischen Lesung aus *Kanak Sprak*, schaltete sich Heide Simonis ins Gespräch ein und zeigte deutliche Vorbehalte gegenüber solchen Sprachpraktiken, wie sie im Buch vorkommen:

> Aber ein Türke, der so redet... [...]. Und ich sage Ihnen, ich würde immer dazwischen gehen, wenn zwei sich auf der Straße so unterhalten, ich sage, ihr Arschlöcher, das ist der Anfang vom Ende, so fangen sie an miteinander zu reden. Das mag auch Kunst sein, aber wenn das die Kunst hervorbringt, daß ich am Ende sage, ich durfte das, weil der andere hat ja auch – dann muß ich Ihnen ehrlich sagen, nee.[85]

Hier nimmt Simonis für ihre Argumentation implizit in Anspruch, dass dieses Sprechen auch ein Handeln ist. Ihre Anspielung auf das Verhältnis von Kunst und Zensur entspricht genau jener in Butlers *Haß spricht* untersuchten Auffassung, die solche Arten des Sprechens als verletzende Handlung einstuft, die einzuschränken oder zu verbieten ist. Aber damit wird die Sprache stillzustellen versucht und eine neue Repression eingeführt. Nach einer Seitenlinie des Gesprächs, in der Wolf Biermann sich einschaltete und an Zaimoglu die „Echtheit" vermisste, entspann sich schließlich der folgende Wortwechsel zwischen Simonis und Zaimoglu:

> H.S.: Also Sie nutzen etwas aus, daß wir sprachlos davorsitzen und sagen: Wenn er das gerne möchte, dann muß er sich so ausdrücken dürfen. Ich darf mich in der Türkei auch nicht so ausdrücken, und deswegen tue ich es nicht, und deswegen erwarte ich auch von Ihnen, daß Sie es nicht tun.
> F.Z.: Sie machen einen großen Fehler. Sie kommen mir wieder einmal damit, Sie kommen mir immer mit der Türkei. Ich bin in diesem Land aufgewachsen...
> H.S.: Sie haben ein Erbe. So wie ich ein anderes Erbe mit mir rumschleppe, schleppen Sie das türkische mit sich rum. Tut mir leid, das ist so.

> F.Z.: Was heißt hier Erbe? Es ist die Musik...
> H.S. ...Nein. Es sind Ihre Eltern, ihre Großeltern, es ist ein Stückchen mehr, als nur nach dem Motto: Ich hab zufällig mal den Bosporus gesehen.[86]

Nachdem Simonis eine Auffassung geäußert hat, die dem Wunsch nach dem Verbot des resignifizierenden Sprechens nahe kommt, weil es die Diskriminierung wieder aufruft, benutzt sie ein neues Argument, das mit dem Vorwurf beginnt, die ursprünglich Diskriminierten nutzten die strukturelle Asymmetrie der Resignifikation aus. Weil es Außenstehenden oder mit den Tätern Verbundenen nicht zukommt, eine Resignifikation vorzunehmen, beklagt sich Simonis darüber, ausgeschlossen zu sein, und wechselt zur moralischen Forderung nach dem Muster über: „Was wir Deutschen nicht in der Türkei dürfen, dürfen die, die sich selbst so nennen wollen, auch nicht in Deutschland", und in der Folge wird ein impliziter Rassismus sichtbar, wenn sie versucht, Zaimoglu auf sein „türkisches Erbe" festzulegen, damit die vertraute Logik der Repression wieder greift. Hier wird deutlich, dass Simonis' Schwierigkeiten damit zusammenhängen, dass Resignifikationsvorgänge immer bedeuten, dass ein Vorgang außer Kontrolle geraten ist. Die sich als Kanaken bezeichnen, können das tun, weil die sprachliche Macht weder zu lokalisieren noch festzuschreiben noch ein für alle Mal zu haben ist (Damit beleidigen sie interessanterweise nicht die Neukaledonier, weil sie mit ihnen die Geschichte teilen, Opfer der Verletzung gewesen zu sein, auch wenn bei den Neukaledoniern die Reihenfolge von Selbstbezeichnung und Diskriminierung durch andere umgekehrt verlief.). Gegen Ende formulierte Simonis das Problem noch einmal in aller Deutlichkeit: „Wieso dürfen Sie Kanake zu sich sagen und ich nicht?", worauf Zaimoglu antwortete „Weil man da draußen uns ständig als Kanaken bezeichnet", und Simonis sich schließlich zum Ausruf hinreißen ließ „Soll ich einem DVU-Menschen, der sagt, ich hau jemand über die Rübe, dasselbe Verständnis entgegenbringen?"[87]

Gegen Simonis ließe sich sagen: Hier sind die oben genannten ‚Grenzen und Risiken' der Resignifikation deutlich sichtbar geworden. „Daß die Sprache ein Trauma in sich trägt" ist aber kein Grund, ihren Gebrauch zu untersagen.[88] Denn damit würde man versuchen, eine Stillstellung herbeizuführen, was erstens ohnehin angesichts der lebendigen Verwiesenheit der Sprache auf Prozesse der Wiederholung erfolglos bleiben müsste, und zweitens auch diskurs- und machttheoretisch naiv wäre.

3. Aboriginal English

Zum literarischen und politischen Projekt der Kanak Sprak gibt es erstens keine direkte australische Entsprechung, und zweitens ist die gesellschaftliche Situation der erst diskriminierten und dann resignifizierenden Menschen eine andere, wenn es nämlich um Aboriginal English und den Umgang mit diskriminierenden Bezeichnungen für die Aborigines geht. Aboriginal English ist daher zunächst einmal kein Resignifikationsgeschehen im genau gleichen Sinne wie die Kanak Sprak, obwohl es sich auch um eine Mischsprache handelt, eine lexikalische, grammatische, phonetische und prosodische Mischung aus Englisch und jeweils unterschiedlichen Sprachen der Aborigines. Diese Mischung wird wiederum von weißen Kindern und Jugendlichen in Teilen übernommen und führt gleichsam zu einer Rehybridisierung des Englischen. Peter Wignell hat die Beispiele für solche Hybridisierungen in drei Kategorien eingeteilt: Erstens solche Ausdrücke, die lexikalisch englisch sind, dann Teil des Aboriginal English wurden, wobei sie eine Bedeutungsverschiebung durchmachten, und schließlich mit der veränderten Bedeutung von einigen SprecherInnen, besonders Kindern und Jugendlichen, ins mainstream-Englisch aufgenommen wurden; zweitens Ausdrücke, die mit Hilfe von Kontraktionsformen aus Wörten der englischen Lexik Begriffe aus Sprachen der Aborigines nachbilden, zuerst im Aboriginal English und dann wieder als Übernahme ins mainstream-Englisch; und drittens Wörter aus Sprachen der Aborigines, die im Aboriginal English vorkommen und von SprecherInnen des mainstream-Englisch übernommen werden.[89] Ein Beispiel für die erste Kategorie ist das Wort ‚deadly', ausgesprochen mit gedehnten Vokalen und einer erst steigenden, dann fallenden Intonation, in der Bedeutung, dass etwas besonders gut oder wünschenswert ist. Ein Beispiel für die zweite Kategorie wäre das Wort Bruz, das eine kreative Übesetzung eines Verwandtschaftsausdrucks ins Englische ist, der ungefähr ‚Cousin-Bruder' bedeutet. Die Kontraktion benutzt Br- aus Brother und Cuz als kontrahierte Form für cousin und wird als Ausdruck benutzt, der Solidarität mit Gruppenmitgliedern signalisiert. Ein Beispiel der dritten Art wäre budju, ursprünglich ein Larrakia-Ausdruck für die weiblichen Genitalien, der dann die Bedeutung von ‚cunt' angenommen hat, etwa in der Beschimpfung You budju!, aber in einer Resignifikation auch etwas Positives wie ‚Mut' oder ‚Mumm' zuschreiben kann und dann dasselbe bedeutet wie ‚She's a real spunk'.[90] Wignell beschreibt den Vorgang als „a kind of meaning-reversal".[91] All dies sind Beispiele dafür, dass es zumindest in Teilen der SprecherInnengemeinschaft des mainstream-Englisch Mode geworden ist, solche hybriden Sprachformen zu verwenden, in denen das Aboriginal English als Sprache durch seine bloße

Verwendung eine implizite Aufwertung erfährt. Hier ist eine ganze Sprache Gegenstand der Resignifikation und enthält darüber hinaus einzelne Wörter, an denen sich Resignifikationsakte zeigen lassen. Aber soweit ist die diskriminierende Anrufung von Aborigines mit Gruppennamen, die dem Wort ‚Kanaken' entspächen, noch nicht berührt. Zwei Beispiele sollen im Folgenden exemplarisch dafür dienen, die in ihnen enthaltene implizite Sprachphilosophie zu dieser Frage zu erkunden: Mudrooroo mit seinem Roman *Doin' Wildcat*[92], und Phillip Gwynnes Jugendbuch *Deadly, Unna?*[93].

Mudrooroo wurde im Jahr 1938 in Narogin als Colin Johnson geboren. Mit seinem 1965 erschienenen Roman *Wild Cat Falling* gilt er als der Begründer der Aborigines-Literatur; er ist Mitglied des Aboriginal Arts Committee des Australia Council und in weiteren Organisationen tätig. Der Roman erzählt von der Titelfigur Wild Cat, einem Aborigine, der aus dem Gefängnis entlassen wird, um nur zwei Tage später wegen versuchten Mordes erneut verhaftet zu werden. 1988 schrieb Mudrooroo die Geschichte noch einmal aus einer neuen Perspektive um[94], sie erschien unter dem Titel *Doin' Wildcat*, und im selben Jahr änderte er auch seinen Namen in Mudrooroo Narogin, mittlerweile nur noch Mudrooroo. Zu seinen Namenswechseln schreibt er:

> Ich wurde in Narrogin (Westaustralien) geboren – daher mein Name. 1988 entschied ich, dass einen englischen Namen zu haben nicht angemessen wäre. Da ich in einem kleinen Ort bei Narrogin, der East Cuballing heißt und aus nicht viel mehr als einer Post besteht, geboren wurde und Narrogin auf meiner Geburtsurkunde steht, entschloss ich mich ‚Narogin' zumindest als Künstlernamen anzunehmen. ‚Mudrooroo' kam zu Stande, als als ich 1988 mit Oodgeroo Noonuccal diskutierte und sie sagte, wir bräuchten ein ‚Arbeitstotem' oder ‚Traum'. Da wir Schriftsteller waren, warum nicht ‚Papierrinden'-Baum. ‚Oodgeroo' heißt Papierrinde in der Noonuccal-Sprache, und ‚Mudrooroo' heißt dasselbe in der Bibbulmum-Sprache, die die Sprache meiner Mutter ist. Daher änderte ich meinen Namen in Mudrooroo. Das entwickelte sich in ‚Mudrooroo Nyoongah', welches der Name meines Volkes ist. Dann war ich es satt, zu erklären, was Nyoongah bedeutet – der Begriff ‚Aboriginal' oder ‚Aborigine' ist eine weiße Täuschung über die Ureinwohner Australiens; ein Nyoongah meint etwas

> anderes als ein ‚Aborigine' zu sein – wir sind eine Mischung verschiedener Rassen aus dem Südwesten Westaustraliens. So ist mein Name jetzt Mudrooroo Nyoongah und mein Künstlername Mudrooroo.[95]

Stiller beschreibt Mudrooroos Verfahren, mit seinen Namen umzugehen, als Dekonstruktion der Identitäten.[96] Interessant ist nicht nur die Abfolge unterschiedlicher Namen mit ihren unterscheidlichen Begründungen (der englische Name mit Vor- und Familiennamen, der selbstgewählte Name Mudrooroo mit Bezug auf den Beruf und die Muttersprache der Mutter), sondern auch Mudrooroos Äußerung zum Namen Nyoongah. Stiller interpretiert sie so, dass sich Mudrooroo abgrenze gegen die „vereinnahmende Bezeichnung ‚Aborigines' für Völker, die sich selbst als verschieden betrachten"[97]; die „weiße Täuschung", die Mudrooroo zurückweist, besteht darin, die verschiedenen Völker, die sich vermischt haben, nicht nur unzulässigerweise zu vereinheitlichen und damit zu vereinnahmen, sondern auch darin, ihre Geschichte der Differenzen und Vermischungen nicht wahrzunehmen. Laut Mudrooroo wird den Aborigines mit solchen verfälschenden Darstellungen nur die nicht akzeptable Alternative zwischen Assimilation und „Tribalization" gelassen[98]; entweder die Aborigines passen ihre Konventionen denen der Weißen an, oder sie werden exotisiert. Mudrooroo kritisiert also die Verwendung des Begriffs ‚Aborigines', gleichzeitig aber benutzen er und viele andere den Begriff sowohl im Rahmen der politischen und kulturellen Gremien zur Repräsentation der mit ihm bezeichneten Menschen, meistens ohne dass es sich um eine aggressive Resignifikation wie im Falle des Ausdrucks ‚Kanake' handelte. Im Vergleich ist ‚Aborigine' ein schillernderer Ausdruck als ‚Kanake', der in bestimmten historischen Phasen eindeutig diskriminierend und nun aggressiv-selbstbewusst resignifizierend verwendet wurde, während jener eine scheinbar ‚neutrale', ‚bloß-klassifikatorische' Bedeutung beansprucht, in der die Diskriminierung auf der Ebene der Sprache selbst verdeckt bleibt. Dadurch sind die Möglichkeiten der resignifizierenden Verwendung durch die Diskriminierten eingeschränkt: Die Resignifikation erfordert eine umkehrbare diskursive Strategie, die sich nicht versteckt. Es gab einen Streit um Mudrooroos Aborigine-Identität, als seine Familie 1996 enthüllte, Mudrooroo sei gar kein „richtiger"[99] Aborigine, denn sein Vater soll ein schwarzer Amerikaner gewesen sein und seine Mutter die Nachfahrin von Weißen. Mudrooroo verwirft jedoch alle Identitätszuschreibungen, die auf Kriterien des Blutes oder des Begriffs der Rasse oder der Gene beruhen: „Was auch immer meine Identität ist, so ruht sie auf meiner über fünfzigjährigen Geschichte, mehr ist dazu nicht zu sagen."[100]

Mit seinem Debutroman *Wild Cat Falling* geht Mudrooroo in *Doin' Wildcat* in ähnlicher Weise um wie mit seiner Identität, indem er ihn aus der Rückschau reinterpretiert und sich in ihn als Autor neu einschreibt. Das lässt sich folgendermaßen beschreiben: „der Autor Mudrooroo wirft dem Autor Colin Johnson vor, einen Aborigine so geschildert zu haben, wie ihn sich Nicht-Aborigines vorstellen."[101] In *Doin' Wildcat* kehrt der Erzähler nach 26 Jahren in das ehemalige Gefängnis, in dem er inhaftiert war, zurück, um einen weißen Regisseur und Produzenten bei der Verfilmung des Buchs zu unterstützen. Der Erzähler ist also in der Position, ein Buch und danach ein Drehbuch geschrieben zu haben und nun bei den Dreharbeiten den Schauspieler beobachten zu können, der ihn als jungen Mann spielt. Das bedeutet, der Erzähler ist in einer privilegierten Position gegenüber allen anderen Figuren des Textes, und trotzdem ist er eine marginalisierte Figur. Er steht mit dem Regisseur hinter der Kamera und ist zugleich die gefilmte Person, er stammt aus der marginalisierten Kultur der Aborigines und benutzt die hegemoniale weiße Kultur als Spielraum seiner Kreativität und Reflexivität[102], und der Text stellt diese vielfältige Konstruiertheit der Identität und des Romans als zentral heraus. Schon der Titel betont den Aspekt der Konstruiertheit des Textes: *Doin' Wildcat: A Novel Koori Script As constructed by Mudrooroo Narogin (Previously known as Colin Johnson)*. Der Text ist darüber hinaus voller linguistischer, textueller und literarischer Anspielungen und Innovationen. Dazu gehört auch der Einsatz des Aboriginal English. Eine häufig, auch von Mudrooroo selbst, zitierte Passage lautet:

> June: I've just got here. Didn't know if you would turn up, or not. I'm at that table with a few friends.
> She takes Ernie by is arm. Ee allows imself to be led to the table. Ee is introduced to the men.
> June: This is the boy I met on the beach yesterday.
> Ernie doesn't say a word. Ee sits nervously on a chair. Ee lights up a cigarette.
> June: Frank and Bill here are doing Social Anthropology. They are really interested in the plight of the Aborigines...
> Even though I ave written these lines, I inwardly shudder at em. I know what's comin, ave bin in such scenes, an know the whole thing. This'll be their first meeting with an Aborigine, and ee'll be expected to be cluey on all aspects of what I've written as 'the plight of

the Aborigines'. Naturally, I've written it to show what
we come up against from even well meanin whites.
Ernie squirms in is chair. There's a few takes an cuts, an
this disrupts the questionin. Still it goes on.[103]

In diesem Zitat gibt es zunächst wieder keine Resignifikation, die mit einzelnen Begriffen nach Art des Ausdrucks ‚Kanake' arbeitete. Webb spricht aber von: "A liberating performance [...] getting out from under the alienated discourse of the earlier work with its European-style idiom", und meint: "Mudrooroo positively positions 'alienated' segments of his earlier novel to achieve new narrative energy."[104] Der Erzähler selbst benutzt Elemente aus dem Aboriginal English und gewinnt damit noch mehr als Narrative Energie: Er stellt sich auf die Seite derer, die von den wohlmeinenden Sozialanthropologen untersucht und entfremdet werden, und verleiht seine sprachliche Handlungsmacht, die er als der Autor in der zentralen Position besitzt, der Figur des Ernie, der seine Sprechmacht im Zitat buchstäblich nicht ausüben kann, weil sie ihm genommen wurde. Die Sätze des Erzählers über Ernie sind durch Merkmale des Aboriginal English gekennzeichnet: D.h. es ist nicht so, dass die Figur einen abweichenden Dialekt spräche und mit der Darstellung durch einen sonst standardsprachlichen Erzähler bloßgestellt würde, sondern der Erzähler spricht gerade die Sprache, die Ernie sprechen würde, wenn er es in dieser Situation könnte. Trotzdem ist es durch die Konstruktionsweise des Textes kein anmaßendes Sprechen-für-andere, weil der Erzähler als Aborigine mit Ernie zusammenfällt. Wenn man bedenkt, dass es sich um einen Text handelt, der von einem Autor geschrieben wurde, der selbst seinen Namen änderte und damit seine ‚Aboriginality' signalisierte[105], kommen hier unterschiedliche Versuche der Konstruktion einer Identität und einer sprachlichen Handlungsmacht zusammen.

Das zweite Beispiel ist Phillip Gwynnes Jugendbuch *Deadly, Unna?* von 1998.[106] Das Buch handelt von einem vierzehnjährigen weißen Jungen, der versucht, sich in der Welt zurechtzufinden, die er als immer komplizierter erlebt; es geht um den kleinen Fischerort, in dem er lebt, die schwierigen Familienverhältnisse mit zahlreichen Geschwistern und einem trinkenden Vater, und um die Beziehungen zu den Aborigines in einem abgetrennten nahegelegenen Ort, deren Jugendliche mit den weißen Jugendlichen in einem Football-Team spielen. Aufschlussreich ist im Gegenzug die aktuelle amazon-Inhaltsangabe der deutschen Übersetzung (mit dem ebenfalls aufschlussreichen Titel *Wir Goonyas, ihr Nungas*):

Gary wird zwar Blacky genannt, aber er ist ein Goonya,
ein Weißer. Mit den Nungas, den Aborigines, hat er

nichts zu tun. Das ändert sich, als Dumby Red, ein Aborigine, neu in Garys Footballmannschaft kommt. Blacky und Dumby werden Freunde, aber in dem kleinen australischen Ort ist das alles andere als normal. Und Blacky muss die Erfahrung machen, dass die Unterscheidung ‚wir Goonyas, ihr Nungas' nicht nur sinnlos ist – sie kann auch tödlich sein.

Der Fokus dieser Inhaltsangabe ist im Vergleich ein ganz anderer als der der zuvor gegebenen: Hier wird, wie auch schon durch den deutschen Titel, das ‚Wir-und-die anderen'-Thema in den Vordergrund gestellt. Eigentlich liegt aber der wichtigste Punkt darin, dass das Buch einen alltäglichen Rassismus zeigt, der zunächst gar nicht so zentral erscheint, weil er in komplizierte soziale Strukturen eingebunden ist. Die Titelfigur wird erst allmählich aufmerksam darauf, wie stark rassistische Muster in seiner Umwelt wirksam sind. Der Originaltitel spielt mit der Mehrdeutigkeit des sprachlichen Ausdrucks ‚deadly': Ein Wort aus dem Englischen, das im Aboriginal English die oben genannte Bedeutung hat, aber brutal auf seine wörtliche Bedeutung aus dem Standardenglisch zurückgeführt wird, als Dumby Red bei einem Überfall auf die Kasse des Ortslokals von einem Weißen erschossen wird; diese Rückführung des Wortes stellt eine Parallele dar zu den Erfahrungen der Hauptfigur, die langsam das Ausmaß des Rassismus in seinem sozialen Umfeld erkennen muss und sieht, dass er beginnen muss, Verantwortung zu übernehmen. Dass diese Verantwortlichkeit zu einem beträchtlichen Teil auch eine für die Sprache und die in ihr enthaltenen (potentiell verletzenden und kränkenden) Anrufungen ist, wird auch dadurch deutlich, dass das Thema der Namensgebung den ganzen Text hindurch extrem präsent ist, zuerst durch die zahlreichen Namensgebungen aus der Perspektive des Ich-Erzählers auf den ersten Seiten. In den zwei kurzen ersten Kapiteln, die zusammen acht Textseiten umfassen, finden sich gleich sechs Beispiele dafür, so dass die LeserInnen sofort auf die Namensgebung als implizites großes Thema des Buches hingewiesen werden: Der Fußballtrainer der Jungenmannschaft wird von Gary, Titelfigur und Ich-Erzähler, nach seiner Sprachauffälligkeit benannt („Ich nenne ihn ‚Arks' [...]. Er sagt nämlich immer ‚sarksen' statt ‚sagen und ‚gesarkst' statt ‚gesagt'"[107], ein Beispiel, dem aber in der deutschen Übersetzung der Kontext fehlt, um als gegenbildliche Diskriminierung zu derjenigen an den SprecherInnen des Aboriginal English gelesen werden zu können); Gary fragt einen körperlich weit überlegenen Aborigine aus seiner Footballmannschaft, warum er einen Mädchennamen trage (‚Carol'); die Bezeichnung für die Aborigines wird von ihm aus ihrer Perspektive reflektiert: „Wir nennen sie

Nungas; so bezeichnen sie sich auch selbst. Sie sind die Nungas und wir sind die Goonyas"[108]; er wird selten mit seinem Vornamen angesprochen, sondern wird nach seinem Familiennamen (einer Institution der englischen Kultur) „Blacky" genannt; einen körperlich überlegenen Jungen aus der gegnerischen Footballmannschaft nennt er den „Thumper (noch so ein Spitzname, den ich mir ausgedacht habe)"[109], usw. Hier präsentiert sich schon auf den ersten Seiten und weiter im gesamten Text ein Ich-Erzähler, der einerseits sehr aufmerksam und sensibel mit Benennungen umgeht. Diese Sensibilität ist es, die schließlich dazu führt, dass die Figur des Gary gegen zahlreiche Vorbehalte und sogar Verbote an der Beerdigung seines Freundes im Ort der Aborigines teilnimmt und zum Befremden etlicher Weißer einige Grußformeln aus dem Aboriginal English übernimmt, als Konsequenz seines Erkennens, dass das Zusammenleben kompliziert und schmerzhaft ist. Andererseits ist er zu Beginn nicht zimperlich im eigenen Austeilen von mindestens respektlosen Anrufungen, was im Laufe der Geschichte im Rahmen der genannten Entwicklung zurückgenommen wird.

Allen untersuchten Beispielen ist gemeinsam, dass die Fiktionalität eine wichtige Rolle spielt: Kannak Sprak ist in Zaimoglus literarisch stilisierter Fassung ein teilfiktionales Unternehmen, das aber auf die Szene derer, die sich Kanaken nennen, bestätigend zurückgewirkt hat; Mudrooroos Reskription seiner Identität und seines ersten Buches, des angeblichen ‚Gründungsdokuments', ist in allen ihren Teilen ein Projekt, in dem die fiktionalen und die nichtfiktionalen Anteile nur schwer auseinanderzutrennen wären, was demonstriert, in welchem Ausmaß Subjekte als Effekte von Diskursen betrachtet werden können; Gwynnes Jugendroman erzählt eine fiktionale Geschichte mit deutlichen Anspielungen auf autobiographische Erfahrungen und real geschehene Verbrechen und demonstriert dabei die große Bedeutung der Anrufungen für die Subjektkonstitution[110] all der Angehörigen der dargestellten mehrkulturellen Gesellschaft, wobei sich die Angehörigen der hegemonialen Kultur nicht aus den verletzenden Geschehnissen heraushalten können.

Betrachtet man den in den Texten vorhandenen expliziten und impliziten Bezug auf Begriffe wie Identität und Authentizität, könnte es so aussehen, als ob diejenigen, die Resignifikationen vornehmen, sich durchaus manchmal auf Modelle des Authentischen, Vordiskursiven berufen, wenn etwa Zaimoglu einen „frei gewählten Zugang" zu Identitätsmöglichkeiten oder persönliche Standpunkte zu fordern scheint und Modrooroo scheinbar souverän seine Namen und Identitäten ändert. Speziell die auffällige Präsenz des Themas der Namen*wahl* im australischen Kontext könnte dazu verleiten, diesem eine vergleichsweise stärkere Berufung auf die Kategorie der Authentizität zuzusprechen. Aber dagegen spricht sehr deutlich Mudrooroos Ablehnung von Identitätszuschreibungen nach Maßgabe der Gene, des Blutes oder der Rasse, wenn er sich auf seine geschichtliche Lebenserfahrung beruft, d.h. die Anrufungen, denen er ausgesetzt war, die er angenommen und die er vorgenommen hat. Die Ablehnung solch unhistorischer Identitätszuschreibungen ist ein gemeinsames Element aller untersuchten Strategien der Resignifikation als eines diskursiven Prozesses: Zaimoglu verwahrt sich gegen die Festlegung auf ein ‚Erbe', die die Logik der Repression und der Zensur wieder in Geltung bringen möchte, Mudrooroo beruft sich auf seine Lebensgeschichte gegen die, die mit einem kontrollierenden Blick auf seine ‚Abstammung' seine Legitimation in Frage stellen möchten, Gwynnes jugendliche Hauptfigur erlebt, wie gerade die festlegenden Zuschreibungen tödlich sein können und entschließt sich vor dem Hintergrund der erkannten diskursiven Anrufungen zu einem verantwortlichen Handeln. Darin liegt eine Chance für das mehrkulturelle Zusammenleben in beiden betrachteten Gesellschaften, zusammen mit der Hoffnung auf gelingende Resignifikationen, die durch Praktiken der Zensur nicht zu verhindern sind, weil die Zensur nur Ausdruck der Angst vor jenen Positionen ist, die für die Gesetzeslogik der Repression bedrohlich sein könnten.[111]

Notes

1. Foucault 1977, 101-106.
2. Ibid, 113, 114.
3. Ibid, 114. Judith Butler fragt, ob Foucaults Beschreibungsversuch nicht ebenso willkürlich verkürzt und stillstellend ist wie der Name ‚Macht' selbst, weist dann aber darauf hin, dass der Name ‚die Macht' noch stärker als Stillstellung des von Foucault beschriebenen variablen und beweglichen Gefüges eingesetzt wird, vgl. Butler 1998, 56-57.
4. Foucault 1977, 115.
5. Ibid, 116.
6. Ibid.
7. Ibid.
8. Ibid, 117.
9. Ibid.
10. Foucault 1973.
11. Foucault 1971.
12. Ich folge hier der Einschätzung, die Foucaults Werk eher im Sinne einer Kontinuitätsthese liest: Dass Foucaults Untersuchungen, die als

,Diskurstheorie' zusammengenommen werden können, sich (freilich mit Sackgassen und Umwegen) kontinuierlich entwickeln. Vgl. Jäger 1999, 120; Lemke 1997. Eine andere Einschätzung vertritt z.B. Isabell Lorey mit ihrer Interpretation, noch in der *Archäologie des Wissens* und in der *Ordnung des Diskurses* sei das Diskurskonzept als der Macht vorgängig und die Macht ausschließlich repressiv gedacht, vgl. Lorey 1999, 87-96. Gegen diese Interpretation kann ich hier nicht ausführlich argumentieren, sondern nur behaupten, dass die *Archäologie des Wissens* auch anders zu lesen wäre.

13. Foucault 1977, 119.
14. Ibid, 120.
15. Ibid, 121.
16. Ibid, 122.
17. Ibid. Hervorhebung von mir, S.H.
18. Ibid, 123.
19. Foucault 1973, 147.
20. Ibid, 148.
21. Ibid, 153.
22. Ibid.
23. Ibid. 150. Hervorhebung i.O.
24. Ibid, 155.
25. Ibid, 149.
26. Butler 1998, 207-210, wo Butler Derridas Tendenz, „die relative Autonomie der strukturellen Verfahrensweise des Zeichens zu betonen" (210) und Bourdieus Machttheorie, der es aber nicht gelänge, die „Logik der Iterierbarkeit zu erfassen" (208), wechselseitig durch einander ergänzt.
27. Link and Link-Heer 1990, 90.
28. Jäger 1999, 125-127.
29. Ibid, 125.
30. Foucault 1977, 156.
31. Das ist der Grund dafür, dass Dreyfus und Rabinow vom methodologischen „Scheitern der Archäologie" sprechen; vgl. Dreyfus and Rabinow 1987, 105.
32. Jäger 1999, 144.
33. Ibid.
34. Ibid, 147.
35. Wittgenstein 1984, 7.
36. Butler 1998, 14. Der Begriff der Anrufung, den sie in modifizierter und kritisierter Weise von Althusser bezieht, kann hier nicht ausführlich dargestellt werden, vgl. ibid, 41-57.

37. Ibid, 14.
38. Ibid, 189.
39. Jäger 1999, 148.
40. Ibid, 148. Hervorhebung i.O.
41. Ibid, 9.
42. Hier ist zu beachten, dass mit Resignifikaton keine simple Umkehrung eines negativen diskriminierenden Werturteils in ein positiv diskriminierendes Werturteil gemeint ist nach dem Muster von ‚Black is beautiful'. An der Frage danach, wer eine Resignifikation vornehmen kann, und zu welchem Preis, wird das unten deutlicher werden. Zur Kritik am 'Black is beautiful'-Modell vgl. Hall 2002.
43. Ibid, 26.
44. Ibid, 27.
45. Ibid, 28.
46. Butler 1997, 40.
47. Butler 1991, 213.
48. Butler 1998, 206.
49. Butler 1991, 203.
50. Ibid, 204.
51. Ibid, 215.
52. Butler 1998, 147.
53. Dafür, dass das eine durchführbare und vielversprechende, aber auch problematische Möglichkeit ist, vgl. z.B. Jäger 1999, 171-187 und Diaz-Bone, der Foucaults Diskurstheorie als eine „(post)strukturalistische Wissenssoziologie" auffasst (Diaz-Bone 1999); einen Überblick über unterschiedliche diskurstheoretische methodische Ansätze gibt z.B. Jäger 1999, 121-124.
54. Foucault 1996, 25.
55. Bublitz et al. 1999, 15.
56. Ibid, 13.
57. Foucault 1993, 17.
58. Vgl. Schlotterbeck 1998 and Baron 2002.
59. Schlotterbeck 1998.
60. Schlotterbeck 1999 and Baron 2002.
61. Schlotterbeck 1998.
62. Butler 1998, 12.
63. Zaimoglu 1995.
64. Ibid, 18.
65. Ibid, 9.
66. Androutsopoulos and Keim 2002.
67. Ibid.

68. Ibid.
69. Römhild 2002.
70. Ibid.
71. Saller 1999.
72. Androutsopoulos and Keim 2002.
73. Zaimoglu 1995, 15.
74. Ibid, 17.
75. Ibid, 18.
76. Ibid, 14.
77. Ibid.
78. Ibid, 16-17.
79. Zaimoglu 2002.
80. Zaimoglu 1995, 25.
81. Gesendet im N3 am 8.5.1998, 22.00-24.00 Uhr, vgl. (N.N. 1999).
82. Ibid, 22.
83. Ibid, 23.
84. Ibid.
85. Ibid, 24.
86. Ibid, 25.
87. Ibid, 26.
88. Butler 1998, 60.
89. Wignell 1997.
90. Ibid.
91. Ibid.
92. Mudrooroo (Narogin) 1988.
93. Gwynne 1998 [dtsch. 2002].
94. Der Streit darum, ob es sich um eine ‚postkoloniale' Perspektive handelt, kann hier nicht ausführlich dargestellt und diskutiert werden, vgl. dazu Webb 1996.
95. Thompson, ed. 1990, 55. Dt. Übersetzung nach Stiller 1998.
96. Stiller 1998.
97. Ibid.
98. Mudrooroo 1990, 148.
99. Stiller 1998.
100. Ibid.
101. Ibid.
102. Ibid.
103. Mudrooroo 1990, 62.
104. Webb 1996.
105. Ibid.
106. Um die Verfilmung, die 2002 herauskam, hat es einigen Streit

gegeben: Schon während der Produktionsphase wurde z.B. von Seiten einiger Vertreter von Organisationen der Aborigines der Vorwurf erhoben, der Film sei rassistisch, diskriminiere vor allem Aborigine-Frauen, und weiße Filmmacher hätten kein Recht, eine Aborigine-Geschichte darzustellen. Diese Debatte wäre aber Gegenstand einer eigenen Diskursanalyse.
107. Gwynne [dtsch. 2002], 6.
108. Ibid, 9.
109. Ibid, 11.
110. Die Frage, ob Gwynne als weißer Autor das Recht dazu hat, eine solche Geschichte zu erzählen, kann hier nicht untersucht werden. Ihr müsste eine eigene Diskursanalyse gewidmet werden, die das Material aus dem o.g. Streit um die Verfilmung einzubeziehen hätte. Mit der hier vertretenen Interpretation des Textes als Jugendentwicklungsroman mit dem Schwerpunkt auf der Bedeutung der Anrufung für die Subjektkonstitution könnte die Antwort auf die Frage möglicherweise positiv beantwortet werden.
111. Butler 1998, 229. Für Hinweise und Kritik danke ich Stephanie Bunk, Thorben Dyk, Uwe Hobuß, Ulrich Lölke und Russell West-Pavlov.

References

Androutsopoulos, Jannis and Inken Keim. „'hey lan, isch geb dir konkret handy.' Deutsch-türkische Mischsprache und Deutsch mit ausländischem Akzent: Wie Sprechweisen der Straße durch mediale Verarbeitung populär werden." 26 January 2000.
<www.archetype.de/papers/tuerkde.html> (24.05.2002).
Baron, Ulrich. „Hereinspaziert, Kanaken frisch eingetroffen." 26 January 2002.
<www.welt.de/daten/2002/01/26/01261w310116.htx> (24.05.2002).
Bublitz, Hannelore, Andrea D. Bührmann, Christine Hanke und Andrea Seier „Diskursanalyse – (k)eine Methode? Eine Einleitung." In *Das Wuchern der Diskurse. Perspektiven der Diskursanalyse Foucaults*, edited by Hannelore Bublitz, Andrea D. Bührmann, Christine Hanke, Andrea Seier, 10-21. Frankfurt am Main: Campus, 1999.
Butler, Judith. *Das Unbehagen der Geschlechter*. Frankfurt am Main: Suhrkamp, 1991.
Butler, Judith. *Körper von Gewicht. Die diskursiven Grenzen des Geschlechts*. Frankfurt am Main: Suhrkamp, 1997.
Butler, Judith. *Haß spricht. Zur Politik des Performativen*. Berlin: Berlin Verlag, 1998.

Diaz-Bone, Rainer. „Probleme und Strategien der Operationalisierung des Diskursmodells im Anschluss an Michel Foucault." In *Das Wuchern der Diskurse. Perspektiven der Diskursanalyse Foucaults*, edited by Hannelore Bublitz, Andrea D. Bührmann, Christine Hanke, Andrea Seier, 119-135. Frankfurt am Main: Campus, 1999.
Dreyfus, Hubert L. and Paul Rabinow. *Michel Foucault. Jenseits von Strukturalismus und Hermeneutik*. Frankfurt am Main: Athenäum, 1987.
Foucault, Michel. *Die Ordnung der Dinge*. Frankfurt am Main: Suhrkamp, 1971.
Foucault, Michel. *Archäologie des Wissens*. Frankfurt am Main: Suhrkamp, 1973.
Foucault, Michel. *Der Wille zum Wissen (Sexualität und Wahrheit I)*. Frankfurt am Main: Suhrkamp, 1977.
Foucault, Michel. „Wahrheit, Macht und Selbst. Ein Gespräch zwischen Rux Martin und Michel Foucault (25.10.1982)." In *Technologien des Selbst*, 15-23. Frankfurt am Main: S. Fischer, 1993.
Foucault, Michel. *Der Mensch ist ein Erfahrungstier*. Frankfurt am Main: Suhrkamp, 1996.
Gwynne, Phillip. *Deadly, Unna?* Australia: Penguin Children's Books, 1998. (Dt.: *Wir Goonyas, ihr Nungas*. Düsseldorf: Sauerländer, 2002).
Hall, Stuart. *Rassismus und kulturelle Identität*. Hamburg: Argument, 2002.
Jäger, Siegfried. *Kritische Diskursanalyse. Eine Einführung*. Duisburg: Duisburger Institut für Sprach- und Sozialforschung e.V., 1999.
Lemke, Thomas. *Eine Kritik der politischen Vernunft – Foucaults Analyse der modernen Gouvernementalität*. Hamburg, Berlin: Argument, 1997.
Link, Jürgen und Ursula Link-Heer. „Diskurs/Interdiskurs und Literaturanalyse." *LiLi* 77 (1990): 88-99.
Mudrooroo (Narogin). *Doin' Wildcat: A Novel Koori Script As constructed by Mudrooroo Narogin (Previously known as Colin Johnson)*. Melbourne: Hyland House, 1988.
Mudrooroo (Narogin). *Writing from the Fringe*. Melbourne: Hyland House, 1990.
N.N „Erbe und Auftrag – Bemerkungen zu einem rassistischen Auftritt." *Karoshi. Zeitschrift gegen die innere Sicherheit des Subjekts* 4 (1999): 22-26.
Römhild, Regina. „Wenn die Heimat global wird." December 2002. <www.zeit.de/2002/12/politik/print_200212_essay.roemhild.html> (24 May 2002).
Saller, Walter. „Brauchst du hart? Geb ich dir korrekt." 28 May 1999. <www.passagiere.de/ha/press/bz28_5_99.htm> (24 May 2002).
Schlotterbeck, Andrea. „Karembeus Urgroßväter wurden im Zoo

ausgestellt." 15 December1998.
<www.berlinonline.de/wissen/berliner_zeitung/archiv/1998/1215/vermischtes/0015/> (24 May 2002).
Stiller. „Vier Namen – welche Identität?" May 1998.
<www.culturebase.net/print_artist.php?598> (22 October 2003).
Thompson, Liz, ed. *Aboriginal Voices: Contemporary Aboriginal Artists, Writers and Performers*. Sydney: Simon and Schuster, 1990.
Webb, Hugh. "Doin' the Post-Colonial Story? Neidjie, Narogin and the Aboriginal Narrative Intervention…" 30 December 1996.
<wwsshe.murdoch.edu.au/cntinuum/litserv/SPAN/32/Webb.html> (22 October 2003).
Wignell, Peter. "The Influence of Aboriginal English." June 1997.
<www.shlrc.mq.edu.au/style/june1997/html> (22 October 2003).
Wittgenstein, Ludwig. *Philosophische Untersuchungen (Werkausgabe Bd. I)*. Frankfurt am Main: Suhrkamp, 1984.
Zaimoglu, Feridun. *Kanak Sprak. 24 Mißtöne vom Rande der Gesellschaft*. Hamburg: Rotbuch Verlag, 1995.
Zaimoglu, Feridun. "Planet Germany. " February 2002.
<www.kanak-attack.de/html/presse/spiegel-reporter.htm> (24 May 2002).

Strategic Uses of Multiculturalism in Germany and Australia

Anja Schwarz

Australian anthropologist Ghassan Hage has cautioned against the kind of knowledge which derives from the analysis of public discourse on multiculturalism and immigration. He maintains that it is impossible to learn anything about 'multicultural subjects' from debates of this kind. Commenting on the Australian context, he suggests such discussions should rather be regarded as "rituals of White empowerment – seasonal festivals where White Australians renew the belief in the possession of power to talk and make decisions about Third-World-Looking-Australians".[1] This paper argues analogously that an analysis of the uses of the term 'multiculturalism', an expression, as will become apparent, employed by actors attempting to dominate public discourse on cultural diversity, cannot be taken to unveil the reality of 'multicultural societies' in Germany and Australia. The knowledge to be extracted from this analysis rather relates to the very speakers who make such statements: Anglo-Celtic Australians or ethnic Germans respectively. It is this managerial position with regard to the nation of these speakers that offers the point of comparison between German and Australian discourses on multiculturalism that this chapter is interested in.

This article thus undertakes an analysis of German and Australian discourse on both nations' de facto cultural diversity by highlighting the different ways in which both societies over the past decades have made sense of socio-political terms such as assimilation, integration and, more importantly, multiculturalism. Such a comparative study situated on the level of political vocabulary gains its significance from revealing the contested nature of political expressions in public discourse. As will become evident, the meaning taken on by these terms does not simply derive from the political reality they are said to address. Rather, the terms' connotations depend on the political convictions and tactics of the respective speakers, as well as their positioning within in the discursive field they engage in. A study of the employment of such terms therefore provides a tableau of the different socio-political groups participating in debates on cultural diversity, as well as their positioning not only vis-à-vis the issue at stake but also in relation to one another in the relevant discursive field.

I employ the term 'cultural diversity' here in order to make possible a distinction between social reality on the one hand and political or popular discourse addressing this reality on the other. Cultural diversity, in the context of this paper, denotes the de-facto multicultural make-up of both countries. This, of course, is a pragmatic decision: the meaning taken on by the term is evidently equally the result of the power/knowledge formation of discourse, as is multiculturalism. It has a discursive history of its own and was introduced to the international debate by French anthropologist Lévi-Strauss in a UNESCO policy paper in 1952.[2] For the purpose of this analysis however, it will nevertheless stand in as a descriptive term for the above-mentioned de-facto diversity of both nations.

    Discourses do not take place in a vacuum but are embedded in both local and global contexts. Contrary to the transnational social reality of the migrants who are addressed by discourses on multiculturalism however, this analysis for the most part ignores such links between Australian and German debates and treats the meanings taken on by the term multiculturalism as being confined to the respective public sphere. A number of obvious fields of social debate such as discourse on immigration but also terrorism and economy will for the most part equally be ignored for the purpose of consistency and only mentioned where necessary.

    Such an analysis, finally, cannot assume a position outside the field it engages with or attempt to offer an impartial evaluation of both countries' discursive fields. Rather, this essay's focus is on the German debate. It first offers a brief history of the Australian employment of the expressions 'assimilation,' 'integration' and 'multiculturalism' up to this day. This chronology will provide the analytical backdrop against which a history of the German use of the term multiculturalism will be offered. This comparative perspective, then, will make the particularities of the German debate more apparent and at least partly explains the expression's highly controversial role in the context of Germany's debate on a proposed immigration law between Spring 2001 and June 2004.

1.   From White Australia to Australian multiculturalism

Since the arrival of the First Fleet in Botany Bay in 1788, marking the beginning of European settlement, until the 1950s the self-perception of the Australian nation state has been predominately white.[3] This was not the inadvertent outcome of history but the result of population politics which, particularly after the founding of the Australian nation state in 1901, aimed at creating and maintaining a nation which was monocultural. As this cultural homogeneity was at the time thought to depend on 'race' as a determinant of culture, one of the first acts of legislation passed by the young nation state's government was the

Immigration Restriction Act.[4] It ensured that non-European immigration was virtually non-existent until the 1940s. The Naturalisation Act, passed two years later, additionally excluded non-Europeans already in the country from obtaining Australian citizenship. The actual 'racial composition' of the nation at the time of Federation had by no means been as monocultural and white as its projected self-image. By 1947 however, these acts of legislation, now jointly known as the White Australia Policy, had made Australia one of the whitest and most monocultural countries in the world.[5] As James Jupp explains, the country "could [now] claim to be 99% white and 96% British, though public statements often put the latter percentage higher."[6] Today, just over 50 years later, Australia regards itself as a multicultural society and announces its diverse population make-up internally as well as internationally as the nation's asset. How can this radical change from administered monoculturalism to an affirmative multiculturalism be accounted for?

Jupp and others identify the shock of the nation's military vulnerability in WWII as the key motivation for a change in Australia's immigration politics in the post-war years.[7] Realising that Britain would not have been able to protect the country from a possible attack by the Japanese, Australia embarked on an immigration scheme that was to increase its population rapidly over the following decades. According to the words of its first Minister for Immigration, Arthur Caldwell, the country was to 'populate or perish' given its increasingly populated Asian vicinity. Largely as a result of this immigration programme, the Australian population increased from 7,5 to 12,7 million in the years 1947 to 1971.[8] While British citizens remained the main addressees of these various immigration schemes and were actively sought through campaigns and with the help of assisted passages, the desired quota could soon no longer be filled with migrants from the British Isles alone. The prior exclusiveness of the White Australia policy was consequently liberalised in order to include 'New Australians' first from Northern and later Southern Europe. The boundary of the 'imagined community' that had formerly been drawn exclusively around those of British heritage was now extended to the point "where a culture ceased to be European."[9] The desired immigrants were subsequently chosen less for racial than for cultural considerations: migrants of European background were thought to be able to assimilate completely to the Australian way of life. They were regarded as already sharing the same set of values that were associated with Europe, while people from other areas of the world and, consequently, of different racial backgrounds supposedly did not.

All 'New Australians' migrating to the country from Federation up until the mid-1960s were targeted by policies of *assimilation* and expected to blend into the dominant culture. For migrants from European countries outside the British Isles, this meant the suppression of any non-Anglo-Celtic characteristics in public and ideally the abandonment of native language, customs or any other attribute which would make the migrant stand out in a crowd.[10] These expectations, already spelt out in the official welcoming material, "included the public use of language others than English, the wearing of unusual clothing, gestures not normally used, physical appearance and anything which prevented the individual from becoming invisible in the majority."[11] It is obvious that these expectations were difficult but easier to overcome for northern Europeans than for those of southern European background whose skin and hair colour made them more visible in the Anglo-Celtic public.

In spite of these visual markers of ethnicity, the 'failure' of southern Europeans to assimilate into mainstream Australia has predominately been attributed to their greater numbers. The Greek and Italian populations in Australia's major cities were soon large enough to form their own social networks.[12] The second phase of Australian policies towards migrant minorities was initiated as a reaction to the emergence of these groups. Devised and implemented from the mid-1960s onwards, the policy of 'integration' no longer assumed that 'new Australians' were to abandon their language and culture so as to become included into mainstream society. Public spending on migrant assistance and welfare rose significantly. A number of programmes, comprising direct assistance such as language classes and structural and financial assistance for ethnic organisations, were designed to enhance participation in Australian society. Nevertheless, the complete absorption into the Anglo-Celtic mainstream at least of second generation migrants remained the implicit objective of these programmes.

The current phase of multicultural policies has often been related to the failure of integrative politics to achieve this complete absorption, which, by the end of the 1960s, could not longer be ignored. Significantly larger and more diverse groups of migrants bargained for representation of their interests through organisations such as the Italian welfare organisation Co.As.It., founded in 1967, and the Greek Welfare Society, founded in 1969. 'Multiculturalism,' a term which had been part of Canadian political discourse since 1968 and which had just been introduced as the Canada's government policy in 1971, seemed to offer a viable concept for addressing this development. Consequently, the term was first mentioned in an Australian context in 1973, when Al Grasby, then Minister for Immigration, delivered a speech titled 'A multicultural society for the future', stating that

> in a family, the overall attachment to the common good need not impose a sameness on the outlook in activity of each member, nor need those members deny their individuality and distinctiveness in order to seek a superficial and unnatural conformity. The important thing is that they are all committed to the good of all.[13]

In subsequent years the actual policy of multiculturalism was elaborated by various government advisory bodies and the 'Galbally Report' of 1978 mapped out its policy consequences subsequently to be implemented by the Fraser Government. It argued that the Australian government was

> convinced that migrants have the right to maintain their cultural and racial identity and that it is clearly in the best interest of our nation that they should be encouraged and assisted to do so if they wish. The knowledge that people are identified with their cultural background and ethnic group enables them to take their place in their new society with confidence if their ethnicity has been accepted by the community.[14]

A number of institutions have since been set up to provide services in accordance with the change to multicultural policies such as the Federation of Ethnic Communities Council of Australia (FECCA) founded 1979, the Office of Multicultural Affairs (OMA) functioning in the Department of Prime Minister and cabinet between 1987 and 1996, the National Multicultural Advisory Council which gave recommendations on the government's *National Agenda for a Multicultural Australia* and reviewed its implementation in 1995, as well as cultural institutions such as the TV channel SBS whose programmes were designed for a migrant audience.

Until the change of government in 1996, most of these multicultural programs and agencies were primarily concerned with easing immigrant settlement and with securing equity for ethnic minority members. Over the years, state sponsored multiculturalism developed from its first mention by Al Grasby in 1973 into "a comprehensive ideology of what Australia was supposed to be and to become".[15] Throughout this time the creation of what was understood to be a multicultural society in Australia initiated by the post-1947 immigration program has always been accepted as an – even desirable – reality by the country's major political parties. In recent years however, there has been a marked decline in enthusiasm for multicultural policies, as well as a change in public discourse about multiculturalism. According to James Jupp the "consistent and bipartisan" support of multicultural policies was already beginning to fracture in the 1980s, when the increasing unpopularity of immigration, caused largely by high unemployment, also undermined support for multiculturalism.[16] The election of the Howard Government in 1996 finally marked a significant change in Australia's multicultural politics. Already before his election, Howard had repeatedly expressed his dislike for the term multiculturalism. Along with the significant reduction in staffing and funding of multicultural agencies, the abolition of the National Advisory Council (re-established in 1997) and the absorption of the OMA into the Department of Immigration and Multicultural Affairs, this change communicated itself in the repeated emphasis on a specific *Australian multiculturalism* which characterises the current government's rhetoric. The term is said to express the government's conviction of the fundamental necessity for certain shared 'Australian' norms and values to be adhered to by all citizens.

The shift in the political discourse on multiculturalism – from a concern for the special needs of certain immigrant groups to an instrument of social cohesion – is most obvious in the government's 2003 policy statement *Multicultural Australia: United in Diversity*. The document updated the *New Agenda for Multicultural Australia* launched in December 1999 and sets strategic directions until 2006. Similarly to earlier policy papers it interprets multicultural policies as an active tool for "successful nation building".[17] Its three main points nevertheless also indicate major changes from previous understandings of multiculturalism outlined above:

A. Focus on individual responsibility rather than group rights:

The policy paper iterates the individual's responsibilities towards the "nation and its democratic institution and values".

> All Australians are expected to have an overriding loyalty to Australia and its people, and to respect the basic structures and principles underwriting our democratic society. These are the Constitution, Parliamentary democracy ... English as the national language, the rule of law...[18]

Whereas multiculturalism formerly referred to a set of mechanisms which provide services for migrant groups and ensure their representation in political bodies, the current policy formulates an individual obligation to the nation state. The recognition of migrant rights is equally relegated to the level of personal recognition of difference, stating that "all Australians have the right to express their own culture and beliefs and have a reciprocal obligation to respect the right of others to do the same".[19]

B. Social cohesion:

A focus on cohesion replaces the former support of diverse social groups. Instead of granting 'special treatment' to these segments of society the policy argues that "the key to the success of Australian multiculturalism is inclusiveness. Every Australian benefits from our diversity...".[20] As Gary Hardgrave, Minister for Citizenship and Multicultural Affairs, explains in his preface to the policy paper, the government "will give increased emphasis to furthering harmonious community relations ensuring equity in the provision of government services".[21] Philip Ruddock, then Minister for Immigration and Multicultural and Indigenous Affairs, equally speaks of "the Government's strong and enduring commitment to community harmony".[22] Several times this envisioned 'community harmony' is linked to a discourse on security. Social cohesion is taken to be the primary weapon not only in the country's national security program but also in the "international effort to combat terrorism" thus making those who argue for special rights into a possible threat to the nation's security:

> Australians now see themselves as directly threatened by terrorism. In this context, community harmony and social cohesion are pivotal elements in enabling Australia to contribute effectively to the international effort to combat terrorism, and safeguarding Australians domestically. The Government believes firmly that Australian multicultural policy provides a framework of national unity and a coherent ethos for a diverse Australia at a time of conflict, as well as in times of peace. National security begins with domestic community harmony.[23]

The *Living in Harmony* initiative, which includes the annual celebration of *Harmony Day* on March 21, is one of the programs initiated by the Howard government to promote this more cohesive, more 'Australian' understanding of multiculturalism.

C. Neo-liberal discourse:

The increasing emphasis placed on economic growth represents a third shift in governmental discourse on multiculturalism. The paper states that "all Australians benefit from productive diversity, that is, the significant cultural, social and economic dividends arising from the diversity of our population."[24] Taking up arguments from neo-liberal discourse the text interprets the country's cultural diversity in terms of an economic resource:

> In the knowledge-based economy of this millennium, where people are the key to a nation's productivity and competitiveness, Australia's multiculturalism is a most valuable resource. It encourages diversity in ways of thinking and stimulates innovation and creativity. It helps us to forge links with the rest of the world that can deliver increased trade and investment through the expansion of markets and development of diverse goods and services.[25]

This brief outline provides an (admittedly oversimplified) chronology of Australian policies regarding cultural diversity – from assimilation and integration to a neoliberal "Australian" multiculturalism. It has shown Australia's discourse on cultural diversity, as well as the meaning the term 'multiculturalism' has come to represent, to rely heavily on government intervention. Al Grasby, as Minister for Immigration, first introduced the term to Australia's public discourse. Subsequent governments in their policy-making function remained crucial in discursive struggles over the term's meaning. The term multiculturalism, broadly speaking, connotes what the respective government deems it to be.

The history of the Australian employment of these expressions provided here will now serve as analytical backdrop for my analysis of the equivalent German debate. Such a comparative view will help to identify the specific features of the German discussion on cultural diversity which peaked in the debate over Germany's first immigration law in 2001.

2. Germany: from denial of immigration via multiculturalism to integration?

Up until the 1990s, Germany's immigration policies relied on the assertion, first made in the 1979 Kühn Memorandum, that Germany was 'not a country of immigration'. Ignoring the social reality of permanent, or at least, long-term immigration, a general public debate over what to expect from migrants – and what migrants could expect from German society in return – did not take place.[26]

If questions of cultural diversity were addressed at all by politicians, academics, intellectuals, as well as teachers or social workers, their statements often took their clues from an international debate which was much more advanced. As I will show in what follows, it is because of this 'time-lag' between the belated recognition of cultural diversity at home and impulses from the international debate that German discussions did not follow the linear progression from assimilation via integration to contemporary politics of multiculturalism which have characterised the Australian debate. The 'delay' resulted in a conglomerate of discursive strands, which appear confusing – and not only from an Australian perspective. At one point for instance, the German discussions on cultural diversity appeared to shift directly from a denial of immigration and the implicit expectation that migrants were to assimilate and disappear into the German mainstream, to calls for multicultural policies. No less confusing were utterances in which the term multiculturalism was treated as if it were synonymous with 'integration', a concept which, at the time, was equally new in the German context. Hartmuth Esser's 1983 statement that "a multicultural society" was "defined by integration, not assimilation," illustrates this confusion of concepts so characteristic for the German context.[27] The history of the German use of the term multiculturalism which is traced on the following pages will outline the significant transformations the term has undergone since its emergence in German discourse in the early 1980s. An analysis of these shifts serves this paper's goal of exploring the particular power relations of those socio-political actors that have determined the German discourse on cultural diversity to this day.

A. The emergence of multiculturalism

Up until the 1980s the term 'multiculturalism' did not play a role at all in German discourse on immigration and cultural diversity. "Only when the pressure exerted by social problems was shaking the country," as Alf Mintzel puts it, did the term start its intensive but short discursive history.[28] Contrary to the governmental dimension of multicultural discourse in Australia, the initiative to talk about multiculturalism first came from speakers in the field of social work, pedagogy, social politics, teaching and health care.[29] Their impulses were subsequently taken up by churches and political parties, thus establishing the term in public discourse.

The date which marks this arrival of multiculturalism in the Federal Republic's public discourse is generally considered to be 1980. Both catholic and protestant churches celebrated the 'Tag des ausländischen Mitbürgers' (Day of the Foreign Citizen) in September that year and used the occasion to promote the notion of "Germany's multicultural society".[30] In the same year, the left-wing intellectual journal

Kursbuch published its volume 'Vielvölkerstaat Bundesrepublik' (Multinational Germany) in which the term was employed on two levels: descriptively, in reference to Germany's social reality, as well as on a normative level, now denoting a desired future policy addressing this reality.[31] Three years later, Hartmuth Esser published his essay *Multikulturelle Gesellschaft als Alternative zu Isolation und Assimilation* (Multicultural Society: An Alternative to Isolation and Assimilation) from which the quotation on the previous page was taken. This text marks the author's attempt to establish a normative reading of the term multiculturalism which is astonishingly close to contemporary definitions of the concept in affirmatively multicultural nations such as Australia:

> [Multikulturalismus bezeichnet] eine Gesellschaft, in der verschiedene ethnische, kulturelle und religiöse Gruppen in einem gemeinsamen wirtschaftlichen und politischen Rahmen jeweils ihre Eigenständigkeit behalten und in geregelten und spannungsarmen Beziehungen zueinander stehen.[32]
> [Multiculturalism refers to] a society in which different ethnic, cultural and religious groups keep their independence within a shared economic and political framework and engage with one another in regulated relations of low conflict potential.

According to Esser a successful multicultural society depends on the shared understanding „dass alle Gruppen bei aller Eigenständigkeit jederzeit im Prinzip für die Begegnung mit anderen Gruppen offen sind und sich auch in gewisser Weise aneinander ‚anpassen'" [...that all groups, in spite of their independence, remain in principle approachable for other groups and are willing to adapt to one another].[33] Esser's concept however, did not become the generally accepted reading of multiculturalism. This failure to establish a normative definition of multicultural politics can be taken as a first indicator of the predominance of certain speaking positions in Germany's public discourse, positions that much more successfully managed to dominate Germany's discussions on cultural diversity. They will be addressed below.

Another prominent and, as will become apparent, rather surprising advocate of multiculturalism in the 1980s was conservative politician Heiner Geißler who, according to his own statements, first employed the term in an 1988 interview in Germany's weekly newspaper *Die Zeit*:

Für ein Land in der Mitte Europas ist die Vision einer multikulturellen Gesellschaft eine große Chance. Deshalb müssen wir das Land offen halten für die Ausländer und Aussiedler. Das sind zumeist mutige und dynamische Menschen, die Risiken auf sich nehmen und anpassungsbereit sind.[34]

For a country in Europe's centre, the vision of a multicultural society is a great chance. This is why we have to keep our country open for foreigners and ethnic German migrants. For the most part, these are brace and dynamic people, who will take risks and are willing to adapt.

Alongside with Geißler's statements there was an overall increase of the term's employment towards the end of the 1980s that can be taken to indicate the term's arrival in Germany's mainstream debates about migration and cultural diversity by this time. In 1989 for instance, the Evangelische Akademie Loccum hosted a symposium titled 'Multikulturell. Oder: Neue Migration – Alte Konzepte? Ausländerpolitik vor neuen Herausforderungen' (Multicultural. Or: new migration – old concepts?).[35] In autumn 1990, more events followed within the framework of the 'Kulturstaat Deutschland' programme further establishing the expression *multiculturalism* in Germany's political centre. The preliminary climax of the term's relevance for German debates on cultural diversity was reached with the publication of two books in the early 1990s which appeared to document the expression's establishment in the general socio-political discourse. In 1990 left wing political scientist Claus Leggewie published his political rather than academically-analytical contribution *MultiKulti. Spielregeln für die Vielvölkerrepublik* (Multikulti. Rules for the Multinational Republic). It was followed in 1992 by a book by two members of the Federal Republic's green-alternative spectrum, Daniel Cohn-Bendit and Thomas Schmidt: *Heimat Babylon. Das Wagnis der multikulturellen Gesellschaft* (Homeland Babylon. The Adventure of a Multicultural Society).

B. The 1990s: shrinking relevance for the term 'multiculturalism'

Five years later, *Der Spiegel*'s cover page from 14 April 1997 communicates an understanding of multiculturalism fundamentally different from the term's German success story of the late eighties and early nineties. Mark Terkessidis describes the image as follows:

> Der Spiegel stellte fest, dass „Ausländer" und Deutsche sich „gefährlich fremd" seien, und verkündete „das Scheitern der multikulturellen Gesellschaft". Auf dem Titelbild sah man im Vordergrund eine junge Frau mit dunklem Teint, die mit geschwollenen Halsschlagadern eine Rote, erst beim zweiten Blick als türkisch zu erkennende Fahne schwang. Links daneben waren Schülerinnen mit Kopftüchern beim Studium des Korans abgebildet. Endlose Bankreihen verloren sich – massenhaften Nachwuchs suggerierend – im weißen Nichts des Hintergrunds. Rechts unter der Fahne wiederum lugte eine mit Messern und Tschakos bewaffnete Jugendgang hervor. In einem Akt perfider journalistischer Zuspitzung fasste der Spiegel das hegemoniale Angstphantasma über Ausländer zusammen: Fanatismus, Fundamentalismus, Kriminalität, Gewalt.[36]

> *Der Spiegel* noted that "foreigners" and Germans were dangerously estranged from one another and announced "the failure of a multicultural society". The title page depicted a young woman of dark complexion in the foreground who, with swollen carotid arteries, waves a red flag which only at a second glance is recognisable as Turkish. On her left the picture showed female students with headscarves studying the Koran. Countless rows of desk – denoting large numbers of offspring – faded into the white background. Then again, under the flag's right hand corner appeared a youth gang armed with knifes and tschakos. Through this act of perfidious journalistic exaggeration, *Der Spiegel* managed to sum up the hegemonic phantasm of fear about foreigners: fanatism, fundamentalism, crime, violence.

This cover page of what was at the time Germany's biggest weekly news magazine illustrates the fundamental changes that Germany's discourse on multiculturalism has undergone since its rather celebratory beginning. By the end of the decade, not only the political right had denounced the term. It became equally discredited amongst the country's political left and the more liberal groupings represented by *Der Spiegel*. In their 1992 contribution Cohn-Bendit and Schmid had already unintentionally predicted the term's future demise when providing a sarcastic account of the expression's political enemies on both sides of the political spectrum.

> Konservative befürchten die Überfremdung, Überflutung und ‚Durchrassung' des Gemeinwesens. Linke befürchten, die wachsende Vielfalt kultureller Traditionen und Wertsysteme komme jenen gerade recht, denen der Imperativ der Menschenrechte und verbindlichen Normen der Republik immer schon ein Dorn im Auge waren. Rechte Besitzstandswahrer erblicken in der multikulturellen Gesellschaft das offene Tor, durch das die Habenichtse aus aller Herren Länder auf uns niedergehen werden. Dritte-Welt-Aktivisten dagegen argwöhnen, die multikulturelle Gesellschaft sei nichts anderes als ein perfides Manöver der hochentwickelten Länder ... Multikulturalismus als Fortsetzung von Kolonialismus und Imperialismus mit anderen Mitteln.[37]

> Conservatives fear the "over-estrangement", flooding and "mixed-racialisation" of society. Left wing critics apprehend, that the growing diversity of cultural traditions and value systems might empower those that have always wanted to attack the Federal Republic's imperative of human rights and binding norms. Right wing protectors of the status quo regard the multicultural society as the open door through which the world's have-nots can enter. Third-World-Activists on the other hand, suspect the multicultural society to be nothing but a perfidious manoeuvre of highly developed countries... Multiculturalism as a continuation of colonisation and imperialism with other means.

Christoph Geulen attributes the increasing unpopularity of multiculturalism in the second half of the 1990s to Germany's overall insecurity in the years following the country's 're-unification'. Increasing levels of immigration, as well as rising numbers of xenophobic attacks on migrants gave the topic new relevance and 'explosiveness'. In this context, multiculturalism came to denote all those problems in the formation of a new collective German identity which dominated German political debate in these post-unification years.[38] The short account of debates from the 1990s which follows provides an overview of attacks on the term multiculturalism from both the political left and right. These attacks contributed to a radical change in the term's perception by the end of the decade.

B.1 Rejection by the political right

A repudiation of multicultural politics was to be expected from the country's political right, since conservatives elsewhere also rejected multiculturalism and argued in favour of the preservation of essentialised national identities. The reaction of German conservatives in the 1990s nevertheless bore some national particularities. Among these were frequent references to ethnic conflicts in other parts of the world to prove that multiculturalism 'obviously did not work'. This argumentative strand was to be found for instance in Erwin Faul's rhetorical question as to whether Germany was threatened by what he perceived to be "Europe's Lebanonisation".[39] Other conservative opponents of multiculturalism referred to the ongoing civil war in former Yugoslavia[40] or, as with Bassam Tibi, one of the nation's most outspoken opponents of multicultural politics at the time, took the 1992 race riots in Los Angeles as proof that multiculturalism was a "dangerous ideology". Tibi went on to ask polemically whether "Europe could possibly pull it off when America had already so obviously failed".[41] One, of course, only needs to take into account the political stability of affirmatively multicultural nations such as Australia and Canada to realise that these nations regard multicultural politics as a preventive instrument for countering social unrest rather than the cause of ethnic conflicts.

Faul, however, spelt out more clearly the convictions underlying the rejection of multiculturalism. Referring to the nation-building slogan of Germany's 'peaceful revolution' of 1989 he claimed that "naturally it was Germans one had in mind and not some ostensibly multicultural society when shouting 'Wir sind ein Volk' (We are one people)".[42] Faul argued that it would be impossible to transplant such an 'American concept' (sic!) to densely populated Europe whose national societies had been forged over the centuries.[43] Apart from the anti-Americanism apparent in this statement (a marker of ultra-conservative discourse) his line of argumentation is typical of a larger group of conservative contributions on cultural diversity. Proponents of multiculturalism had politicised 'culture' in terms of a regulated co-habitation of different groups within the framework of the nation state. Conservative and right wing discourse of the Faul variety likewise made 'culture' central to its argument. Here, 'culture' stands in as a substitute for 'race', a category that has become discredited over the years. And while its speakers concede that all cultures are of equal value, they argue for an 'ethno-pluralism' which keeps these cultures distinguishable and outside Germany's imagined community.[44]

B.2 Rejection by the political left

While the rejection of multiculturalism by Germany's conservatives was to be expected, a surprisingly large number of critical interventions also came from left wing discourse participants. This is at least partly due to the fact that although Germany was late to embark on debates on multiculturalism these never took place in an empty discursive space. In their critical position on multiculturalism these left-wing opponents in particular often referred to arguments that had earlier been discussed in an international context such as Canada or Australia. Most of these contestations belong to one of the following lines or argumentation.

Representatives of cultural pluralism argued that multiculturalism was nothing but "reverse racism" since it emphasises differences between and not within cultures.[45] For these speakers, multiculturalism was based on the fallacious assumption that "all cultures are unique, clearly distinguishable, as well as classifiable".[46] Within this "racism of distance" other cultures were said to be regarded as "self-contained entities" in the face of which "the multiculturalist could assert his own privileged, universal position of distance".[47]

Others criticised the "romantic idealisation of social reality" and the "limitation of everything social to the realms of culture" that came with the shift towards a politics that emphasing the importance of all things cultural.[48] In their eyes, this "culturisation" of economic and social differences expressed the growing "instrumentalisation of culture" and the "abuse of culture's moral capital for political-ideological goals."[49] Shifting the focus from class to culture, these speakers argued, meant that multicultural politics ignored the actual needs of those it sought to address.

A third group finally found fault with the discourse's proximity to and interrelatedness with consumer culture in late capitalism. Multiculturalism was deemed to combine "neoliberal market affirmation ... with a consumerist discourse of difference" since only those differences which are regarded as "enriching to one's own culture" would be recognised.[50] This complicity of multiculturalism with consumer culture was claimed to be most clearly expressed in those very examples of 'successful multiculturalism' celebrated by the concepts' advocates such as ethnic restaurants and businesses, musicians and writers.

C. Why did German multiculturalism 'fail'?

Klaus Bade argues that it was this 'negative constellation' of opponents at the left and right ends of Germany's political spectrum that contributed to the failure of multicultural programs in Germany. While Bade is certainly correct in his observations, discourse-theoretical considerations might provide more persuasive explanations for the final demise of a multicultural vocabulary in the German context. Such a perspective helps to identify those aspects that have contributed to the term's disappearance from German discourse on immigration and cultural identity after its initial 'discursive success' in the 1980s.

A repeated complaint regarding the employment of the term multiculturalism was its perceived 'elusiveness'.[51] The expression was said to be too "inexact, ambiguous and vague", or too "blurry ... and spectacular"[52], for it ever to represent any tangible political programme. Interestingly, accusations such as these are very seldom heard in Australian discourse on multiculturalism. The reasons for this discrepancy in the perception of the same expression are obvious: in Australia, the term has been part of a state sanctioned vocabulary since the 1970s and is agreed upon as the name given to certain policies and regulations addressing the country's cultural diversity. It has therefore always been understood and conceptualised in the context of these actual laws and regulations. Its meaning has been determined by what Pierre Bourdieu calls "official nomination",

> an act of symbolic imposition that has behind it all the strength of the collective, the consensus, the common sense, because it is performed by a delegated agent of the State, the holder of the monopoly of legitimate symbolic violence.[53]

In the German context multiculturalism never acquired this status of state-sanctioned stability and the term's meaning was therefore left open to contradictory interpretations by different political interest groups. As Alf Mintzel explains, this conceptual openness "allowed everyone to project their understandings and world views into it and, in doing so, to render the term as something positive or negative."[54] In the course of the 1990s the term multiculturalism thus retained less and less value for political discussion. Rather than being associated with certain political ideals and concepts, it had become, in Rainer Geißler's summary of the development in a recent overview of Germany's debates on multiculturalism, "an emotive word full of clashing ideals".[55]

D. 'Integration' – the new magic word?

I wish to close with a survey of Germany's debate over the nation's first Immigration Act. Such an overview on the one hand delivers a portrait of the current state of Germany's discourse on cultural diversity. However, it also serves to illustrate the role of the term multiculturalism in these debates after its difficult discursive history in the 1990s. The public debates over the Immigration Act lasted from Spring 2001 right up to June 2004 when the law was finally passed by both chambers of Germany's parliament. Because these debates reached a climax in summer/autumn 2001 however, the focus will be on statements made during this period of time.

First of all, it is striking to observe the virtual disappearance of the term multiculturalism from the German debate. This absence should however not necessarily be taken to indicate a lessening of social debate on issues such as immigration and cultural diversity. On the contrary, the term's disappearance coincides interestingly with the passing of regulations that are much closer to the legislation labelled 'multicultural' in Australia than any previous regulation. However, the term which came to label this new phase in Germany's immigration politics is not multiculturalism but rather integration, an expression widely rejected in the Canadian and the Australian context.

This shift in political vocabulary is clearly reflected in statements made not only by the country's political parties but also by all of Germany's major socio-political pressure groups such as churches, welfare organisations and human rights groups. Of of the more than thirty statements available from these groups not more than even three do so much as mention the term multiculturalism: Germany's conservative party, the CDU, Germany's Turkish Community and the Greens. While this 'coalition of multiculturalism' across the political spectrum might initially seem surprising, an analysis of the term's employment quickly reveals the groups' differing motivation for their employment of the term. Indeed, their manner of using the expression makes even more apparent the diminishing relevance of multiculturalism and the 'rise' of integration in Germany's socio-political discourse. Here, it is important to repeat that one would be mistaken in associating a shift in political goals with this change of political vocabulary. Contrary to the Australian context in which integration is associated with certain outmoded political programmes, the term integration has never acquired such a definite meaning in the German context and can now, similarly to multiculturalism in its earlier discursive career, come to carry a vast variety of meanings and serve a broad range of political agendas.

On 7 June 2001, the CDU's federal commission passed a resolution in which the heated debates of the late 1990s still resonate, and in which the politicians spoke of "multiculturalism in the sense of an enduring, non-committal coexistence of different social and ethnic groups" which they found to be "inacceptable, since it would lead to the loss of cohesion and identity of German society."[56] Instead, the CDU advocated the concept of integration. The term was mentioned 120 times in the resolution's text making it central to the CDU's new approach to cultural diversity in contrast to the single reference to multiculturalism.

Germany's Turkish Community also referred to multiculturalism in its statement on the future Immigration Act. Here, the term was employed not to denote possible future politics addressing the interests of Germany's migrants but was used solely to describe Germany's de facto culturally diverse society: "Germany has long since and irreversibly become an immigration country and a multicultural society. The state's politics must be oriented towards this reality."[57] Apart from this assertion the text, similarly to the CDU's statement, only speaks of integration in the sense of a set of policies and regulations. Again, in contrast to the single reference made to 'multiculturalism', the term 'integration' is employed 32 times.

Germany's Green Party, finally, appeared to be the only political group to have stuck to multiculturalism in their political vocabulary, employing it to refer to both socio-political goals, as well as the reality of cultural diversity in Germany. Their paper made a case for a "multicultural democracy".[58] Similarly to both other groups however, their text also refered to the term integration and employs this expression considerably more often (22 mentions) than multiculturalism (9 mentions). In the political vocabulary of Germany's Greens therefore, both terms appear not to contradict and exclude one another but rather to stand for the same concepts.

The final draft of the Immigration Act' passed by the Lower House of the German Parliament on 20 June 2002[59] but subsequently blocked, redrafted and, two years later in June 2004, passed a second time, this time by both, the Lower House and the Federal Assembly[60] does not so much as mention the term multiculturalism. This is remarkable for the an expression that had dominated any German discussion on immigration and cultural diversity just a decade earlier.

What is to be learnt from such a comparative perspective? A preliminary result appears to be the impossibility of comparisons that remain merely at the level of political vocabulary. Expressions employed in various nations' discourses on cultural diversity do not signify the same concepts. As this paper has shown, the rewards of a comparative perspective are to be found at another level. By turning the respective other country into the backdrop against which the actual analysis may be staged, the particularities of national debates are rendered more transparent and, hopefully, can be opened up to productive questions.

Notes

1. Hage 1998, 241.
2. Lévi-Strauss 1975. For a discourse analytical look at the term 'cultural diversity' in recent German discourse see Schmalfeld 2004.
3. The Australian continent, of course, never was 'white'. This article however, is interested in the self-image of the Australian state which first denied indigenous Australians the right to the continent under the policy of terra nullius and excluded them from the 'imagined community' of the nation until the public referendum in 1967.
4. See Ang 1999, 191.
5. Jupp 2002, 9. My argument follows closely the historical chronology of Australian immigration policies suggested by James Jupp. For a more recent account of Australian immigration history see Tavan 2005.
6. Jupp 1998, 132.
7. Jupp 2002, 11.
8. Ibid, 13.
9. Castles 1988, 45.
10. See White 1981, 160.
11. Jupp 1998, 134.
12. Ibid, 137-138.
13. Quoted in Theophanous 1995, 9.
14. Quoted in Ibid, 18.
15. Castles 1988, 4. Several scholars have pointed out that the major reason for these changes was not necessarily stimulated by a shift in the national self-image but rather in the country's international economic position, since the importance of Japan and South-East Asia as trading partners increased rapidly throughout the 1950s and early 1960s. "For obvious reasons, the White Australia policy in its crude from was an embarrassment in this process" (Ibid, 53). See also Freeman and Jupp 1992, 18-19.
16. Jupp 2001, 261.
17. Agenda, 2.
18. Ibid, 6.
19. Ibid.
20. Ibid, 5.
21. Ibid, 3.
22. Ibid, 2.
23. Ibid, 7.
24. Ibid, 6.

25. Ibid, 8.
26. My paper only refers to the West-German and, since 1990, united German debate on cultural diversity. A parallel look at the way in which GDR politics and public discourse addressed these issues while obviously necessary for a more rounded picture of the topic, cannot be provided here. For a summary of these issues in GDR history see Bade and Oltmer 2004, 90-96.
27. „Das Konzept der multikulturellen Gesellschaft ließe sich dann schließlich unter der Kombination subsumieren, bei der es Integration aber keine Assimiliation gibt" (Esser 1983, 28). All translations my own.
28. Mintzel 1997, 10.
39. „Der Diskurs wurde zunächst „von denjenigen Instanzen geführt, die in der bundesrepublikanischen Gesellschaft mit der Integration, der sozialen Kontrolle und der Normalisierung beschäftigt sind, also der Sozialpolitik, Sozialarbeit/Sozialpädagogik, der Schulpädagogik und des Gesundheitswesens" (Radtke 1991, 82).
30. Mintzel 1997, 25.
31. Michel and Spengler 1980.
32. Esser 1983, 30.
33. Ibid, 33.
34. Geißler, H. 1988, 9. In subsequent statements, Geißler additionally contributed to the term's development in Germany's political discourse from a rather demographical-instrumental reading (Radke) to an understanding that focussed on communal values and norms expressed Germany's contribution while at the same time welcoming the cultural identity of migrants (See Geißler, H. 1996). He still insisted on the term's use in a 1998 interview with Germany's news magazine *Der Spiegel* (Der Spiegel 1998).
35. Mintzel 1997, 26.
36. Terkessidis 2001, 201-202.
37. Cohn-Bendit and Schmid 1992, 17.
38. Geulen 1998, 17.
39. „Droht eine Libanonisierung Europas?" (Faul 1993, 62).
40. Bade 1996, 10.
41. „Kann Europa leisten, woran Amerikaner scheinbar gescheitert sind?" (Tibi 2001, 24).
42. „Natürlich hatte man mit dem Ruf ‚Wir sind ein Volk' *Deutschland* im Sinn und nicht eine sogenannte ‚multikulturelle' Gesellschaft, wie sie in Westdeutschland, sicher auch im Gegenzug, neuerdings verstärkt, wenn nicht geradezu hektisch propagiert wird" (Faul 1993,

45).
43. „Ungeachtet der schweren Besorgnisse über den Verlust an gesellschaftlicher Kohäsion, die sich selbst im weitläufigen Amerika mit der Perspektive einer multikulturellen Separierung verbinden, ist sie in dem erwähnten deutschen Resonanzspektrum sogar im Sinne einer beabsichtigten Zielorientierung auf unseren dichtbesiedelten Kontinent übertragen worden, in dem wir schon seit vielen Jahrhunderten festkonstruierte Volksidentitäten vorfinden" (Faul 1993, 56).
44. See Terkessidis 2000, 19.
45. Ackermann 1998/1999, 57.
46. Oberndörfer 1996, 136.
47. Žižek 1997, 166.
48. Bade 1996, 17.
49. Wolfgang Kaschuba, quoted in Bade 1996, 20.
50. Terkessidis 2000, 199.
51. Mintzel 1997, 21.
52. „unscharf ... oder spektakelhaft" (Geißler, H. 1996, 138); „schillernd, vage und mehrdeutig" (Mintzel 1997, 21).
53. Bourdieu 1985, 723.
54. „erlaubt es jedem, seine eigenen Vorstellungen und Weltbilder hineinzudeuten und ihn damit positiv oder auch negativ besetzen" (Mintzel 1997, 21); see also Geißler, H. 1996, 138 and Robertson-Wensauer 1993, 13.
55. „wert- und emotionsgeladene(s) Reizwort" (Geißler, R. 2003, 19).
56. „Eine multikulturelle Gesellschaft im Sinne eines dauerhaften, unverbundenen Nebeneinanders unterschiedlicher gesellschaftlicher oder ethnischer Gruppierungen ist nicht akzeptabel und führt zum Verlust des Zusammenhalts und der Identität einer Gesellschaft" (CDU 2001).
58. „Deutschland ist längst unumkehrbar ein Einwanderungsland und eine multikulturelle Gesellschaft geworden. Die Politik muss sich an dieser Realität orientieren" (Türkische Gemeinde 2001).
59. Grüne 2001.
60. Bundesgesetzblatt, 2002.
61. Bundesgesetzblatt, 2004.

References

Ackermann, Andreas. „Globalität, Hybridität, Multikulturalität. Homogenisierung der Kultur oder Globalisierung der Differenz." *Jahrbuch des kulturwissenschaftlichen Institut im Wissenschaftszentrum NRW* (1998-1999): 50-82.

Ang, Ien. "Racial/Spatial Anxiety. 'Asia' in the Psycho-Geography of Australian Whiteness." In *The Future of Australian Multiculturalism. Reflections on the Twentieth Anniversary of Jean Martin's 'The Migrant Presence'*, edited by Ghassan Hage and Rowanne Couch, 189-204. Sydney: The Research Institute for Humanities and Social Sciences, 1999.

Bade, Klaus J. „Grenzerfahrungen. Die multikulturelle Herausforderung." In *Die multikulturelle Herausforderung. Menschen über Grenzen – Grenzen über Menschen*, edited by Klaus J. Bade, 10-22. München: Beck 1996.

Bade, Klaus J. and Jochen Oltmer. *Normalfall Migration*. Bonn: Bundeszentrale für politische Bildung, 2004.

CDU. „Beschluss des Bundesausschusses der CDU Deutschlands: Zuwanderung steuern und begrenzen. Integration fördern." 7 Juni 2001. <http://www.bpb.de/zuwanderung> (30 July 2003).

Bourdieu, Pierre. "The Social Space and the Genesis of Groups." In *Theory and Society* 14(6) (1985): 723-744.

Bündnis 90/Die Grünen. "Einwanderung gestalten, Asylrecht sichern, Integration fördern." 17 February 2003.
<http://www.bpb.de/zuwanderung/> (30 July 2003).

Castles, Stephen. *Mistaken Identity. Multiculturalism and the Demise of Nationalism in Australia*. Leichthardt NSW, Pluto Press, 1988.

Cohn-Bendit, Daniel and Thomas Schmid. *Heimat Babylon. Das Wagnis der multikulturellen Demokratie*. Hamburg: Hoffmann und Campe, 1992.

Esser, Hartmut. „Multikulturelle Gesellschaft als Alternative zu Isolation und Assimilation." In *Die fremden Mitbürger. Möglichkeiten und Grenzen der Integration von Ausländern*, edited by Hartmut Esser, 25-38. Düsseldorf: Patmos, 1983.

Faul, Erwin. „Multikulturelle Gesellschaft in Deutschland." In *Migration und Toleranz. Fakten, Herausforderungen, Perspektiven*, edited by Bayrische Landeszentrale für politische Bildung, 43-66. München 1993.

Freeman, Gary P. and James Jupp. Eds. *Nations of Immigrants: Australia, the United States and International Migration*. Melbourne: Oxford University Press, 1992.

Geißler, Heiner. „Interview mit Heiner Geißler." *Die Zeit* 44, 28 Oktober 1988.

Geißler, Heiner. „Bürger, Nation, Republik – Europa und die

multikulturelle Gesellschaft." In *Die multikulturelle Herausforderung. Menschen über Grenzen – Grenzen über Menschen*, edited by Klaus J. Bade, 125-146. München: Beck, 1996.
Geißler, Heiner. „Interview mit Heiner Geißler." *Der Spiegel* 14 (1998): 48-52.
Geißler, Rainer. „Multikulturalismus in Kanada – Modell für Deutschland?" *Aus Politik und Zeitgeschichte* 26 (2003): 19-25.
Geulen, Christian. „Die Ordnung der Unordnung. ‚Multikulturalismus' als Modell und als Problem." *Jahrbuch des kulturwissenschaftlichen Institut im Wissenschaftszentrum NRW* (1997/1998): 15-35.
Jupp, James. *From White Australia to Woomera. The Story of Australian Immigration*. Port Melbourne: Cambridge University Press, 2002.
Jupp, James. "The Institutions of Culture. Multiculturalism." In *Culture in Australia: Politics, Publics and Programs*, edited by Tony Bennett and David Carter, 259-277. Oakleigh, VIC.: Cambridge University Press, 2001.
Lévi-Strauss, Claude. „Rasse und Geschichte." In *Strukturale Anthropologie II*, 363-407. Frankfurt am Main: Suhrkamp, 1975 [1952].
Michel, Karl M. und Tilman. Spengler. Eds. *Vielvölkerstaat Bundesrepublik. Kursbuch* 62. Hamburg: Rotbuch Verlag, 1980.
Mintzel, Alf. *Multikulturelle Gesellschaft in Europa und Nordamerika. Konzepte, Streitfragen, Analysen und Befunde*. Passau: Wiss.-Verl. Rothe, 1997.
N.N. „Gefährlich fremd. Ausländer und Deutsche. Das Scheitern der multikulturellen Gesellschaft." *Der Spiegel*, 16 (1997).
N.N. „Gesetz zur Steuerung und Begrenzung der Zuwanderung und zur Regelung des Aufenthalts und der Integration von Unionsbürgern und Ausländern." *Bundesgesetzblatt* 1(38) (2002).
Oberndörfer, Dieter. „Assimilation, Multikulturalismus oder kultureller Pluralismus. Zum Gegensatz zwischen kollektiver Nationalkultur und kultureller Freiheit der Republik." In *Migration, Ethnizität, Konflikt*, herausgegeben von Klaus J. Bade, 127-147. Osnabrück: Universitätsverlag Rasch, 1996.
Radtke, Frank-Olaf. „Lob der Gleich-Gültigkeit. Zur Konstruktion des Fremden im Diskurs des Multikulturalismus." In *Das Eigene und das Fremde. Neuer Rassismus in der Alten Welt*, edited by Uli Bielefeld, 79-96. Hamburg: Junius, 1991.
Robertson-Wensauer, Carolin Y. „Grundsätzliches zur aktuellen Diskussion über die multikulturelle Gesellschaft." In *Multikulturalität – Interkulturalität. Probleme und Perspektiven der multikulturellen Gesellschaft*, edited by Carolin Y. Robertson-Wensauer, 12-30. Baden-Baden: Nomos, 1993.

Schmalfeldt, Tim. *Diskurs und Politik der kulturellen Diversität: die Auseinandersetzungen über das GATS-Abkommen.* Universität Lüneburg: unveröffentlichte Magisterarbeit, 2004.

Tavan, Gwenda. *The long, slow death of White Australia.* Carlton North, VIC.: Scribe Publications, 2005.

Terkessidis, Mark. „Wir selbst sind die Anderen. Globalisierung, multikulturelle Gesellschaft und Neorassismus." In *Zuwanderung im Zeichen der Globalisierung*, edited by Christoph Butterwegge und Gudrun Hentges, 188-209. Opladen: Leske+Budrich, 2000.

Theophanous, Andrew. *Understanding Multiculturalism and Australian Identity.* Carton South, VIC., Elikia Books, 1995.

Tibi, Bassam. „Leitkultur als Wertekonsens. Bilanz einer missglückten deutschen Debatte." *Aus Politik und Zeitgeschichte* 1-2 (2001): 23-26.

Türkische Gemeinde in Deutschland. „Die Eingewanderten sind fester Bestandteil der Gesellschaft. Zur Perspektive der multikulturellen Gesellschaft." *Frankfurter Rundschau*, 7 Mai 2001.

White, Richard. *Inventing Australia. Images and Identity 1688-1980.* Sydney: Allen & Unwin, 1981.

Žižek, Slavoj. „Das rassistische Schibboleth." In *Probleme des Postkolonialismus und der globalen Migration*, edited by Peter Weibel und Slavoj Zizek, 145-169. Wien: Verlag, 1997.

Privileged Discourses of Hate in Australia and Germany: the Holocaust and the Stolen Generation

Katharine Gelber

1. Introduction

In Australia and Germany public discourse often raises historical issues in terms of their impact on contemporary cultural identity and public policy. In Australia, one of the most pertinent of these issues is that of indigenous children removed from their families by government policy, known as the 'stolen generation'. In Germany, the issue of responsibility for the Holocaust has been a recurring and controversial theme, especially since the mid 1980s. This paper investigates and compares two contemporary examples of discourse around these themes, which are connected by their attempts to link past practice with contemporary responsibility, interpretation and identity. This is not to suggest that the two events are comparable in and of themselves. Rather, this paper argues that discussion of past practices is a means by which current identities can be reshaped, reconstituted and reaffirmed. More specifically, it is the argument of this paper that how that discussion occurs has a direct bearing on the kind of contemporary identity being sought by the speaker.

The texts to be examined here are both products of members of parliament from a major political party. The Australian example is a submission by the then Minister for Aboriginal Affairs, Senator John Herron, in March 2000 to a parliamentary inquiry into the removal of indigenous people by government.[1] The German example is a speech made by Martin Hohmann, CDU representative for the electoral district of Fulda and member of the Bundestag since 1998, on the occasion of the anniversary of German reunification on 3 October 2003, a national holiday.[2] Therefore another linking theme between these two examples is that they were communicative events engaged in by parliamentary representatives of a major political party. This, arguably, gives them a certain weight in political discussion not afforded everyday members of a polity as I will clarify in the argument below.

I will first outline the discourse analytic method to be adopted in this paper in order to examine the two texts which I have outlined. Following this an analysis of both examples will be undertaken, focussing first on the word-use in the texts themselves, secondly on the means by which specific claims are made within those texts and thirdly on the general social context within which the events took place. This method is derived from a discourse analytic approach as outlined below.

I will argue that a discourse analysis reveals the nature of these texts as discursive attempts to achieve a particular kind of reconstruction of the past, one which denies the link between the past and contemporary practices of discrimination, harm and violence. This is done from a position of relative power, and in a manner which denies the contestability of the claims. In so doing, these texts reaffirm the very harms whose past and present meaning they seek to reconstruct.

2.   Method

Discourse is a word used frequently in the social sciences, often in a relatively undeveloped or undefined way in the sense of ideas (or a set of ideas) expressed by speakers. Discourse analysis tries to categorise and functionalise language use, including by defining "communicative events" as events which do something rather than just say something.[3] Discourse analysis arguably has particular import within the field of politics because the study of politics is ultimately the study of power[4] or more specifically, the study of interactions of unequal power. If language use represents an attempt to achieve a particular communicative or discursive act, then developing an understanding of the intended meaning, force and effect of the speech requires examining the communicative act within its context. That context includes relativities of power between the speaker, other potential speakers and the audience. It has been acknowledged that the positioning of the speaker as "an authoritative narrator and messenger and as a decisive actor is crucial".[5] So when the speaker uttering a communicative act is a member of parliament within a representative liberal democracy, it can be argued that her or his communicative actions have potentially greater force than those of ordinary citizens. A speaker from a parliament in a liberal democracy possesses the communicative power to command wide media coverage and therefore reach a broader audience than ordinary citizens, and the legitimacy of public office within a representative and liberal democracy. For these reasons the communicative acts of members of parliament possessing institutional power warrant close consideration within a discourse analytic framework.

Having made this claim for an application of the method generally to the discourse of members of parliament, however, there is considerable dispute about what a discourse analytic framework might look like. An immense body of work has developed in this field. Some of this attempts to delineate the areas within which discourse analysis may be applied by providing discrete discussion of theoretical approaches including linguistic, psychological, social psychological, sociological, mathematical, sociocultural and philosophical approaches.[6] Alternative analytical frameworks have been proposed including pragmatics, conversation analysis, institutional, cultural, political and critical analytical perspectives.[7] Attempts to disaggregate (for the purpose of clarifying and studying) an area of study which is complex and multifaceted can nevertheless lead to a false separation of theoretical and analytical tools. It can be argued that analyses which result from a disaggregated methodological position are likely to produce only partial pictures of the meaning and force of communicative events, or at the least pictures that are more partial than is necessary.

An alternative is to adopt an "eclectic"[8] approach which merges analytical insights from a range of perspectives. While no single analysis can possibly combine all of the theoretical and analytical perspectives which make claim to the area of 'discourse', it may be possible to produce better results by combining elements of more than one approach. This kind of work has been undertaken by Carol Johnson[9], who focuses on key government documents and speeches to analyse how contemporary issues are framed, constructed and debated within political discourse in Australia. In doing so, Johnson cautions against the simplistic application of theoretical and analytical tools derived from discourse analysis to the Australian experience without in-depth contextualisation of the analysis within the circumstances of specific case studies, in order to prevent over generalisation. Each theoretical perspective, she argues, can present a partial response to the question of what a particular discursive event is trying to achieve and might therefore mean. Adding insights from a range of relevant perspectives, then, is crucial to developing an accurate picture of the effects of discourse within political communities.[10]

In this context, the discourse analytic approach to be adopted in this paper draws from a range of insights. The first is a broad conception of discourse that acknowledges that the study of discourse is an attempt to uncover "socially constructed" meaning. This means that discourse analysis sees meaning as contested, as a "site and object of struggle" over the production of meaning.[11] This is a more specific claim than the general one that discourse is "a shared way of apprehending the world"[12] because the latter can lead one to overlook the specific contestation that is a feature of discourse analysis, whereas the former situates discourse within contestation over meaning. It is precisely such a contestation over meaning, or more specifically a set of claims by politicians to a certain kind of (reconstructed) meaning, that is the focus of this paper.

Secondly, the approach taken here also draws from work by Norman Fairclough, whose propound of critical discourse analysis is a theory and method for "studying language in its relation to power and ideology".[13] A method which seeks to study the relationships between power and discursive practice seems eminently suitable for conducting a study into the discourse of members of parliament. More specifically, Fairclough acknowledges that participants have unequal power over the production, distribution and consumption of communicative events and that these inequalities may be examined by studying the properties of texts.[14] A salient component of examining these inequalities is produced by examining what he calls the "technologization of discourse"[15], a top-down, discursive attempt to restructure or reconstruct a belief or set of beliefs which are dominant. These events take place within a broader context of changes in institutional and political practice as societies change and develop ideologically.[16] This idea renders the activities of a state at the level of parliament as a form of representative democracy vulnerable to a discourse analysis which can reveal change at that higher level.

His notion of a technologised discourse represents a struggle "on the part of dominant social forces to modify existing institutional discursive practices"[17], but this does not render it an over-simplified, deterministic account of state power. Rather, it is an account which (drawing from Gramscian notions of hegemony) examines the reshaping of cultural and societal beliefs, through the means of discourse. In society, diverse constitutive discourse practices converge and contest one another. This produces a "hegemonic struggle"[18], which can be understood through a three dimensional framework. An attempted technological discourse can be examined by describing the language text used, interpreting the discourse practice which gives rise to it, and explaining the sociocultural practice within which it is embedded.[19] This will be undertaken here.

As an overall method for studying the discourse of members of government, this methodological approach appears particularly illuminating. In particular, although Fairclough discusses technologised discourse at a micro level by seeking to examine technical, skills-based and workplace-based changes in a way which may be too specific for the analysis undertaken here, one further element of this method may prove salient and fruitful. That is his acknowledgement that an element of technologised discourse is the positioning of those undertaking the communicative event as experts with privileged access to scientific information, who are attempting to distil and propagate "truth".[20] An attempt to do this can be identified in part by examining the strategic choices made by the speaker in terms of word-use and vocabulary.[21]

The notion of truth is a difficult one in the social sciences. Other discourse and speech-act analysts have identified the difficulty of discerning 'truth', and instead acknowledge the existence of truth claims. This recognises both the contestability of the communication as a claim to truth and at the same time the speaker's assertion that it is a 'truth' that needs to be told. For example, Carol Johnson argues that Foucault's project was to "detach" the power of truth from the forms of hegemony, social, economic and cultural, within which it operates.[22] Similarly, Habermas argued that in a communicative action (that is, a communication whose meaning may be comprehended by reaching understanding on the context-dependent and use-dependent meanings of utterances), a speaker raises "validity claims".[23] These are made on three levels: the truth of an objective world, the rightness of inter-subjective norms and values, and the sincerity of his/her subjectivities. Reaching agreement on these validity claims would enable utterances to be effectively employed, in such a way that the speaker and hearer would be able to agree on what was meant.[24] Even though such agreement is rare, investigating the claims raised by speakers enables one to attempt to understand the meaning of the utterance.

This overall framework appears to be useful for examining the utterances of members of parliament. The approach I will take rests on the presumption that a study of discourse is a study of competing meanings, a struggle over meaning. Secondly, this struggle takes place in contexts of unequal power, in which some participants attempt to attain hegemonic discourse-use. Although such attempts are made possible by the continuous development of ideas within society, they are not as benign as simply another development in the history of ideas. Rather, some discursive events represent attempts to reconstruct a set of beliefs as dominant by appealing to 'truth' from a position of expert access to 'scientific' information. By examining the contexts within which such claims are made at several levels it is possible to discern the proposed meaning (although not the relative 'success' in the sense of achieving shared agreement on that meaning) of the communicative event.

Below, this approach will be applied to two texts in comparative perspective. The first is a submission by the Australian federal government concerning indigenous children who had been removed from their parents, known colloquially as the 'stolen generation'. The submission was written by Senator John Herron in March 2000. The second is a speech made by a member of the governing party federally in Germany concerning German guilt for the Holocaust, made in 2003 by Martin Hohmann. An application of this discourse-anlaytic approach to these two communicative events provides illuminating evidence of the discursive appeals made by the two speakers, and an insight into discourse around past abhorrent government practices, and their contemporary reconstruction.

A. Herron and the stolen generation
A.1 The text

In 1997 the Australian Human Rights and Equal Opportunity Commission reported the results of an inquiry into the separation of indigenous children from their families in past Australian government policy. The report, entitled *Bringing Them Home*[25] concluded that the policy had affected between one in three and one in ten indigenous children between approximately 1910 and 1970. It argued that the policy had infringed indigenous people's rights at best, and possibly even that it had represented an attempted genocide. The report recognised that the policies were continuing to have detrimental effects within indigenous communities, in the form of ongoing disadvantage and community dysfunction.

In November 1999 the Senate Legal and Constitutional References Committee established an 'Inquiry into the Stolen Generation' to inquire into the federal government's response to the *Bringing Them Home* Report. In March 2000 then Minister for Aboriginal and Torres Strait Islander Affairs, Senator John Herron, made a submission on behalf of the federal government to the inquiry.[26] Part I of the submission will be examined here. This part contains Herron's statements in direct response to the HREOC report, thus providing a counterpoint to the claims made by HREOC regarding the stolen generation. This is a clear example of the presentation of competing claims to truth in terms of the construction of the meaning and definitions of the 'stolen generation', which is the relevant issue here. Blocks of the text have been reproduced below. Part II of the submission outlined the terms of reference of the Senate Inquiry. Because it focussed primarily on the specific legal question of whether compensation should be paid to indigenous people for past practices, rather than on a construction of the meaning and 'truth' of past practices, it is less directly relevant to the analysis here and will not be discussed.

In Part I of the submission, under the heading 'Key Issue 1: Who are the 'stolen generation'?, Herron argued,

> ...the evidence that a proportion of those removed fitted within the stereotype of 'forcible removal' is only anecdotal and has not been subjected to proper scrutiny. <u>Although not used in the BTH [*Bringing Them Home*] report, the term 'stolen' is now used interchangeably with the term 'forcibly removed', as used in the HREOC inquiry.</u> [emphasis in original]
> The terms of reference for the HREOC inquiry, which directed it to conduct the widest of investigations into

the separation of indigenous children from their families, have contributed to the construction of a simplistic concept of a 'stolen generation'...[27]

In pursuing this broad approach, HREOC discussed the concepts of 'compulsion, duress and undue influence' and used the term 'forcible removal' throughout the report to include all three aspects. Importantly, the inquiry did not consistently differentiate between reasons for removal, or treat separately removals which may have been justified whether by the child protection standards of the day or by reference to modern understanding of the need to remove children from their homes. Although at times the inquiry recognised that removal may, in some circumstances, have been justifiable, and agreed that:
Due to the dispossession and dependence of indigenous families, many children's physical and sometimes psychological well-being was endangered.
It [sic] concluded that:
These children nevertheless fall within our terms of reference because they were separated from their indigenous families and communities, typically by compulsion...' The issue of justification may be relevant to any remedy that might be contemplated.
While the stereotype of the child snatched from his or her mother would fit within the scope of the inquiry, it by no means represents the full range of circumstances considered by HREOC. The terms of reference of the BTH report would equally cover the case of a teenage child leaving his or her local community to go to school in circumstances where his or her parents had reservations about the move and were persuaded by the local priest that education was an important opportunity. Also all the statistics cited by HREOC include children who were not forcibly separated and those who were forcibly separated for good reason. Clearly such cases do not fit within the widely understood notion of the 'stolen generation'.
The BTH report also specifically includes situations where further contact between the child and his or her parents was not precluded....

> The HREOC inquiry's terms of reference also included the circumstance of any child at real risk of physical harm in his home: circumstances which would also today warrant emergency court sanctioned removal. Even today Aboriginal children are 5-8 times (depending on the jurisdiction) more likely to be the subject of care and protection orders, and 5-14 times more likely to be in out-of-home placements. Nobody would regard these as 'stolen' or unreasonably separated children.[28]
>
> ...Such a lack of differentiation represents a fundamental methodological flaw in the BTH report...
> The government is concerned that the confused methodology and its consequential simplistic 'stolen generation' terminology has [sic] distorted public understanding of the historical record. The dangers of classing such a broad range of circumstances under the 'stolen generation' heading are evidenced by the facts of three cases which have recently been the subject of judicial consideration, and which are discussed further below in this submission under the issue of compensation.
> This is not to say that children separated in circumstances other than the archetypal 'stolen child' scenario have not suffered trauma as a result of having spent a proportion of their childhood away from their families and communities...
> Nonetheless, consideration of the recommendations contained in the BTH report must have regard to the varied circumstances which fell within the inquiry's terms of reference, rather than to any inaccurate and monolithic view of the so-called 'stolen generation'. To do otherwise would be to base government policy on a falsely constructed past'.[29]

In the submission, Key Issue 2 is 'Why were indigenous children removed? Standards of the time?'[30] which argues that the motivations of government representatives and others involved in the period under study were more benign, even aimed at "improving the lot"[31] of indigenous people, than the HREOC report implies. This is followed by Key Issue 3: 'Was there a stolen generation? How many children were stolen?' Here,

Herron argues,
> A further concern with the term 'stolen generation' is the issue of how many people were removed under past policies and practices. The term 'generation' carries with it the impression of vast numbers. Public comment has included reference to 100,000 'stolen children' and an assertion that every indigenous family has been affected. Putting this rhetoric to one side, the actual evidence as to the number of Aboriginal children who were removed from their families is slim. The government is concerned that there is no reliable basis for what appears to be a generally accepted conclusion as to the supposed dimensions of the 'stolen generation'. HREOC was unable to quantify the number of children separated from their families. The BTH report discussion the question of numbers in a mere one page of its 600 page report. It makes the point that 'it is not possible to state with any precision how many children were forcibly removed' but goes on to 'conclude with confidence [sic] [Note 'sic' here was in original] that between one in three and one in ten Indigenous children were forcibly removed from their families and communities in the period from approximately 1910 until 1970'.
>
> The government has serious reservations as to the accuracy of this estimate and its usefulness in developing policies to deal with the issue of past practices of removing Aboriginal children from their families. None of the sources referred to by HREOC support a figure of any more than 1:10 indigenous children having been removed for whatever reason (good or bad) and under whatever circumstances (forcibly or with consent).
>
> In fact, the estimates of the extent of the removals are the weakest part of the HREOC report. They are, when analysed, based on considerably uncertain guestimates and shoddy research, totally inappropriate to the weight of the argument which is based on the construction of the conclusion.[32]

In the conclusion to this Key Issue section of the submission, Herron states, "[t]he phrase 'stolen generation' is rhetorical."[33]

A.2 Textual analysis

In making these arguments Herron was explicitly questioning both the methods and findings of the *Bringing Them Home* Report. Moreover, this questioning was done in a specific discursive manner. The federal government's submission was wide-ranging, but for the purposes of the discussion here it raised two key claims. First, it questioned the validity of describing the method of removal of indigenous children from their families as "forcible", arguing that there may have been valid reasons for the government's actions at the time. Secondly, it argued that it was erroneous to describe the removals as a 'stolen generation', because fewer than 10% of children were removed and this did not constitute a generation. What were the methods by which these two claims were made? There appear to be three: the use of scientific, specifically mathematical, methods to claim truth; the imputation of methodological carelessness on the part of HREOC in their report; and a particular choice of vocabulary and tone. I will investigate each of these in turn.

Herron's submission clearly attempts to appropriate the language of 'truth'. He says the broad classification of the term 'stolen generation' by HREOC carries "dangers" which are "evidenced by the facts of three cases", thus citing hard evidence. He openly calls HREOC's view "inaccurate". He refers to the term stolen generation as "so-called", thereby explicitly calling into question its validity in terms of its truthfulness and saying it is a misnomer. Importantly, Herron's submission implies that since the reasons for the removal of children may in several cases have been benign or even philanthropic, this negates the description of their removal as 'stolen'. He thus reinscribes the same act of removal cited by HREOC in a new way. He is not so much disagreeing with what took place here, but rather reinscribing its meaning by restating its intent. In ascribing the events of removal with benign or philanthropic intent, he prioritises his view over the view expressed in the HREOC report that removal was not only harmful to indigenous communities at the time, but that it led directly to ongoing disadvantage and community dysfunction today. The reinterpretation of a past event as benign or philanthropic is used to challenge the truth of the idea of 'stolen' and, by extension, the truth of the extent to which the government is responsible for ongoing community disadvantage and dysfunction. This is a clear attempt to use reinterpretation of past events to reinscribe the contemporary meaning and consequences of the removal of indigenous children for Australian society.

Herron refers to the numbers utilised by HREOC as "rhetoric", calling instead for "actual evidence". His submission argues there is "no reliable basis" for the conclusion that the term 'generation' is appropriate, in part because HREOC was "unable to quantify the number of children separated from their families". The submission makes an issue of the "lack of precision" in the data and calls instead for "accuracy". Elsewhere, the report says HREOC did not subject the claims of those who gave evidence to the inquiry to "scrutiny", "corroboration or verification". Herron advocated looking at the historical record, in an area which the HREOC stated in its report is heavily reliant on anecdotal and oral forms of evidence. These forms of evidence are defined by Herron as inherently unreliable, and therefore lacking scientific basis and validity to the claim of truth, because they do not derive from historically verifiable hard forms of data storage. This dismisses and decontextualises the forms of evidence utilised and relied upon within the indigenous communities under discussion. In emphasising a formal, documented evidence-based method of enquiry, the Herron submission is overlooking the anecdotal nature of much evidence regarding the removal of children, and the consequences of their removal. Australian indigenous legal systems rely on the spoken word as a form of evidence, and requiring indigenous people to provide hard evidence when making claims against governments about past practices may in and of itself constitute a breach of their legal system.[34]

Herron calls the calculations made by HREOC "guestimates", a colloquial word which infers that guess-work is what led to HREOC's estimates of the numbers of children removed. Herron's submission interpolates the linguistic term "[sic]", meaning "in error", into a quotation from the HREOC report regarding the confidence of its conclusions. Yet within this context, Herron's submission itself chooses the lowest of the possible quantities cited by HREOC itself (the 1 in 10 figure) as the most likely 'truth'.

The use in the submission of an evidence-based claim to truth which is superior to the claims made by HREOC is supported by accusations of methodological carelessness on the part of HREOC. Herron's submission accuses HREOC of careless methodology, both in investigating and substantiating claims made by indigenous peoples regarding their removal, and in drawing conclusions from the evidence used. He says this overtly, referring to a "confused methodology", as well as more covertly by calling their research methods "shoddy". As well as questioning HREOC's methodology, the Herron submission makes claim to its own 'modern' interpretations of evidence. This is an overt attempt to locate his own claims within the period of enlightened and scientific modernity, and to juxtapose his scientific method against the unscientific method adopted by HREOC and by indigenous communities themselves. In some ways this represents an attempt to reimpose the dominant values of the coloniser-culture on indigenous communities, even though it took place in the year 2000.

The choice of vocabulary in the submission is of particular interest. Words such as "stereotype" imply a false construction. The word stereotype is defined in the Oxford English Dictionary as a "preconceived and oversimplified idea of the characteristics which typify a person or situation". This is a deliberate slur on the concept of the 'stolen generation' as oversimplified and preconceived. This implies HREOC (and other members of the public who use the term) decided the 'stolen generation' existed before it conducted its research. Other word-use which is arguably demeaning and dismissing of the work undertaken by HREOC in conducting its investigations and writing its report includes terms such as "rhetorical", "weakest", "considerably uncertain guestimates", "falsely constructed past", "whatever reason" and "whatever circumstances".

Although the Herron submission accuses the HREOC report of 'rhetoric', it also uses rhetorical devices in significant measure. Clear examples of this include the use of superlatives and finites such as "nobody", "by no means", "clearly", "none", "totally inappropriate" and "monolithic". These words admit no qualification, in an area of enquiry one would expect to be imbued with qualification. The use of these words is of particular interest given the contestability of the evidence being examined. Whereas HREOC acknowledged the difficulties and contestabilities of claims made in the area, and openly admitted to drawing conclusions based on its own interpretation of the events under discussion, the Herron submission makes no such admission. Herron claims not to be drawing his own interpretation of events, but rather the only possible interpretation of events. This is linked in clearly with the claims to scientific validity and truth, which by definition (if one believes in the superiority of and adopts a modernist, scientific methodology) are objective and 'true'.

A.3 Social and political context for the Australian study

Since its election in 1996 the federal Coalition government, and Prime Minister John Howard in particular, have argued against the capturing of the resources of the state by 'special interests', identified as "elite professional advocates rather than an organisations and movements representing legitimate grievances by marginalised groups".[35] One of the special interest groups targeted by the government has been indigenous people, and one of the themes of the government's discussions has been the question of the responsibility or 'shame' to be borne by the current generation of Australians for past government practices. Howard has campaigned against what he describes as the 'black armband' view of history. For example, he stated in parliament in 1996 that, "I profoundly reject the black armband view of Australian history. I believe the balance sheet of Australian history is a very generous and benign one ... I think we have been too apologetic about our history in the past".[36]

The Coalition government has drawn from and built upon feelings of uncertainty in the electorate, proposing a series of reforms to social policy which have sought to reinforce traditional conservative certainties around the family and Australian identity. One of the ways this was attempted was by portraying indigenous-specific programs as discouraging participation in the 'mainstream'[37] and by promoting the 'mainstream' as the core place of security for all Australians. Aborigines were not the only 'special interest' to be targeted, with others including feminists, multiculturalists and gays and lesbians.[38] In deliberately neglecting to acknowledge difference and diversity, it has been argued the government has promoted a particular Australian identity based on masculinist, heterosexual, conservative social values.

The years of Coalition government have seen some of the most vociferous 'race' debates in Australian politics for some years. In August 1998, Australia became subject to the Committee on the Elimination of Racial Discrimination's (CERD) 'early warning procedures' – the first Western government to do so – and was asked to provide information to the committee regarding amendments to the Native Title Act 1993. After considering Australia's report, in 1999 the CERD concluded that the amendments were racially discriminatory and amounted to a contravention of Australia's obligations under the racial discrimination convention.[39] In particular, the CERD was concerned about the extinguishment of native title rights and the lack of participation in the formulation of the legislative amendments by indigenous peoples.[40]

The CERD continued to criticise Australia's native title regime after the passage of the Native Title Amendment Act 1998, as well as other policies including mandatory sentencing in Western Australia and the Northern Territory (which was regarded as disproportionately affecting indigenous people, especially youth), the lack of an entrenched protection against racial discrimination, the government's unwillingness to apologise to or consider compensation for the stolen generation, over-representation of indigenous people in jail, low standards of living in indigenous communities, the winding back of funding and powers of the Human Rights and Equal Opportunity Commission,[41] and the Australian government's position regarding their responsibilities towards international bodies and treaties.[42]

Statistics provided by the Human Rights and Equal Opportunity Commission show that the indigenous community suffers in comparison with the non-indigenous community in a range of measures of standard of living. This includes a life expectancy approximately 20 years lower than non-indigenous people, a death rate more than twice that of the whole Australian population, an infant mortality rate twice the rate of all Australians, twice the likelihood of hospitalisation for serious health problems, half the rate of continuation at school to Year 12, more than three times the unemployment rate, 60% of the average weekly income as all Australians, half the home ownership rate, and sixteen times the adult imprisonment rate of non-indigenous adults.[43]

In this context, the release of the *Bringing Them Home* Report opened up a "sustained and intense" public debate.[44] A component of this debate was the question of whether the Australian government should pay compensation to indigenous communities for past practices. The HREOC report recommended that legislation be passed to implement a compensation scheme which would be available to relatives and families of stolen children, as well as those directly affected. Herron clarified in his submission that the government felt compensation was not appropriate and would not be paid. He said, "[t]he government does not support the payment of cash compensation" and that "monetary compensation is inappropriate and improper unless a legal liability can be established in individual cases through a proper process of claims assessment. In addition, the prospective Australia-wide cost of compensation, as proposed, is conservatively estimated (on the premise that only 5 percent of children were *forcibly and wrongly* [emphasis in original] removed) as in the order of $3.9 billion and probably more".[45]

Having analysed at a textual level some of the important elements of the Herron submission, as well as the context within which the submission was made in terms of public debate around indigenous policy, I will now investigate the Hohmann text in the same way. Following this, broader conclusions will be able to be drawn regarding the import, significance and interpretation of both communicative events as a (re)construction of past practices.

B. Hohmann and the Holocaust
B.1 The text

On the thirteenth anniversary of German reunification, 3 October 2003, Martin Hohmann gave a speech to his local party, the CDU-Neuhof. Hohmann was a member of parliament and backbencher in the conservative opposition party. His speech was placed on the web site of the party branch where it remained available until the news media publicised its existence on 30 October, and it was removed.

Hohmann's speech began with a preliminary discussion about "immediate events" in Germany, in relation to the provision of social welfare to non-citizens. These preliminary paragraphs utilise phrases like "everyday Germans" [*normaler Deutscher*] and "Germans in Germany" [*Deutscher in Deutschland*] to establish his audience. He claims to be speaking for everyday Germans in asking questions of the German government, such as whether payments to the European Union or compensation to (as he puts it "primarily Jewish") forced labourers and other victims of National Socialism should be limited or halted due to economic decline in Germany. These preliminary paragraphs, although interesting types of claims in and of themselves, are not directly relevant to his later claims which form the basis for this paper and will therefore not be further investigated.

In the 12th paragraph of his speech, Hohmann asks what the reason is for this "lopsided position" [*Schieflage*] and argues it lies in German history. From this point on, he says:[46]

> Ladies and gentlemen, no experienced or thoughtful person could seriously attempt to whitewash or forget German history. No. We all know the devastating and unparalleled crimes which were committed under Hitler's orders. Hitler, as an executor of evil and pure and simply the German people with him, have together become the counter-symbol of the last century. One speaks of a 'past which will not pass'. Even today the Hitler phenomenon is granted an uncannily high presence in public representations. Thousands of mediocre films, especially in Anglo-Saxon countries, ensure that the cliché of dumb, brutal and criminal German soldiers is kept alive and renewed.
>
> Merely making mention of the fact that also a great many Germans during the last century have been the victim of foreign violence, is already considered to be breaking a taboo. The discussion about the Centre against Expatriation makes this very clear. The danger of compensation is immediately invoked. Reference is made to the fact that the Hitler regime started the Second World War. Hans-Olaf Henkel, Vice President of the Federal Association of German Industry, has recently in an interview clearly enunciated the fact, and the consequences, of this negative relationship with the past. He said: "Our inherited sins are paralysing the country".[47]

... It is not the brown hordes, which are gathering under the symbols of Good, which are the main problem. The real problem is the pervasive destruction of spirit in the national consciousness, which was triggered off by the after effects of Hitler. The crime of the destruction of human beings in an industrial scale, which he set in motion, especially of the European Jews, weighs heavily in the German story. The guilt of ancestors for this crime against humanity has almost led to a new self-definition of Germans. In spite of a unanimous declaration that there is no such thing as collective guilt, in spite of the nuanced creation of new terms like 'collective responsibility' or 'collective shame': at heart the reproach remains: the Germans are a perpetrator-people [*Tätervolk*].

Every other country tries to portray the dark pages of their history in a favourable light. Blinkers are put up in front of shameful events. Others are given a new interpretation. A perfect example of reinterpretation is the portrayal of the French revolution. A large massacre in Paris and the provinces took place, especially in the Vendee. This led to the resumption of power by a single leader whose conquering war had brought death to millions in Europe. The majority of French and non-French voices have reinscribed the revolution and its terror as an emancipatory act and Napoleon as a mild, enlightened father of modern Europe.

Such favourable reconstructions or reinterpretations are not permitted the Germans. This forcefully hinders the contemporary dominant political class and science. They 'almost neurotically adhere to German guilt', as Joachim Gauck expressed it on 1.10.2003.

With virtually neurotic eagerness, new generations of German scientists research the tiniest ramifications of the NS-time.

It is surprising that no-one has as yet proposed that we should stop using knives and forks, since it is generally known that these instruments served the physical strength of the perpetrators of criminal events of that time. The Germans as perpetrator-people [*Tätervolk*] – that has become an image with great international visibility. The rest of the world has on the other hand comfortably settled into the role of innocent lambs – at least relatively innocent lambs. Those who do not simply accept this clear division of roles – here the Germans as the greatest perpetrators of all time, there the morally superior nations – get into difficulties. Difficulties come precisely from those who as 1968ers, with great personal success, made 'Questioning, Criticising, Exposing' [*das Hinterfragen, das Kritisieren und das Entlarven*] their primary occupation. As is well-known, some of the exposees have entered the highest positions of public office.

Ladies and gentlemen, in order to avoid any misunderstanding: with them I stand for clarity and truth. It should and may not be withheld and glossed over. 'Hehle nimmer mit der Wahrheit, bringt sie Leid, nicht bringt sie Reue', says the poet. Yes the uncomfortable, the unbelievable, the shameful about truth, that is what is worth bearing. We Germans have borne it, we have borne it for decades. Many however question whether the plethora of truths about the criminal and calamitous 12 years of the National Socialist dictatorship:
a) are being used as a propaganda instrument and
b) might not turn into an underlying defensive attitude within general education.
Over and over, the same dreadful truths. This can result in, and by now must have produced, psychological damage. We know that this is so from rehabilitation psychology.

It is especially bad when a US junior Professor (Daniel Jonah Goldhagen) as the result of his research labels our entire people as 'murderers from birth'. This thesis, as shrill as it is false, has produced media notoriety and honoraries for the author – especially in Germany. Other nations would have contemptuously shunned him.
As a matter of fact, young people are rebelling against

being held responsible for the misconduct of their grandfathers and great-grandfathers, and against being labelled 'members of a perpetrator-nation'.

There is no doubt about the following: the German people, after the criminal exploits of the Hitler period, have occupied themselves in an unparalleled, relentless manner with this matter, have asked for forgiveness, and within the limits of what is possible, have paid billions in compensation, especially to the Jews. I am referring to the agreements between the Federal Republic of Germany and the state of Israel, under the guidance of Adenauer and Ben Gurion. The majority of the German people have very clearly declared themselves in favour of the compensation agreement, even though immense suffering and death can not be undone.

Against this background I am provoked to ask the following question: is there also amongst the Jewish people, whom we exclusively perceive in the role of victim, a dark side in recent history, or were Jews exclusively the victims?

Ladies and Gentlemen, it will surprise you to know that the American car king Henry Ford in 1920 published a book with the title 'The International Jew'. This book had a circulation in the USA of 500,000 copies. It became a worldwide bestseller and was translated into 16 languages. In it, Ford paraded a generalisation of Jews as 'World Bolsheviks'. He claimed to be able to account for an 'all Jewish stamp on red Russia', where at the time the Bolshevik revolution was rampaging. He denoted the Jews in 'enormous numbers' as 'Revolutionaries', thereby alluding to Russia, Germany and Hungary. Ford expressed in his book an alleged 'equality of character' between Judaism and communism, in this case Bolshevism.

How did Ford develop this thesis, which to our ears is similar to the Nazi propaganda about 'Jewish Bolshevism'? Listen to what the Jew Felix Teilhaber said in 1919: 'Socialism is a Jewish idea ... for millenia our religious leaders have preached socialism'. He also said that Jewish thinkers sit in the cradle of communism and socialism. Karl Marx descended from Rabbis on both parents' sides. His portrait hung in the living room of a Jewish researcher on women, who by the way admitted that: 'I have been raised to know that a Jewish person stands for social equality, and is progressive and socialist. Socialism was our religion.' Over and over again in the literature of the early communist period, quasi religious elements are evoked. Many of the Jews who were engaged with Bolshevism felt themselves to be so-called 'faithful soldiers of the world revolution'. This is why Kurt Eisner already by 1908 expected that the 'religion of socialism' would be the 'despair of the piteous' and would overcome the 'loss of hope of worldly fate'. Leo Rosenberg even exalted the proletariat in 1917 as a 'world messiah'.

We must ask ourselves precisely the following question: How many Jews were then members of the revolutionary cells? Out of a seven member Politbureau of the Bolsheviks in 1917, four were Jews: Leon Trotsky, Leon Kamenjew, Grigori Sinowjew and Grigori Sokolnikow. Those who were not Jews were Lenin, Stalin, Bubnow. Amongst the 21 members of the revolutionary central committess in Russia in 1917, 6 were of Jewish nationality, that means 18.6%. The high proportion overall of Jews amongst the communist founding fathers and the revolutionary cells was not limited in any way to the Soviet Union. Ferdinand Lassalle was also a Jew, as were Edward Bernstein and Rosa Luxemburg. In 1924 out of six communist party leaders in Germany, four (therefore two-thirds) were Jewish. Among 48 people's commissars in Hungary, 30 were Jewish. Also among the revolutionary soviet secret police, the Cheka[48], the Jewish proportion was extraordinarily high. While the Jewish proportion of the population in 1934 in the Soviet Union lay around the 2% mark, 39% of the leaders of the Cheka were Jewish. By way of further explanation, Jews were considered a nationality in the Soviet Union. That is why we can say the Jewish proportion of the Cheka was 36% higher than the Russian proportion. In the Ukraine 75% of the Chekists were Jews.

These findings lead to a conclusion which ensured the monstrous insurrection of that time. The murder of the Russian Tsar and his family was arranged by the Jew Jacob Swerdlow and carried out on Tsar Nicholas II by the Jew Chaimowitz Jurowski. This raises a further question, whether Jews in the communist movement were just followers or had a leadership role. The latter is the case [*Letzteres trifft zu*]. Leon Trotsky in the USSR, Bela Kun in Hungary.

... We can inquire further into the revolutionary zeal and determination of the Jewish communists. Now these revolutionary elites were serious, as expressed by Franz Koritschoner from the Communist Party of Austria: 'to lie and to steal, yes even to kill for an idea, that is courage, and greatness belongs there'. Grigori Sinowjew declared in 1917: '90 out of 100 Million Soviet Russians will follow us. As far as the rest are concerned, we have nothing to offer them. They will have to be exterminated' (Page 138). 'Similarly, Moisei Wolodarski formulated it thus: 'The interests of the revolution demand the physical annihilation of the bourgeoisie' (Page 138). In much the same manner, Arthur Rosenberg in 1922 said: 'Soviet power has the obligation to put an end to its implacable enemies' (Page 163).

Undoubtedly, these expressions of Jewish communist revolutionaries were not empty threats. They were serious. They were deadly serious. According to a statistical study undertaken by a Professor and reported by Churchill in 1930, the number of people who fell victim to the Soviets up to 1924 were: 28 orthodox bishops, 1,219 orthodox clerics, 6,000 Professors and teachers, 9,000 doctors, 12,950 landowners, 54,000 officials, 70,000 police officers, 193,000 workers, 260,000 soldiers, 355,000 intellectuals and tradespeople, and 815,000 farmers.

Later in the speech, Hohmann drew his conclusions:

> we have now seen how strong and enduring the Jewish stamp is on the revolutionary movement in Russia and middle European states. Even the American President Woodrow Wilson in 1919 made the assessment that the Bolshevik movement had been 'led by Jews'. Looking back to the millions of dead from the first revolutionary phase, we can with authority now ask about the 'guilt' [*Täterschaft*] of the Jews. Jews were active in great number in the leadership as well as in the Cheka-firing squads. Thus one could describe the Jews with some justification as a 'perpetrator-people'. This may sound shocking. But it would follow the same logic with which one describes the Germans as a 'perpetrator-people'.

B.2 Textual analysis

In making these arguments, Hohmann was revisiting a highly controversial debate. He was positioning himself, arguably, as a seeker of the truth and a presenter of factual knowledge rather than opinion. He was deliberately questioning the idea of whether Germans should be held guilty for the Holocaust, and although he began by talking about contemporary Germany the bulk of his argument was concerned with the historical record. In this sense, he was making an argument linking the historical record with contemporary German identity. The essence of his argument was that it was just as logical to describe Jews as a perpetrator-people as it is to describe Germans in that way. In making this claim, many of the same discursive techniques can be identified as those which appeared in the Herron text analysed earlier.

First, Hohmann's speech attempts to appropriate the language of 'truth'. Hohmann frequently uses phrases including "truth" [*Wahrheit*] which is used repeatedly throughout the speech, "clarity and truth" [*Klarheit und Wahrheit*], something being "the case" [*etw. trifft zu*], findings [*Feststellung*], and "with authority" [*mit einer gewissen Berechtigung*]. These represent overt claims to fact and to truth, in an area imbued with interpretation. By analogy, Hohmann claims the moral high ground. He claims that his account is not political (in the sense of being instigated by a desire to present a people in a particular light), but rather than it is objective and factual.

Hohmann supports these claims to truth with an appeal to mathematics. He provides figures, both in the form of calculations of the number of Jewish people within Bolshevik revolutionary organisations and the number of dead. In doing so, he attempts to deduce from the provision of hard data, ie numbers, that Jews could be logically described as 'responsible' for the actions of those organisation. He makes this argument despite the fact that those revolutionary organisations professed atheism and carried out their deadly programs for any number of reasons. Importantly for the purposes of this analysis, he presents a very small amount of data, or evidence, from which he draws extremely wide-ranging conclusions unsupported by the actual evidence presented. In other words, Hohmann implicitly appeals in the same way Herron did to a modernist scientific method by citing statistics and numbers. Yet Hohmann does not implement such a method himself in drawing his conclusions, in the sense that his deductions are too far removed from the evidence he presents. A modernist, scientific, method of enquiry requires that the conclusions are directly and causally supported by the evidence presented. Conclusions must be cautiously stated, alternative explanations considered and if rejected, proper reasoning provided for their rejection. Findings should not be over-stated or exaggerated. Yet this is precisely what Hohmann does.

Hohmann belittles his opposition, suggesting at one point that those who decry the Holocaust might even suggest abolishing knives and forks, such is their desire to banish instruments that were useful to the Nazi regime from everyday German life. This claim makes light of the seriousness of the issue and exaggerates the claims of those who support serious accounts of the Holocaust. He uses similar techniques in labelling those who speak of German guilt as "shrill" [*schrill*] and "false" [*falsch*], and in describing those who hold to theories of German guilt as neurotically eager to do so [*mit geradezu neurotischem Eifer*]. The denigration of alternative viewpoints, instead of addressing them in the context of the argument, is again contrary to the scientific method to which Hohmann appeals. In this sense, the denigration of alternative viewpoints therefore weakens Hohmann's claims, rather than strengthens them because he does not address his opponents, rather he paraphrases and caricatures them.

Hohmann implies that he has hitherto been prevented, by public disapprobation, from speaking the truth. He bemoans that "favourable reconstructions or reinterpretations are not permitted the Germans", drawing a comparison with the French revolution. In doing this, Hohmann emphasises claims of large numbers of casualties over and above other elements in both events – such as the reasons for the casualties, or the targetting of victims on the basis of their nationality and religion – in order to draw a comparison which would otherwise not make any sense.

Hohmann makes use of superlatives as a linguistic technique, in a similar manner to that employed by Herron above. Examples include his description of the idea of Germans as Tätervolk and the rest of the world as 'innocent lambs' as a 'clear division of roles' which is dichotomised between the Germans and the rest of the world. He refers to some who express these views as holding the "highest positions of public office" [*bis in höchste Staatsämter getragen*]. He often uses unqualifiable terms such as "precisely", "exclusively" [*ausschließlich*], "undoubtedly" [*zweifellos*]. He uses the term "exclusively" twice in the same sentence when considering the possibility that Jewish people could be other than victims, i.e. perpetrators.

An element in the Hohmann speech which is absent from the earlier Australian example is his tendency to contradict himself. Although initially conceding that Ford's claims sounded like Nazi anti-Jewish propaganda, Hohmann then nevertheless repeats and adds to those claims to establish his 'case' regarding the number of Jews involved in the crimes of early Bolshevism. In so doing, Hohmann is both distancing himself from claims which appear motivated by hatred of Jews rather than fact, and yet citing further evidence which attempts to establish his views as 'facts'. He appears oblivious to this apparent contradiction in his argument. Such a torturous and convoluted logic is interestingly not employed in the Australian example. Since Hohmann's argument is itself internally contradictory, this adds to the analytical conclusion that his speech was more obviously a discursive strategy, rather than a statement of objective 'truth'.

B.3 Social and political context for the German study

Germany's post World War II social reconstruction has arguably been dominated by the issue of dealing with the horrors perpetrated in the Holocaust. There is a plethora of scholarship on this issue, but in the 1980s the specific question of 'guilt' was debated vehemently in the national media. This *Historikerstreit* of 1986 debated attempts to 'revise' the Holocaust and led to accusations of claims being made for political, rather than scientific, motivations.[49] It involved claims by the historian Ernst Nolte offering a revised analysis and explanation of the Holocaust. Nolte concluded that the Holocaust had been an – albeit irrational, horrifying and more repulsive – copy of the Soviet destruction of the kulaks whom they considered a threat. A counter position was presented by Jürgen Habermas, who argued that rather than trying to reconstruct the meaning of the historical record, we must recognise the inevitability and appropriateness of applying contemporary analytical frameworks to historical events. Thus, a morally informed reading of the past is unavoidable, one within which contemporary German identity is ineradicably linked with the Holocaust experience.[50]

It is clear from even this cursory summary of the *Historikerstreit* that Hohmann's speech took place within a broader, and long-term, debate about contemporary German identity. It cannot be seen in isolation. The ideas he expressed are held by others. The scientific method which he appealed to was central to the Historikerstreit itself. My purpose here is not to resolve the debate about whether science is capable of providing an explanation for the Holocaust or not, but to examine how appeals to a scientific method and scientific facts support a particular (re)interpretation of past events and their impact on contemporary identities.

In Germany today, incidences of anti-semitism and hatred towards foreigners are still high. Information on the activities of extreme right-wing organisations is maintained by the Federal Office for the Defence of the Constitution [*Bundesamt für Verfassungsschutz*] which produces regular reports detailing anti-semitic violence and behaviour. Statistics are kept on offences against the constitutional provisions banning propaganda of unconstitutional organisations (§86 of the Criminal Code: *Kennzeichen*), the use of symbols of unconstitutional organisations (§86A of the Criminal Code: *Propagandamittel*), and vilification ('Agitation of the People', §130 of the Criminal Code: *Volksverhetzung*), as well as statistics on violent offences on the basis of hatred. For example, it was reported in Berlin that the number of right-wing-extremist acts of violence had increased substantially in the first half of 2003 with 41 violent offences, compared with the whole of 2002 with 52 violent offences.[51] In this context, Hohmann's comments amounted to more than a scientific enquiry because they interacted with this other contemporary evidence.

After Hohmann's speech became public, the CDU party distanced itself from his comments. Hohmann himself initially refused to apologise, however on 31 October he retracted his remarks in part, saying he had not intended to characterise Jews as a nation of perpetrators. He was eventually expelled from the parliamentary party, but retained his seat in parliament. There were approximately 20 attempts to have him indicted under the vilification provisions in the Criminal Code, but these were unsuccessful on the grounds that he had used the phrase Tätervolk in the conjunctive and in a relativised sense. Moreover, in other passages in his speech he had clearly distanced himself from the views of the Nazi period.[52] In January 2004 an expert jury in Frankfurt am Main chaired by Horst Dieter Schlosser denoted Tätervolk as the 'Unword of the year 2003' on the grounds that Hohmann had, with that word, "without exception made an entire people responsible for the actions of a few individuals". The selection was made by a jury of linguists out of 1,160 nominated terms.[53]

C. Herron and Hohmann: reconstructing the past to what future?

In seeking to draw conclusions from the textual analysis conducted, it is useful to revisit the broader framework established earlier in this paper. The first analytical element outlined was that of the speaker as an 'authoritative narrator and messenger'. In both the examples provided, the speakers were members of parliament. They carried the authority and legitimacy of public office. Their statements were made in the context of broader public debates on the issues, and they therefore represented much more than an expression of their individual opinions. Rather, the making of these statements by the speakers made visible inequalities of power in public debate. These speakers attempted to make use of their positions of public office to present evidence and claims to truth in such a way as to sway public opinion in their favour. Although arguably all speakers could be regarded as trying to do this, the particular weight afforded parliamentary representatives adds a dimension to their communications not available ordinary citizens. It also contributed to the level of public engagement with (and indeed contestation with) the views presented by the speakers and in this way, the analysis has also been able to reveal inequalities in the production and consumption of communicative events.

The second element of the overall framework provided here is that the study of discourse is an attempt to uncover socially constructed meaning, in a site of struggle over meaning. The two examples provided here are exemplary in demonstrating that discourse is more than a claim to a particular world-view. Rather, that claim is counterposed to other world views, it is claim to truth against other claims to truth, it is a site of contestation and struggle over meaning. Issues as controversial as the stolen generation in Australia and the Holocaust in Germany will continue to provoke controversy and dispute. The point is to engage in these disputes in such a way as to expose that they are contestations over meaning and interpretation. Recognising this helps one to understand what the competing claims are, and to uncover the viability of the evidence underlying the claims. This allows the audience to make clearer and more informed choices about which arguments are more viable. In this sense, undertaking a discourse analysis uncloaks the text.

Earlier I also argued, after Fairclough, that a discourse analysis is capable of showing how a technologised discourse can be regarded as a top-down attempt to restructure beliefs, and that this can occur where the speakers position themselves as experts with privileged access to scientific information. Again, the examples analysed above demonstrate this clearly. In both cases the speakers made claim to the reproduction of hitherto unknown, obscured or suppressed (and selective) data in order to bolster their claims. The analysis undertaken here has attempted to reveal these as discursive techniques, rather than fact. The speakers claimed both overtly, and through linguistic devices, to be simply putting forward facts and evidence which others may not be aware of, in other words they presented themselves relatively speaking as experts.

In sum, these texts amount to attempts by speaker with relatively high levels of power to reconstruct the meaning of past events and reinterpret those events to absolve current generations of guilt. The Australian example referred to a text produced by a member of the governing party, whereas the German example referred to an opposition member of parliament and these contexts may have contributed to the ways in which the intended and unintended audiences reacted to the statements. Nevertheless, the common theme of both texts is the reconstruction of the past in a way which obscures and seeks to deny its impact on the present. In this way both speakers avoid taking on the harder questions of ongoing dysfunction within, or hardship caused to, specifically targeted communities caused by past practices which reach into the present in their effect and ongoing practice. Indeed, the claims made by the speakers to reinterpret past events in some senses amount in themselves to the deployment of the practices of the past in the present. The speaker re-enacted the meaning of the past practices in a sense by trying to deny them with spurious arguments in the present.

The contemporary consequences of the stolen generation in Australia and the Holocaust in Germany – while by no means equivalent events in and of themselves – manifest in ongoing discrimination and violence. In discussing past practices, it is important to recognise that the links between past and present practice are neither discontinuous nor benign. Whether dressed up as 'science' or not, discursive practices of the kind engaged in in these two examples, re-enact discrimination and harm just as surely as they reinterpret how it once took place.

Notes

1. Herron 2000.
2. Hohmann 2003.
3. van Dijk 1997a, 1-2.
4. Dahl 1964, 2.
5. Chilton and Schäfner 1997, 219.
6. van Dijk 1985.
7. van Dijk 1997b; van Dijk 1997c.
8. Johnson 2000, 2.

10. Johnson 2000. For an overview of some the most important discourse analytic contributions in relation to Australian public discourse, see Johnson 2000, 8-11.
10. Ibid, 2000, 1-2.
11. Best and Kellner 1991, 26 cited in Johnson 2000, 15-16.
12. Dryzek 1997, 8.
13. Fairclough 1995, 1.
14. Ibid, 1, 2.
15. Ibid, 3.
16. Ibid, 87.
17. Ibid, 91.
18. Ibid, 92-95.
19. Ibid, 97.
20. Ibid, 103.
21. Chilton & Schäffner 1997, 216.
22. Rabinow cited in Johnson 2000, 101.
23. Habermas 1984, 305.
24. Habermas 1979, 26; see also the elucidation of this as a discourse analytic method in Gelber 2002, 60-65.
25. HREOC 1997.
27. Herron 2000.
27. Ibid, 2.
28. Ibid, 3.
29. Ibid, 4-5.
30. Ibid, 5-12.
31. Ibid, 5.
32. Ibid, 13.
33. Ibid, 18.
34. Gray 1998.
35. Johnson 2000, 7.
36. Cited in McKenna 1997, 6.
37. Johnson 2000, 39.
38. Ibid, 40.
39. Evatt 2001, 4.
40. Gelber 2001, 2.
41. CERD 2000a.
42. CERD 2000b.
43. HREOC 2003.
44. ATSISJC 1998, 14.
45. Herron 2000, 18.
47. Translation of most of the text was undertaken by the author, a

qualified NAATI Paraprofessional Translator (German-English). Some sections were translated by the UNSW Institute of Languages' Translation and Interpretation Service, University of New South Wales, Sydney, Australia (31 May 2004).
47. HÖRZU 21/2003, 16ff.
49. The Soviet secret police.
49. Peacock 2001, 87.
50. Ibid, 88-94.
51. Kopietz 2003.
52. N.N. 2004a; N.N. 2004b.
53. N.N. 2004c.

I wish to thank Matt McDonald for endless discussions on my emerging thoughts around this project, Jeni Whalan for research assistance, Gary Smith, Russell West-Pavlov and Annett Baumgaertel.

References

Aboriginal and Torres Strait Islander Social Justice Commissioner (ATSISJC). *Social Justice Report 1998. Sixth Report.* Sydney: HREOC, 1998.
Best, Steven and Douglas Kellner. *Postmodern Theory: Critical Interrogations.* Houndsmills: Macmillan, 1991.
CERD. "Summary record of the 1393rd Meeting." *CERD/C/SR.1393*, 29 March 2000a.
CERD. "Summary record of the 1395th Meeting: Australia, Tonga, Zimbabwe." *CERD/C/SR. 1395*, 3 April 2000b.
Dahl, Robert A. *Modern Political Analysis.* 3rd edition. New York: Prentice-Hall, 1964.
Dryzek, John. *The Politics of the Earth: Environmental Discourses.* New York: Oxford University Press, 1997.
Evatt, Elizabeth. "How Australia 'Supports' the United Nations Human Rights Treaty System. Comment." *Public Law Review* 12 (March 2001): 3-8.
Fairclough, Norman. *Critical Discourse Analysis: The Critical Study of Language.* London: Longman, 1995.
Gelber, Katharine. "Human Rights Treaties in Australia – Empty Words?" *The Drawing Board: An Australian Review of Public Affairs.* 12 April 2001. <http://www.econ.usyd.edu.au/drawingboard/archive_digest.html> (3 December 2003).

Gelber, Katharine. *Speaking Back: The Free Speech versus Hate Speech Debate*. Amsterdam: John Benjamins Ltd., 2002.
Gray, Peter. "Saying it like it is. Oral Traditions, Legal Systems and Records." *Archives and Manuscripts*, 26(2) (1998): 248-269.
Habermas, Jürgen. *Communication and the Evolution of Society*. Translated and with an introduction by Thomas McCarthy. London: Heinemann, 1979.
Habermas, Jürgen. *The Theory of Communicative Action, Volume 1: Reason and the Rationalization of Society*. London: Heinemann, 1984.
Herron, Senator the Hon. John. *Federal Government Submission to the Senate Legal and Constitutional References Committee's Inquiry into the Stolen Generation*. (March 2000).
<www.australianpolitics.com/issues/aborigines/2000-govt-submission-on-stolen-generations.doc.> (March 2000).
Hohmann, Martin. *Gerechtigkeit für Deutschland. Ansprache von MdB Martin Hohmann zum Nationalfeiertag*. 3. Oktober 2003.
<http://www.heise.de/tp/deutsch/inhalt/co/15981/1.html?q=null> (3 December 2003).
Human Rights and Equal Opportunity Commission (HREOC). *Bringing Them Home: National Inquiry into the Separation of Aboriginal and Torres Strait Islander Children from Their Families*. Sydney: HREOC, 2003.
Human Rights and Equal Opportunity Commission (HREOC). *Face the Facts: Questions and Answers about Aboriginal and Torres Strait Islander People*. Sydney: HREOC, 2003.
<http://www.hreoc.gov.au/racial_discrimination/face_facts/atsi_txt.htm> (3 December 2003).
Johnson, Carol. *Governing Change: From Keating to Howard*. St Lucia: University of Queensland Press, 2000.
Kopietz, Andreas. "Neonazis schlagen öfter zu." *Berliner Zeitung*, 4 December, 2003.
McKenna, Mark. "Different Perspectives on Black Armband History." *Parliament of Australia Parliamentary Library Research Paper* 5 (1997-98).
<http://www.aph.gov.au/library/pubs/rp/1997-98/98rp05.htm#BLACK> (3 December 2003).
N.N. "Entscheidung über Hohmann-Anklage noch diesen Monat." *Sternshortnews*. 6 January (16:17) 2004a.
<www.shortnews.de/start.cfm?id=495082&9=Hohmann> (10 Feburary 2004).
N.N. "Staatsanwaltschaft: Hohmann-Rede enthält keine Strafbestände." *Sternshortnews*. 5 February (19:17) 2004b.

<www.shortnews.de/start.cfm?id=500033&q=Hohmann> (10 February 2004).
N.N. "Tätervolk ist das Unwort des Jahres 2003." *Stern*. 20 January 2004c.
<http://www.stern.de/unterhaltung/buecher/index.html?id=519105&q=Hohmann> (20 January 2004).
Peacock, Mark S. "The Desire to Understand and the Politics of Wissenschaft: an Analysis of the Historikerstreit." *History of the Human Sciences* 14(4) (2001): 87-110.
van Dijk, Teun A. Ed. *Handbook of Discourse Analysis: Vol. 1 – Disciplines of Discourse*. London: Academic Press, 1985.
van Dijk, Teun A. "The Study of Discourse." In *Discourse as Structure and Process. Discourse Studies: A Multidisciplinary Introduction* [Volume 1], edited by Teun A. van Dijk, 1-34. London: Sage Publications, 1997a.
van Dijk, Teun A. Ed. *Discourse as Structure and Process. Discourse Studies: A Multidisciplinary Introduction* [Volume 1]. London: Sage Publications, 1997b.
van Dijk, Teun A. Ed. *Discourse as Social Interaction. Discourse Studies: A Multidisciplinary Introduction* [Volume 2]. London: Sage Publications, 1997c.

Discourses of Uprooting, Discourses of Re-Routing: Autobiographical Discourse and Cultural Nomadism in Foucault, Castro and Flusser

Russell West-Pavlov

"Je ne sais rien de moi. Je ne sais même pas la date de ma mort."[1] – with this ventriloquised self-mocking dismissal of the (auto)biographical discourse, taken from the introduction to Borges' *Fictions*, Jean-Marie Auzias opens an early study on the 'archaeologist' of discourse, Michel Foucault.[2] Auzias' subject would himself probably have approved of this fictional attribution of Borges' words to himself, having said, in a 1982 interview with Stephen Riggins,

> I'm ... boring in my personal life. ... It's a bore to live with me. ... my personal life is not at all interesting. As far as my personal life is uninteresting, it is not worthwhile making a secret of it. ... By the same token, it may not be worthwhile publicizing it.[3]

Foucault's sceptical stance with regard to auto/biography is understandable, for it was he who contributed crucially to a historical discourse analysis of the emergence of the Western subject as we know it today – a subjectivity constituted centrally by the quasi-autobiographical reflex of confession.[4] Foucault's work on discourse implies that autobiographical writing does not so much reflect the facts of a life, as constitute a set of collective, historicised discursive conventions which offer individuals frameworks in which to construct and articulate narratives of an interior life and its temporal trajectory. Foucault's account of the relations between subjectivity and discourse is particularly pertinent to autobiographical discourse:

> Dans l'analyse proposée, les diverses modalités d'énonciation au lieu de renvoyer à *la* synthèse ou à *la* fonction unifiante d'*un* sujet, manifestent sa dispersion. Aux divers statuts, aux divers emplacements, aux diverses positions qu'il peut occuper ou recevoir quand il tient un discours. A la discontinuité des plans d'où il parle. Et si ces plans sont reliés par un système de rapports, celui-ci n'est pas établi par l'activité synthétique d'une conscience identique à soi, muette et

> préalable à toute parole mais par la spécificité d'une pratique discursive. On renoncera donc à voir dans le discours un phénomène d'expression – la traduction verbale d'une synthèse opérée par ailleurs; on y cherchera plutôt un champ de régularité pour diverses positions de subjectivité. Le discours, ainsi conçu, n'est pas la manifestation, majestueusement déroulée, d'un sujet qui pense, qui connaît, et qui dit: c'est au contraire un ensemble où peuvent se déterminer la dispersion du sujet et sa discontinuité avec lui-même.
>
> In the analysis proposed here, the various modalities of utterance, rather than pointing to the synthesis or the unifying function of a subject, point to its dispersion – to the diverse statuses, to the diverse contextualisations, to the diverse positions which it can occupy or receive when it holds forth – and to the discontinuity of the levels on which it might speak. And if these levels are linked by a system of relationships, this system is not established by the synthesising activity of a consciousness which is identical with itself, mute but pre-existing all speech, but by the specificity of a discursive practice. It is necessary to give up seeing discourse as an expressive phenomenon – the translation of a synthesis achieved elsewhere. Rather, it is necessary to see it as a field of regularities for various positions for subjectivity. Discourse understood thus is not the manifestation, unrolling majestically, of a thinking, knowing, speaking subject. On the contrary, it is an ensemble where the dispersion of the subject, its discontinuity with itself, can be determined.[5]

The analysis of discourse, in this quintessentially Foucauldian formulation, does not show the subject telling its own story – on the contrary, discourse analysis lays bare the subject's discontinuity and its dispersal within the very discursive field which constitutes it.

In this essay, I attempt to work in the interstices the tension between the patent artifice of autobiographical writing, and the overwhelming desire for such discourse which characterises our individualist culture. I argue for a notion of life-writing which stresses the disparate, heterogeneous character of the autobiographical text, a 'strangeness' at the heart of the 'familiarity' of autobiographical constructions of selfhood – a 'strangeness' which becomes explicit in transcultural autobiographies. Such transcultural life-writing causes turbulence in broader streams of discursive production, in particular to a generalised 'will to (auto/biographical) knowledge' in our culture. I suggest that transcultural autobiographies both participate in, and productively deconstruct, current hegemonic discourses of autobiographical self-presentation, in particular with regard to the manner in which they are co-opted by discourses of national identity. I begin by sketching the links between discourse analysis, the autobiographical impulse and the rupture caused by cultural heterogeneity by taking Foucault himself as an example of this fraught nexus of discourse, subjectivity and alterity. In the rest of the essay I go on to analyse transcultural autobiographies from the German-speaking and the Australian contexts – although the burden of my argument will be to demonstrate that these works themselves promblematise such bounded categorisations.

1. Foucault and the discourse of the subject

Given his scepticism with regard to subjectivity, it comes as no surprise to hear Foucault, at the very period where he reached celebrity, declaring his desire to disappear back into the discourse, whence, according to his analysis, the subject had come.[6] For Foucault's analysis of the manner in which the Western individual subject gained consistency is based upon the notion of "redoublement empirico-transcendental"[7] – "cette étrange figure où les contenus empiriques de la connaissance délivrent, mais à partir de soi, les conditions qui les ont rendus possibles."[8] The empirical data of human existence are both the stuff of the new discourse of subjectivity, and at the same time, the pre-conditions of that self-same discourse: its content and the larger conditions which brought that discourse into being. The subject which looks at itself is constituted by that which it sees – the facts of its own life. Its existence as narrative is predicated upon "[la] possibilité ... d'être à la fois sujet et objet de sa propre connaissance."[9]

If we may interpellate to the larger context of autobiographical discourse, it is possible to say that the autobiographical form in which it casts its narratives of itself both describes and produces or indeed determines the very possibility of such narratives. Well before the early modern epistemological analyses of *Les Mots et les choses*, Foucault had sketched the *productive* entanglement of selfhood, self-reflexivity and discourse in his portrait of Raymond Roussel, whose life ended with the auto/bio/*graphical* text entitled "comment j'ai écrit certains de mes livres."[10] Such processes of autobiographical feedback loops have been found to be at work, for instance, in the diaristic practices of early modern Puritans, who in the process of writing their experience, then reading that writing of experience, and finally re-writing that writing, engaged in a genuine "redoublement empirico-transcendental" out of which a proto-modern individualism emerged.[11] The Western subject truly emerged thus as "author of itself', dictated by a self-imposed "necessity | [which] Commands me name myself", to quote Shakespeare's Coriolanus, at the historical moment identified by Foucault.[12]

From the moment of its emergence as a 'discursive effect', self-authorising individual subjectivity has been traversed and invested by relations of power. Indeed, it was the very constitutive definition of their 'subjectivity' which produced the terms of their 'subjection' as docile, disciplined 'subjects':

> Cette forme de pouvoir s'exerce sur la vie quotidienne immédiate, qui classe les individus en catégories, les désigne par leur individualité propre, les attache à leur identité, leur impose une loi de vérité qu'il leur faut reconnaître et que les autres doivent reconnaître en eux. C'est une forme de pouvoir qui transforme les individus en sujets. Il y a deux sens au mot 'sujet': sujet soumis à l'autre par le contrôle et la dépendance, et sujet attaché à sa propre identité par la conscience ou la connaissance de soi. Dans les deux cas, ce mot suggère une forme de pouvoir qui subjugue et assujettit.
>
> This form of power is exercised upon immediate everyday life, placing individuals in categories, designating them by their own individuality, attaching them to their identity, and imposing on them a law of truth which they must recognise and which others must recognise in them. This is a form of power which transforms individuals into 'subjects'. There are two meanings to the word 'subject': a subject which is subjected to the other via control and dependence, and a subject attached to its own identity by consciousness and by self-knowledge. In both these cases, the word suggests a form of power which subjugates and subjects.[13]

Here it is clear that the constitution of subjectivity – eminently through the work of confession, of diaristic writing, and of autobiographical self-inscription – is not a neutral process, but is part and parcel of struggles for power over the lives of individuals – via the manner in which they are persuaded to represent their lives to themselves. This, in fact, is Althusser's celebrated definition of ideology. However, according to Althusser, ideology does not merely provide the terms with which individuals represent the conditions of their own existence to themselves (potentially in narrative or autobiographical form), but more radically, calls them into existence as subjects: "L'idéologie interpelle les individus en sujets."[14] In other words, ideology constitutes the subject in its subjectivity, making a subject out of the raw material of an individual, producing the subject through the agency of a highly tendentious set of narratives.[15] In our contemporary society, autobiographical discourses in all their multifarious forms are one of the most potent forms of ideology. These discourses constitute subjects and endow them with a subjectivity in which ideological *Weltanschauungen* are embedded from the outset as if natural. The 'givenness' of these discourses appears so ineluctable for the simple reason that they provide the very fabric of that subjectivity and its conditions of existence. Autobiographical discourses are one of the places where late modern subjects are most at the mercy of strategies of manipulation and coercion, because such discourses are the sites of subjects' emergence and ongoing construction.

In Foucault's works of the mid-1970s, *Surveiller et punir* (1975) and *Histoire de la sexualité 1: La Volonté du savoir* (1976), the nexus of power and discourse came to the forefront. The nineteenth-century discursive accumulation of knowledge 'about' subjects which simultaneously 'created' them as social beings, what Foucault named 'bio-power', gave impetus to the auto/biographical impulse in modern societies. As far back as 1968, however, at the moment when Foucault was formulating his theoretical account of discourse analysis, in anticipation of *L'Archéologie du savoir* which he was writing at the time, he had already sketched out the ways in which discourse analysis, subjectivity and power might interlock. In an open letter to the journal *Esprit*, Foucault criticised a 'reactionary' politics of nineteenth-century provenance which sees knowledge as the instrument of progress and sovereign human consciousness. In contrast, he envisaged a 'progressive' politics which would acknowledge the weight of discourse in producing consciousness and subjects, and form its strategies with an eye to the agency of discourses as well as that of political actors. He concluded his polemic by expressing his understanding for those who were under shock at the dismantlement of sovereign subjectivity operated by the work of discourse analysis. His last words were mockingly 'autobiographical' in their tenor:

> Il faudrait que je suppose que dans mon discours il n'y vas pas de ma sur-vie? Et qu'en parlant je ne conjure pas ma mort, mais que je l'établis; ou plutôt que j'abolit toute intériorité en ce dehors qui est si indifférent à ma vie, et si *neutre*, qu'il ne fait point de différence entre ma vie et ma mort?'

> Ought I to assume that my discourse has nothing to do with my survival/what comes after me? That in speaking I do not conquer my death, but reinforce it? Or rather, that I abolish all possible interiority in this outside which is so indifferent to my life, and so neutral, that it does not differentiate between my life and my death?[16]

Here the theoretician-deconstructor of the 'selfhood' of the 'author-function' hollows out the auto/biographical discourse, identifying it as a central element of a reactionary politics unaware of the role of discourse as a force for forming the putative agents of political action and moulding their range of action.

Ironically for an author who caustically analysed 'the author' and 'the author's life' as so many strategies for the stabilisation of textual dispersal, there are a number of excellent biographies of Foucault now available.[17] I shall play upon this paradoxical situation by briefly pursuing my biographical train of thought in reference to Foucault the enemy of auto/biography.

Foucault wrote the open letter to *Esprit* during a two year stay in Tunisia from 1966 to 1968 when he was teaching in the philosophy department at the University of Tunis. It was during this same period that *L'Archéologie du savoir* was written. Further, Foucault's famous lecture "Qu'est-ce qu'un auteur"[18] was given in February 1969, only a few months after his return from Tunisia. Foucault's Tunisian sojourn also marked the beginning of his political activism after his having witnessed the savage repression of student protest by the Tunisian authorities; Foucault found himself obliged to come out in support of his own students. The period during which Foucault thus theorised his discourse analysis up until then and began to forge its political cutting edge was one in which he was away from his native France. The moment of *L'Archéologie du savoir* thus perpetuated the nomadic condition under which he had lived until the publication of his first major study, *Histoire de de la folie* and his return to his first tenured appointment in French academia in 1961.

Such biographical details may appear trivial unless one appreciates their symptomatic character for the wave of radically innovative literary and cultural theory which swept through the French intellectual context in the 1960s and 1970s. Almost all of the major thinkers who forged French structuralist and poststructuralist theory came from outside the closed and insular French higher education system, or had spent formative periods of their careers beyond its borders. The anthropologist Lévi-Strauss spent the decisive years of his early career in Brazil; the literary theorists Todorov and Kristeva (who has spoken openly of the stuffiness of the Paris she discovered in 1966[19]) came from Bulgaria, bringing with them a familiarity with the hitherto-unknown Russian Formalist tradition; the ethical philosopher Lévinas, who had studied in Freiburg, was from Lithuania, as was the semiotician Greimas (Roland Barthes met him when both of them were teaching at the University of Alexandria); the deconstructionist philosopher Derrida and the literary theorists Cixous both grew up in Algeria, where the sociologist Bourdieu had also worked as a school teacher. And Foucault had held appointments in Uppsala, Hamburg and Warsaw before taking up a chair of philosophy at Clermont-Ferrand and the later appointment at the University of Tunis.[20] In 1960s and -70s France, radical thought went hand in had with cultural displacement. Derrida's Indian-Canadian translator Gayatri Chakravorty Spivak has put her finger on this conjunction in remarking,

> What I liked in [*De la grammatologie*] was that I had thought I was resonating with someone who was not quite French in the way in which I was not quite British. Such a person, a sort of insider/outsider, knowing it in a very specific way, was exploring what he called Western metaphysics from that position ...[21]

The retrospective theorisation of the 'applied' discourse analysis which Foucault had undertaken in his works on madness, medicine and the 'human sciences', in which discursive genealogy of the modern individual subject was carried out, thus intersected with a symptomatic and systematic disruption of the subject's 'national' affiliation. At the historical juncture at which discourse analysis announced itself as a method and a discipline in the very act of turning towards the (autobiographical) subject to genealogise and historicise it, the spatial displacement at work in that analytical process can be clearly glimpsed. This nexus of critical discourse analysis, an acerbic account of the constructability of subjectivity, and the displacement of an otherwise seamless match between the subject and its cultural-linguistic 'homeliness' is by no means accidental, but rather, was constitutive of the radical paradigm shift in poststructuralist thought.

Foucault's discourse analysis, I shall suggest in the remaining sections of this paper, permits a critical anatomy of autobiography as the diachronic fiction of a unified subject, and of the homogeneous national space and nationality as the synchronic place in which that subject belongs. Intercultural autobiographies, whose temporal trajectories sketch the transgression of national and linguistic borders, tend to question both these interlinked fictions – that of the narrative of selfhood and that of the homogeneous subject as a synecdoche of the homogenous nation.

2. Nomadism and subjectivity

The migrant experience in its literary codification is frequently judged as an inadequate capacity to intervene in the symbolic order. The flatness of some immigrant autobiographies or fictions such as those of the Australian Judah Waten are often complicit in this verdict.[22] Migrant writing is often judged as being closer to the immediacy of speech rather than of the artifice of writing.[23] This putative 'naturalness' of migrant or ethnic autobiographies endows them with the seal of 'authenticity', thus naturalising and recuperating the potentially disturbing resonance of such autobiographical narratives.[24]

In this essay I want to rescue and revalorise that element of disturbance. I will do this by reading in combination two central axes of discursive production in our society: on the one hand, discourses of national identity and homeland rootedness, what in German would be described by the term 'Heimat' ['homeland']; and on the other hand, discourses of stable selfhood, most evidently encoded in the manifold biographical and autobiographical discourses which circulate in the various media of our time. These discursive streams can be seen to converge in discourses of citizenship, patriotic loyalty, and so on. I am particularly interested, however, in reading these discourses across examples of their negation, namely, across discourses of homelessness and nomadism and rootlessness on the one hand, and discourses of the process-character of selfhood on the other. Diane Macdonell has commented that

> A 'discourse', as a particular area of language, may be identified by the institutions to which it relates and by the position from which it comes and which it marks out

for the speaker. That position does not exist by itself, however. Indeed, it may be understood as a standpoint taken up by the discourse through its relation to another, ultimately an opposing, discourse.[25]

Opposition among discourses would appear to go hand in hand with mutual entanglement and implication. Both the hegemonic discourses of rootedness and their opposing emergent discourses of nomadism, or alternately, hegemonic discourses of centred selfhood as opposed to emergent discourses of selfhood-in-process would thus appear to be intimately connected to one another.

Of particular relevance in this context is manner in which emergent discourses of 'nomadic subjectivity' as elaborated by Gilles Deleuze and Félix Guattari can be traced across contemporary discursive confrontations.[26] The notion of 'nomadic subjectivity' is taken up by more recent theoreticians such as Rosi Braidotti in a manner which always already represents a eminently societal engagement with discourses of national, rooted subjectivity:

> The nomad is my own figuration of a situated, postmodern, culturally differentiated understanding of the subject in general and of the feminist subject in particular. This subject can be described as post-modern/industrial/colonial, depending on one's locations. In so far as axes of differentiation such as class, race, ethnicity, gender, age, and others intersect and interact with each other in the constitution of subjectivity, the notion of the nomad refers to the simultaneous occurrence of many of these at once. [...] The nomadic subject is a myth, that is to say a political fiction, that allows me to think through and move across established categories and levels of experience: blurring boundaries without burning bridges.[27]

Braidotti uses nomadism as a figure of a flexible way of rethinking subjectivity today. I want to take her metaphor as genuinely describing something of the real experiences of nomadism, and of the subjective configurations that arise out of that nomadism – configurations which ought to be created consciously in order to better allow us to come to terms with the multicultural reality in which we live:

> Though the image of 'nomadic subjects' is inspired by the experience of peoples or cultures that are literally nomadic, the nomadism in question here refers to the kind of critical consciousness that resists settling into socially coded modes of thought and behavior. Not all nomads are world travelers; some of the greatest trips can take place without physically moving from one's habitat. It is the subversion of set conventions that defines the nomadic state, not the literal act of traveling.[28]

In the light of such programmatic statements, much is to be learnt from the ways in which contemporary authors harness the real experience of living between the cultures, and endow it, in a sense, with a normative force which would allow it to become the subject of a critique deployed within the field of competing discourses so as to serve the interests of tolerance and pluralism. Because such discursive undertakings are inherently situated in the conflicted public sphere, we need to ask such question as, Where are such discourses situated on the discursive landscape? How broadly distributed are they and according to what parameters? Which networks of circulation do they travel along? Are they still residual, or genuinely emergent? How influential are they in moulding the everyday practices of those subjects for whom they make available discourse positions?

In this essay I seek to provide answers to such questions by reading the work of two contemporary authors from the English- and German-speaking world who both combine in their writerly personas a critique of nationalist rootedness. Both use the platform of the autobiographical text to combat notions of stable subjectivity as the basis for exclusive national identity, or conversely, the notion of national boundaries as a model for individual subjectivity. In what follows I analyse autobiographical works by two intensely nomadic writers – the Hong Kong-born, Australian writer Brian Castro, who has gained prominence since publishing his first novel *Birds of Passage* in 1983, and the German-speaking, Prague-born Vilém Flusser, who spent the great part of his adult life in Brazil as Professor of Communication Philosophy at the University of São Paulo.

The manner in which they present themselves in their respective autobiographical works – Castro's collection of occasional autobiographical and essayistic pieces *Looking for Estrellita*, and Flusser's 'philosophical autobiography' *Bodenlos*, both published in 1999 – are strikingly similar. Indeed, the two writers' inaugural thumbnail-portraits of themselves are in many ways programmatic for the tasks undertaken in their respective life stories. Castro writes:

> I grew up [in Hong Kong] as part of a minority. My father was Portuguese, Spanish and English, my mother English and Chinese. I went to school with Indians, English, Fijians, Pakistanis, Chinese, Iraqis, Filipinos and everyone else in between. ... There were no racial slurs in the schoolyard. I spoke three languages fluently and never had to use the word 'identity' except when displaying my bus pass. Nobody else there seemed to care much, either, about this strange construct called identity, until recently. The miscegenation was such that it may have become rather boring to have had a Russian-speaking grandfather with a Chinese mother and an unpronounceable name. ... My Liverpudlian grandmother spoke fluent Cantonese, and I was brought up in a household which used a mixture of English, Cantonese and Portuguese.[29]

One of the essays in Flusser's *Bodenlos* is striking in the similarity of its structure, themes and formulation:

> Ich bin gebürtiger Prager, und meine Ahnen scheinen seit über tausend Jahren in der Goldenen Stadt gewohnt zu haben. Ich bin Jude, und der Satz 'Nächstes Jahr in Jerusalem' hat mich seit meiner Kindheit begleitet. Ich war jahrzehntelang an dem Versuch, eine brasilianische Kultur aus dem Gemisch von west- und osteuropäischen, afrikanischen, ostasiatischen und indischen Kultur zu synthetisieren, beteiligt. Ich wohne in einem provenzalischen Dorf und bin in der Gewebe dieser zeitlosen Siedlung einverleibt worden. Ich bin in der deutschen Kultur erzogen worden und beteilige mich an Ihr seit Jahren. Kurz, ich bin heimatlos, weil zu zahlreiche Heimaten in mir lagern. Das äußert sich täglich in meiner Arbeit. Ich bin in mindestens vier Sprachen beheimatet und sehe mich aufgefordert und gezwungen, alles Zu-schreibende wieder zu übersetzen und rückzuübersetzen.
>
> I am a native of Prague by birth and my ancestors

> appear to have lived in the golden city for over a thousand years. I am a Jew, and the sentence 'Next year in Jerusalem' has accompanied me since my childhood. I participated for decades in the attempt to synthesise a Brazilian culture from a mixture of Eastern and Western European, Africa, East Asian and Indian culture. I live a village in Provence and have been absorbed into the fabric of this timeless settlement. I was raised in the German cultural tradition and have participated in that tradition for decades. In short, I am homeless, because too many homelands are stored within me. That is expressed from day to day in my work. I am at home in at least four languages and see myself required, indeed forced, to translate and re-translate everything that I write [with a pun on 'ascription'].[30]

Both writers stress the spatial nomadism and the cultural hybridity which has fundamentally structured their lives; the Babelian range of languages in which they express themselves underlies these nomadisms and hybridities and continues to leave its print on their writing. In what follows, I claim that the very manner in which these cross-cultural selves are presented represents a discursive intervention in which the hegemonic public discourses of selfhood and nationalism are subverted and inverted, with a view to mobilising 'counter-discourses' that offer alternative subject positions and thus a platform for agency and resistant political action.[31] These counter-discourses constitute a 'rupture' within the unitary discourses of the bounded nation and its synecdoche the bounded self, a rupture driven by the demise of the notion of the 'self's sovereignty' over its own monolingual territory.[32]

3. Discourses of the un/stable nation

Such discourses of rootedness have a long tradition in Australia, paradoxically, with a generalised and historical suspicion of those who do not subscribe to the normative sense of stability. Paul Carter speaks of "patriots who preach a unique provenance and urge us to settle down peaceably (and quietly)."[33] Geoffrey Blainey traces this suspicion of 'birds of passage' back as far as white hostility towards the Chinese miners on the 1850s goldfields, who were accused of taking the gold they had found out of the country.[34] Ien Ang describes the unsettling effect of "transnational connections and diasporic linkages in the cultural identifications of migrants" and the manner in which, even today, "[t]hese relations frequently become a source of anxiety in public discourse about the risks of migrants ... maintaining political and economic loyalties elsewhere."[35] These discourses draw upon older discursive traditions such as the 'cosmopolitan' Wandering Jew of the Eastern European anti-semitic imagination, "whose rootlessness was a condemnation and a proof of nonbelonging precisely *there*."[36] Such discourses have influenced state policy, with pressure increasingly put upon migrants to Australia to take up citizenship, that is, to demonstrate their loyalty to their host country in a public act of allegiance.[37] In Germany, the earlier rhetoric of repatriation of the 'Gastarbeiter' has ceded to a rhetoric of 'integration' and of acceptance of 'mainstream culture' (Leitkultur), though actually gaining citizenship in many cases remains difficult, despite recently modified citizenship legislation. Both Brian Castro and Vilém Flusser subject these discourses of national belonging to a scathing critique. Castro satirically describes "the way [in Australia] almost everyone uses the word 'we' unquestioningly; the obsession with a territorialised landscape rather than with its spirituality; ... *above all, a fear of being seen as unpatriotic"*.[38] Similarly, Flusser deconstructs the notion of 'Heimat', based in the notion of 'stability':

> Die sogenannte Werte, die wir dabei sind, mit der Seßhaftigkeit aufzugeben, also etwa den Besitz, die Zweitrangigkeit der Frau, die Arbeitsteilung und die Heimat, erweisen sich dann nämlich nicht als ewige Werte, sondern als Funktionen der Ackerbaus und der Viehzucht. ... Die geheimen Codes der Heimaten sind nicht aus bewußten Regeln, sondern größtenteils aus unbewußten Gewohnheiten gesponnen. Was die Gewohnheit kennzeichnet, ist, daß man sich ihrer nicht bewußt ist. ... Wird jedoch der Code bewußt, dann erweisen sich seine Regeln nicht als etwas Heiliges, sondern als etwas Banales. Der Einwanderer ist für den Beheimateten noch befremdender, unheimlicher als der Wanderer dort draußen, weil er das dem Beheimateten Heilige als Banales bloßlegt.
>
> The so-called values which we are in the process of abandoning along with stability and rootedness – for instancepossessions, the second-class status of women, the division of labour and the homeland – prove to be not eternal values but merely functions of agriculture. ... The secret codes of the homelands are not woven out of

conscious rules, but for the most part of unconscious habits. What marks habit is the fact that one is not aware of it. ... As soon as one becomes aware of the code, its codes prove to be something banal, not something holy. The immigrant is even more perplexing for the native than the wander without because he lays bare to the native the banality of that which is holy.[39]

Flusser's last words here, which stress the immigrant's capacity to disturb received notions of homeland and belonging, are given flesh by the self-reflexive turn of his account, for in the last analysis he is describing himself. To this extent, he makes an implicit illocutionary statement in which the discursive act itself, that of autobiography, the self-writing itself, is highlighted as an intervention in the homeland-context which it deconstructs.[40]

4. Discourses of the un/stable self

This brings me to the second strand of my critique, that of the way in which hegemonic discourses of centred selfhood are contested by emergent discourses of selfhood as process.[41] In modern Western culture, as Foucault's historical analyses made clear, autobiography has functioned as a mode of fixing of selfhood, of confirmation of subjectivity as stability. Autobiography is an enshrined literary discourse which first emerged together in the eighteenth century with the modern novel and was consolidated in the context of romanticism, particularly in texts such as Wordsworth's *The Prelude* and Rousseau's *Confessions*. Philippe Lejeune's much disputed formula for the strict definition of an autobiographical discourse forming the basis of the 'autobiographical pact' (the equivalence of author, protagonist, and the narrating 'I'[42]), can be ratified historically as an emergent function within Western society: namely, that of the individual subjectivity endowed with coherence through the recursive force of its own autobiographical narration. Autobiography in its traditional form depends upon the fixing of identity via the fixing of a fluid range of discourses of selfhood in favour of a single version which is then attributed truth value through the double agency of the author underwritten by the critic.[43] It is this historical function which has made the autobiography such a valued form of writing in our culture, cementing as it does a bounded, stable version of selfhood.

Recent criticism has fundamentally questioned the fixity of self ostensibly reflected by autobiographical writing, positing a fragmented self merely cast as an illusory unity within the text.[44] A forerunner of this trend is Virginia Woolf's quirky critique of autobiographical writing in *A Room of One's Own*:

> But after reading a chapter or two a shadow seemed to lie across the page. It was a straight dark bar, a shadow shaped something like the letter "I". One began dodging this way and that to catch a glimpse of the landscape behind it."[45]

The 'I' as a entity 'barring' a wider mode of perception might remind one of Lacan's notion, in his playful algebra of psychoanalysis, of the bar which keeps the unconscious safely at bay from the conscious mind, thus guaranteeing the cohesion of the individual subject. The bar represents the barrier of repression, which maintains the 'signified' of the subject's 'signifiers' in a state of inaccessibility. The subject is constituted by the constant metonymic jostling of 'signifiers', and their metaphoric transformation from signifiers into associated signifieds likewise relegated to the bric-a-brac of the subconscious.[46] Reading Virginia Woolf via Lacan, we arrive at a notion of autobiography which buys subjective stability at the price of the repression of multiple, contradictory narratives within the self.

In contrast, an alternative possibility for autobiography is posited by Elspeth Probyn, who suggests that an autobiographical speaking position can be sustained without it solidifying into an identity, in the hope that stories can "be told though selves and through emotions without being at the expense of other stories and other selves."[47] A concrete example of such parallel autobiographical narratives can be found in Luc Sante's *The Factory of Facts*, whose opening chapter, 'Résumé', offers the same autobiographical incipit in nine versions, each time with minimal but accumulating variations.[48]

Given the massive cultural role of biographical and autobiographical discourse in contemporary capitalist societies,[49] the explosive force of 'unruly' autobiographical discourses can hardly be underestimated. This subversive force is all the more pregnant when discourses of nationalism and autobiographical discourses converge, only to be corroded by their counter-discourses in the form of texts by writers like Castro and Flusser.

We need to understand one function of traditional autobiography as buttressing notions of national identity to assess the immense didactic power possessed by autobiographical modes of writing. Anna Johnston has analysed recent Australian autobiographies which tend to offer powerful narratives of national identity, thus eliding the reality of many

Australian experiences of expatriation or exile and the fundamentally heterogeneous character of 'Australia' as a nation.[50] A representative example of this mode of autobiographical writing in the Australian context would be A. B. Facey's bestselling *A Fortunate Life* from 1981, hailed by one reviewer as "a microcosm of the earlier life of this country, with those mighty totems of ours – the Bush and the War – looming monolithically over everything else."[51] The enlistment of autobiography in the service of the jingoistic nation calls forth a caustic response from Brian Castro:

> Ironic, then, that some writers cannot see that they unwittingly act as homogenising agents for a national consciousness steeped in a fabricated idea. *National writers*. These oxymorons are welded painfully together ... as if all were involved in a single project. And these writers aren't even dead yet."[52]

Against such writers participating in discourses of national coherence and stability, authors such as Castro and Flusser offer exemplary illustrations of the creation of a counter-discourse.

Such counter-discourse is generated in alternative autobiography as a potent deconstruction of discourses of national identity. Recent discourse theory has taken care to link discursive streams to material locations and specific historical and socio-political sites of production and transmission. Foucault suggests that "un savoir, c'est aussi l'espace dans lequel le sujet peut prendre position pour parler des objets auxquels il a affaire dans son discours."[53] The notion of the discursive space, which has been the target of heavy criticism by a number of theoreticians,[54] becomes a genuinely relevant concept in this context. As Linda Anderson observes,

> discursive positions and material locations are imbricated in each other, without ever forming a unity or a connection that is absolute or unchanging. However, we need now to ask what happens when the very notion of 'location' starts to change, when 'place' becomes layered with numerous crossings.[55]

The 'placedness of discourse' implies that subjects who shift between places also shift between discourses – and vice versa. Such subjects are discursive producers who inevitably participate in several discursive domains, tending to contaminate one domain (an "espace commun" ["common space"] in Foucault's formulation) with discursive activity from another (thus generating what he calls "'systèmes de dispersion" ["systems of dispersal"]).[56]

5. Autobiography in the public realm

What results might be obtained were one to regard autobiographical discourse as such a 'space of dispersal'? What would occur if autobiography revealed the true mobility and fragmentariness of its signifying components, customarily pulled into line by authorial and critical disciplinary action? Such an autobiography would inherently point towards the mobility of cultural identity, the tendency of subjects to shift across borders, the inevitability with which culture is perennially being formed at the interstices of geographical and linguistic spaces. Such a form of autobiography would 'naturally' speak of a culture of nomadism. In an autobiographical-theoretical passage which shifts from the analytical to the subjective mode almost imperceptibly, Braidotti offers an example of the mode a 'nomadic' autobiographical practice might take. Such autobiography would foreground the arbitrariness of the sign, so as to speak of the mobility of culture, itself in turn embodied in mobile subjects:

> The polyglot also knows intimately what de Saussure teaches explicitly: that the connection between linguistic signs is arbitrary. The arbitrariness of language, experienced over several languages, is enough to drive one to relativist despair. Thus the polyglot becomes the prototype of the postmodernist speaking subject; struck by the maddening, fulminating insight about the arbritariness of linguistic meanings and yet resisting the free fall into cynicism. ... My experience as a polyglot taught me the courage to face this arbitrariness and still not to jump to the conclusion that anything goes, that arbitrary does not equate absurd and polyvalence does not mean anarchy.[57]

Vilém Flusser describes, in terms far removed from those of Braidotti's structuralist linguistics, a similar autobiographical experience of the abritrariness of place-specific discourses of homeland and belonging:

> Die Heimat ist zwar kein ewige Wert ... aber wer sie verliert, der leidet. Er ist nämlich mit vielen Fasern an seine Heimat verbunden, und die meisten dieser Fasern sind geheim, jenseits seines wachen Bewußtseins. Wenn die Faser zerreißen oder zerrissen werden, dann erlebt er dies als einen schmerzhaften chirurgischen Eingriff in

sein Intimstes. Als ich aus Prag vertrieben wurde (oder den Mut aufbrachte zu fliehen), durchlebte ich dies als ein Zusammenbruch des Universums; denn ich verfiel dem Fehler, mein Intimstes mit der Öffentlichkeit zu verwechseln. Erst als ich unter Schmerzen erkannte, daß mich die nun amputierten Faser angebunden hatten, wurde ich von jenem seltsamen Schwindel der Befreiung und des Freiseins ergriffen, den angeblich den überall wehenden Geist kennzeichnet. .... Es sind zumeist geheime Fasern, die den Beheimateten an die Menschen und Dinge der Heimat fesseln. Sie reichen über das Bewußtsein des Erwachsenen hinaus in kindliche, infantile, wahrscheinlich sogar in fötale und transindividuelle Regionen; ins nicht gut artikulierte, kaum artikulierte und unartikulierte Gedächtnis. ... Der Heimatverlust lüftet dieses Geheimnis, bringt frische Luft in diesen gemütlichen Dunst und erweist ihn als das, was er ist: der Sitz der meisten (vielleicht sogar aller) Vorurteile – jener Urteile, die vor allen bewußten Urteilen getroffen werden.

The homeland may not be an eternal value ... but whoever loses it suffers. For he is connected by many threads to his homeland, and most of these threads are secret, beyond his conscious awareness. When these threads break or are broken, he experiences this as a painful surgical operation upon his most intimate world. As I was driven away from Prague (or gathered the courage to flee) I experienced that as the end of the world; for I made the mistake of confusing my intimate world with the public world. As I recognised that the amputated threads had actually kept me in bondage, I was seized by a weird dizziness of freedom, the freedom which ostensibly characterises the mind everywhere. ... It's mostly secret threads which bind the native to the people and the things of home. They go back beyond adult consciousness towards the childhood, infantile and probably even the foetal, transindividual regions; into the partly articulable, barely articulable and even inarticulable memory. ... The loss of the homeland lays bare this secrecy, brings fresh air into this dusty atmosphere and shows it up for what it is: the site of

> most (perhaps even all) pre-judices – those judgements
> which precede all conscious judgement.[58]

The merit of Flusser's critique of the sense of homeliness is that he accurately pinpoints the psychic roots of the sense of belonging which allows public discourse ('die Öffentlichkeit') to infiltrate and mould selfhood ('mein Intimstes') by anchoring itself in the archaic, pre- or unconscious realm of 'pre/judice'. Flusser suggests that the process by which the public discourse of 'homeliness' ('Heimat') is revealed as just that, be it through the most painful processes of existential loss, may free the individual from the hegemony of such discourses in the *subjective* realm.

In this context, a comment by Brian Castro is highly significant. Castro claims that autobiography

> is a form which is not only unstable in itself and which has undergone intense transformation, but which has the potential to transgress the furthest. This is the auto/biographical form. The slash is already an implosion of multiple forms, dividing the conjunction of prefixes and yet allowing the crossing over between self, life and writing.[59]

The 'slash' introduced by Castro cleaves the apparent unity of the public-private discourse of autobiography and introduces a problematic note hitherto absent and conducive to critical thought in the domain of nationalism and its subjective avatars. Castro's 'slash' mimics Flusser's brutal uprooting and its concomitant liberation from the 'pre/judices' of 'homeliness'.

One could well complicate Flusser's scenario by a chiastic gesture, and examine the manner in which a discourse of *intimate* selfhood, that of autobiography in this case, functions as a *public* discourse which moulds the subjective configurations of nationalist sentiment. What effects would be obtained where the disjunctions which Flusser himself claims to have experienced in his own private experience through the traumatic experience of exile, were effected directly within the public discourse which he here appears to leave intact? That, indeed, is the role of autobiography to which Brian Castro draws attention in his own writing in that mode – and a role which Flusser's own autobiographical writing, as we will see subsequently, also takes on.

Castro is fully aware that autobiography is a genre constituted of "highly inventive acts of dissimulation which sometimes had real or unfortunate consequences."[60] In other words, autobiography is an acknowledged fictional discourse – but whose *effects* may be anything but fictional – which occupies a prominent space within the public space. Castro elaborates:

> An 'autobiography' ... does make some claims. Claims about oneself, one's family, lineage, history. This is usually done within the 'grammar' of an accepted system, a cultural norm imposed by families, societies, nations. A novel (*The Satanic Verses* aside) rarely incurs wrath. But an 'autobiography', by the very nature of its definition, invokes a kind of dogma about what can and can't be written.[61]

Thus autobiography as a public discourse is clearly an ideologically heavily loaded genre. This is so because in Western societies the individual subject figures, sociologically as the basic building block of the nation, and symbolically as its synecdoche (whence the importance, in recent Australian debates, and in negative form in Germany, where the debate centres upon 'assimilation', of citizenship). The subject, like the nation-state, is ostensibly closed, unified, homogeneous and stable. Autobiographical texts frequently bear the burden of confirming the stability of the subject as a necessary pre-condition of the stability of the nation.

In an extended consideration of the ways in which autobiography is read according to the rules of genre so as to elide its "hybrid instability,"[62] Castro notes that "from the nineteenth century we have inherited a necessity to imperialise interpretation, to link it with the cultural history of the nation-state."[63] Autobiography is constructed by hegemonic meta-literary discourse as a stabilising instance and thus takes on its role as a building block in the rhetoric of nationalism.

Castro frequently employs tropes of public monumentalism to express the synedochic relations between the state and the individual (or more frequently in his work, the family, which places the individual within a historical lineage, a function which is highly germane to the diachronic and chronological character of autobiography): "The family of the nation can be monumentalised into an absurdly phatic utterance: *the friendliness of our people*"[64]; "I thought of national anthems, marbled memorials ..."[65] For Castro, the individual, particularly within the family, is the guarantor of the historical continuity of a national myth. He places the notion of 'inheritance' clearly in the public domain when exploring its semantic relative 'heritage', albeit here in its predominately negative form for Asian Australians such as Castro himself: "The *heritage* of Australian film and television occupies a museum-space where Asians are depicted as never having left the Burma Railway or the Killing Fields. ... they have no narrative position. ... They are either silent, or they make strange noises."[66] The notions of heritage and inheritance belong equally to the semantic field of rigid, ossified, stultifying monumentalism.

6. Transgressive autobiography in the public sphere

Logically, then for Castro, *alternative* autobiography constitutes a problematizing, resistant intervention in the public sphere. He refers to 'the element of risk' incurred by the critical autobiographer[67] – referring to the risk to the self and its representations in an age of individualism, to the self and its national avatars in an era of patriotism. "He thinks: An autobiography which is outside the parameters of this patriotic dependency stands against the nation and its single, imagined and hypothetic community."[68] The allusions to Bendict Anderson are unmistakeable, and given the influence of this last writer in recent years, point to the representative importance of alternative autobiography as a discursive intervention in the domain of nationalism at the nexus of public discourse and discourses of subjective identity.

Flusser assigns to the status of the exile, what he names 'Bodenlosigkeit' – the fact of having 'no ground under one's feet', an existential state of which he makes a life-long vocation with the title of his autobiography, *Bodenlos* – a similarly prominent role in public discourse. Flusser's conception of 'Bodenlosigkeit'/exile is one that reserves it such a subversive force that it can only appear as an anti-discourse:

> Sobald nämlich die Bodenlosigkeit ein öffentliches Thema wird, ist sie es nicht mehr. Sie ist eine Erfahrung von Einsamkeit und zerfließt, wenn öffentlich besprochen, zu leerem Gerede. Sie ist grundsätzlich anti-kulturell und kann daher nicht zu Kulturform erstarren.
>
> Man kann die Erfahrung der Bodenlosigkeit in Literatur, Philosophie und Kunst nicht niederschlagen, ohne sie zu verfälschen. Man kann nur versuchen, sie in diesen Formen zu umschreiben, sie einzukreisen und so einzufangen. Oder aber man kann versuchen, sie direkt zu bezeugen, indem man autobiographisch seine eigene Lage schildert, in der Hoffnung, daß sich in der Schilderung andere erkennen. Das eigene Leben wird sozusagen zu einem Laboratorium für andere, um die

Lage der Bodenlosigkeit von außen erkennen zu können. Das, und hoffentlich nicht Eitelkeit und Selbstbehauptungstrieb, ist das Motiv dieses Buches.

Jeder kennt die Bodenlosigkeit aus eigener Erfahrung. Wenn er vorgibt, sie nicht zu kennen, dann nur, weil es ihm gelungen ist, sie immer wieder zu verdrängen: ein Erfolg, der in vieler Hinsicht sehr zweifelhaft ist. Aber es gibt Menschen, für die Bodenlosigkeit die Stimmung ist, in der sie sich sozusagen objektiv befinden. Menschen, die jeden Boden unter den Füßen verloren haben, entweder weil sie durch äußeren Faktoren aus dem Schoß der sie bergenden Wirklichkeit verstoßen wurden oder weil sie bewußt diese als Trug erkannte Wirklichkeit verließen. Solche Menschen können als Laboratorium für andere dienen. Sie existieren sogar intensiver, falls man unter 'Existenz' ein Leben in der Bodenlosigkeit verstehen will. Eine in diesem Sinn intensive Existenz sei nun geschildert.

As soon as groundlessness becomes a public theme, it is no longer a theme. Groundlessness is an experience of isolation and evaporates, as soon as it is discussed in public, into empty discourse. It is fundamentally anti-cultural and therefore cannot solidify into a cultural form. One cannot inscribe the experience of groundlessness in literature, philosophy and art without falsifying it. One can merely try to paraphrase it in these cultural forms, to circumscribe it and to capture it. Or one can try to bear witness directly to that experience, by describing in autobiographical form one's own position, in the hope that others will recognise this description. One's own life becomes, so to speak, a laboratory for others, so as to make the situation of groundlessness recognisable from outside. That, and hopefully not vanity and egoism, is the motivation for this book.

Everyone knows groundlessness from their own experience. Whoever claims not to have experienced it can only do so by having repressed it: a success in many respects of doubtful value. But there are people for whom groundlessness is the mood in which they are, objectively, so to speak, located. People who have lost this ground under their feet, either because external factors shoved them out of the lap of comforting reality or because they have consciously recognised this reality as a deception. Such people can serve as laboratories for others. They exist even more intensively than most, if one decides to understand 'existence' as a life in groundlessness. One such experience of intensive existence in that sense will be described in this book.[69]

Flusser's concept of 'exile' is a double one. On the one hand, he stresses the impossibility of describing 'Bodenlosigkeit', the notion that 'exile' constitutes an 'outside' beyond all the discourses which endow us with identity, a sort of black hole of identity-loss. Here he is close to Foucault's claim that the discursive 'place' in which our own current 'archive' is to be found can only be located with reference to its own 'outside', the horizon of what cannot be said.[70] On the other hand, 'exile' can be imported into the domain of the social, in a manner somewhat akin to the Kristevan 'semiotic' which erupts within the 'symbolic'. Just as Kristeva's 'semiotic' can only be evinced within the textual and linguistic order of the 'symbolic', Flusser selects autobiography as the privileged site in which 'exile' can emit its disruptive shock-waves.[71]

It is significant that Flusser, though somewhat ingenuously denying descriptions of the experience of exile the status of public discourse, ascribes to the exile her- or himself, or as a collective agent, a pedagogical role which cannot but take effect in the discursive realm (pedagogy without discourse would be an absolute non sequitur). Correspondingly, Flusser endows the immigrant or exile with a representative, modelling function in society:

> Wir, die ungezählten Millionen von Migranten (seien wir Fremdarbeiter, Vertriebene, Flüchtlinge oder von Kornseminar zu Kornseminar), erkennen uns dann nicht als Außenseiter, sondern als Vorposten der Zukunft. Die Vietnamesen in Kalifornien, die Türken in Deutschland, die Palästinenser in den Golfstaaten und die russischen Wissenschaftler in Harvard erscheinen dann nicht als bemitleidenswerte Opfer, denen man helfen sollte, die verlorene Heimat zurückzugewinnen, sondern als Modelle, denen man, bei ausreichendem Wagemut, folgen sollte.

> We, the countless millions of migrants (whether we be

> migrant workers, displaced persons, refugees, or those who commute from one seminar such as this [where the lecture was given] to another), do not see ourselves as outsiders, but rather, as heralds of the future. The Vitenamese in California, the Turks in Germany, the Palestinians in the Gulf States, ort he Russian scientist at Harvard do not figure then as pitiful victims in need of assistance in regaining their lost homeland, but rather as models which one, with enough courage, ought to emulate.[72]

But what sort of modelling function does Flusser envisage here? What he proposes is in no wise a comforting confirmation of the nationalist notions of identity which societies inevitably generate in their own interests. Rather, says Flusser in a typically complicating formulation, "Der Migrant [...] ist zugleich Fenster, durch welches die Zurückgebliebenen die Welt erschauen können, und Spiegel, in dem sie sich, wenn auch verzerrt, selbst sehen können."[73] These statements about the migrant are also, implicitly, statements about migrant autobiography, the immediate performative context in which they are made: autobiography, suggests Flusser, is one of the few contexts in which exile and migrancy can be genuinely made available within public discourse – a discourse, however, to which they none the less remain inimical.

Both Castro and Flusser are thus concerned with the form in which an inherently centrifugal experience such as that of migrancy can possibly be inscribed within centripetal discourses of the nation-state and national belonging. The 'monumentalist' discourses of 'homeliness' and 'patriotism' cannot but be shattered by those of migrancy. Homi Bhabha writes:

> Increasingly, national cultures are being produced from the perspective of disenfranchised minorities. ... The Western metropole must confront its postcolonial history, told by its influx of postwar migrants and refugees, as an indigenous or native narrative internal to its national identity ... Such cultures of a postcolonial *contra-modernity* may be contingent to modernity, discontinuous or in contention with it, resistant to its assimilationist technologies; but they also deploy the cultural hybridity of their borderline conditions to 'translate', and therefore reinscribe, the social imaginary of both metropolis and modernity.[74]

Castro imagines writing as a process of 'disfigurement of monuments' in which he "found a vehicle for resistance."[75] "His sisters complained that he was defacing the epitaph of his father."[76] What comes in place of these monuments for writers such as Castro and Flusser is something more fragmentary: "a montage built by blasting out the myth of the past"[77] – *"An essay on disinheritance crumbles around the family."*[78] The autobiography, reformulated in the tentative mode of the 'essay', becomes itself a monument caught in a process of entropy and transformation. Similarly, Flusser claims that "Es gibt kein Selbst, das verloren gehen könnte. Das Selbst ist nichts als ein Haken, auf den Masken gehängt werden können." This attitude, we will subsequently see, is crucial for Flusser's experimentation with various 'masks' of autobigraphical writing, upon which he embarks without regard for "das scheinbare Problem dabei, der Selbstverlust hinter den Masken" for precisely the reasons given above.[79]

One of Castro's favourite terms to describe the corrosive effect of migrant discourse upon the monuments of national identity is that of the oxymoron: "Ironic then, that some writers cannot see that they unwittingly act as homogenising agents for a national conscious steeped in a fabricated idea. *National writers*. These oxymorons are welded painfully together ... as if all were involved in a single project. And these writers aren't even dead yet."[80] Writing within the discourses of national cohesion involves a strained binding-together of diversity and multiplicity so as to create a forced homogeneity. Such oxymorons will be blasted apart by 'writing'. Autobiography is the privileged site for that blasting operation: "I knew that the word *autobiography* carried a freight of meaning it didn't really deserve: real life; true stories; family secrets. Writing, of course, makes oxymorons of all these."[81] Autobiography, suggests Castro, when wielded as 'writing' in its true sense, and thus to unfold its genuinely turbulent effects, can lay bare all the tensions inherent in such pairs of pairs of terms, making them pull apart from each other. The genre itself is conducive to such oxymoronic ruptures: "The word *autobiography* signifies an impossible act," claims Castro, suggesting that one must 'uncouple' "the *auto* and *bio* from writing."[82] Castro's insertion of slashes into the word 'auto/bio/graphy' has already been mentioned above. At the level of his autobiographical writing, he exploits the multiplicity of pronominal positions to split the autobiographical self, following Barthes' example in *Roland Barthes par Roland Barthes*. Castro is clear about the mechanisms of transgressive autobiography, which he places in the realm of 'dispossession' and 'disinheritance', notions which seek to explain the manner in which an individual may leave the closed family community, crossing the borders into a space of exile and thus disturbing the linear continuity of the 'family history' within which the traditional autobiography receives its standard configuration:

> Disinheritance may be the cause or consequence of autobiography, whose riches depend on nothing. ... Along with yourself, you say, families, nations, sugary-sweet celebrations and ideologies, are all cast into the fire. Your ashen hair. Somewhere you had read Celan and had never shaken him loose.[83]

The act of dispossession is traced here via the modulation through the indicative statement, the subsequent movement of uncertain second-person discourse (does it connote the impersonal 'one', an address to the reader, or a genuinely recursive communication with a self mirrored in the autobiographical text?), and the final fall into citation. The self is dislodged by the act of writing, in which an other voice, that of the writer of cultural strangeness and exile par excellence, Paul Celan, comes to the fore. *"Whenever we write, we write an other."*[84]

In Flusser, autobiography as a mode of writing and the experience of migrancy interlink in a manner not dissimilar to that found in Castro's writing. Flusser's notion of migrancy begins with the painful experience of exile, which frees the migrant from the pre/judices of home, and allows her or him to embrace a new reality, a reality in which the 'freedom-from' of exile becomes the 'freedom-to' of new engagement in the new country. However, this movement of engagement may well in turn become embedded in new notions of 'homeliness', and thus must likewise be followed by a subsequent movement of re-disengagement if the migrant is to continue to act in a creative way. Nonetheless, the movement of engagement never loses its validity. For only once a movement towards an object has occurred can a movement away from it occur. This dual model is of course, as often in Flusser, a spatial one, based upon the dialectical model of distole and sistole.[85] Such meditations are themselves formulated within a stylistic context in which the modes of expression chosen by Flusser for his autobiographical text are highly significant.

Flusser's decision to use the impersonal 'one' (the German 'man') as the mode of enunciation of his autobiographical voice, constitutes a means of combating the egotism of autobiography. In his meditations upon his background of Prague Jewishness, Flusser discusses his decision not to write in the autobiographical mode: „Die erste Konsequenz, die der Text aus diesen Antworten zu ziehen hat, ist der Entschluß, alles Autobiographisches zu vermeiden. Das Prager-Jude-sein wird intersubjektive, nicht subjektiv, mit dem Blick nach außen, nicht nach innen aufgenommen werden müssen".[86] Yet two pages later, Flusser writes: "Wenn auch alles Autobiographisches in diesem Text zu vermeiden ist, so heißt das nicht, daß ein objektiver Standpunkt zu der spezifischen Bedingung 'Prager-Jude-sein' eingenommen werden muß."[87] The avoidance of personal detail, of the privileging of a speaking selfhood, does not make the text an objective one, for it remains engaged:

> Der Text wird weder autobiographisch noch objektiv sein dürfen, sondern er wird sich zu bemühen haben, ein noch für kurze Zeit lebendiges Zeugnis für eine untergangene Welt abzulegen; Der Text wird vom Schreibenden weg (wenn auch vom Schreibenden aus) auf die zahlreichen Toten und wenigen Überlebenden zu blicken haben.
>
> The text must be neither autobiographical nor objective, but rather, will try to bare witness for a short time yet to a world now gone'; 'The text will have to gaze away from the writer (even when it emerges from the writer) and towards the many dead and the few survivors.[88]

A witness is not interested in her or his subjective reality, but this does not make her or him objective, rather, it points to an inter-subjective reality. In this movement towards others, sistole and distole are reconciled. In the central section of the autobiography, entitled "Dialoge" and devoted to short portraits of influential friends from his time in Brazil, Flusser's work is at its most 'intersubjective' – and also describes the moment of crisis in the early 1970s following the military coup d'état in Brazil. This reconciliation of sistole and distole at the end of Flusser's autobiography, and almost at the end of his life, confirms the recurrence of the gesture of engagement through the act of writing at the very moment of describing the gradual process of disengagement from the Brazilian situation. The "Dialoge" are capped off by the section on "Die Terrasse", which describes Flusser's increasing sense of helplessness to offer his students any solutions to the situation in which they found themselves after the coup d'etat of 1964. This sense of powerlessness led to his definitively leaving Brazil in the early 1970s.[89] Paradoxically, it is here, at a textual moment which melds engagement and disengagement, that the autobiographical 'I' reappears in the text. The 'I' re-emerges in the three "Dialoge" preceding the moment of departure, devoted to Romy Fink, Miguel Reale and Mira Schendel. The "man" cedes to the "ich" precisely at the opening of the description of the friendship with Romy Fink, that is, at the moment where, in the personalised "Dialoge" section, the movement of 'Dégagement' takes up. Here, at the very moment of departure, the failure of the Flusser's political engagement in Brazil, the speaking self appears to recognise the situatedness of itself, its engagement for other people. The "I" is an expression of a relationship to others.

Interestingly, the decision to reintroduce the 'ich' into the autobiographical narrative arose out of Flusser's acceptance of a challenge issued to him by his French publisher:

> Sie werden in den beiden Texten 'Reale' und 'Mira' bemerkt haben, daß ich Ihre Kritik annahm. Ich habe mich 'angenommen' (assumé), habe in der Ich-Form geschrieben und habe bewußt, mich ebenso wie meine Partner zu Wort kommen lassen. Das bedeutet, daß ich die ganze Sache von neuen zu schreiben habe.
>
> You'll notice in two texts 'Reale' and 'Mira' that I've accepted your criticisms. I accepted/took responsibility for myself, wrote in the 'I'-form and consciously allowed myself and my partners to speak. This means that I must write the whole thing anew.[90]

The abrupt eruption of a speaking self hitherto elided in the text expresses, in formal terms, the tension inherently present in the act of writing, the tension between engagement and disengagement, between proximity and distance, between the freedom to leave 'homeliness' and the freedom to re-engage in a new political context. Flusser's autobiography thus evinces a constant movement away from selfhood to others, and back to selfhood as the site of proximity with others, resulting in the decision "mich ebenso wie meine Partner zu Wort kommen lassen".[91] These stylistic oscillations within the autobiographical enterprise are homologies of the movements of the migrant subject her- or himself. The refusal or acceptance of the autobiographical mode of self-expression provide subjective models for the rejection of national models of civic identity and the assumption of new modes of intersubjective identity-in-process. Thus the text as 'laboratory' gives concrete stylistic expression to Flusser's notion of the migrant subject as a 'laboratory' for new modes of social existence.[92]

7. **Language and transgressive autobiography**
Castro ascribes to the transgressive autobiography an inherently

spatial function which is that of vitiating borders and boundaries: "auto/biography demonstrates the impossibility of totalisation and closure of any written text."[93] The oxymoronic slash through auto/biography symbolises the explosive force inherent within the genre, its tendency to generate heterogeneity, to cross borders:

> Genres nurture an implicit contradiction because they enforce boundaries which writing is obliged to cross ... because writing will always transgress genre and will always use genre to exercise its own coming into being. I write precisely because I want to write myself out of an artificially imposed corner. The autobiographical element leads the way because it is the most direct form of transgression. The "I" deliberately invokes multiplicity. Declares itself against authority. Places itself at the very juncture of risk. ... Mainly because hybridity, a mixture of forms, a mixture of character types and ethnicities, is what I bring to writing. It is what the "I" is. A proliferation of selves. A juxtaposition of differences.[94]

Lest one think these are merely theoretical declarations, it is instructive to return a second time to the accumulation of identities which Castro displays in his self-descriptions: "*I am not only Portuguese, English, Chinese and French, but I am writing myself out of crippling essentialist categories, out of the control exerted over multiplicities.*"[95] Castro as an autobiographical writer defines his own identity – performatively – in playful, productive Joycean terms: "And the sea, the sea speaks back in an idle gurgle, transporting me, violator of languages, traducer and transgressor from over the short wave, translator of tongues lodged cheek by jowl in happy confusion and good taste."[96] A comparison with Flusser's self-presentation, also cited at the beginning of this essay, makes the point more forcefully, multiplying not only the subordinate adjectives, but the instances of 'I', to the point where it is necessary to ask whether these 'I''s are identical with one another:

> Ich bin gebürtiger Prager ... Ich bin Jude ... Ich wohne in einem provenzalischen Dorf und bin in der Gewebe dieser zeitlosen Siedlung einverleibt worden. Ich bin in der deutschen Kultur erzogen worden und beteilige mich an Ihr seit Jahren. Kurz, ich bin heimatlos, weil zu zahlreiche Heimaten in mir lagern. ... Ich bin in mindestens vier Sprachen beheimatet und sehe mich

150   Autobiographical Discourse and Cultural Nomadism

> aufgefordert und gezwungen, alles Zu-schreibende wieder zu übersetzen und rückzuübersetzen.
>
> I am a native of Prague by birth ... I am a Jew ... I live a village in Provence and have been absorbed into the fabric of this timeless settlement. I was raised in the German cultural tradition and have participated in that tradition for decades. In short, I am homeless, because too many homelands are stored within me. ... I am at home in at least four languages and see myself required, indeed forced, to translate and re-translate everything that I write [with a pun on 'ascription'].[97]

Both writers reflect the splintering of their selves in the splintering of their work on language.

Flusser's description of his encounter with Brasilian Portuguese demonstrates the manner in which the encounter with an other culture is an encounter with an other language which transforms the self:

> Im Fall des eigenen Erlebnisses der brasilianischen Kultur stand die portugiesische Sprache schon darum im Mittelpunkt, weil man sich zu ihr entschlossen hatte, als man sich entschloß, sich in Brasilien zu engagieren. Das bedeutete, daß man diese Sprache vor allem als Rohmaterial erlebte, das dazu herausforderte, bearbeitet und verändert zu werden, und zwar so, daß diese Veränderung einen selbst realisieren und mit anderen in Verbindung bringen möge. Das heißt, man erlebte die portugiesische Sprache als Herausforderung und als Lebensaufgabe. ... Gefühlsmäßig bedeutete es, daß man diese Sprache zu lieben begann, je mehr man ihre Schönheit entdeckte, und zu hassen, je mehr sie sich wehrte, verändert zu werden. ... Man versuchte die Sprache zu beherrschen, um von ihr beherrscht zu werden, und das tat man, um durch die Sprache anders zu werden und zu anderen vorzudringen. Kurz, man begann, brasilianischer Schriftsteller zu werden.
>
> In the case of my own experience of Brazilian culture, the Portuguese language was central, because one had decided for that language, at the same moment as one decided to commit oneself in/to Brazil. This meant that

> one experienced this langauge above all as a raw
> material which challenged one to reworked and
> transformed, in such a way that this change would fulfil
> oneself and bring one into contact with others. This
> means that one experienced the Portuguese language as
> a challenge and as an existential task for life. ... In
> emotional terms, it meant that one began to love this
> language more and more as one discovered its beauty,
> and began to hate it more and more as one discovered
> how it resisted change. ... One tried to master the
> language so as to be mastered by it, and one did this in
> order to be become an other through the language and to
> reach others. In short, one was beginning to become a
> Brazilian writer.[98]

Flusser implicity suggests that the engagement in a language means that the self is transformed, because it accepts that the very condition of its existence as a social being is changed. The subject finds itself determined by a different paradigm of things that can be said, and a different syntax of the ways theses things can be combined in meaningful structures.

Translation plays a privileged role here, as a mode of cultural border-crossing which transforms the self. Multilingualism, that built-in version of translation, is praised by Castro as the royal way towards border-transgression:

> [T]he benefits of being able to speak another language
> are manifold. Language marks the spot where the self
> loses its prison bars – where the border crossing takes
> place, traversing the spaces of others. When one speaks
> or translates Chinese, one metaphorically becomes
> Chinese; when one speaks Japanese one 'turns'
> Japanese. Each language speaks the world in its own
> way. The polyglot is a freer person, a person capable of
> living in words and worlds other than the narrow and the
> confined one of unimagined reality. When we translate
> from one language to another we not only reinvent
> ourselves but we free up the sclerotic restrictions of our
> own language.[99]

It is significant that the language used to describe the expanded self via the impact of polyglot heterogeneity is the language of territorial transgression: "it is only through curiosity about language, through wilful misunderstanding and obliquity, that we are able to live within a multiplicity of selves and to encounter new worlds. It is through constant translation that we are able to cross borders."[100] Flusser gives Castro's notions of "wilful misunderstanding" and "obliquity" a very concrete significance when he writes:

> Portugiesisch schöpferisch schreiben heißt, verborgene Bedeutungen aufdecken, und das kann man tun, indem man versucht, die Regeln der Sprache zu brechen. Diese Entdeckung läßt sich für die brasilianische Kultur überhaupt generalisieren: Sich in ihr engagieren heißt, ihre verborgene Bedeutung (zum Beispiel ihren Mystizismus und Messianismus) aufzudecken, und dies kann man tun, indem man versucht, die Regeln der Kultur (zum Beispiel ihren offiziellen Positivismus) zu brechen.
>
> To write Potuguese creatively means discovering hidden meanings, and this can only be done by breaking the rules of the language. This discovery can be generalised for the entire Brazilian culture. To commit oneself to that culture means discovering its hidden meanings (for instance its mysticism and messianism) and this can only be done by breaking the rules of the culture (for instance it offical positivism).[101]

What might this mean in practice? The answer, for Flusser, was to import a transgressive mode of translation, a cross-cultural linguistic contact-zone into his writing itself:

> So sah, in Kürze, die subjektive Seite der Dialektik aus: Man trat an das Portugiesische heran, um es mit dem Deutschen und dem Englischen zu manipulieren, wobei das Deutsche vom Tschechischem, lateinischen, Griechischen und Hebräischen in Frage gestellt wurde. Ortega diente dabei als Vorbild. Das war eine Lebensaufgabe. Das Leben konnte erst wirklich beginnen.
>
> The subjective side of the dialectic was, in brief, as follows: one approached Portuguese in order to manipulate it with German and English – with a

> German, however, which was interrogated by Czech, Latin, Greek and Hebrew. Ortega was the model fort his process. That was a task for life. Life could now finally begin.[102]

Each language disturbs and disrupts the others - each shift in place is a shift in the language which subsequently changes other sites of linguistic identity. Rosi Braidotti writes similarly of such processes:

> The nomadic polyglot practices an aesthetic style based on compassion for the incongruities, the repetitions, the arbitrariness of the languages s/he deals with. Writing is, for the polyglot, a process of undoing the illusory stability of fixed identities, bursting open the bubble of ontological security that comes from familiarity with one linguistic site. The polyglot exposes this false security [...] Writing in this mode is about disengaging the sedentary nature of words, destabilizing commonsensical meanings, deconstructing established forms of consciousness.[103]

The genre of autobiography wielded by Castro and Flusser thus constitutes a direct recursive attack on the material of which the self is made, language, by the mode of language itself. Autobiography as a cross-cultural genre and as a discursive intervention thus offers a response to the dilemma described by Blanchot in *L'Écriture du désastre*. There, he posits an irreconcilable contradiction between a social engagement in which writing is the polemical instrument of politics, and an autotelic ethics of writing in which the ineluctable alterity of language itself is given free reign.[104] In cross-cultural autobiography these apparently opposed literary imperatives can be reconciled: it is the "strangeness" of all literary texts, in Lévesque's terms,[105] which comes to the fore in the exile or the migrant's discursive interventions, a strangeness which undermines the unholy alliance of public discourses of coercively bounded selfhood and rigorously policed national boundaries.

Notes

1. ["I know nothing of myself. I don't even know the date of my own death."] All translations in square brackets mine.
2. Auzias 1986, 11.

3. Foucault 1983, 4-9, here 7, 9.
4. See Foucault 1976, in particular 25-49.
5. Foucault 1969, 74.
6. Foucault 1971, 7-8.
7. ["empirical-transcendental doubling"].
8. Foucault 1966, 323. ["this strange figure where the empirical contents of knowledge make available, of their will, the conditions which made them possible"].
9. Foucault 1988, 201. ["the possibility of being, simultaneously the subject and the object of its own knowledge"].
10. Foucault 1963, 7, 10. ["how I wrote some of my books"].
11. See Nussbaum 1989; Schlaeger 1999, 22-36. For a further analysis of autobiographical discourse as an instantiation of 'negative feedback' (and thus of 'systemic self-perpetuation') see my essay "Selfhood as System" (West 2004).
12. Shakespeare *Coriolanus*. 4.5.57-58.
13. Foucault 1994a, 227.
14. ["Ideology interpellates individuals as subjects"].
15. Althusser 197, 122-123.
16. Foucault 1994b, 692-695.
17. Foucault 1980, 141-60; Idem, 1994, I, 789-821. For recent biographies of Foucault, see, in descending order of interest, Eribon 1991; Macey 1993; Miller 1993.
18. ["What is an author"].
19. Kristeva 1983, 41.
20. See also Bourdieu 1984, 142-144.
21. Spivak 1996, 70.
22. See for instance, Waten 1968.
23. Gunew 1988, 5-8; Idem 1990, 113; Idem 1994, xii, 11.
24. Huggan 2001, 155-157.
25. Macdonell 1986, 3.
26. Deleuze and Guattari 1972, 1980.
27. Braidotti 1994, 4.
28. Idem, 5.
29. Castro 1999, 149, 152.
30. Flusser 1999, 247.
31. See Terdiman 1985; Tiffin 1995, 95-98.
32. See Foucault 1969, 272.
33. Carter 1992, 6.
34. Blainey 1983, v.
35. Ang 2000, xx.

36. Brennan 1997, 21.
37. See Stratton 1998, 107-114.
38. Castro 1999, 221; my emphasis.
39. Flusser 1999, 248, 250.
40. I depend for my analysis here upon Ricœur 1990, 55-72, in particular 58-59.
41. See, for the classic locus of this formulation, Kristeva 1977, 55-106.
42. Lejeune 1975, 14-15.
43. See Anderson 2001, 6.
44. For representative texts see Marcus 1994, and Smith 1995, 58.
45. Woolf 1973, 98.
46. See Lacan 1970, 273-5; Grosz, 1990, 101-103.
47. Probyn 1993, 84.
48. Sante 1999 3-11.
49. See in particular Evans 1999, Ch. 1.
50. Johnston 1996, 75.
51. Facey 1981 back cover blurb.
52. Castro 1999, 219.
53. Foucault 1969, 238. ["Knowledge is also the space in which a subject can position itself in order to speak of the objects it deals with in its discourse"].
54. See Lefebvre 1974, 10ff; Smith and Katz 1993, 67-83.
55. Anderson 2001, 114.
56. Foucault 1969, 52-53.
57. Braidotti 1994, 14-15.
58. Flusser 1999, 249-250.
59. Castro 1999, 105-106.
60. Ibid, 205
61. Ibid, 205-206.
62. Ibid, 109.
63. Ibid, 113-114.
64. Ibid, 219.
65. Ibid, 207.
66. Ibid, 213.
67. Ibid, 205.
68. Ibid, 222.
69. Flusser 1999, 11.
70. Foucault 1969, 172.
71. Kristeva 1974.
72. Flusser 1999, 248-249.
73. Ibid, 263.

74. Bhabha 1994, 5-6.
75. Castro 1999, 206.
76. Ibid, 209-210.
77. Ibid, 214.
78. Ibid, 218.
79. Flusser 1999, 214.
80. Castro 1999, 219.
81. Ibid, 205.
82. Ibid, 222.
83. Ibid, 214.
84. Ibid, 217.
85. See also Flusser 1994, 31-34.
86. Flusser 1999, 268. ["The first consequence which the text must draw from this reply is the decision to avoid everything autobiographical. The identity of the Prague Jew must be registered in a manner which is intersubjective, not subjective, and with the gaze directed outwards, not inwards."]
87. Ibid, 270. ["Even though everything autobiographical is to be avoided in this text, this does not mean that an objective perspective on the specific conditions of the "Prague Jewish identity" needs to be assumed."]
88. Ibid, 271, 268.
89. Ibid, 207-214.
90. Ibid, 290.
91. ["allowed myself and my partners to speak"].
92. Ibid, 11.
93. Castro 1999, 121.
94. Ibid, 214-215.
95. Ibid, 115.
96. Ibid, 130.
97. Flusser 1999, 247.
98. Ibid, 78-79.
99. Castro 1999, 152-153.
100. Ibid, 132.
101. Flusser 1999, 87.
102. Ibid, 84.
103. Braidotti 1994, 15.
104. Blanchot 1980, 125-127.
105. Lévesque 1978.

References

Althusser, Louis. "Idéologie et appareils idéologiques d'état." *Positions*, 78-137. Paris: Editions sociales, 1976.

Anderson, Linda. *Autobiography*. London: Routledge, 2001.

Ang, Ien. "Introduction: Alter/Asian Cultural Interventions for 21st Century Australia." In *Alter/Asians: Asian-Australiian Identities in Art, Media and Popular Culture*, edited by Ien Ang, Sharon Chalmers, Lisa Law and Mandy Thomas, xiii-xxx. Annadale, NSW: Pluto Press, 2000.

Auzias, Jean Marie. *Michel Foucault: Qui suis-je?* Lyon: La Manufacture, 1986.

Bhabha, Homi K. *The Location of Culture*. London: Routledge, 1994.

Blainey, Geoffrey. *The Blainey View*. Quoted in Brian Castro, *Birds of Passage*. St Leonards, NSW: Allen & Unwin, 1983.

Blanchot, Maurice *L'Écriture du désastre*. Paris: Gallimard, 1980.

Bourdieu, Pierre. *Homo academicus*. Paris: Minuit, 1984.

Braidotti, Rosi. *Nomadic Subjects: Embodiment and Sexual Difference in Contemporary Feminist Theory*. New York: Columbia University Press, 1994.

Brennan, Timothy. *At Home in the World: Cosmopolitanism Now*. Cambridge, Mass.: Harvard University Press, 1997.

Carter, Paul. *Living in a New Country: History, Travelling and Language*. London: Faber & Faber, 1992.

Castro, Brian. *Looking for Estrellita*. St Lucia: University of Queensland Press, 1999.

Deleuze, Gilles and Félix Guattari. *Capitalisme et Schizophrénie: L'Anti-Œdipe*. Paris: Minuit, 1972.

Deleuze, Gilles and Félix Guattari. *Capitalisme et Schizophrénie: Mille Plateaux*. Paris: Minuit, 1980.

Eribon, Didier. *Michel Foucault (1926-1984)*. Paris: Flammarion/Champs, 1991.

Evans, Mary. *Missing Persons: The Impossibility of Auto/Biography*. London: Routledge, 1999.

Facey, Albert B. *A Fortunate Life*. Ringwood, VIC: Penguin, 1981.

Flusser, Vilém. "Für eine Philosophie der Emigration." *Von der Freiheit des Migranten. Einsprüche gegen den Nationalismus*. Mannheim: Bollmann, 1994.

Flusser, Vilém. *Bodenlos. Eine philosophische Autobiographie*. Frankfurt am Main: Fischer, 1999.

Foucault, Michel. *Raymond Roussel. Preface de Pierre Macherey*. Paris: Gallimard/Folio, 1963.

Foucault, Michel. *Les Mots et les choses. Une archéologie des sciences*

humaines. Paris: Gallimard, 1966.
Foucault, Michel. *L'Archéologie du savoir.* Paris: Gallimard, 1969.
Foucault, Michel. *L'Ordre du discours.* Paris: Gallimard, 1971.
Foucault, Michel. *Histoire de la sexualité. 1: La volonté de savoir.* Paris: Gallimard, 1976.
Foucault, Michel. "What is an Author?" In *Textual Strategies: Perspectives in Post-Structuralist Criticism*, edited by Josué Harari, 141-160. London: Methuen, 1980.
Foucault, Michel. "Qu'est-ce qu'un auteur?" In *Michel Foucault: Dits et écrits 1954-1988*, edited by Daniel Defert and François Ewald, I, 789-821. Paris: Gallimard, 1980.
Foucault, Michel. "An Interview by Stephen Riggins." *Ethos* 1(2) (1983) : 4-9.
Foucault, Michel. *Naissance de la clinique.* Paris: PUF/Quadrige, 1988.
Foucault, Michel "Le sujet et le pouvoir." In *Michel Foucault: Dits et écrits 1954-*1988, edited by Daniel Defert and François Ewald, 223-243. Paris: Gallimard, 1994a.
Foucault, Michel "Réponse à une question." In *Michel Foucault: Dits et écrits 1954-1988*, edited by Daniel Defert and François Ewald, 673-695. Paris: Gallimard, 1994b.
Grosz, Elizabeth. *Jacques Lacan: A Feminist Introduction.* London: Routledge, 1990.
Gunew, Sneja. "Women's Experimental Writing." In *Telling Ways: Australian Women's Experimental Writing*, edited by Anna Couani and Sneja Gunew, 5-8. Adelaide: Australian Feminist Studies, 1988.
Gunew, Sneja. "Denaturalizing Cultural Nationalisms: Multicultural Readings of 'Australia.'" In *Nation and Narration*, edited by Homi K. Bhabha, 99-120. London: Routledge, 1990.
Gunew, Sneja. *Framing Marginality: Multicultural Literary Studies.* Melbourne: Melbourne University Press, 1994.
Huggan, Graham. *The Post-Colonial Exotic: Marketing the Margins.* London: Routledge, 2001.
Johnston, Anna. "Australian Autobiography and the Politics of Narrating Post-Colonial Space." *Westerly* 41(2) (1996): 73-80.
Kristeva, Julia. La Révolution du langue poétique. Paris: Seuil, 1974.
Kristeva, Julia. "Le sujet en procès." In *Polylogue*, 55-106. Paris: Seuil, 1977.
Kristeva, Julia. "Mémoire." *L'Infini* 5(1) (1983): 39-54.
Lacan, Jacques. *Ecrits I.* Paris: Seuil/Points, 1970.
Lefebvre, Henri. *La Production de l'espace.* Paris: Editions Anthropos, 1974.
Lejeune, Philippe. *La pacte autobiographique.* Paris: Seuil, 1975.

Lévesque, Claude. *L'étrangeté du texte: Essais sur Nietzsche, Freud, Blanchot et Derrida.* Paris: 10/18, 1978.
Macdonell, Diane. *Theories of Discourse: An Introduction.* Oxford: Blackwell, 1986.
Macey, David. *The Lives of Michel Foucault.* London: Hutchinson, 1993.
Miller, James. *The Passion of Michel Foucault.* London: HarperCollins, 1993.
Marcus, Laura. *Auto/biographical Discourses: Criticism, Theory, Practice.* Manchester: Manchester University Press, 1994.
Nussbaum, Felicity. *The Autobiographical Subject: Gender and Ideology in Eighteenth-Century England.* Baltimore, MD: Johns Hopkins University Press, 1989.
Probyn, Elspeth. *Sexing the Self.* Gendered Positoins in Cultural Studies. London and New York: Routledge, 1993.
Ricœur, Paul. *Soi-même comme un autre.* Paris: Seuil, 1990.
Sante, Luc. *The Factory of Facts.* New York: Vintage, 1999.
Schlaeger, Jürgen. "Self-Exploration in Early Modern English Diaries." In *Marginal Voices, Marginal Forms: Diaries in European Literature and History*, edited by Russell West and Rachael Langford, 22-36. Amsterdam/Atlanta, GA.: Rodopi, 1999.
Shakespeare, William. "Coriolanus." In *The Complete Works*, edited by Stanley Wells and Gary Taylor. Oxford: Clarendon Press/Oxford University Press, 1988.
Smith, Neil and Cindy Katz. "Grounding Metaphor: Towards a Spatialized Politics." In *Place and the Politics of Identity*, edited by Michael Keith and Steve Pile, 67-83. London: Routledge, 1993.
Smith, Robert. *Derrida and Autobiography.* Cambridge: Cambridge University Press, 1995.
Spivak, Gayatri Chakravorty. "Transnationality and Multiculturalist Ideology." In *Between the Lines: South Asians and Postcoloniality*, edited by Deepika Bari and Mary Vasudeva, 64-89. Philadelphia, PA.: Temple University Press, 1996.
Stratton, Jon. *Race Daze : Australia in Identity Crisis.* Annadale, NSW.: Pluto, 1998.
Terdiman, Richard. *Discourse/Counter-Discourse: The Theory and Practice of Symbolic Resistance in Nineteenth-Century France.* Ithaca, NY.: Cornell University Press, 1985.
Tiffin, Helen. "Post-Colonial Literatures and Counter-Discourse." In *The Post-Colonial Studies Reader*, edited by Bill Ashcroft, Gareth Griffiths and Helen Tiffin, 95-98. London: Routledge, 1995.
Waten, Judah. *Alien Son.* Melbourne: Sun Books, 1968.
West, Russell. "Selfhood as System: Autobiography and Poetic

Subjectivity in Wordsworth's The Prelude." *Arbeiten aus Anglistik und Amerikanistik* 29(1) (2004): 23-40.
Woolf, Virginia. *A Room of One's Own*. Harmondsworth: Penguin, 1973.

Towards another Modernity?
Multicultural Discourse in German and Australian Film from the 1970s to the 1990s

Tim Mehigan

1.

The question of multiculturalism – a topic of increasing importance in the white settler societies of Australia and Canada since the Second World War – has received renewed attention in European countries of late as Europe moves further, and with a rising sense of conviction, along the path of political, economic and social integration. A vigorous engagement with the nature and value of multiculturalism has taken centre-stage in several of those countries, in particular, France, Germany and Great Britain. In part, this engagement has brought forth arguments already registered in similar debates in Australia and Canada in recent years. In part, also, it has gone further. Not only have questions arisen in the domain of practical politics – questions that have accompanied the establishment of multiculturalism as a matter of governmental concern in Australia[1] and Canada.[2] Issues have also been raised that go to the heart of foundational concepts in the West such as liberalism and social democracy.

These concepts, as we now understand them, took shape in the eighteenth century – a century in which "science and taste"[3], that is to say, nature and society, came together in the imagination of individual women and men of that century in a unique coalescence that lent them moral force. In arguments that revisit the eighteenth century and the project of "Enlightenment" that is presumed to be at its core, this moral force is still strongly felt. It is encountered in the current debate about multiculturalism in Britain, where Brian Barry's *Culture and Equality* has stimulated reflection on whether the values promoted by Enlightenment rationality – values such as freedom and equality – endure to a point where they can be considered universal[4], or whether, as the romantic reaction to Enlightenment at the turn to the nineteenth century implied, all values are subject to revision and change through time and circumstance and depend for their meaning on the cultural environment that brought them into being.[5] Any state constructed on the basis of immutable, rational principles – so the first argument goes – need have no especial interest in the cultural values of its citizens. In fact, the cultural values of some citizens might be considered antithetical to those principles. However, if there is no such thing as normative principles – this is the countervailing argument – the cultural values of citizens assume importance and may even be antecedent to principles arising from social agreement. From this standpoint, the voluntary aspect of rationalist principles forged on the basis of rational argument appears less compelling than the identity of citizens founded on age-old cultural tradition. In the debate about multiculturalism at the start of the twenty-first century, then, romanticism and Enlightenment are again at the fore, but they have changed positions in relation to each other. Two centuries after this major cultural debate first took place, the romanticism that underlies multiculturalism is now ascendant, and it is rational liberalism that finds itself in reaction.[6] How this new version of the old romanticism-Enlightenment controversy will be decided, is emerging as one of the key political questions of the present era.

Given the resilient nature of the multicultural debate, and its long history, it is instructive to consider how multiculturalism as a critical discourse has been inflected in the medium of film – a significant site of cultural reflection in the modern era. In putting this question, I follow what Jaworski and Coupland refer to as the "forensic task" of discourse analysis, namely to "track how various forms of discourse, and their associated values and assumptions", are incorporated into texts.[7] At the same time, Fowler's idea of 'criticism', which acknowledges both the artificial quality of cultural categories and the possibility of conceiving the world in hitherto unexplored ways, serves as a model for my analysis.[8] Particularly instructive in this regard is a comparison of German and Australian film where multiculturalism has been approached from different starting points and where, accordingly, different insights into its problems and opportunities have been advanced. In the case of Germany, a critical discourse of multiculturalism first emerged from economic imperatives in the immediate aftermath of the Second World War. Political agreements struck with various southern European and northern African countries from the late 1950s onward brought cheap migrant labour into Germany to aid the postwar reconstruction effort. These 'Gastarbeiter', or guest-workers, as they were soon called, entered an old European society ill-prepared to deal with them, and ill-inclined to face the social issues that their arrival brought with them. By the early 1970s, when the deployment of cheap labour in Germany was at its greatest extent, Rainer Werner Fassbinder made the important film *Angst essen Seele auf* (Fear Eats the Soul) about a Moroccan guest-worker in Germany. By the 1980s, when issues of integration had come to be seen as part of a wider failure of western society to structure life within a sustainable physical and social ecology, Werner Herzog directed *Where the Green Ants Dream*, a film about the land rights of Aborigines in

Australia. When these films were made, both directors were at the height of their fame as filmmakers; both films shaped the German and European discourse of multiculturalism in ways still relevant today.

While these German directors offered a pessimistic assessment about minority rights in mainstream German and Australian society of the 1970s and 1980s, the multicultural discourse had already shifted markedly by the 1990s, if Baz Luhrmann's *Strictly Ballroom* (1992) and Steve Thomas's documentary *The Hillmen* (1996) are taken as a guide. In these films, the Australian director Luhrmann and the Anglo-Australian Thomas are more sanguine about the prospects of urban multiculturalism in modern society. Their characters are young people on the threshold of maturity, whose outlook is shaped both by the tradition they inherit from their migrant parents and the new life that beckons for them in mainstream Australian society. These films suggest that a dialogue between cultural tradition and rational liberalism – which in turn are derived from the older debate between romanticism and Enlightenment – is certainly conscionable.

2.

Rainer Werner Fassbinder and Werner Herzog are two important members of the postwar tradition of German film that rose to prominence in the 1970s. Films such as the Fassbinder trilogy *Die Ehe der Maria Braun* (1978), *Lola* (1981) and *Die Sehnsucht der Veronika Voss* (1982) and the Herzog films *Aguirre, die Rache Gottes* (1972), *Das Enigma des Kaspar Hauser* (1974) and *Woyzeck* (1978) are trenchantly critical in outlook, drawing attention, among other things, to the social cost of Germany's 'Wirtschaftswunder' or economic miracle which had gathered momentum in the 1950s and brought a decade or more of booming economic growth. Whilst most of these films engage directly with questions of social alienation, there are some, like Herzog's *Woyzeck*, that approach the same topic from a literary point of view (Herzog's *Woyzeck* is a film version of Georg Büchner's 1834 play of the same name). Other films explore issues of social alienation and marginalisation in the context of a wider historical discussion of postwar German society (Fassbinder's *Maria Braun*) or, reconstruct actual historical events such as the Spanish conquest of South America (Herzog's *Aguirre*) to ask more general questions about the propensity of human beings to dominate, intimidate and tyrannise in pursuit of material gain. In all cases, Fassbinder and Herzog take issue with the type of civilization model that has established itself in the West and with the values that underlie it. Their films may be understood as strategic interventions in a critical discourse they seek to influence, if not fundamentally change. In doing so, they have elicited a mixed reaction among audiences, inspiring both admiration among those who share their criticisms of Western values and indignation among those who don't.

Herzog, in particular, was widely criticised for his attempt to politicize the question of Aboriginal land-rights in the later film *Where the Green Ants Dream* (1984). As Cheesman notes, the film "was regarded not only as falling between the stools of ethnographic-environmentalist documentary and exotic fiction, but also as showing, above all, a manipulative, egomaniac director who 'moves the Aborigines before his camera in much the same way as the mining company threatens to have them moved by the police'".[9] Close analysis of the film appears to bear out the claim that the aesthetic 'shaping' of the film recedes into the background. Instead, the director highlights the political question of the failure of the Australian higher courts of the day to acknowledge Aboriginal title to ancestral lands in any serious way.[10] This already suggests Herzog's main concern – the failure of the argument from (cultural) tradition to command any favour in political debate in Australia at this time. Herzog's film, in other words, examines not only the conditions of exclusion – the exclusion of the Australian Aborigines from the cultural discourse of mainstream Australia – but enquires into the legality of this exclusion. This is taken up in the long courtroom scene in the film, which presents a comparative cultural discussion of the issue of native title. While hearsay can serve as a basis for asserting native title in the legal systems of certain African countries, for example, it does not constitute a compelling argument for the Aboriginal plaintiffs in the film, who are obliged to accept the intrusion of a large uranium mining company on their land. The fact that intrusion ultimately leads to displacement and that the displacement of this Aboriginal community from ancestral lands had been foretold in Aboriginal mythology – the dreaming of the green ants from the title of the film – adds poignancy and a sharpened political focus to the ending of the film.[11]

The politicised nature of Herzog's approach to the issue of Aboriginal land-rights notwithstanding, the real story in Herzog's film is the journey from unquestioning naivety to political and even spiritual awareness of the story's protagonist, the geologist Hackett. At the start of the film, Hackett is the somewhat guileless employee of Ayer's Mining who administers test-drilling on the company's mining lease. He has no axe to grind with the local Aborigines; he would rather just get along with them. Their defiant attitude towards further drilling, however, gets under his skin. As the film progresses, Hackett develops not just a sympathetic understanding of the political position of the Aborigines, but indeed an affinity with them, to a point where, in the midst of delicate discussions between the executive director of the mining company and two Aboriginal elders at the company's big city offices, he is transported into a dreaming of his own that subverts his received Western sense of reality. "We're still stuck in the lift", he says, referring to the uncertain technology that brought them to the nineteenth floor of the office block. "We're not really at this table at all".

Herzog's point here is not merely to launch a scornful attack on a technology-dependent Western world. Rather, he explores the idea that all reality is culturally mediated, which is to say, a construct. When the dominant assumptions underpinning normative culture shift, as they do so for Hackett in the lift, the sense of reality shifts with it. Moreover, a local anthropologist, who already has been through the spiritual journey Hackett now undertakes, points to a moral deficit attaching to the Western value system and therefore outlines the case for change: "Your civilization destroys everything", he charges, "including yourself". In a reference, perhaps, to the short story *Der Tunnel* by the Swiss author Friedrich Dürrenmatt – a story first published in 1952 and republished in a revised version in 1978 – the anthropologist compares Western civilization to a train unable to arrest its imminent plunge into an abyss.[12] As the student notes at the end of the 1978 version of Dürrenmatt's story: "Wir saßen noch in unseren Abteilen und wußten nicht, daß schon alles verloren war".[13] That this self-annihilation of civilization is by no means a recent event, is implied in a sub-theme at the start of the film relating to a dog that has strayed down a mineshaft (a "tunnel", as his owner, an old lady, calls it). The unfortunate dog goes by the name of Benjamin Franklin – an oblique, and of course ironic, reference to that Benjamin Franklin of the eighteenth century: thinker and scientist of the Enlightenment, pioneer in the use of electricity, one of the chief authors of the constitution of the United States. As Herzog tells us by such suggestive means, the once great Benjamin Franklin of the eighteenth century is now – more than two centuries later – lost down a tunnel his technology and industry helped usher into being. Furthermore, the dog's owner – old Miss Strehlow – shares her name with the Lutheran missionary Carl Strehlow who worked for many decades at the end of the nineteenth and the start of the twentieth century with the Loritja and Aranda peoples in central Australia. This bastard stray dog born of Enlightenment and Protestantism – those twin pillars of modern European civilization – never returns to the light of day in the film.

A further intertextual reference concludes the film. As Hackett prepares to renounce his employment with the mining company and seek out an alternative life in the desert, a blaring radio beams coverage of the final of the 1978 world cup of soccer from Argentina. Such a device was first used by Fassbinder in *Die Ehe der Maria Braun* as a backdrop to Maria Braun's self-immolation at the end of that film.[14] In *Where the Green Ants Dream* a similarly apocalyptic atmosphere is created: the green RAAF Caribou airplane offered to the Aborigines as a placatory gift by the mining company flies off over the hills with its Aboriginal pilot on board, as if in fulfilment of the mythical prophecy of the green ants. News of the plane's demise in the desert reaches Hackett only moments after a goal is struck in the soccer final, presumably signalling the victory of the Argentinian team. The irony of such a conclusion is clear – this 'victory' of western culture, now exported to the most remote regions of the globe by the technology of the West, is anything but a triumph for the indigenous communities of the Australian outback, and seems part of a wider sacrifice of human-centred values to technological progress under the paradigm of modernity discussed by the film.

Herzog's use of the soccer coverage as a cinematic quotation is part of a general homage to the work of Fassbinder evident in his films. Whereas Herzog is drawn to broad themes that he treats mythically, and, as we have seen, also somewhat polemically, Fassbinder's scope is more circumscribed and at the same time more sociological. This is certainly true of *Angst essen Seele auf* (1974) which is far and away the most searching and profound treatment of the issue of guest-workers in German film. In the film, Ali, a young Moroccan guest-worker, is taken in by an elderly German widow, Emmi, who meets Ali in a pub after sheltering there from rain. This unlikely friendship soon blossoms into a physical and emotional relationship, much to the frustration of Ali's female admirers in the pub, who are drawn to Ali's raw physicality, and very much to the irritation of Emmi's children, who, despite their own cross-cultural background – Emmi's first husband was a Pole – uniformly condemn Emmi's attachment to this "filthy foreigner". In this way, Fassbinder enters the debate about multicultural issues in German society of the early to mid 1970s, and specifically engages with questions of the social integration of guest-workers in a society whose rules of citizenship were (and are still) governed by the principle of racial consanguinity.

As with Herzog's *Where the Green Ants Dream*, a mixture of fiction and close attention to empirical detail is evident in the film. For example, the film ends with a sequence in a local hospital. Ali has succumbed to a stomach ulcer, a typical ailment of foreign guest-workers in Germany. As the doctor explains to Emmi, ulcers reflect the heightened stress levels to which guest-workers find themselves subjected on a daily basis. Instead of undergoing treatment in a health resort to reduce the stress, he points out, the guest-workers choose the far more radical means of a surgical intervention, "but in six months they are back here again".

The film, which on one level is an engaging and unusual love story, is at the same time a forensic reconstruction of the circumstances leading to hospitalisation for the guest-worker. The narrative time of the story is measured against the period of six months it takes for the ulcer to appear and burst, following the doctor's diagnosis and prognosis.

Ali's story – and the wider affliction of which it reports – is brought to light by the amiable, but lonely Emmi. It is this sharp sense of loneliness that leads her to observe the same in Ali, and it soon overcomes her caution about involvement with a younger man. Ali, for his part, is not drawn to Emmi through any sense of opportunism. He does not want for the attention of women his own age, and he cheerfully agrees to marry Emmi when Emmi uses the pretext of impending marriage to keep the landlord at bay. Nevertheless, this love is unable to overcome the obstacles that confront it. Emmi finds herself ridiculed by family members when she declares that she has a boyfriend; later, when she presents Ali to her two sons and daughter and their spouses, their reaction is uncontrolled and even violent – one son kicks in the television set in Emmi's apartment. When news of Emmi's relationship reaches her cleaning lady colleagues, their disgust is made plain at meal breaks when they ensure that Emmi eats on her own. Emmi is only reinstated to the circle after one of their number, Frieda, is summarily fired because of stealing. Among the hierarchy of prejudices that characterises these average Germans, then, a thief is worse than someone who consorts with filthy foreigners (although perhaps not by a great margin).

In Ali's case, reactions to his liaison with Emmi are of two types. Ali's fellow guest-workers are warmly supportive, gladly accepting Emmi's invitation to celebrate news of their wedding in Emmy's apartment. The Germans Ali meets, however, are almost universally condemnatory: Emmi's local grocer refuses to serve Ali a new brand of margarine, ostensibly because Ali fails to make himself understood in German. When Emmi later appears at the vehicle repair place where Ali works, distraught that Ali has not come home the previous night, Ali's colleagues make fun of "die Großmutter aus Marokko" after she leaves. Even the German barmaids who have taken a shine to Ali at the local pub keep up constant background pressure on Ali, eager that he renounce a relationship that they are convinced is sure to "end badly".

A bad end of sorts indeed occurs. Certainly it is bad for Ali, who will make even further demands on the devoted Emmi if he is to return to full health and the semblance of a normal life after his sudden hospitalisation. Furthermore, a note of sober reflection accompanies the end of the film, for hostility toward the foreign guest-worker remains both profound and widespread in the society Fassbinder depicts. The grocer who mends bridges with Emmi after the incident with Ali in his shop, for example, does so to keep a client happy, but not out of any sense of regret about his actions. Similarly, Emmi's son apologises for the television set he has destroyed and offers to buy a new one, but it is really his need for a babysitter that moves him to contrition, rather than any understanding of how he has wronged Emmi or Ali. We sense the persistence of xenophobia in German society and the fact that its root causes remain unchallenged. In 1970s Germany, then, Emmi is the exception that proves the rule of the German loathing of foreigners. Emmi remains – along with the foreigner to whom she is drawn – very much "draußen vor der Tür".[15]

Herzog and Fassbinder's films are thus decidedly morose about the social experiment of multiculturalism. As Fassbinder shows, the guest-worker in Germany inhabits a second society with few points of connection with mainstream culture. Like the Australian Aborigines, he has been systematically excluded from the dominant culture; he has no access to social power. In fact, as Ali says in the opening scene of the film when declining to go off with a girlfriend: "Schwanz kaputt". Marginalisation, therefore, means emasculation. Any adjustment to the presence of foreigners in German society that does occur is entirely pragmatic, and, we assume, short term. There is no sense in the film *Angst essen Seele auf* of a mixing of cultures to promote the goal of social cooperation. In *Where the Green Ants Dream*, the outcome of the encounter between white and black culture is positively apocalyptic. As with the guest-worker in Germany, the economic interests of white society precede any cultural interest in the other, and these remain predominant. In this case, the rule of social exploitation of the other for financial gain appears as the guiding assumption of civilisation in the West since the Enlightenment. The dominance of the extractive economic interest creates a condition of voluntary blindness toward the other that in Herzog's view will surely bring about social ruin. Striking a parallel note of alarm towards the civilisation project in the West, Dürrenmatt observes in the new 1978 version of the short story *Der Tunnel*: "Es hatte sich noch nichts verändert, wie es schien, doch hatte uns in Wahrheit der Schacht nach der Tiefe zu schon aufgenommen".[16]

3.

In the 1990s in Australia, a new direction in the discourse of multiculturalism clearly emerges. In part this is because the legal and political climate itself has changed. In the case of *Mabo v Queensland* brought before the Australian High Court in 1992, old assumptions about native title that had proved an obstacle for the Aboriginal plaintiffs in

Where the Green Ants Dream have been overturned. Whereas Aboriginal communities had been obliged to demonstrate that they were the traditional owners of land to which they laid claim, under the Mabo decision it was the Crown which was now so obliged. This not only reduced the importance of procedural questions about the admissibility of oral evidence. It also ended the old doctrine of *terra nullius*, according to which the territory of Australia had been declared empty of land tenure upon the arrival of white settlers in 1788. This doctrine was now found impossible to support, even, as Henry Reynolds observed, "iniquitous and wrong".[17] In the Mabo judgement, the High Court held that Aborigines maintained native title over their land in spite of the arrival of Europeans. Moreover, in the specific instance of *Mabo v Queensland*, nothing had been done by the Queensland Government to extinguish the traditional ownership of the Murray Islanders of the Torres Strait since the advent of white settlement.

Steve Thomas's early documentaries engaged sympathetically not just with this legal context of long denied Aboriginal claims to native land, but also with the actual social situation of Aboriginal groups and individuals. In *Harold* (1994), Thomas tells the story of an Aboriginal opera singer who went to New York in the 1950s to pursue an operatic singing career. Caught between an indigenous black culture to which he no longer wholly belonged and a white society that he perhaps never wholly wished to become a part of, the life the film posthumously reconstructs ends prematurely. Harold's dream of operatic success is only partly realised. In *Black Man's Houses* (1993) a similar forensic interest in the past is apparent. In this case, the film follows a small group of Aborigines from Flinders Island, who probe the past to answer questions about self and identity, and who, in the process, uncover a history of exploitation and displacement at the hands of white settlers on the island that stretches back to the nineteenth century. In the later documentary *The Hillmen* (1996), Thomas moves from Aboriginal themes to the urban setting of a local soccer club, yet the interest in questions of tradition, integration and individual identity remains undiminished.

These questions impact heavily on the lives of the dozen or more fifteen year-old boys whom the film follows during the course of a full winter season of soccer in Melbourne. These boys mostly come from immigrant families, and most speak a language other than English at home as well as in the school playground. While traditionally Greek in membership, the soccer club depicted in the film has recently decided to throw open its doors to boys from the nearby Housing Commission flats. The film thus describes what results from the bold social experiment that throws together Vietnamese, Greek, Turkish and English children of the first generation in Australia, and where the main, and in some instances, only, thing that unites them is a common love for the game of soccer.

The season begins badly for the boys, and all but two of the first eleven games end in ignominious defeat. The manager of the side, an elderly 'die-hard' soccer fanatic, struggles with the names of the Vietnamese boys. Some of the boys seem more interested in making a show of their performances for their girlfriends on the sideline than in working to establish a team ethic. Alex, the Greek coach of the side, who is more committed to the multicultural experiment lying behind the team than to week-to-week successes, repeatedly draws attention to the importance of team solidarity and the sense of collective injury that each team member should feel when goals are conceded. More than anything else, it is this 'soft' approach to guiding the team and Alex's willing spirit that, from uncertain beginnings, slowly communicates an idea of common destiny to the team, as well as loyalty to that destiny.

Nevertheless, this fledgling sense of common identity is sorely tried. Two new Turkish recruits add skill and strength to the side, but one of them is hotheaded. An incident on the soccer field soon sees him suspended, and when he returns to play a few weeks later, the manager is reluctant to readmit him into the fold. Since the two new Turkish boys will stick together, a minority flank is created in the side. Later, the entire Vietnamese contingent of five or six boys arrives late one day for a game – they have been held up by local police for questioning. This appears heavy-handed, as it seems obvious that the boys are on their way to a soccer game. As one Vietnamese boy explains after the incident, the police do not distinguish between Asians of different backgrounds, "they think everyone looks the same". As attendance at training during the week is poor, and the number who turn up for weekend games on the wane, the entire season – and with it, the social experiment lying behind the team – appears threatened.

It is the incident with the police, however, that proves to be the pivotal moment for the team and indeed of the film. In a decisive show of support for the Vietnamese boys, the coach visits the police station; the police appear to regret their action and now wish to present a trophy at the end-of-season team awards. The mood of the crusty old manager now also lifts; he is shown sparring warm-spiritedly with the Vietnamese boys, with whom he has established a paternal bond. He also relents with the hotheaded Turkish boy, who rejoins the team to play the last game of the season. While defeats are still registered, the team chalks up several notable victories over the second half of the season and finishes the season fourth out of six teams (they had been last at the half way point).

After an unpropitious start for the team, then, the season is turned round and finishes on a positive note. There is warm atmosphere at the presentation of awards; a threshold of sorts is laid for the season to come.

And what can be said of the social experiment that the film describes? While no final conclusions can be drawn, it is clear that the boys get on well with each other and learn more about playing together as the season progresses. Any tensions witnessed occur not within the team, but between the team and their opponents, and, as such, must rather be linked to the competitive ethic that governs sporting competition in general. While the boys rarely move out of their cultural groupings within the team, arriving with their friends and leaving with them, no 'ghettoisation' is evident either. And when John Ho – a youth leader within the Vietnamese community and the team's main goal scorer – responds to a jibe from an opponent before the last game of the season with a jibe in English of his own, we sense that an important milestone has been achieved. Language provides a point of access where social difference is mediated and – for a split second – overcome. No longer merely 'other' to the dominant culture, this Vietnamese boy forges a connection through language with the mainstream, at that moment adding something intangibly real to that majority culture that, only now, we recognise as lacking from the beginning.

Like *The Hillmen*, Buz Luhrmann's *Strictly Ballroom* is set in a competitive sporting environment, but in this case the competitive aspect is not diminished by any benevolent social engineering. Rather, competition is cut-throat and the need to master formal technique paramount: it is every man and woman for themselves. These ballroom dancers aspire to first place not only at the next competition, but ultimately at that pinnacle of dancing excellence, 'the Pan Pacifics' (the Pan Pacific Grand Prix). It is here, indeed, that the film reaches its culmination.

The ballroom dancing milieu, as depicted in the film, is exclusive and predominantly 'waspish' (white Anglo-Saxon Protestant) in nature. It is overseen by Barry Fife, the corrupt President of the Australian Dance Federation, whose favourites invariably carry off the important medals in the major competitive events. Currying favour with Barry, therefore, is an inevitable part of a duo's success. A current favourite is the talented Scott, whose destiny, it appears, is to win gold in the Latin finals of the Pan Pacific Grand Prix. Yet this ambition runs aground when Liz, his partner, deserts him after a competition event – Scott had used unconventional steps and 'crowd pleasing' manoeuvres that had alienated the judges (chief among them, of course, being Barry Fife). When the champion dancer Tina Sparkle becomes available, Scott's fortunes seem unexpectedly restored, yet Scott does not want to abandon his secret ambition to "dance his own steps", that is, to realise his own notion of dancing success. He faces a difficult choice between pursuing success in the expected way, or finding an independent path to his art, and to the singular, passionate life that he senses goes with it.

His ally in this undertaking comes from an unlikely quarter. It is the demure, bespectacled Fran who understands Scott's heart better than he does himself, but who in dancing terms is a beginner. Moreover, she comes from a migrant Spanish family living down by the railway tracks at the poor end of town. She is too low profile to arouse any interest among the Australians, and she is certainly not taken seriously as a dancer. Of course the film is also a love story, and Scott and Fran do eventually fall in love, but the passage to love for both is as thorny and uncertain as the road to master the new steps. Fran repeatedly falls back into self-doubt – after all, she, a beginner, has dared to approach Scott, an open amateur. Scott, for his part, must learn to relinquish a strong mental attachment to his own culture and to allow new rhythms to enter his heart and soul. For this is a journey not just to a new dancing technique, but to a new idea of self, and nothing less than a cross-over into another culture and another life will tutor him in the new way of being he seeks – he must learn, as it were, inside-out, he cannot command the new form from the outside looking in. When the Pan Pacifics finally come round, Scott and Fran plan to dance the *paso doblé* in the new language of expression learnt from Fran's father and grandmother by the railroad tracks.

At the decisive moment, however, Scott's confidence wilts, his partnership with Liz is restored and Fran is consigned back to beginners. Barry Fife urges him to stride the conventional path to dancing success. As the open Latin finals are announced, it is Scott's father, whose story had not been told to its end, who now provides the breakthrough. Finally gaining Scott's attention long enough to explain the consequences of failing to be true to self, he exhorts: "We lived our lives in fear".

In light of this importance of the father, *Strictly Ballroom* has usually been interpreted as being about awakening masculinity. Scott, it is argued, masters the *paso doblé* and learns to become "a kind of bullfighter – proud, forceful, and dominating".[18] Moreover, in the exaltation that accompanies Scott's achievement of his ambition in the final scenes, Doug and Shirley (his domineering wife and former dance partner) dance again, "him leading, as we are told should be the case in ballroom dancing, and therefore in life".[19] David Buchbinder provides a similar reading of the end of the story, noting that Scott and Fran dance the *paso doblé* "as it should be performed", lending "a new phallicism" to a dance culture dominated by the flaccid principles of Barry Fife and the Dance Federation.[20]

Without connection to questions of culture that otherwise clearly animate the film, these insights, however valuable on their own, remain one-sided and partial. For Scott's disempowerment is not ultimately to be read sexually, but culturally. The film asserts the desirability of cultural inclusiveness as a way to achieve the social goal of individual and collective success. The instruction that Scott must undergo to realise his dream of artistic independence comes not only from the poor end of town, but also from the rich end of a culture that mainstream Australian society downgrades or forgets entirely. Moreover, Fran – the beginner who dares to approach an open amateur – asserts the role of woman in a powerful way, and it is Fran's grandmother as much as Rico, her father, who instructs Scott in the new way to sense life's rhythms.

More than anything else, the film highlights aspects of a debate now encountered in recent theorising about multiculturalism. As Scott's dance teacher opines, the old steps have been passed down from one generation to the next; they cannot suddenly count for nothing. Yet Scott declares himself "bored" with them. They no longer speak to the new reality he senses and ultimately embraces. This is the reality of a world in which minority cultures are found in profusion in new societies, such as Australia and Canada, as well as in older ones. These minority cultures follow traditions that enrich mainstream, adding a stock of directly lived experience that would otherwise be missing. Moreover, as *Strictly Ballroom* illustrates on a technical level, dance should not be about the slavish imitation of form without reversion to the content that enlivens and precedes it. The *paso doblé*, in that case, would simply be laughable – a trivialisation of cultural expression, an impoverishment of life itself. Above all, it is the trivialisation and impoverishment of cultural life that constitutes the true flaccidity of the mainstream.

The multiculturalism portrayed both in Luhrmann's *Strictly Ballroom* and in Thomas's *The Hillmen* therefore represents a debate between competing traditions – the old steps of mainstream culture, and the new (old) steps of minority culture. The hope that the experiment of multiculturalism appears to hold is witnessed at the end of *Strictly Ballroom*, where beginners and open amateurs, and everyone from six years of age to sixty, all take to the dance-floor. Admittedly, this is not the vision of 'culture and equality', that is, culture informed and led by the mainstream, that the political scientist Brian Barry has in mind. In the film, the custodian of the dominant culture, Barry Fife, has been knocked from his chair, and the Federation, accordingly, now loses control of proceedings. Yet the film casts forward, however fleetingly, even beyond this moment of dethronement of dominant culture. As the camera prepares to sweep to the dance-floor in a closing pan, Barry Fife is shown not so much defeated as overwhelmed. In the new celebration of culture and difference at the end, we sense, there is a place for him as well.

The price for countenancing this new cross-cultural reality is perhaps not any diminution or watering down of the mainstream so much as its greater complexity. Societies that choose to go down this path of cultural inclusiveness make demands on the imagination of individual citizens and social institutions. As multiculturalism cuts against other questions such as globalisation and postcolonialism in these societies, nations can take on a "haunted" appearance as they enter debates as protracted and perhaps unsolvable as "who owns modernity[?]"[21] While film must on some level fall short of representing these debates in any comprehensive sense, it does engage with the individual imagination in ways not possible in political debate. Both Thomas and Luhrmann in their films, for example, portray the subtle changes that serve as points of access to the mainstream – the Greek coach's appearance at the local police station in *The Hillmen*, for example, or the beginner's challenge to the open amateur in *Strictly Ballroom*. Herzog and Fassbinder, equally, are eloquent in the portrayal of the cultural perspective of minorities, and resolute in mounting arguments that call for new complexity to be admitted into the mainstream. Moreover, there can be no final certainty that the paradigm of modernity on which mainstream culture in western society has been premissed has been an unambiguously good thing. Perhaps, as Herzog argues, it is now to possible to envisage positions that will transform it.

Notes

1. See, for example, The Australian Law Reform Commission 1992.
2. E.g. Alberta Task Force 1991.
3. Cf. Gibbon 2000, 64.
4. Barry 2001.
5. For an overview, see Haddock and Sutch 2003.
6. This swapping of positions has made of former adversaries strange bedfellows. Liberal rationalists, for example, now find themselves allied with political positions from the far right that have also mounted opposition to romantic multiculturalism. Thus one can observe a curious alliance between adherents to the old Enlightenment, such as Brian Barry in Britain, and reactionary opponents of multiculturalism such as Pauline Hanson in Australia.
7. Jaworski and Coupland 1999, 9.
8. Fowler 1981, 25. See also Jaworski and Coupland 1999, 33.
9. Cheesman 1997, 288.

10. According to a judgement of the 1972 Supreme Court of the Northern Territory, unless Aboriginal people could demonstrate that they had been granted land by the Crown, they had no rights to the ownership of land. The Land Rights Act of 1976 in the Northern Territory restated this position. For a discussion, see Reynolds 2003.
11. The myth of the green ants, however, is a controversial contrivance of the director.
12. In the short story, the two main characters (the student and the train conductor) move forward down the train to the engine, which plunges ever faster to its doom.
13. Dürrenmatt 1991, 229.
14. The soccer game, in this case, is the 1954 world cup final in which Germany defeated Hungary in Switzerland and thereby symbolically reestablished its position among European nations for the first time since the end of the Second World War.
15. This is a reference to Wolfgang Borchert's 1947 play *Draußen vor der Tür*. It is referred to obliquely in the film when Emmi visits her daughter Krista in order to reveal her relationship with Ali. When Emmi rings the doorbell, Krista asks, somewhat unidiomatically, who that might be ringing the doorbell "draußen vor der Tür".
16. Dürrenmatt 1991, 229.
17. Reynolds 2003.
18. Butterss 2001, 82.
19. Ibid, 2001, 83.
20. Buchbinder 1998, 62.
21. Gunew 2004, 39.

References

Alberta Task Force. *The Main Report*. 1991.
Barry, Brian. *Culture and Equality: An Egalitarian Critique of Multiculturalism*. Cambridge, Mass.: Harvard University Press, 2001
Buchbinder, David. *Performance Anxieties: Re-Producing Masculinity*. St Leonards, NSW: Allen & Unwin, 1998.
Butterss, Philip. "Becoming a Man in Australian Film in the Early 1990s: *The Big Steal*, *Death in Brunswick*, *Strictly Ballroom* and *The Heartbreak Kid*." In *Australian Cinema in the 1990s*, edited by Ian Craven, 79-94. London: Frank Cass, 2001.
Cheesman, Tom. "Apocalypse Nein Danke: The Fall of Werner Herzog." In *Green Thought in German Culture: Historical and Contemporary Perspectives*, edited by Colin Riordan, 285-306. Cardiff: University of

Wales Press, 1997.
Dürrenmatt, Friedrich. *Gesammelte Werke in sieben Bänden. Bd. 5 Erzählungen*. Zürich: Diogenes Verlag, 1991.
Fowler, Roger. *Literature as Social Discourse: The Practice of Linguistic Criticism*. London: Batsford Academic, 1981.
Gibbon, Edward. *The History of the Decline and Fall of the Roman Empire* (abridged version). London: Penguin Books, 2000.
Gunew, Sneja. *Haunted Nations: The Colonial Dimensions of Multiculturalism*. London and New York: Routledge, 2004.
Haddock, Bruce and Peter Sutch. *Multiculturalism, Identity and Rights*. London: Routledge, 2003.
Jaworski, Adam and Nikolas Coupland. *The Discourse Reader*. London: Routledge, 1999.
Reynolds, Henry. *"The Mabo Judgement – Its Implications."*
<www.caa.org.au/publications/reports/MABO/implications.html> (2003).
The Australian Law Reform Commission: *Multiculturalism and the Law*. Report No. 57, 1992.

"We will decide who comes to this country": Inclusion, Exclusion and the National Imaginary

Fiona Allon

The last thirty to forty years have seen unprecedented levels of global change associated primarily with migration and the movements of people. These changes have not only dramatically reconfigured the relations between nation-states, leading to an increasingly transnational system of interconnection and exchange, but have also radically transformed the societies within their borders. Although immigration has a long history in most Western countries, the pressures caused by these more recent social and cultural processes of globalisation have led to intense debates around questions of culture, identity and citizenship. In a globalised world, national identity becomes a particularly difficult terrain, a site of tension upon which nations, predicated historically as politically sovereign and culturally homogenous, must now negotiate new realities as culturally heterogeneous multicultural states.[1]

In Europe, for example, the last ten to fifteen years have seen a range of mixed responses to the increasing numbers of non-Europeans living there: from an implicit expectation of assimilation to extreme and xenophobic rejection and, more recently, a recognition of the *de facto* multicultural makeup of most European countries. This is the position in which Germany currently finds itself. Australia, by contrast, is one of the few countries in the world to declare itself officially multicultural. An official government policy of multiculturalism, however, is not without its own problems. Recent challenges, including the present government's withdrawal of support for an explicitly multicultural stance, and populist political movements such as One Nation rallying against cosmopolitan elites, have led to a period of sustained critique of multiculturalism in Australia. This reassessment has also occurred alongside the emergence not only of anit-immigration agendas race, but of race and ethnicity as key terms in contemporary political debates more generally.

The question of how exactly to engage with cultural difference and diversity is one, therefore, which most Western nation-states are still grappling with. It is a question that assumes some urgency in an era of globalisation, where the form of the nation-state and the national identity and culture that has usually represented it, are radically redefined and reconfigured. Until fairly recently, the fundamental principle for political identification in Western societies has been through national identities, through citizenship of the nation-state. Yet this allegiance is now being increasingly undermined, and we are seeing the emergence of new conceptions of citizenship and new forms of belonging, expressed as affinities rather than affiliations, and frequently across a range of scales that only sometimes, and sometimes never, includes the national. The geographical dynamics of contemporary patterns of spatial restructuring, in particular the rise of transnational communication networks that often completely bypass the framework of the nation, also play a significant role in these transformations. It is commonly held that the modern nation-state is characterised by three distinct elements: territory, people, and sovereignty. Yet globalisation creates disjunctures between precisely these three dimensions. As Appadurai argues "the isomorphism of people, territory, and legitimate sovereignty that constitutes the normative character of the modern nation-state is under threat from the forms of circulation of people characteristic of the contemporary world."[2] Diasporas, transnational cultures, refugee and migrant communities that both exist within the boundary of a country and frequently cut across its borders challenge the traditional form of the nation-state. But they also complicate traditional categories of identity and difference, belonging and citizenship, leading to strong debates over how these should be conceptualised and understood, especially within national spaces fractured by discontinuities between community, culture and language.

Multiculturalism – a policy to manage cultural diversity within pluralist societies – has been the political response most Western liberal states have adopted, or at least considered adopting, as a way of negotiating this situation. Put simply, multiculturalism is premised on what Charles Taylor has called a "politics of recognition".[3] It is an official and formal recognition of the co-presence of multiple cultures within the space of the nation-state. Multiculturalism has become extremely popular over recent decades, providing liberal pluralist democracies with the means of managing the increasing cultural diversity within their borders. Yet the *management* of diversity offered by multiculturalism is also where one finds its discursive limit, and its limitations as a way of actually *living with difference*. As Homi Bhabha suggests, multiculturalist discourse works simultaneously as "a creation of cultural diversity and a containment of cultural difference". The discourse of multiculturalism, therefore acts as if it simply "resolves the tension between two cultures ... in a dialectical play of 'recognition'".[4]

The crisis of multiculturalism in Australia, a country that was once referred to as a multicultural nation in Asia, illustrates clearly the limitations of multiculturalism as a policy of simultaneous celebration and containment.[5] Meanwhile, recent debates about multiculturalism in European countries like Germany, where the term itself is also strongly contested, provide an opportunity to consider the complexities of framing national identity within the context of globalisation and increasing cultural diversity during a similar process of transition.

Guided by these themes of culture, language and representation, this chapter will explore discourses of inclusion and exclusion in contemporary political debates in Germany and Australia. Both countries are struggling to find new national cultures that negotiate the desire for a common culture, a desire that over recent years has been frequently expressed by multiple groups within both countries, at exactly the same time as global forces unsettle and disrupt all claims for commonality and sameness. Through reference to different framings of multiculturalism, the chapter will focus on the way in which imagese and symbols of national identity have been deployed as practices of identity-formation and exclusion. The chapter will also explore other strategies of representation circulating within the national imaginary. It will consider whether alternative conceptions of community, belonging and citizenship can actually overcome the limitations of bith the nation-state form – a form that inevitably leads to systems of exclusion, not only between majorities and minorities, but also between populations considered national and those considered foreign – and discourses of multiculturalism.

1. National narrations

National identities, in a similar manner to all collective cultural identities, must be maintained through a complex mapping of territories, frontiers and borders, and through principles of inclusion and exclusion that define us against them. Constructions of national identity, however, are also always played out over a symbolic field involving language and imagery. Different versions of national identity are continually promoted and contested, and it is through this process that a nation develops and projects a certain image or representation of itself. Nationhood, like national identity, is therefore not given; rather it is something that must be realised. This process is, necessarily, a continuous one involving perpetual contestation. Definitions of national identity, therefore, always involve the construction of an imaginary homogeneity of culture apparently shared by all belonging to the national community. This process inevitably involves mechanisms of inclusion and exclusion whereby one definition of the nation is privileged, while others are marginalised. National identity is then a question of the kinds of stories societies use to make sense of both the past and the future as a way of constructing identities in the present. The nation is always narrated, in other words. It is sustained through the kinds of stories and narratives it tells of itself.

Contemporary public and political debates are versions of these kinds of stories and narratives, and are fundamentally important to the ways in which national identities are constructed and contested. These debates serve to establish the symbolism and iconography of nationhood, as well as the range of meanings and interpretations that coalesce around ideas of national identity at any particular time. The symbolic order of national culture and identity has a profound affect, therefore, on how these categories are materially experienced, and the kinds of material effects that flow on from the acceptance and legitimation of certain representations. Within the stories, narratives and invented traditions that provide the foundations of national identity, the symbolic and the material are irreducibly interrelated.[6] Invention, however, should not be understood as fabrication and falsity, but rather, as Benedict Anderson suggests, as imagining and creation. Communities are to be understood and analysed, he adds, not by their falsity/genuineness, but by the style in which they are imagined.[7] The point then is not which versions get it wrong and which get it right, but how they actually work and who is actually mobilising them, and what this achieves. As Richard White has also argued, "When we look at ideas about national identity, we need to ask, not whether they are true or false, but what their function is, whose creation they are, and whose interests they serve".[8]

Another way to approach these stories, narratives and debates about identity is to see them as discourses. In this sense, discourses produce or construct the national culture; the nation is then an effect of these various discourses. So, rather than the nation as the origin of these various cultural technologies, it is apparatuses of discourse in fact which actually work to produce what is generally recognised and experienced as the national. The sense of nationness and the national culture produced, however, is not unitary or unified, nor does it have a single identity. It is, potentially, comprised of a multitude of different narrations and stories. But the requirements of collective identity always call for some degree of closure, and the fixing of a fictional unity. This is what Etienne Balibar calls the "fictive ethnicity" or "fictive identity" that is an essential feature of national consciousness. As Balibar notes, this fictive ethnicity must be "produced in such a way that it does not appear as fiction", but rather "as the most natural" of processes.[9]

The concept of discourse is, therefore, very useful, emphasising the constructive and productive elements of the interaction of material conditions with knowledge, politics and society. The notion of discourse also provides an analytical construct for looking at the contested nature of power relationships among groups in society. As Foucault explains:

> In a society such as ours, but basically in any society, there are manifold relations of power which permeate,

characterise, and constitute the social body, and these relations of power cannot themselves be established, consolidated nor implemented without the production, accumulation, circulation and functioning of a discourse. There can be no possible exercise of power without a certain economy of discourses of truth which operated through and on the basis of this association.[10]

Discourses, in this sense, are not only the sites where objects of knowledge are constructed but also sites governing the production of truth, that is, the systems of thought which circulate as common sense, as natural and obvious. Foucault's own work highlights the multiplicity of discourses that continually overlap with each other and compete for dominance. A discourse however cannot be reduced to a system of representation or a language. Although discourses engage and use linguistic and symbolic forms, they have material effects and are enacted through the micropolitical struggles taking place in material conditions. A discourse then, combines language and metaphors, practices and technologies, and as a result they actually *produce* power and knowledge, individual behaviour and institutional authority.

Once the nation is posed in terms of discourse, the distinction between politics and poetics, material and symbolic, is effectively elided. The notion of discourse provides an analytical construct that enables us to link the politics of material change and the realities of social power with the politics of representation, seeing both as the mutually interrelated and connected elements of the politics of culture. It is this interplay that is most relevant here.

2. Australian Psycho-Geography

Australia is predominantly an immigrant country and settler society, a result of European colonial expansion, produced from successive waves of migration and settlement. An island-continent, Australia is also the most recent European settler colony, and this intersection of geography and history has had a profound effect on how conceptions of national culture and identity have developed and been played out. The history of Australia's development as a modern nation-state is inseparable from its status as a European settler society geographically located in south-eastern Asia. This distinctive psycho-geography has greatly influenced the ways in which Australia has constructed its identity: the unique situation of being a far-flung outpost of Europe on the edge of Asia has given rise to a particular antipodean sense of place and self. The idea of Australia as specifically an island-continent, as a separate and distinct white European settlement in a non-European arena of the globe, has also meant that natural borders have easily mapped onto, and thus worked to legitimate, the boundaries of the nation-state. To use Balibar's terms, the external borders of the state had to become internal borders, producing together "a projection and protection of an internal collective' that enabled the fledgling Australian nation, as a people, 'to inhabit the space of the state".[11]

But more than this, Australia's psycho-geography has especially influenced the ways in which Australians see their geopolitical position in relation to the rest of the world. It is, I would suggest, responsible in particular for the fears of invasion that have always played a role during its relatively short history. The relative geographical isolation of the country has also led to the idea that it was "possible to control contact with the rest of the world in a manner not possible for most other nations".[12] Both Australia's sense of itself and its place in the world have, in other words, been shaped by this fundamental tension between its white, European identity and its Asian, non-European geographic location. The effect of this psycho-geography, especially the sense of vulnerability accompanied by the fear or threat of invasion, by non-European neighbours, an 'invasion anxiety', is still being felt today. As Ien Ang puts it, a racial anxiety, one that has tended to focus intensely on imagining Asia as the primary threat or invader, has always been and continues to be articulated with a distinctively Australian, equally formative spatial anxiety.[13]

Although geographically Australia was on the other side of the world, it was impossible for this land to exist outside of the principles of European modernity, even if it was a space outside of Europe. First as a colony, and later as an independent nation-state, Australia was positioned firmly within the framework of European imperialism and thereby reproduced these values and these ideologies: namely, the universalisation of the nation-state as the most desirable form of political community. This is, of course, the political form whose unity can only ever be predicated on the imposed assimilation, containment, even eradication, of difference, of minorities, migrants and foreigners. It is a form realised through an imagined community, a community that must be maintained through the performative work of nation-building, through constantly-rehearsed anxieties of national identity, and also through the constant policing of borders.

Although clearly an export of the universalising projects of European modernity and colonial expansion, the settler colony also simultaneously established an identity for itself as a new society, a land of opportunity far removed from the strictures of tradition and constraint found in the old world. It was seen as literally a place in the sun, where a new civilisation could be developed. But it was also imagined as racially pure, a bastion of British-derived cultural homogeneity that had to be protected and regulated in order to be maintained. The Immigration Restriction Bill, introduced in 1901, and also known as the White Australia Policy, was the first piece of legislation passed by the newly-federated Commonwealth of Australia, and one of the first steps taken to ensure the exclusion of racially and ethnically different people. The bill prohibited non-Europeans and the 'coloured races' from entering the country, and was seen as an important measure in asserting the sovereignty of the new Australian state. It was in this sense a nationalist policy bound to the desire to establish a distinctive and modern national identity, and is in many ways the basis of the provincial, anti-internationalist, protectionist agenda that has played such a foundational role in Australian economic and cultural history. It is also, I would argue, a key effect of the many contradictions that lie at the heart of Australian nation-building: the need to maintain racial purity and British-heritage, while at the same time asserting a specific and separate new national identity. By repressing the racial difference of the indigenous owners, and by extending the exclusion of difference through the White Australia policy, the new nation grounded cultural homogeneity in racial homogeneity and thereby enunciated a national identity that was wholly racialised. [14]

Narratives of national culture are a salient site for working through exactly these kinds of contradictions and ambivalences that will consequently adhere to any proposed model of nationhood or nationness. Yet unlike more conventional forms of European nation-building and nationalism, Australian national identity has had to negotiate a difficult path through these two related yet opposing demands: enunciating difference – from the British Empire and more generally the Western world (Australia has always had a strong, though unrealised, republican tradition) – while simultaneously claiming sameness, unity and commonality (through an assimilation policy which stressed not only white identity but also European identity). This in turn entailed a further displacement of identity, as Aborigines were constructed and excluded as Other to a supposedly civilised, benign Europeaness. White Australia carries with it this heritage of double displacement: a history of displaced Europeans who are neither wholly displaced nor wholly European, struggling to achieve settlement in an inhospitable land in the Antipodes by various means including the violent displacement and dispossession of others.

Over the last twenty five years a monocultural national identity based on a unitary model of culture and tradition fixed, however tenuously, in myths of place (White Australia) has been replaced by a recognition of cultural diversity and an official policy of multiculturalism (Multicultural Australia).[15] Multiculturalism in Australia is a government policy directed towards the inclusion of ethnic minorities within the national culture. Underpinned by the central tenet of cultural maintenance, it emphasises the acceptance of diverse ethnic groups and the rights of those groups to maintain their cultural identities and lifestyles. It was also championed as a radical break with the exclusionary project of assimilation and monoculturalism, and the adoption instead of an inclusionary politics that recognises the distinct cultures and identities of ethnic communities within the boundaries of the nation. A symbolic politics aimed at redefining national identity, multiculturalism in Australia has been predicated on an image of harmonious cultural diversity. However, it is also worth remembering that the experience of multiculturalism as an official policy of managing cultural difference, has, almost since the time of its inception, been criticised as simply the dominant culture's strategic deployment of a liberal pluralist discourse of tolerance.[16]

The translation of the fear of cultural difference into governmental policy has therefore a long history in Australia. Arguably, the first move away from institutionalised xenophobia came in 1966 with the abandonment of the White Australia policy. The removal of this racially discriminatory law was inevitable after the large-scale immigration program of the 1940s, 50s and 60s, introduced to meet labour shortages and develop national infrastructure. From the mid-1970s such changes accelerated, reaching a peak with Paul Keating's Labor government in the early 1990s. Intensely internationalist in outlook, Keating pursued a vision of Australia as a 'post-modern republic', a political entity that negotiated local diversity, pluralistic citizenship and the realities of global connectedness. Keating claimed such policies as necessities – as the inevitable product of the new cultural and political landscapes produced by economic internationalisation, globalisation and new communications technologies.

The election of the conservative government of John Howard in 1996 brought about a reassessment of these policies. Confronted by the proliferation of cultural difference at home, and by the continued fragmentation of the polity through so-called identity politics, and faced with the spectre of an Australia increasingly integrated with the Asia-Pacific region Howard sought to construct instead a defensive and exclusive definition of Australianness. It is a definition explicit in its rejection of cultural difference. As Howard observed: "I want people to feel comfortable and relaxed about their identity as Australians ... I think we should be more relaxed about who we are. We've spent too much time navel-gazing and worrying about our identity."[17] Howard's successes over the past ten years, and his subsequent election victories in 1998, 2001 and 2004, are indicative of the effective spread of this rhetorical realm of comfort and relaxation, of sameness and familiarity, even as Australian society as a whole has suffered increasing levels of dislocation and inequality. The reasons for Howard's success are complex, but one crucial issue has been his effective mobilisation of ethnicity and race as terms of political debate, and his obvious distance from policies of multiculturalism.

Although Howard has stated his "absolute, unqualified embrace of a culturally diverse, harmonious and tolerant Australian community", he has consistently refused to use the term multiculturalism in relation to his political outlook. Actions speak louder than words, and Howard's intent has never been unclear: when he became Prime Minister, his government abolished the Office of Multicultural Affairs and the Bureau of Immigration, Multicultural and Population Research. It reduced health, job training, employment, and language services to immigrants in general, and restricted access for new immigrants to a range of crucial welfare benefits. A government-commissioned report *Multicultural Australia: the Way Forward*, gave legitimacy to Howard's own long-standing ambivalence about multiculturalism, when it asked "Is multiculturalism an appropriate term to describe a policy for managing cultural diversity or has it outlived its usefulness?"[18]

In the face of what he called multiculturalism's encouragemt of "minority fundamentalism", "special interest groups", and "hyphenated identities",[19] Howard asserted the "sentiments of mainstream Australia". In the 1996 election, the Liberal Party's campaign slogan was 'For all of Us', a statement articulating in no uncertain terms an appeal to those disenfranchised groups who felt excluded from a vision of Australia as a cosmopolitan, multicultural utopia embracing international interconnectedness and ever greater degrees of economic globalisation. It is important to note here that at this time, immigration, multiculturalism and globalisation were concepts that were often collapsed together, especially within the populist-nationalist discourse used by both Howard and One Nation, each becoming a shorthand for the other, and together suggesting an image of Australia as divided, as insecure and vulnerable, and as threatened by exposure to outside forces which it was powerless to control or contain.

In 2001 the international context again played a crucial role in Australian politics, helping to bring about another election victory for

Howard and the Liberal Party. The so-called '*Tampa* crisis' in August of that year, when 438 asylum seekers rescued from a sinking ship were refused entry to Australia, brought to a head the long-standing fears about invasion by non-Europeans, though this time they were focused on refugees arriving by boats. Boat people, mainly Vietnamese, had first started arriving on Australian shores in the 1970s. The attitude towards these 'uninvited' refugees was essentially the same as to the Chinese and other 'coloured races' before Federation, and marginally less hostile than that displayed toward the Afghans who would arrive in the late 1990s: they were not welcome. As one former diplomat stated: "They simply turned up, uninvited, asking for refuge." In words echoing older, foundational, spatial anxieties, he continued "For Australia, history and geography had merged, causing a shiver of apprehension".[20]

It was of course much more than a shiver of apprehension, however, that greeted the asylum seekers who had been rescued by the *Tampa*. Like the other boat people who had arrived in the preceding few years, they were branded 'queue jumpers' and 'illegals'. For the Howard Government, the most important questions raised by these boats arriving in Australian waters were not about the status of refugees and the processes of asylum seeking, but about threats to security and sovereignty. As then Minister for Immigration Phillip Ruddock put it, the Government was determined to "safeguard the integrity of our immigration program", just as much as it was determined to "safeguard the integrity of the nation's borders"[21]. The Government's response to 'illegal immigrants' was extremely popular: for example, a poll in 1998 showed that the average Australian overestimated by 70 times the number of boat people arriving each year. The events of September 11, occurring less than a month after the Tampa events, intensified these fears of invasion even further, with the added dimension that these Afghani (mainly Muslim) asylum seekers were now seen as potential terrorists.

Howard fully exploited the timing of the two events, bringing both together under the rubric of national security. The *Tampa* also provided him with a key statement for the November election campaign: "We will decide who comes to this country and the circumstances in which they come".[22] This message was played and replayed again and again on television and radio, it appeared as full-page advertisements in newspapers, on large posters distributed from one end of Australia to the other, and on handbills dropped into letter boxes across the nation. On the day of the election, the words WE DECIDE covered polling booths in electorates all over the country. Accused of playing the 'race card', and with attention focusing on the ways in which 'race' was being exploited in the campaign, Howard responded by saying that it was simply "a question of protecting our borders", and that accusations of racial prejudice were a "self-flagellation of the Australian spirit".[23]

3. **Germany: From Integration to Multi-Kulti**

In Germany, by contrast, immigration has never really been considered as a constitutive or important feature of national identity. Although, as in Australia, immigration has been essential to nation-building and economic prosperity, at the symbolic level of the national imaginary, migrants and national identity have tended to be seen as mutually exclusive. The different lifestyles and languages that migrants and so-called 'guest workers' have brought with them over the years have generally been viewed as the somewhat unfortunate consequences of large-scale immigration, and as practices that exist outside or at least on the margins of the dominant, mainstream culture. It was always expected that if these groups were to settle permanently they would have to integrate into German society and adopt 'German values'. So, despite having had some of the largest immigration programs and policies in the world (over 20 million people have entered the country since 1945), and a relatively open and generous refugee policy, Germany has never regarded itself as a 'country of immigration'.[24] This belief finds expression in the oft-repeated mantra "Germany is not an immigration society", a phrase that has featured regularly in recent debates over citizenship laws and immigration policies. In the run-up to the 2002 election, in which the issues of immigration and the 'integration of foreigners' played a central role in the campaigns of most political parties, the mantra surfaced again, associated in particular with the Presidential candidate and Premier of Bavaria, Edmund Stoiber.[25] The conservative Stoiber's political agenda included opposition to the new naturalisation and citizenship laws, a commitment to restrict immigration, and opposition to Turkey's admission to the EU on the grounds that it is non-Christian country. In an article "Deutsche Identität statt Multi-Kulti" (German Identity against Multiculturalism), Stoiber reiterated his well-known position:

> Deutschland ist kein Einwanderungsland. Klares Nein doppelten Staatsangehörigkeit. Wer die Grenzen der Integrationsfähigkeit der deutschen Gesellschaft überschreitet, derfördert damit (faktisch, wenn auch meist ungewollt) ausländerfeindlische Tendenzen.[26]

> Germany is not a country of immigration. A clear No to dual citizenship. Whoever crosses and therefore goes beyond the borders of Germany's ability to be an

integrated society, actually creates (even though often unintentionally), the xenophogic problems of today.

In the context of such assertions, it is therefore no surprise that multiculturalism as a concept has historically been regarded with at least deep ambivalence, if not outright censure. One of the most persistent critiques of multiculturalism to emerge in the debates on cultural diversity is that it leads to 'parallel societies' and 'ghettoes'. Politicians such as Stoiber refer to the threats to Germany's national unity posed by 'parallel societies' in which migrants maintain their own communities and culture. The concern articulated here is that integration has been unsuccessful and that social cohesion in general is somehow in jeapordy. As one article, "Integration: Ghetto im Kopf" from the newspaper *Die Zeit* put it "Integration? ... all in all that seems to have failed. During the past four decades, a "parallel society" seems to have established where Turks stay Turks and the Germans stay Germans".[27]

Similar themes emerged in the debates over the idea of 'Leitkultur'. The debates were triggered by comments made by several politicians from the CDU/CSU parties suggesting that, in essence, immigration would only be successful if migrants adapted to and followed the German 'Leitkultur'. Made in the context of ongoing debates over the Government's planned changes to immigration laws, the comments sparked a controversial discussion not only about the obligations of migrants to integrate and adapt, but about what German 'Leitkultur' (leading, or hegemonic, culture) might actually mean. While some commentators suggested that any definition of the new German Leitkultur most certainly had to incorporate such things as the "Love Parade", "Big Brother" and a "good Techno beat",[28] other supporters of the term mentioned the more traditional identity foundations of German law and language. For the CDU/CSU, though, speaking German and obeying laws do not automatically qualify immigrants' admission into society; rather, they have to show a willingness to adopt what the party platform defines as 'Western-European values':

> Integration means more than being able to speak German and recognize our legal system. It also includes acceptance of the norms and customs that the native population feels obliged to obey. This means accepting the system of values of our Western, Christian culture, which has been influenced by Christianity, ancient philosophy, humanism, Roman law, and the Enlightenment.[29]

In a similar manner to the term 'un-Australian', the distinguishing thing about the concept 'Leitkultur' is its semantic emptiness.[30] But in many ways this is precisely the point: the meaning of such terms is always vague and unclear. In fact, both terms actually say more about the people employing them, and about the amount of social power they wield, than about what they attempt to describe or delimit. Users of such terms position themselves as having a privileged relationship to the discourses on national identity, and therefore to national space.

What these debates over integration, 'parallel societies' and 'Leitkultur' demonstrate, then, are struggles over spatial/national belonging. As Hage argues, such debates are practices of 'spatial management', and are nearly always concerned with the policing of national space as the imagined space of the nation. They function, therefore, as practices of nationalist exclusion, establishing both the legitimate and illegitimate occupiers of national space, and reinforcing the privileged relation between the imagined national 'race' and 'culture' and the national space it claims and defines as its own.[31]

A similar dynamic underpins the calls for integration. With every demand for integration, the idea of an internally cohesive national community is reasserted and reinforced. The national space is automatically conceptualised as a homogenous community, into which the immigrant has to be 'integrated'. In this way, the concepts of nation and national space result not only in the racial and cultural stigmatisation of the foreign and heterogeneous, but are also used pragmatically to deny immigrants the right of full political participation and citizenship. Yet the contemporary reality is in fact unprecedented heterogeneity – ethnically, religiously, culturally, linguistically – throughout German national space. With flexible borders and markets, and increasingly mobile populations, we now live in a world where all traces of homogeneity seem to be disappearing. These changes have transformed Europe from a continent of emigration into a continent of immigration. Many of the groups who existed historically as the Others against which Europe defined itself and who were previously racialised outside Europe, are now literally in Europe. For Germany, the least homogenous country in Europe, mobile, deterritorialised groups such as immigrants, asylum seekers and refugees are not only challenging what it means to be German, but what it means to be a citizen in an increasingly multicultural and diverse world.

The result is a considerable disjuncture between different imaginaries of citizenship: a 'flexible' or 'transnational' citizenship configured by the spatial transformations of global capitalism must compete with the highly restrictive form of citizenship tied to the territorially bounded nation-state.[32] Today, though, every nation-state is forced in some way, through the continuing pressures of globalisation, to confront the exclusions underpinning racial ideology and the fantasy of an ethnically pure national identity.

4. Familie Deutschland

In Germany over the last few years, and especially since the 1998 election of the Social Democrat-Green coalition, there has been a growing acknowledgement of the undeniably multicultural make-up of German society, and a corresponding recognition of the need to reform discriminatory immigration and naturalisation legislation. These changes were seen as essential in order to encourage the extension of citizenship – and the full and active participation in democratic life that this implies – to immigrants and ethnic minorities. The key issue however, is how could immigrants become citizens when Germany's historical model of national identity and nationality is based on a unity of culture and place and descent by blood?

In response to the resurgence of racist nationalism and the marginalisation of foreign residents, particularly immigrants and refugees, that accompanied German unification, a number of public education campaigns appeared which sought to normalise or mainstream the issue of cultural diversity. These campaigns were premised on the understanding that the project of integration and assimilation had failed and that multiculturalism – the acceptance of cultural difference – was the best option for a liberal, pluralist democracy situated at the centre of 'the new Europe'. I would like now to take a detailed look at one of these campaigns.

Familie Deutschland was a campaign established by the Federal government to showcase its family policy and programs.[33] The slogan attached to the campaign reads "Mehr Chancen, mehr Rechte, mehr Sicherheit" (More opportunities, more rights, more security). The campaign includes a series of photographs of 'real German families' taken by the photographer Herlinde Koelbl. One image that particularly interests me in this context shows a mixed race family of two adults and a child. The woman in the plate – blonde-haired and 'white' – stands alongside her 'black' partner, a man recognisably of African ethnicity. Their daughter stands behind them, arms outstretched, as though both proudly and defiantly introducing and announcing her family. The message behind the image is clear: this is a typical German family, and also (by way of the family as a metaphor for the nation-state), this is the future of Germany, as a kind of family. The power of this image resides in the fact that this is a family, that there is a relationship, a blood connection, between mother, father and child. The image would have an altogether different meaning if, as in a Benetton ad, these were three autonomous individuals from different cultural backgrounds, coming together spontaneously in the 'united colours of cultural diversity'. This Benetton-inspired imagery is all too frequently used in official promotions of multiculturalism as simply a celebration of cultural diversity and as the achievement of unity-in-diversity. By presenting a family as the site of irreducible cultural difference, the campaign directly addresses the intensely charged concepts of race and sexuality, culture and nation, as well as racist notions of miscegenation and racial impurity.

Yet by using the trope of the family, and a particular kind of family at that, this image also unconsciously references and reproduces the long-standing connection between heterosexuality and nationalism, whereby the implicit gender hierarchy of the heterosexual family is constructed as integral not only for the reproduction of a certain form of society but also for the reproduction of the form of the nation.[34] This connection between the heterosexual family unit and nationalism has figured throughout modern German history, finding its most extreme expression in the idealisation of the family within National Socialism, where it was positioned as the foundation of German racial purity and, together with the female body, became the site that was seen as crucial to the reproduction of the 'pure' German race and nation. The image, either self-consciously or inadvertently, speaks to this history.

But the image is confronting not only for directly invoking the categories of sexuality and race, but because it engages directly with traditional conceptions of identity and 'Germanness'. The 1913 law on citizenship, which remained unchanged until 1999, enshrined a conception of national identity that was based on blood, descent and common culture, as expressed by the Latin term ius sanguinis: literally 'power/law of blood'. This blood principle of citizenship has meant that German nationality is only available to those interrelated by blood; immigrants born in Germany do not, unlike in Australia, automatically acquire citizenship status. Determined by the principle of descent rather than, as in Australia, the principle of territory, this conception of German nationality has meant that anybody who can prove German ethnicity or ancestry has a right to claim German citizenship. This logic of racial ethnicity not only predisposes the nation towards "racial closure"[35], but also has determined that German national identity is seen as actually derived from a community bound together by blood and descent. German national consciousness has been shaped by these notions of culture and race, which have to a great extent been naturalised and normalised through the categories of identity and nationality.

This has resulted in a powerful national imaginary that has effects extending even beyond the nation. For example, many of the ethnic Germans from eastern Europe 'returning' to Germany in the wake of unification and the end of the cold war feel that they are being reunited with their 'homeland'. Although the ancestors of these people settled several hundred years ago in Russia in response to an invitation to fill labour shortages, and although many speak antique German dialects, and many others only speak Russian, they can claim their 'blood tie' to the German nation and thus are immediately granted citizenship. They also often have a very specific idea of what Germany should be like, and express attitudes and sentiments that appear to have been shaped by a particular understanding of a German nation configured as a community of shared-heritage and purity of descent. Many arrive puzzled to find that actually-existing Germany is not like they imagined, and that they are not always welcomed back 'home' by their fellow German citizens. One German woman from Kazakhstan, arriving at Frankfurt airport, declared "We are in heaven". Another young woman however, complained (in Russian because she speaks no German) "I thought I was coming to Germany ... Instead it's Turkey".[36]

In 1998, with the prospect of an integrated Europe fast approaching, Chancellor Schroeder introduced changes with the explicit aim of creating "an open society, with flexible borders, to make Germans capable of joining the European Union".[37] In a similar manner to the official transition from monocultural to multicultural Australia, the nation's racially restrictive nationality laws were seen as incompatible with the realities and requirements of globalisation. The Social-Democrat/Green Coalition aimed to introduce major changes, including dual citizenship and the granting of citizenship to the children of immigrants. But, with strong opposition from other political parties, the proposed changes were unsuccessful and a compromise had to be reached. The significant point of contention raised in the opposition to the reforms was the concept of dual citizenship, acquired by ius soli territory/residence). As Uli Linke argues, "[Dual citizenship] was read as a signifier of alterity, marking a life of displacement and uprootedness."[38] Despite the reforms that were eventually adopted, however, the accompanying public debates demonstrated clearly that there still exists a particular politics of identity associating migrants with the inauthentic and impermanent. As Linke states, the result is

> a two-tiered, caste-like system of national belonging: by blood (descent) and by space (residence). One native-German, based on cosanguinity, which is presumed natural, authentic, and permanent; the other foreign-German, based on territorial affinity, which is deemed artificial, inauthentic, contractual, and impermanent.[39]

In addition, eligibility for citizenship is now strictly tied to the immigrant's ability to demonstrate a sufficient knowledge of and fluency in the German language: Germanness, traditionally configured by descent, is now configured by language. So, paradoxically, while promoting inclusion, the reforms have also succeeded in producing other, subtler, mechanisms of segregation and exclusion.

Within this context, the radical content of the *Familie Deutschland* campaign is significantly reduced. This image of a hybrid, mixed-race family certainly unsettles the traditional configuration of German identity and Germanness. Yet these complex structural inequities are exactly the kinds of difficulties that tend to be suppressed by the image of harmonious cultural diversity that is endorsed by the multicultural idea. As Hage argues, "the practices of tolerance, like the practices of intolerance and exclusion, are nationalist practices aimed at management of national space ... If the nationalist practices of exclusion emphasise a capacity to remove the other from national space, the nationalist practices of tolerance emphasise a capacity to position them in specific places so that they can be valued and tolerated".[40] In other words then, practices of tolerance that are implicit to the multicultural fantasy of accepting and celebrating everyone's cultural difference does nothing to actually change structures and relations of power.

Implicit in the concept of multiculturalism, therefore, is a narrative of progressive transformation, charting the nation's progress from a racist, exclusionary past to a multicultural inclusionary present. Yet what this tends to do is actually suppress the continuing constitutive role of processes of racialised and ethnicised othering that have simply been transformed in the multicultural era. As Ien Ang suggests, what we are witnessing then is no longer the simple mechanisms of rejection and exclusion, but an ambivalent and contradictory process, including the very construction of difference and otherness, which in essence amounts to a process of inclusion by making Other.[41]

It is multiculturalism's role in actually constructing difference and constructing the difference of 'others', who are then, through a process of tolerance and inclusion, brought into the nation envisaged as a harmonious multicultural family, which brings me to the next section.

5.   Welcome to Sydney

Welcome to Sydney is a series of photographs by the Australian artist Anne Zahalka. The series was commissioned by Sydney Airport to "celebrate artistic and cultural diversity in Australia".

The large photographs were intended for the arrivals lounge at the airport, placed where they could be seen by disembarking visitors. In this way, the images would provide an introduction to Australian multicultural life and the diversity of cultures that could be potentially encountered. Zahalka is a photographer known for drawing upon and deconstructing images from the field of Australian popular culture and myth-making. By removing an image from the original context in which it has developed significant symbolic value, and by using a visual style that combines photographic techniques borrowed from advertising and marketing, she not only

Fiona Allon 195

deconstructs the image's naturalness but highlights the constructedness of the image and the myth-making role it has served. Zahalka's photographs show that the power to represent the nation is the power to dominate it, and that the power to contest this representation often has to involve the same strategies as used in the very processes of domination, sometimes successfuly and sometimes not.

In the series *Welcome to Sydney* Zahalka employs her usual method of questioning iconic images of national identity, though here her attention is directed towards representations of cultural difference in multicultural Australia. Each image shows an individual or family from a non-Anglo background, positioned within a landscape or setting that relates to them in some way. Each image is accompanied by a caption that states a welcome greeting in the language of the person or group depicted. For example, in the image (previous page) 'Cabramatta', featuring the young Vietnamese-Australian woman Catherine Phan, the caption in Vietnamese has an English translation that reads "Welcome gladly valued personages to Sydney".

In all of the images, the individuals wear 'traditional' ethnic dress or costume. Catherine wears Vietnamese dress and holds a traditional Vietnamese hat, which we find out from the accompanying information, was brought by her grandparents when they came to Australia in 1990. In the photograph Catherine stands in a scrubby, undeveloped block of land, on the fringe of what appears to be a new housing development in Cabramatta, in the Western suburbs of Sydney, where, we are also told, a large Vietnamese community resides. The timber frame of a house under construction is in the background, and behind a row of tall gum trees we see the edge of the suburb. Catherine stands amidst the overgrown grass and weeds, a figure of displacement and dislocation within the landscape. In two of the other photographs, the positioning of the subjects is the same. In 'Parramatta Park', four young Aghan women, again in traditional dress, crouch on the dry grass, amidst a similar backdrop of gum trees (previous page).

In the photograph 'Bondi Beach', Rabbi Mendel Kastel wears religious dress and holds a Russian samovar which, we are told, has come to represent his Russian heritage and memories of tea being served as Judaism was taught to him.

The effect of positioning these non-Anglo people in landscapes which have been so over-determined as signifiers of Anglo-Celtic national identity is visually striking and arresting. Bondi Beach, for example, is internationally recognised as an Australian icon; yet it is also home to a large Jewish community. The symbol of the beach in the Australian national imaginary has historically been one that has usually defined national identity through a culture of surf and sun. The clearing of land, and the construction and development of Australian suburban life have, similarly, become images synonymous with a particular version of national identity; the building of a suburban house is still today constructed as a personal symbol for the 'social progress' of the nation as a whole. The aim of situating these individuals who are so visibly culturally different in these settings is, it seems, to challenge the mythical nature of these sites and landscapes, and the exclusions upon which their identity as 'white' Australian symbols depend.

The series as a whole also appears to challenge reified and essentialist depictions of ethnic identity. By both presenting and subverting stereotypical representations in the same image, Zahalka arrests the tendency to generalise and essentialise identity, while at the same time significantly decontextualising the sites and places in which contemporary, everyday experiences and practices of diverse groups are played out. These are, of course, important strategies for any identity politics. Yet the images can also be read in another way: as the staging of the ethnic other as an object. Within each photograph, cultural difference is not only associated with authenticity and traditional dress and costume, but is presented as something isolated within each individual. Difference is not about interaction and change and the interrelations with others, but is a unique essence bound to the individual person. It seems that not only are these people subsumed within static landscapes, they are also trapped within tradition and the static category of ethnic identity.

This suggests, therefore, a version of multiculturalism that simply associates migrants with folklore and custom or with folkloric traditions such as food, dress and dance. We see this often at multicultural festivals where cultural diversity is openly celebrated and championed. What is stressed here is the traditional and the stereotypical, and what tends to be reproduced is a picture of multiculturalism as a grid of distinct 'ethnic communities', bounded and closed, each with their own separate 'culture', and with little in common. The problem with this conception of the multicultural society, in which differences are neatly classified and organised as distinct and separate, reduced and contained within the category of 'identity', is that it ignores change and dynamism, and the new forms of cultural practice and expression that emerge when cultures meet and mix. The multicultural order depends in this way on the fixing of mutually exclusive identities and the masking of socio-economic inequalities behind an image of happy togetherness and harmonious diversity. But more than this, it downplays the constitutive role of the multicultural grid in actually constructing this difference.

The emphasis on cultural difference as simply folkloric traditions and customs also produces what Hage calls "cosmo-multiculturalism", where ethnicity largely exists as an exotic object of consumption, a "multiculturalism without migrants" as he puts it.[42] Rather than a process of real intercultural interaction and the interactive experience of living with difference, multiculturalism simply increases the diversity of consumption choices on offer. Cultural difference is an increasingly marketable commodity, and officially sanctioned versions of multiculturalism, which have historically 'contained' expressions of difference with private spheres and activities – food, dance, music etc. – are now often complicit in the packaging of difference for an increasingly undifferentiated class of global consumers.

6. Conclusion

The transformation of the national experience of the nation-state is by no means unique to Australia or Germany. All Western countries are experiencing these changes in some way, as a result of the reorganisation of global capitalism. Multiculturalism succeeds in substituting the ideal of national homogeneity, framed in racial and cultural terms, with the ideal of cultural diversity. But more often than not, multiculturalism in fact produces and then maintains the boundaries between the diverse cultures it encompasses, and an overall boundary of the nation-state as a whole. In this sense, multiculturalism establishes itself as a more complex form of nationalism, employing more flexible strategies of inclusion and exclusion. Through such flexible strategies, the policies of multiculturalism present, therefore, as uniquely suited to the contemporary regime of 'flexible capitalism', as well as a more effective way of securing national boundaries in an increasingly borderless world. It is perhaps because of these reasons that a recent survey found that although multicultural policies and programs have existed since the 1970s, in the national imagination Australian identity and 'Australianness' are still generally defined as white, Anglo-Celtic.

In today's multicultural societies, a host of differences (religion, race, ethnicity, class, gender, and so on), including those differences increasingly forged by translocal and transnational connections, create complex and dynamic articulations and multiple modes of belonging that disturb the neat and static categories of managerial multiculturalism. The question for diverse cultural groups is, at the very least, the recognition and acceptance of cultural difference. Yet as so often with such liberal models, the actual result of an avowed policy of tolerance for others is the subsuming, and absorption, of a range of differences within either the identity of the ethnic community or at the level of national identity. The grand narrative of multiculturalism as a national identity is, within this approach, simply the calculated management, administration and containment of difference on the terms of the structurally dominant. It displays little concern for real differences and inequalities of power, or for changing entrenched and discriminative power relations. Essentially, heterogeneity – the practice of living with and through pluralism and diversity – cannot be realised within a bipolar model of abstract sameness versus abstract difference. When multiculturalism becomes a legitimate model of national identity, as it has in Australia, this does not eliminate questions of difference and heterogeneity; rather it makes a politics of difference (for whom, and for whose benefit and in whose interest, and how?) all the more crucial.

The reality of changed economic and geopolitical circumstances in both countries has rendered an older, protectionist and culturally homogenous national identity untenable and unviable. The policy of multiculturalism and the recognition of cultural diversity are in this sense inevitable, as programs of economic restructuring are aimed specifically at internationalising the economy and achieving increasing levels of integration within neighbouring markets, Asia in Australia's case, the European Union in Germany's.

In this globalising world characterised by flexible markets and transnational alliances, what is now needed are new images of identity, belonging and citizenship that are adequate to the plurality, heterogeneity and mobilities of the new global context. The key question for both countries is whether they can in fact move to a modern form of civic identity, which allows the admission of immigrants and minorities to full citizenship and acceptance, while still recognising cultural difference. But in another sense, formal citizenship is not enough. What is needed is a conception of cultural attachment and belonging that is open and flexible and not reducible to singular and exclusive notions of 'home' or national community. The challenge then is to recognise ways of belonging which are not closed, insular and unitary, and which do not automatically presuppose a 'fixed address' or locate 'origins' as the only condition of possibility for identity. It is also the challenge to be able to conceptualise a citizenship without myths of identity and without the fictive ethnicities characteristic of national identity and the nation-state.

Notes

1. See Bennett 1998.
2. Appadurai 1996, 43.
3. Taylor 1992.
4. Bhabha 1990.
5. This was a phrase used by Paul Keating, Prime Minister (1991-1996).
6. Hobsbawm and Ranger 1983.
7. Anderson 1983, 15
8. White 1981, viii.
9. Balibar 1995, 96. For a discussion of 'fictive ethnicity' in relation to Europe, see also Balibar 2004.
10. Foucault 1980, 93.
11. Balibar 1995, 95.
12. Evans et al. 1901, quoted in Ang 2000, 131.
13. See Ang 2000, 130.
14. See Stratton and Ang 1998.
15. See Castles et. al. 1988.

16. For a critique of multiculturalism as 'tolerance' see, Bauman 1991; Hage 1994; Idem, 1996; See Stratton and Ang 1998.
17. John Howard, quoted in Grattan 1996, 71.
18. National Multicultural Advisory Council 1997.
19. Howard makes numerous references to these entities. See for example, Howard 1995, 5 and Howard 1996, 8.
20. Bruce Grant, quoted in Marr and Wilkinson 2003, 34.
21. Philip Ruddock, quoted in ibid, 32.
22. Liberal Party 2001.
23. John Howard, quoted in Marr and Wilkinson, 279.
24. See Castles 1999.
25. N.N. 2002, 27.
26. Edmund Stoiber, quoted in Ramsauer 2003.
27. Bittner 2003.
28. Mrozek 2000.
29. Quoted in Nichols 2002. "Germany grapples with immigration: as an influx of immigrants challenges what it means to be German, particularly within the Muslim community, politicians fumble with a potentiallu explosive issue."
30. See Schwarz 2004.
31. See Hage 1998.
32. See Ong 1999; Balibar 2004.
33. The campaign can be seen at <www.familie-deutschland.de> (November 2004).
34. See for example Gilroy 1991 [1987].
35. Günter Frankenberg, quoted in Linke 2003,153.
36. Quoted in Morley 2000.
37. Thomas Därnstadt quoted in Linke 2003, 154.
38. Linke 2003, 154.
39. Ibid.
40. Hage 1998, 94-95.
41. Ang 2001, 139.
42. Hage 1997.

I would like to thank Urte Böhm for bringing the Familie Deutschland campaign to my attention.

References

Anderson, Benedict. *Imagined Communities: Reflections on the Origin and Spread of Nationalism.* London: Verso, 1983.

Ang, Ien. *On not speaking Chinese: Living Between Asia and the West.* London and New York: Routledge. 2001.

Appadurai, Arjun. *Modernity at Large.* Minneapolis: University of Minnesota Press, 1996.

Balibar, Etienne. "The Nation Form: History and Ideology." In *Race, Nation, and Class: Ambiguous Identities*, edited by Etienne Balibar and Immanuel Wallerstein, 86-106. London and New York: Verso, 1995.

Balibar, Etienne. *We, the People of Europe: Reflections on Transnational Citizenship.* Princeton and Oxford: Princeton University Press, 2004.

Bauman, Zygmunt. *Modernity and Ambivalence.* Cambridge: Polity Press, 1991.

Bennett, David. Ed. *Multicultural States.* London and New York: Routledge, 1998.

Bhabha, Homi. "The Third Space." In *Identity*, edited by Jonathan Rutherford, 207-221. London: Lawrence & Wishart, 1990.

Bittner, Jochen. "Integration: Ghetto im Kopf." *Die Zeit*, 28 August 2003.

Castles, Stephen. *Mistaken Identity: multiculturalism and the demise of nationalism in Australia.* Sydney: Pluto Press, 1988.

Castles, Stephen. "Challenges to National Identity and Citizenship: A Comparative Study of Immigration and Society in Germany, France and Australia." *CAPSTRANS-CEDA Information Paper* (68), 1999.

Foucault, Michel. *Power/knowledge: selected interviews and other writings 1972-1977*, edited by Colin Gordon. New York: Pantheon, 1980.

Gilroy, Paul. *There ain't no black in the Union Jack: The Cultural Politics of Race and Nation.* Chicago: University of Chicago Press, 1991 [1987].

Grattan, Michelle. "Home-Grown PM." *The Financial Review Magazine*, (November 1996).

Hage, Ghassan. "Locating Multiculturalism's other." *New Formations* 24 (1994): 19-34.

Hage, Ghassan. "At Home in the entrails of the West: multiculturalism, 'ethnic food' and migrant home building." In *Home/World: Space and Marginality in Western Sydney*, edited by Helen Grace, Ghassan Hage, Leslie Johnson, Julie Langsworth and Michael Symonds, 99-153. Annandale: Pluto Press. 1997.

Hage, Ghassan. *White Nation: Fantasies of White Supremacy in a Multicultural Society.* Sydney: Pluto Press, 1998.

Hobsbawm, Eric and Terence Ranger. *The Invention of Tradition.* Cambridge: Cambridge University Press, 1983.

Howard, John. *Politics and Patriotism: A Reflection on the National Identity Debate.* 13 December 1995.

Howard, John. *Election Campaign Launch Speech*, 18 February 1996.

Liberal Party. *Launch of the Liberal Party's Election Campaign*, Sydney

Recital Hall, 28 October 2001.

Linke, Uli. "'There is a Land where Everything is Pure': Linguistic Nationalism and Identity Politics in Germany." In *Race, Nature and the Politics of Difference*, edited by Donald S. Moore, Anand Pandian and Jake Kosek, 149-174. Durham and London: Duke University Press, 2003.

Marr, David and Marian Wilkinson. *Dark Victory*. Crows Nest: Allen & Unwin, 2003.

Morley, David. *Home Territories: Media, Mobility and Identity*. London and New York: Routledge, 2000.

Mrozek, Andrea. "Heavy on the Leitkultur." *Central Europe Review* 2(42) (4 December 2000).

National Multicultural Advisory Council. *Multicultural Australia: The Way Forward*. Canberra: AGPS, 1997.

Nichols, Hans S. "Germany Grapples with Immigration. As an Influx of Immigrants Challenges what it means to be German, particularly within the Muslim Community, Politicians Fumble with a potentially explosive Issue." *Insight on the News*. 30 September 2002. <http://findarticles.com/cf_0/m1571/36_18/92589540/print.jhtml> (November 2004).

N.N. "Immigrants loom large in election." *The Australian Financial Review*. 20 September 2002.

Ong, Aihwa. *Flexible Citizenship*. Durham: Duke University Press, 1999.

Ramsauer, Peter. "Deutsche Identität statt Multi-Kulti." December 2003. <www.konservativ.de/epoche/138_138e.htm> (December 2003).

Schwarz, Anja. "Modes of 'un-Australianness' and 'un-Germanness': Contemporary Debates in Cultural Diversity in Germany and Australia" *Journal of Australian Studies* 80 (New Talents) (2004): 211-220.

Stratton, John and Ien Ang. "Multicultural Imagined Communities: Cultural Difference and National Identity in Australia and the USA." *Continuum* 8(2) (1994): 124-158.

Stratton, John and Ien Ang. "Multicultural Imagined Communities: Cultural Difference and National Identity in the USA and Australia." In *Multicultural States: Rethinking Difference and Identity*, edited by David Bennett, 135-162. London and New York: Routledge, 1998.

Taylor, Charles. *Multiculturalism and the Politics of Recognition*. Princeton, NJ: Princeton University Press, 1992.

White, Richard. *Inventing Australia: Images and Identity 1688-1980*. Sydney, Allen & Unwin, 1981.

Von der Expansion zur Lokalisierung der Wissenschaften in multikulturellen Gesellschaften: Australische und europäische Erfahrungen

Ulrich Lölke

My chapter addresses the question of the reciprocal relationships and influences which have existed and continue to exist between polyculturalism and science. I am particularly interested in the cultural plurality which results today from the European expansion which came about in the wake of colonialism, and the impact this plurality may have upon conceptualizations of science. He contrasts universalistic and specific, localized models of science, suggesting that contemporary reflection upon the epistemologies of scientific knowledge-production will gain much by scrutinizing the specific epistemological economies at work in various cultural contexts. I focus on the one hand upon the German context, asking about the manner in which European science developed on the basis of early German voyages of discovery. In von Humboldt's and Forster's travel accounts there is still in evidence a 'dialectical tension' between the universalist aspirations of the scientist-explorers and the rising consciousness – brought about by the journey itself and the 'places' it traversed – of the obstacles to such a project. On the other hand, I examine the contemporary power constellations of competing knowledge systems which become visible when various epistemic traditions collide with one another. My example is taken from the Australian indigenous context, in which European scientific and indigenous knowledge meet in school syllabi. In such epistemological 'contact zones', scientific discourse could possibly relinquish its policing function and instead become one of several equal discursive instances in dialogical interaction.

Die Frage nach einem schlüssigen Konzept multikultureller Gesellschaften kann sehr einfach mit einem Verweis auf die Gesellschaften beantworten, in denen wir leben. Damit ist die These verbunden, alle gegenwärtigen Gesellschaften verfügten über multikulturelle Erfahrungen. Kolorierungen ergeben sich zum einen durch die Unterschiedlichkeit der Erfahrungen als auch aus den unterschiedlichen Bedeutungen, die diese Erfahrungen erlangen. Die Prozesse von Migration, Vertreibung, Integration, Abgrenzung, nationaler Identitätenbildung sowie von Sezessionen werden unterschiedlich stark bewertet und sie werden unterschiedlich stark in die narrativen Strukturen lokaler und nationaler Erzählungen aufgenommen. So können zum Beispiel Integrationsprozesse als nationale Erfolgsgeschichten bewertet werden (*the melting pot, the rainbow nation, usw.*). Kultur kann aber auch in ihrer nationalen Reichweite als (vermeintlich) ontologische Einheit gefasst werden, deren *Wesen* (Volksgeist) in Leitkultursätzen festgeschrieben wird. Einheit oder Integration entscheidet nicht darüber, *ob* es sich um multikulturelle Gesellschaften handelt, sondern nur darüber, *wie* Multikulturalität begriffen wird und in den nationalen Narrationen repräsentiert wird.

Ich möchte im folgenden weder eine Vereinheitlichung des Begriffs vorschlagen, noch eine Kritik der bisherigen Ansätze betreiben, sondern statt dessen fragen, welchen Einfluss die Multikulturalität gegenwärtiger Gesellschaften auf die Entwicklung der Wissenschaften hat und andersherum, welchen Einfluss die Wissenschaften auf die Entwicklung multikultureller Gesellschaften genommen haben und heute nehmen. Mein Interesse gilt also nicht in erster Linie den in der Multikulturalismus-Kontroverse zentralen Begriffen Identität, Kultur, Nation und Gesellschaft, sondern einer *von ihrem Selbstverständnis* transnationalen und transkulturellen Struktur: den Wissenschaften. Ich möchte auf die Wechselverhältnisse hinweisen, die zwischen Wissenschaften und Kulturentwicklungen bestehen und mich dabei auf die Konsequenzen konzentrieren, die die Multikulturalität heutiger Gesellschaften für unsere Wissenschaftsvorstellung hat.

1. Expansion und Nationenbildung in Europa

Nationen beanspruchen definierte Territorien, die sich in der Wahrnehmung ihrer Multikulturalität als porös und kontingent erweisen können.[1] Wissenschaften verstehen sich als transnationale Gemeinschaften, die bei genauerem Hinsehen lokale, kulturelle und nationale Besonderheiten aufweisen können. Die Frage nach der Multikulturalität der Wissenschaften[2] irritiert, weil sie die Wissenschaften, jenen Ort allgemeiner und transkultureller Wahrheitsansprüche, mit ihren lokalen Bezügen konfrontieren. Hier ist ein Forschungsbereich entstanden, der zwar bei Vertretern der „harten" Wissenschaften mitunter auf größtes Unverständnis stößt[3], dem aber zu gute gehalten werden muss, dass er die wichtige Frage der Repräsentation unterschiedlicher Wissensformationen in multikulturellen Gesellschaften aufnimmt und versucht zu beantworten. Für die Wissenschaftsforschung mindestens so interessant ist die Frage nach der Multikulturalität der Wissenschaften selbst. Theorien und Hypothesen können untereinander unverträglich sein. Wissenschaftliche Gemeinschaften setzen sich zudem aus Mitgliedern zusammen, die selbst noch einmal unterschiedliche Kulturen vertreten können: so können zum Beispiel Mikrobiologen Buddhisten sein oder analytische Philosophen US-Amerikaner. Es ist also ratsam, mit weniger komplexen Modellen zu beginnen.

Unsere Moderne, als eine Voraussetzung multikultureller Strukturen, wird mit drei Ereignissen in Verbindung gebracht: europäische Expansion, Nationenbildung sowie Entstehung der modernen Wissenschaften. Die Dynamik des Modernisierungsprozesses und die Entstehung multikultureller Gesellschaften als eine Folge dieses Prozesses ergibt sich aus einem Zusammenspiel dieser drei Phänomene. Es müssen Geschichte (europäische Expansion), Politik (Nationenbildung) und Wissenschaftsphilosophie (Entstehung der modernen Wissenschaften) zusammengebracht werden.[4] In der Multikulturalismus-Kontroverse ist der letzte Aspekt bisher wenig beachtet worden.

Europa hat mit der Expansion in der frühen Neuzeit und dem Kolonialismus zwischen den Regionen der Erde Verbindungen hergestellt, Wege und Routen entdeckt, diese militärisch und strategisch beherrscht und genutzt. Mit der europäischen Expansion hat eine totale Mobilmachung[5] eingesetzt, die heute zu Gesellschaftsformen führt, die häufig unter Missachtung ihrer historischen Voraussetzungen als multikulturelle Gesellschaften bezeichnet werden.

Dabei müssen die Expansionsprozesse vor dem Hintergrund der Nationenbildung in Europa gesehen werden. Expansion und Nationenbildung gehören zusammen, wenn sie auch in ihren Bewegungsrichtungen gegeneinander zu laufen scheinen: Bildung von Innerlichkeit und Volksgeist bei der Konstitution des Eigenen einerseits und die Erfahrung des Fremden als Konfrontation, aber auch als Neugier für das Fremde andererseits. Verbunden sind sie durch spezifische Formen der Gewalt: die Konstitution des Eigenen als nationale Einheit wird erkämpft als Territorium, Sprache, Fahne, Identität, Regierung, Krieg mit den Nachbarn. Und es ist hinzuzufügen: *Kolonie*.

Betrachtet man die Geschichte multikultureller Gesellschaften vor dem Hintergrund der europäischen Expansion, dann fällt auf, dass als Gegenbewegung zum Expansionsprozess nach innen jenes Modell nationaler Einheit und Identität entstanden ist, das jetzt von dem Modell multikultureller Gesellschaften ersetzt zu werden droht. Der Umstand, dass die Expansion die Bedingungen dafür schafft, dass die Idee einer einheitlichen nationalen Kultur in Frage gestellt wird, kann als Ironie der Geschichte angesehen werden.

Mit der Expansion entsteht nicht nur in der europäischen Phantasie eine äußere Welt des Fremden, sondern auch eine gegenseitige Wahrnehmung. Die Anderen sehen uns. Und sie sehen uns anders, als wir uns selbst sehen. Es entsteht die lange in Europa übersehene Spiegelung des Eigenen im Fremden.[6] Eduardo Galeano berichtet von einem Gespräch mit dem spanischen Pfarrer Ignacio Ellacuriá, der behauptet:

> Es ist der Unterdrückte, der den Unterdrücker entdeckt. Er glaubte sogar (Ellacuria, UL), dass der Unterdrücker noch nicht einmal fähig sei, sich selbst zu entdecken. Die eigentliche Realität des Unterdrückers lasse sich nur aus der Sicht des Unterdrückten erkennen.[7]

Mission und Handel schaffen die Kontaktzonen[8] in denen Kulturen aufeinander stoßen. Wissenschaft (und Literatur) sind die Routen, auf denen eine kritische Auseinandersetzung mit Europa in das Zentrum gelangte. Der haitianische Schriftsteller und Politiker Aimé Césaire hat sich in seinem *Discours sur le colonialisme* (1955) mit der europäischen Verantwortung angesichts des moralischen Desasters der europäischen Expansion befasst. Er stellt fest: „Une civilisation qui s'avère incapable de résoudre les problèmes que suscite son fonctionnement est une civilisation décadent."[9] Er schließt daraus, dass Europa nicht zu „verteidigen" sei („*L'Europe est indéfendable*"). Er verweist aber auch auf die Chance, die von Europa ausging und die auf fatale Weise vertan wurde. Diese Chance hätte nach Césaire darin bestanden, die mit der Expansion außen entstandenen multikulturellen Strukturen, auch nach innen, in die Prozesse der Nationenbildung, hinein zu nehmen:

> ... la grande chance de l'Europe est d'avoir été un carrefour, et que, d'avoir été le lieu géométrique de toutes les idées, le réceptacle de toutes les philosophies, le lieu d'accueil de tous les sentiments en a fait le meilleur redistributeur d'énergie.[10]

Diese Frage Césaires, warum Europa nicht zum Kraftzentrum jenes Prozesses geworden ist, den es selbst mit seiner Expansion initiiert hat, ist eine Frage, die sich meines Erachtens an die Wissenschaften richtet, die sich über einige hundert Jahre mit dem Sammeln und Verstehen von Wissen fremder Kulturen befasst haben. Dieses Verstehen und Erfassen kann heißen, dass Wissen importiert wird und seine Herkunft überschrieben wird, es kann aber auch heißen, dass das Wissen als das Wissen dieser Fremden den Status eines fremden Wissens erhält. So wie sich multikulturelle Gesellschaften mit den Erinnerungen ihrer kulturellen Gruppen konfrontiert sehen und der Frage der (angemessenen) Repräsentation der Erinnerungen nachgehen, deren Erzählungen in der Phase der Expansion überschrieben wurden, genauso kann in Bezug auf die Wissenschaften von einer „Krise der wissenschaftlichen Repräsentationen" gesprochen werden.[11] Wissenschaften übernehmen die

Funktion, Kulturen und ihre Geschichten zu repräsentieren, das heißt aber auch, ihre Geschichten und Wissenstraditionen anzueignen, zu interpretieren und zu systematisieren, also zu überschreiben und damit Prozesse der Marginalisierung fortzuführen. Hier liegt ein wichtiger Schnittpunkt kultureller und wissenschaftlicher Diskurse.

Seit mindestens 150 Jahren sind die westlichen Wissenschaften unterwegs. Sie treffen in ihrer weltweiten Verbreitung auf Kulturen und Wissensformationen und durchlaufen Prozesse lokaler Anpassung. Hier stellt sich die Frage der Repräsentation erneut. Wie lösen Wissenschaften in postkolonialen Gesellschaften die Konfrontationen, die dadurch entstehen, dass indigene Gruppen einen Anspruch auf Selbstvertretung erheben, dass sie für endogene Wissensformationen den Status einer Wissenschaft beanspruchen und dass sie die (westlichen) Wissenschaften anklagen, sich Wissen unrechtmäßig angeeignet zu haben bzw. dies weiter tun?

Um diese Frage zu beantworten, sollen im Folgenden die Prozesse der Anpassung wissenschaftlicher Wissensformationen in postkolonialen Gesellschaften dargestellt werden. An einem australischen Beispiel werden die Schwierigkeiten im Umgang mit divergierenden Wissensformationen verdeutlicht.

2. Situierte Wissenschaften

Bevor ich auf die Expansionsprozesse der Wissenschaften eingehe, ist es erforderlich zwischen zwei wissenschaftshistorischen Ansätzen zu unterscheiden. Zum einen zeichnet die Geschichte der Wissenschaften Bewegungen eines dekontextualisierten Diskurses einzelner Disziplinen und ihrer Entdeckungen (und Irrtümer) nach, ihre Strategien, Begriffe, Debatten, Ergebnisse, Um- und Holzwege. Dabei bezieht sie sich auf einen imaginären Ort des Diskurses, der zwischen Labor, Universität und Text liegt. Die Eigenart dieses Wissenschaftsdiskurses ist sein ‚utopischer' Charakter. Sie zeichnet einen Diskurs nach, der entweder ortlos, nämlich utopisch ist oder zumindest eine eigenwillige Orthaftigkeit besitzt.[12] Zum anderen aber ist Wissenschaftsgeschichte eine Kulturgeschichte des Wissens, die die Entwicklung der Wissenschaften zwischen den Bewegungsrichtungen europäischer Expansion und nationaler Identitätsbildung darstellt. Die Herausbildung des Eigenen entsteht vor dem Hintergrund einer Expansion der Wahrnehmung und einer systematischen Erfassung von Wissen in einem globalen Maßstab, an dem die Wissenschaften beteiligt sind.[13] Diese zweite Wissenschaftsgeschichte ist in ihrer Beschäftigung mit Bewegungen an den Orten und den Ortswechseln des Wissens interessiert (Expansion, Verbreitung).[14] Somit ist es auch kein Zufall, dass diese stärker in Regionen vertreten ist, *in* die die Wissenschaften exportiert wurden und in denen zum Teil schwierige und langwierige Anpassungsprozesse statt gefunden haben, die oftmals nicht abgeschlossen sind oder noch nicht einmal in einem nennenswerten Umfang begonnen haben. Mit diesen Anpassungsprozessen wird ein Konflikt sichtbar, der zwar auch Teil der Entstehungsgeschichte der Wissenschaften in Europa war, hier aber weitestgehend unbeachtet geblieben ist: gemeint ist die Spannung zwischen wissenschaftlichem Wissen und nicht-wissenschaftlichem (lokalem, endogenem, indigenem) Wissen. Sie behandelt das Problem der Entwertung, Zerstörung und Transformation anderer Wissensformationen durch die Wissenschaften und zwar unter Berücksichtigung der Spezifik der einzelnen Regionen (Australien, Afrika, Lateinamerika, Indien).[15] Mit der wissenschaftlichen Aneignung lokalen Wissens verbunden sind Gegenbewegungen, die wiederum aus der politischen Wortmeldung indiger Gruppen in multikulturellen Gesellschaften hervorgegangen sind. Nach der politischen Verfassung indiger Gruppen, die auch im Rahmen internationaler Organisationen aktiv sind, hat eine Debatte über *local knowledges* bzw. *indigenous knowledges* eingesetzt, die sich, neben der Frage der Speicherung und Bewahrung dieses Wissens, mit seiner Konzeptualisierung befasst.[16] Was ist lokales Wissen? Wo verlaufen die Grenzen zwischen Wissensformationen (wissenschaftlichen und nicht-wissenschaftlichen)? Worin bestehen ihre Differenzen und wo liegen Überschneidungen? Dabei ist die Konzeption eines lokalen Wissens auf der Grundlage eines Differenzmodells insofern problematisch, als lokales Wissen als Gegenmodell eines nicht selten recht einfachen Wissenschaftsverständnisses konzeptualisiert wird. Lokales Wissen bleibt in dieser Konstellation das Andere der Wissenschaften. Ein Grund hierfür ist, dass es allzu häufig als Wissenschafts- und Zivilisationskritik gegen die epistemologischen Modelle des Zentrums instrumentalisiert wird.[17]

Ich möchte im Folgenden die Ordnungen des Wissens in multikulturellen Gesellschaften von der historischen Perspektive wissenschaftlicher Expansionsbewegungen aus untersuchen. Dabei interessieren mich die historischen Aneignungen und Überschreibungen lokalen Wissens, die mit der Expansion westlicher Wissenschaften in der Welt einhergehen sowie die damit gleichfalls verbundenen regionalen Anpassungsprozesse der Wissenschaften, die heute von einem wachsenden Interesse für lokale Wissensformationen begleitet werden.

3. Die Ausbreitung der westlichen Wissenschaften

Zwischen Expansion und Nationenbildung stehen die Wissenschaften, die an beiden Prozessen partizipieren, beide Seiten beeinflussen und von beiden profitieren. Wissenschaft erfährt in der Zeit der Expansion und mit dem Zugang zu neuem Wissen einen erheblichen Auftrieb. Gleichzeitig beginnt mit der Expansion eine Globalisierung der Wissenschaften. Es entstehen im 19. Jahrhundert externe Zentren der Wissenschaftsentwicklung, mit eigenen Traditionsbildungen und eigenen methodischen und inhaltlichen Schwerpunkten. Karl Popper schreibt noch 1948 über seine Erfahrungen mit der Wissenschaftsentwicklung in Neuseeland:

> Certain types of tradition of great importance are local and cannot easily be transplanted. These traditions are precious things, and it is very difficult to restore them once they are lost. I have in mind the scientific tradition, in which I am particularly interested. I have seen that it is very difficult to transplant it from the few places where it has really taken root. ... Similarly, recent attempts to transplant it from England overseas have not been too successful. Nothing is more striking than the lack of a research tradition in some of the countries overseas.[18]

Dennoch waren die Wissenschaften lange darum bemüht, ihre Geschichte unabhängig von der Spannung zwischen Expansion und Nationenbildung und unter Missachtung ihrer eigenen Traditionalität darzustellen. Mit dem expansiven Moment der Wissenschaften und ihrer Umwandlung in regional verankerte Wissenschaftstraditionen beschäftigt sich eine Debatte der Wissenschaftsgeschichte, die durch einen Artikel von George Basalla ausgelöst wurde, der 1967 in der Zeitschrift *Science* erschien.[19] Basalla schlägt ein Modell vor, das auf die Frage zu antworten versucht: „How did modern science diffuse from Western Europe and find its place in the rest of the world?"[20] Sein Modell beansprucht zum einen allgemeine Geltung in allen Regionen der Erde. Allerdings unter der Prämisse, dass Wissenschaften an soziale und kulturelle Bedingungen gebunden sind und in diesen eine eigene regional-spezifische Tradition ausbilden: „... science exists in a local social setting."[21]

In dem Modell werden drei Phasen der Expansion unterschieden, die sich ablösen und überlagern können. In *Phase 1* begibt sich der europäische Wissenschaftler in die Neue Welt, um dort Flora, Fauna und Landschaft zu studieren und die Ergebnisse nach Europa zurückzutragen. Oft handelt es sich bei den Reisenden nicht tatsächlich um Wissenschaftler, sondern um Amateure: Entdeckungsreisende, Missionare, Diplomaten, Ärzte, Händler, Offiziere und Abenteurer. Es entsteht ein Rückstrom von Wissen aus der Neuen Welt und den Kolonien nach Europa, der Teil der wissenschaftlichen Revolution wird. Basalla zitiert Bischof Sprat aus seiner *History of the Royal Society of London* von 1667, der die Bedeutung maritimer Nationen darin sieht, „ ... to bring home matter for new science, and to make the same proportion of discoveries ... in the intellectual globe, as they have done in the material."[22] Die Entdeckung der Welt und die systematische Klassifizierung ihrer Tiere, Pflanzen und Landschaften bildet sich in einem parallelen Prozess der Ausbreitung der Wissenschaften ab. *Phase 1* bleibt auf Europa als ihr Zentrum bezogen.

> All of the plant, animal, and mineral specimens collected in the foreign lands, as well as the information amassed there, were returned to Europe (or, at a later date, to the United States) for the benefit of its scientists.[23]

Phase 2 wissenschaftlicher Expansion bezeichnet Basalla als koloniale Wissenschaft, die allerdings nicht notwendig das Ergebnis einer kolonialen Situation sein muss. Es entstehen eigene wissenschaftliche Institutionen außerhalb des europäischen Zentrums, die aber, in ihrer methodischen Ausrichtung und ihrer materiellen und apparativen Ausstattung, von einem der alten Wissenschaftszentren abhängig bleiben: „... the scientific activity in the new land is based primarily upon institutions and traditions of a nation with an established scientific culture."[24] Alle Wissenschaftler erhalten ihre Ausbildung im Zentrum und beziehen sich auf dessen wissenschaftlichen Diskurse und ihre Publikationsorgane.[25]

Basalla bezeichnet *Phase 2* als einen Übergang zu *Phase 3*, in der unabhängige wissenschaftliche Traditionen entstehen: „Colonial science ... is ... being able to utilize the resources of existing scientific traditions while it slowly develops a scientific tradition of its own."[26]

Der Übergang zu *Phase 3* sei ein „bewusster Kampf, um einen unabhängigen Status zu erreichen".[27] So befinden sich die Wissenschaften in den USA Ende des 19. Jahrhunderts im Übergang zu *Phase 3*. Es werden Forschungsreisen in Amerika finanziert und durchgeführt. Interessant ist in diesem Zusammenhang, dass sich die Institutionen der Ostküste der USA auch an den Forschungsreisen in das Innere Afrikas beteiligen. Henry M. Stanleys Reisen etwa werden von Zeitungen in den USA finanziert und erhalten in den USA eine ähnlich starke Aufmerksamkeit wie in Europa.[28] In den USA war eine Wissenschaftstradition entstanden, die zwar bis in die ersten Jahrzehnte des zwanzigsten Jahrhunderts hinein von den Ausbildungsmöglichkeiten in Europa abhängig blieb, aber im Übrigen eine eigenständige Forschungstradition etabliert hatte: „This region [der Osten der USA, U.L.] ... was now in a position to act as a centre for the diffusion of modern science."[29]

4. Von Phasen zum Raum, vom Diffusionsmodell zum Diskurs

Aus dem Zentrum wird die Geschichte des Wissens als eine Geschichte europäischer Erfahrungen erzählt, die auch hier ihre Orte hat: Bibliotheken, Museen, Universitäten, Kolonialinstitute, Archive, Kongresse und Zeitschriften. Es entstehen jene kolonialen Diskurse, die die kulturellen, politischen, sozialen und geographischen Landschaften der Peripherie strukturieren. Insbesondere unter Berücksichtigung der These Basallas der sozialen und lokalen Einbettung von Wissenschaftstraditionen ist es 25 Jahre nach der Erstveröffentlichung von *The Spread of Western Science* interessant, seine wissenschaftshistorischen Analysen der Expansionsprozesse westlicher Wissenschaften auf Gesellschaften zu beziehen, die sich heute als multikulturell verstehen und in denen Anpassungsprozesse der Wissenschaften statt finden, die sich von denen in den alten Zentren unterscheiden.

Die Wissenschaften sind dem Weg der Expansion gefolgt, soweit sie nicht selbst diese Wege ausgekundschaftet haben, was sich an den Forschungsreisetätigkeiten zwischen dem 17. und frühen 20. Jahrhundert aufzeigen lässt. Basallas Modell macht deutlich, dass es am Ende des 20. Jahrhunderts eine Landschaft wissenschaftlicher Traditionen gibt, in der einigen der Übergang zu *Phase 3*, mit der Ausbildung eigener wissenschaftlicher Zentren (z.B. USA, Australien und Japan) gelungen ist. Andere Regionen befinden sich weiterhin in einem Zustand ‚kolonialer Wissenschaften'. Basallas Modell legt nahe, diese Transformationsprozesse als lokale Ereignisse zu verstehen und sie als Traditionen in Bezug zu einem Ort oder einer Region zu interpretieren.

Die Kritik an Basallas Modell richtet sich vornehmlich gegen diese *Phase 3*. Sie sei nicht mehr als ein Kriterienkatalog für die Etablierung eigenständiger Wissenschaftstraditionen und könne die neuen Anpassungsprozesse der Wissenschaften nicht zufrieden stellend erklären. So könnte man ihm vorwerfen, er wechselte in seiner Darstellung von *Phase 2* zu *Phase 3* von der Analyse eines Historikers zu der Perspektive eines Entwicklungshelfers, der auf der Grundlage US-amerikanischer Erfahrungen Prognosen für einen erfolgreichen Übergang gibt.

Roy MacLeod, Wissenschaftshistoriker der *Universität Sydney*, stellt die neuere Beschäftigung mit dem kolonialen Unternehmen der

Wissenschaften als einen Versuch dar, „die europäische Erfahrung der Wissenschaft zu lokalisieren"[30]. Basalla habe für diese neuen Forschungsfragen die Richtung angegeben, aber weder die Methode noch die Begriffe gefunden, mit Hilfe derer diese Prozesse der Lokalisierung einer europäischen Erfahrung erfasst werden können. Die Aufgabe, die sich der neueren Forschung stellt, bestehe nun darin, so MacLeod, die regional unterschiedlichen Geschichten der *Phase 3*-Transformationen zu rekonstruieren. Mit der Forderung nach dezentralisierten Geschichten globaler Wissenschaftsentwicklungen gehen jedoch so gravierende methodische Schwierigkeiten einher, dass ihnen eine Klärung der Frage nach den Bedingungen der Möglichkeit lokalisierter historischer Rekonstruktionen vorangehen muss. Unklar bleibt, wer wessen Geschichte, von welchem Zentrum aus und aus wessen Perspektive erzählt. Welche Diskursformationen, Machtdispositive und Bezüge strukturieren und gestalten diese Erzählungen?[31] Basallas Modell stützt sich auf die These der Diffusion der Wissenschaften von ihrem europäischen (respektive US-amerikanischen) Zentrum aus in die Welt. Mit der Entstehung neuer Zentren entstehen entsprechend neue Diffusionsprozesse. Die Schwäche des Modells ist, dass es Wissensformationen, die nicht Teil jenes „reisenden Wissens"[32] der westlichen Wissenschaften sind, nur als fremdes Wissen erfassen kann, als nicht-wissenschaftliches Wissen oder durch den ungesicherten Status außer-europäischer Wissenschaftstraditionen.[33] So weist Basalla zwar darauf hin, dass es bei der Ausbildung wissenschaftlicher Kulturen in China, Indien und Japan Schwierigkeiten mit den vorhandenen endogenen Wissenssystemen gegeben habe: „The slow development of science in China can be explained, in large measure, by the inability of modern science to displace Confucianism as the prevailing philosophy."[34] Die zentrale Forderung der aktuellen Debatten in der Wissenschaftsgeschichte zur Entwicklung unabhängiger Wissenschaftstraditionen in der ‚Peripherie' ist allerdings die Überwindung dieses Modells der Diffusion mit seinem Dualismus von Zentrum/Peripherie. Roy MacLeod spricht davon, dass hier eine „komplexere Lesart der kolonialen Wissenschaften"[35] entstanden sei. Für die zentralen Kategorien bisheriger Erklärungen gelte:

> [they are, U.L.] no longer merely a phase, but rather a space, a complex of legacies, a combination of motives, and a role in the discourse of development. How else, after all, to deal with the obvious differences in the relationship between Ottoman science and European science, or between science in Europe and science in

premodern China and Japan?[36]

Der Wandel in der Wahrnehmung dieser Prozesse vollzieht sich in den Konzepten, die den Modellen zugrunde liegen. Diffusionsmodelle bleiben an ein Zentrum gebunden. Statt dessen schlägt MacLeod vor, Wissensformationen in ihren lokalen Bezügen darzustellen. Also keine Phasen der Diffusion mehr, sondern Räume, lokale Bezüge, ein gleichzeitiges Nebeneinander unterschiedlicher Wissenstraditionen:

> [C]olonial histories once written from Europe are in fact often histories about Europeans abroad, which must be rewritten in terms familiar to local narrators. [...] Today, locality and place are now being constituted as legitimate 'centers' for historical reconstruction.[37]

MacLeod verweist im Zusammenhang dieses relativ neuen Forschungsfeldes auf zwei interessante Aspekte: Erstens haben die Wissenschaftshistoriker lange die Bedeutung der Kolonialgeschichte übersehen (so wie diejenigen Geschichtswissenschaftler, die sich mit der Kolonialgeschichte befassen, die Rolle der Wissenschaften unterschätzt haben). Zweitens zeigt MacLeod, dass eine koloniale und postkoloniale Wissenschaftsgeschichte bzw. Geschichte des Wissens, die mit einem Differenzmodell und Zentrum/Peripherie–Dichotomien arbeitet, auf die Erfahrungen Europas beschränkt bleibt. Eine Lokalisierung der europäischen Erfahrung hieße, abweichende Erfahrungen mit den europäischen Wissenschaften einzubeziehen, aus den dichotomen Strukturen sich ausschließender Wissensformationen auszusteigen und die Geschichte des Wissens, anstatt sie als Siegeszug des Modells ‚Griechenland' darzustellen und mit der weltweiten Durchsetzung einer europäischen Wissenschaft enden zu lassen, als regional-spezifische Geschichte lokalisierter Erfahrungen, auf der Grundlage hybrider (postkolonialer) Epistemologien zu erzählen. Die australische Wissenschaftsphilosophie hat hierzu Vorschläge erarbeitet, auf die ich später zurückkomme.[38] Ähnlich vertritt der Inder Dhruv Raina die These, dass etwa in der neueren theoretischen Physik durch das Zusammentreffen unterschiedlicher epistemischer Kulturen (*cultural hybridization*) bedeutende Erkenntnisfortschritte gemacht werden konnten. Wichtige Impulse hat eine Wissenschaft wie die theoretische Physik an den Grenzen des Faches aufgenommen, die aber in der Historiographie des Fachs vergessen und marginalisiert wurden:

Big Picture historiography suffers from this inherent optical scotoma: not only is Boyle's technician invisible, but so are knowledge forms that enrich the epistemic and cognitive dimensions of modern science, but are marginalized politically and institutionally.[39]

5. Lokalisierung des Zentrums

Postkoloniale Perspektiven sind dadurch entstanden, dass sich unabhängige Wissenschaftstraditionen herausgebildet haben. Diese werden seit den 1990er Jahren auch zunehmend in Europa wahrgenommen. Ein Merkmal postkolonialer Ansätze ist, dass sich ihre Bindungen an das Zentrum verschoben haben und sie ihre Erfahrungen regional lokalisieren. Während Césaire noch 1955 mit starken Metaphern des Raumes (carrefour, lieu géométrique, réceptacle, lieu d'accueil) in Europa die Schnittstelle aller Erfahrungen sieht, haben sich die heutigen postkolonialen Autoren von dieser Vorstellung entfernt. Damit ist Europa zurückgeworfen auf seine Erfahrungen der Entwicklung der Wissenschaften zwischen Expansion und Identitätsbildung. Europa ist aufgefordert, seine Erfahrungen der Wissenschaftsentwicklung und der Wissensakkumulation historisch neu zu lokalisieren. Aber in welchem Sinne lassen sich diese Erfahrungen lokalisieren? Wie sähe ein solcher Prozess aus? Welche (neuen) Positionen kann das alte Zentrum in einer dezentrierten Wissenschafts- bzw. Wissenslandschaft übernehmen?

Am Anfang stünde eine erneute Interpretation europäischer Akkumulations- und Transformationsprozesse globalen Wissens sowie eine Rückkehr zu den Anfängen europäischer Expansion in den Wissenschaften. Der hannoveraner Literaturwissenschaftler Leo Kreutzer hat vorgeschlagen, den Prozess der Selbstverständigung europäischer Wissenschaftsentwicklung mit der Analyse der Anfänge europäischer und hier insbesondere deutscher Forschungsreisetätigkeiten zu beginnen. Am Anfang stehen Georg Forster und Alexander von Humboldt. Vor allem die Südamerikareise des Letzteren wird häufig als ein „Modell"[40] späterer Forschungsreisen angesehen. Humboldts und Forsters Berichte lassen noch die Unsicherheit erahnen, die für die Autoren mit der literarischen Fassung ihrer Erfahrungen des Fremden verbunden war. Kreutzer spricht von einer „dialektischen Spannung" zwischen einer wissenschaftlichen Aneignung, die Bezug nimmt auf eine universalistische Ordnung der Welt, und einem Bewusstsein für die mit dieser vorgestellten Ordnung verbundenen Schwierigkeiten. Aneignung von Natur und Wissen war einer ästhetischen Orientierung geschuldet. Humboldt ist nicht weit entfernt von den heute aktuellen Ansätzen einer *writing culture* in der Anthropologie, wie auch Kreutzer betont.[41] Humboldt löst den Konflikt dadurch, dass es in seinem Buch *Ansichten der Natur, mit wissenschaftlichen Erläuterungen* eine ästhetische Darstellung im Haupttext gibt und in den Anmerkungen der wissenschaftliche Diskurs beigefügt wird. Der Haupttext besteht aus jenem, was Humboldt seine „Naturgemälde" nennt. „Schüchtern," so beginnt Humboldt die Vorrede zur ersten Ausgabe von 1808,

> übergebe ich dem Publikum eine Reihe von Arbeiten, die im Angesicht großer Naturgegenstände, auf dem Ocean, in den Wäldern des Orinoco, in den Steppen von Venezuela, in der Einöde peruanischer und mexicanischer Gebirge, entstanden sind. Einzelne Fragmente wurden an Ort und Stelle niedergeschrieben, und nachmals nur in ein ganzes zusammengeschmolzen. Überblick der Natur im großen, Beweis von dem Zusammenwirken der Kräfte, Erneuerung des Genusses, welchen die unmittelbare Ansicht der Tropenländer dem fühlenden Menschen gewährt: sind die Zwecke, nach denen ich strebe. ... Diese ästhetische Behandlung naturhistorischer Gegenstände hat, trotz der herrlichen Kraft und der Biegsamkeit unserer vaterländischen Sprache, große Schwierigkeiten der Composition. Reichthum der Natur veranlaßt Anhäufung einzelner Bilder, und Anhäufung stört die Ruhe und den Totaleindruck des Gemäldes. Das Gefühl und die Phantasie ansprechend, artet der Styl leicht in eine dichterische Prosa aus.[42]

Offensichtlich sucht Humboldt nach einem literarischen Verfahren, das in seiner Strenge naturwissenschaftlichen Methoden gleich kommt. In Bezug auf die literarische Form der Naturgemälde verlangt er, die Möglichkeiten der deutschen Sprache einzubeziehen, aber zugleich die Grenze zu einer dichterischen Prosa einzuhalten. Humboldt spricht von einem „Beweis von dem Zusammenwirken der Kräfte", für dessen Darstellung er eine eigentümliche wissenschaftliche Prosa entwickelt.

Der etwas ältere Georg Forster, Lehrer Humboldts in Sachen Forschungsreisen – Forster war selbst Teilnehmer der zweiten Weltumseglung James Cooks –, sieht neben der Naturvermittlung die Bedeutung der Kulturvermittlung. Er reflektiert sogar die mit den Transformationsprozessen in die wissenschaftlichen Sprachen Europas verbundene Frage einer späteren Rückerstattung eines jetzt universalisierten Wissens. Auf diesen Umstand geht Kreutzer ausführlich ein:

> Forster stellt sich vor, wie Europa das Wissen, das es weltweit erbeutet hat, den „übrigen Geschlechtern der Menschen" zurückerstatten werde. Und obwohl es dann mit dem „Salz europäischer Universalkenntniß" gewürzt und „mit dem Stempel der Allgemeinheit neu ausgemünzt" sei, werde das an seine Ausgangsorte zurückfließende Wissen als ursprünglich Eigenes *wiedererkannt* werden können. Forster ist also zuversichtlich, alles lokale Wissen werde im Laboratorium europäischen Denkens auf eine Weise verallgemeinert, daß es noch in seiner Universalisierung, aber nunmehr in einer dialektischen Spannung zu dieser, repräsentiert werde.[43]

Vielleicht ist Europa nicht mehr jener größte Energieverteiler, von dem Césaire spricht, aber noch immer ist es das größte Archiv für Weltwissen. Die Beispiele Humboldts und Forsters sollen verdeutlichen, wie Europa zu einer Art kulturellem Zwischenlager für die Kulturen der Erde geworden ist, ohne dass es dieses archivierte Wissen alleine nutzen könnte. Hier setzt ein Prozess der Rückgabe ein, der darin besteht, die Archive wieder in ihre jeweiligen Kontexte zu bringen. Leo Kreutzer hat dafür einen Begriff der Weltwissenschaft vorgeschlagen, der sich gegen delokalisierende und dekontextualisierende Aspekte der westlichen Wissenschaften wendet und sich an Goethes Vorstellung und Begriff einer Weltliteratur anlehnt. Die Lokalisierung des Zentrums bestünde nun darin, die Wege der Aneignung zurückzuverfolgen, um ihre Bedingungen und Motivationen nachzuvollziehen. Eine derartige Geschichtsschreibung der Aneignungsprozesse steht noch aus. Die Analyse der wissenschaftlichen Diskurse der Aneignung von Wissen könnte zeigen, dass die universale Ordnung der Welt, wie sie von den europäischen Wissenschaften im Zeitalter der Expansion und der wissenschaftlichen Revolution entworfen wurde, viel stärker auf die Erfahrungen außereuropäischer intellektueller Traditionen rekurriert, als es die Erzählungen des europäischen bzw. westlichen Zentrums sichtbar machen. Eine Neubewertung der europäischen Geschichte globalen Wissens soll als ein Äquivalent zu Basallas These von der Ausbreitung der westlichen Wissenschaften verstanden werden. Zur weltweiten Diffusion westlicher Wissenschaften gesellt sich eine Unterströmung im Sinne eines Transfers von Wissen nach Europa. Ohne dessen Berücksichtigung ist die Geschichte der europäischen Wissenschaften unvollständig. Diese Unterströmung ist ein wesentlicher Aspekt einer Situierung des Zentrums.

6. Contested spaces

Während die Wissenschaften des Zentrums in erster Linie historisch lokalisiert werden, stellt sich die Situation in solchen Regionen als grundlegend anders dar, die westliche Modelle von Wissenschaft importiert haben. Hier ist der Konflikt zwischen den Wissenschaften und anderen, lokalen Wissenssystemen nicht auf epistemologische und historische Fragen zu beschränken. Die Gesellschaften, deren Wissen von den Wissenschaften die Geltung entzogen wurde, Repräsentationen einer Welt zu sein, existieren weiter. Seit zwei Jahrzehnten erfährt dieses Wissen eine wachsende Aufmerksamkeit.[44] Indigene Gemeinschaften als Träger und Archive eines besonderen Wissens haben einen selbstbewussteren Umgang mit ihrem Wissen entwickeln können und beanspruchen intellektuelle Eigentumsrechte. Es ist in Australien vor allem Helen Verran vom Department of History and Philosophy of Science der Universität Melbourne, die sich mit Fragen der Integration indigener Wissenstraditionen in den Wissenschaften bzw. der Annäherung von wissenschaftlichen und indigenen Wissensformationen in Australien heute beschäftigt. Sie geht von einer grundsätzlichen Gleichberechtigung epistemischer Traditionen aus und billigt den Wissenschaften keine exponierte Stellung zu.[45] Sie stützt sich bei ihren Arbeiten auf die Annahme, dass Wissenssysteme generell, über alle epistemologischen, methodischen und sozioökonomischen Differenzen hinweg, sich in dem Umstand ihrer Lokalität ähneln.[46] Somit gilt für alle Wissenssysteme, dass sie über lokale Bezüge verfügen und sie generell als eine *Assemblage* (Deleuze und Guattari) lokalen Wissens bezeichnet werden können. Eine ähnliche Position vertritt Dhruv Raina mit seiner Forderung, „....the history of science will be transformed into the history of ever so many knowledge forms".[47] Mit dem Ziel, getrennte Wissenssysteme „zusammen zu arbeiten", sucht Helen Verran zusammen mit David Turnbull nach den Macht-Konstellationen, in die Wissensformationen eingebunden sind. Dazu suchen sie Bereiche aus, in denen Wissenssysteme „überlappen".[48]

Ein eindrucksvolles Beispiel für die schwierige Verbindung differierender Epistemologien ist die Umsetzung eines komparativen Mathematikunterrichts in der Yirrkala Gemeinde in Australiens Bundesstaat Northern Territory. Unter dem Motto der Selbstbestimmung (*self-determination*), seit 1972 Politik der australischen Regierung, haben sich Mitglieder der Yolngu Aborigines dafür eingesetzt, dass neben der westlichen Arithmetik ein Yolngu System *gurrutu* unterrichtet wird. Während beide Systeme nebeneinander unterrichtet werden, lassen sich komparative Strukturen sichtbar machen, die auf die Merkmale beider

218   Von der Expansion zur Lokalisierung der Wissenschaften

Modelle anwendbar sind und somit ihre Vergleichbarkeit ermöglichen.
Die Schwierigkeiten, die entstehen, wenn disparate Epistemologien zusammengebracht werden, machen die Macht-Konstellationen sichtbar, in die Wissenssysteme eingebunden sind. Helen Verran vermutet, dass der anfängliche Widerstand gegen die Yolngu Wissenssysteme auf Seiten der australischen Administration einem bestimmten Verständnis von Wissen geschuldet war.[49] Übergänge zwischen disparaten Wissensfeldern sind mit schwierigen Übersetzungen und Interpretationen verbunden, die von beiden Seiten gleichermaßen geleistet werden müssen. Hierbei ist es wichtig, die jeweiligen „intellektuellen Räume" zu respektieren. Ein Beispiel für eine Praxis der Überwindung epistemischer Demarkationen ist der Bericht des Workshops *Working disparate knowledge systems together*[50]. Hier beschreiben Helen Verran und David Turnbull für die australische Seite, wie komparative Modelle in der Epistemologie verhandelt werden können. Es ist bemerkenswert in welchem Ausmaß dabei Positionen in Bewegung geraten.

Die Übersetzung disparater Epistemologien wird in sozialen Räumen ausgehandelt. Diese Räume sind umkämpft, es handelt sich um *contested spaces*. Sie sind mit ihren besonderen Strukturen spezifisch für multikulturelle Gesellschaften. Es kann festgehalten werden, dass die Bezüge disparater Wissensformationen in solchen Räumen ausgehandelt werden, in denen die Wissenschaften nicht mehr als Ordnungsmacht auftreten, sondern lediglich als Spieler. Diese Räume müssen jetzt genauer beschrieben werden.

Notes

1. Vgl. Hannerz 1987.
2. Vgl. Harding 1998.
3. Vgl. z.B. Levitt 1999.
4. Vgl. Pyenson 1985; Krishna 1992; Raj 2000; Burke 2001 [1997].
5. Jünger 1981, 157.
6. Vgl. Lips 1983 [1937]; Kramer1987; Riesz 2003; Därmann et al. 2004.
7. Galeano1992, 195.
8. Der Ausdruck *contact zone* stammt von Mary L. Pratt 1992.
9. Césaire 1955, 7 „Eine Zivilisation, die sich als unfähig erweist, die Probleme zu lösen, die ihr Funktionieren hervorruft, ist eine dekadente Zivilisation." [Übersetzung nach der deutschen Ausgabe 1968, 5].

10. Ibid, 9. „... die große Chance Europas war es, ein Ort der Begegnung zu sein; und damit geometrischer Ort aller Ideen, Sammelbecken aller Philosophien, Empfangsstation aller Gefühlsregungen, so hat es zum bedeutendsten Energieverteiler werden können." [Übersetzung verändert, U.L.].
11. Vgl. für die Ethnographie Berg und Fuchs 1995.
12. Zur Kritik dieses wissenschaftlichen Selbstverständnisses aus einer feministischer Sicht siehe Haraway 1996 [1988], 108-128.
13. Burghartz et al. 2003.
14. Basalla 1996 [1967], 1-21.
15. Vgl. UNESCO 1998; Gaillard et al. 1997; Emeagwali 1992; Alvares 1994.
16. Die Debatte habe ich ausführlich behandelt in Lölke 2002.
17. Vgl. meine Kritik dazu, ibid.
18. Popper 1961, 121.
19. Basalla 1996.
20. Ibid, 1.
21. Ibid, 18.
22. Ibid, 6.
23. Ibid, 5.
24. Ibid, 5.
25. Der Béniner Philosoph Paulin Hountondji beschreibt die Situation der Wissenschaften in den meisten afrikanischen Ländern heute in diesem Sinne und spricht von einer „Logik der Extroversion"; vgl. Hountondji 1997, 1.
26. Basalla 1996, 8.
27. Ibid, 12.
28. Stanley 1872.
29. Basalla 1996, 4.
30. MacLeod 2001, 3.
31. Vgl. stellvertretend für eine anhaltende Debatte Said 1995 [1978] und Mudimbe 1988.
32. Vgl. Said 1983.
33. Vgl. auch Raina 1999.
34. Basalla 1996, 12-13.
35. MacLeod 2001, 8.
36. Ibid, 8-9.
37. Ibid, 9, 10.
38. Vgl. zur Debatte Chambers [ohne Jahr]; Chambers und Gillespie 2001.
39. Raina 1999, 510; vgl. auch Raj 2000.

40. So von Raby 1996, 12.
41. Kreutzer 2004.
42. Humboldt 1859, v-vi.
43. Kreutzer 2004. Zitate im Text aus Forster 1963.
44. Geertz 2000 [1983]; Brokensha et al. 1980; Warren et al. 1989; Warren et. al. 1995.
45. Watson-Verran und Turnbull 1995a.
46. Ibid, 116.
47. Raina 1999, 511.
48. "Working were knowledge systems overlap." Watson-Verran und Turnbull 1995a, 131.
49. Watson-Verran und White 1993, 69.
50. Watson-Verran und Turnbull 1995b.

Wie immer gibt es Personen, die bereit waren, den Text zu lesen und sich über meine Ideen und Formulierungen Gedanken zu machen. Ich danke Constanze Schmaling, Leo Kreutzer und Steffi Hobuß sowie den Herausgebern für ihre Kritik an diversen früheren Versionen des Textes.

References

Alvares, Claude. *Science, Development and Violence: The Revolt Against Modernity*. Dehli: Oxford University Press, 1994.

Basalla, George. "The Spread of Western Science." In *Scientific Aspects of European Expansion*, edited by William K. Storey, 1-21. Aldershot: Variorum, 1996 [1967].

Berg, Eberhard und Martin Fuchs. Eds. *Kultur, soziale Praxis, Text. Die Krise der ethnographischen Repräsentation*. Frankfurt am Main: Suhrkamp, 1995.

Brokensha, David, D.M. Warren and Oswald Werner. Eds. *Indigenous Knowledge Systems and Development*. Washington: University Press of America, 1980.

Burghartz, Susanne, Maike Christadler und Dorothea Nolde. Eds. *Berichten, Erzählen, Beherrschen. Wahrnehmung und Repräsentation in der frühen Kolonialgeschichte*. Frankfurt am Main: Klostermann, 2003 [Zeitsprünge. Forschungen zur frühen Neuzeit, Bd.7, Heft 2/3].

Burke, Peter. *A Social History of Knowledge*. Cambridge: Polity Press, 1997 [dtsch.: Papier und Marktgeschrei. Die Geburt der Wissensgesellschaften. Berlin: Wagenbach, 2001].

Césaire, Aimé. *Discours sur le Colonialisme*. Paris: Présence Africaine,

1955. [dtsch: *Über den Kolonialismus*. trans. Monika Kind. Berlin: Wagenbach, 1968].

Chambers, David Wade. "Locality and Science. Myths of Centre and Periphery." In *Mundializacíon de la Sciencia y Cultura Nacional*, edited by Antonip Lafuente, Alberto Elena and M.L. Ortega, 605-617. Madrid: Doce Calles, 1993.

Chambers, David Wade and Richard Gillespie. "Locality in the history of science. Colonial science, technoscience, and indigenous knowledge." In *Nature and empire: Science and the colonial enterprise*, edited by Roy MacLeod, 221-240. Chicago: University of Chicago Press, 2001 [Osiris, 2nd. series, vol.15, 2000, special issue].

Därmann, Iris, Steffi Hobuß und Ulrich Lölke. Eds. *Konversionen. Fremderfahrungen in ethnologischer und interkultureller Perspektive*. Amsterdam: Rodopi, 2004.

Emeagwali, Gloria Thomas. Eds. *Science and Technology in African History with Case Studies from Nigeria, Sierra Leone, Zimbabwe and Zambia*. New York: Edwin Mellen, 1992.

Forster, Georg. „Über lokale und allgemeine Bildung." In *Forsters Werke*, bearbeitet v. Gerhard Steiner [Band 7: Kleine Schriften zu Kunst und Literatur. Sakontala], 45-56. Berlin: Akademie Verlag, 1963.

Gaillard, Jacques, V.V. Krishna and Ronald Waast. *Scientific Communities in the Developing World*. New Dehli: Sage, 1997.

Galeano, Eduardo. *Von der Notwendigkeit, Augen am Hinterkopf zu haben*. Wuppertal: Hammer, 1992.

Geertz, Clifford. *Local knowledge. Further Essays in Interpretive Anthropology*. New York: Basic books, 2000 [1983].

Hannerz, Ulf. "The World in Creolisation." *Africa* 57(4) (1987): 546-559.

Haraway, Donna. "Situated Knowledges: The Science Question in Feminism and the Privilege of Partial Perspective." In *Human Geography: An Essential Anthology*, edited by John Agnew, David Livingstone and Alisdair Rogers, 108-128. Oxford: Blackwell, 1996.

Harding, Sandra. *Is Science Multicultural? Postcolonialisms, Feminisms, and Epistemologies*. Bloomington: Indiana University Press, 1998.

Hountondji, Paulin J. "Introduction: Recentring Africa." In *Endogenous Knowledge: Research Trails*, 1-39. Dakar 1997.

Humboldt, Alexander von. *Ansichten der Natur, mit wissenschaftlichen Erläuterungen*. Stuttgart: J.G. Cotta'scher Verlag, 1859.

Jünger, Ernst. *Der Arbeiter. Herrschaft und Gestalt*. Stuttgart: Klett-Cotta, 1981 [1932].

Kramer, Fritz W. *Der rote Fes. Über Besessenheit und Kunst in Afrika*. Frankfurt am Main: Athenäum, 1987.

Kreutzer, Leo. „Depp im globalen Dorf? Lokales Wissen und das Wissen der Wissenschaft." In *Konversionen. Fremderfahrungen in ethnologischer und interkultureller Perspektive*, edited by Iris Därmann, Steffi Hobuß und Ulrich Lölke, 231-49. Amsterdam: Rodopi, 2004.

Krishna, V.V. "The Colonial 'Model' and the Emergence of National Science in India: 1876 – 1920." In *Science and Empires*, edited by Patrick Petitjean, Catherine Jami and Anne Marie Moulin, 57-72. Dordrecht: Kluwer, 1992.

Levitt, Norman. *Prometheus Bedevilled: Science and the Contradictions of Contemporary Culture*. New Brunswick, NJ: Rutgers University Press, 1999.

Lips, Julius. *Der Weiße im Spiegel der Farbigen*. München: Carl Hanser, 1983 [1937].

Lölke, Ulrich. *Zur Lokalität von Wissen. Die Kritik der local knowledge-Debatte in Anthropologie und internationaler Zusammenarbeit*. Hamburg: Institut für Afrika-Kunde, 2002 [Reihe Focus Afrika, Nr.21].

MacLeod, Roy. "Introduction." In *Nature and Empire: Science and the Colonial Enterprise*, edited by Roy MacLeod, 1-13. Chicago: University of Chicago Press, 2001 [Osiris, 2nd. series, vol.15, 2000, special issue].

Mudimbe, Valentin Y. *The Invention of Africa: Gnosis, Philosophy, and the Order of Knowledge*. Bloomington and London: Indiana University Press and James Currey, 1988.

Popper, Karl R. "Towards a Rational Theory of Tradition." In *Conjectures and refutations*, 120-135. London: Routledge and Kegan Paul, 1961.

Pratt, Mary L. *Imperial Eyes: Travel Writing and Transculturation*. London: Routledge, 1992.

Pyenson, Lewis. *Cultural Imperialism and Exact Sciences: German Expansion Overseas 1900 – 1930*. New York: Peter Lang, 1985.

Raby, Peter. *Bright Paradise: Victorian Scientific Travellers*. Princeton, NJ: Princeton University Press, 1996.

Raina, Dhruv. "From West to Non-West? Basalla's Three-Stage Model Revisited." *Science as culture* 8(4) (1999): 497-516.

Raj, Kapil. "Colonial Encounters and the Forging of new Knowledge and National Identities: Great Britain and India, 1760 – 1850." In *Nature and Empire: Science and the Colonial Enterprise*, edited by Roy MacLeod, 119-134. Chicago: University of Chicago Press, 2001 [Osiris, 2nd. series, vol.15, 2000, special issue].

Riesz, János. Ed. *Blick in den schwarzen Spiegel. Das Bild des Weißen in der afrikanischen Literatur des 20. Jahrhunderts*. Wuppertal: Hammer, 2003.

Said, Edward W. "Travelling Theory." In *The World, the Text, and the Critic*, 226-247. Cambridge, MA: Harvard University Press, 1983.

Said, Edward W. *Orientalism: Western Concepts of the Orient*. London:

Penguin Books, 1995 [1978].
Stanley, Henry M. *How I found Livingstone: Travels, Adventures, and Discoveries in Central Africa*. London: Sampson Low, Marston, Low, and Searle, 1872.
UNESCO. Eds. *World Science Report*. Paris: UNESCO, 1998.
Warren, Michael D., Jan L. Slikkerveer and Oguntunji Titilola. Eds. *Indigenous Knowledge Systems: Implications for Agriculture and International Development*, Ames: Iowa State University Press, 1989.
Warren, D. Michael L. Jan Slikkerveer and David Brokensha. Eds. *The Cultural Dimension of Development: Indigenous Knowledge Systems*, London: Intermediate Technology Publications, 1995 [*Studies in Technology and Social Change* (11)].
Watson-Verran, Helen and David Turnbull. "Science and other Indigenous Knowledge Systems." In *Handbook of Science and Technology Studies,* edited by Sheila Jasanoff, Gerald Markle, James Petersen, and Trevor Pinch, 115-139. Thousand Oaks: Sage, 1995a.
Watson-Verran, Helen and David Turnbull. "Talking about Science and other Knowledge Traditions in Australia." *HASN* (34) (1995b). <http://www.asap.unimelb.edu.au/hasn/no34/r34knowl.htm> (23.01.04).
Watson-Verran, Helen and Leon White. "Issues of Knowledge in the Policy of Self-Determination for Aboriginal Australian Communities." *Knowledge and policy* 6 (1993): 67-78.

Negotiating Nationhood in Multi-Ethnic Germany: an Australian Perspective

Nicholas K. White

1.   Introduction

'Negotiating nationhood in multi-ethnic Germany' is intended to evoke both conversations with others and conducting oneself in order to clear or pass certain obstacles. The subjects of this study, teachers in a secondary school in former West Germany, were engaged in conversations with those seen to be different from themselves and in navigation through the difference and common ground thus constructed. One might say that the latter process, the finding of a way in multi-ethnic Germany, is also a conversation: a conversation not only with people but with German history and institutions.

It was as Germans that teachers at the school formed a community of actors for my analytical purposes. The voices I present are particular voices, but they negotiate the shared reality of being German. I am not suggesting that the ways my subjects negotiated German nationhood were representative of those of teachers in Germany, much less of Germans more generally. Nor do I claim that being German was an important self-identity category for them, just that by certain criteria it was something they shared. For my purposes, it was sufficient that being German was central to the teachers in the following ways: first, they were aware that they were in the business of forming German citizens; second, an awareness of their 'Germanness' remerged out of contact with and construction of others, namely immigrant students and me; third, awareness of German identities is heightened in these contexts borne of the historical circumstances to which I allude in this paper. I make my perspective explicit because a systematic reflexivity provides the source of unique ethnographic insights[1] and because my being an Australian influenced how I was treated and how I responded.

At the beginning of the 1998-1999 school year teachers at the *Gesamtschule* in Osnabrück were aged between thirty-seven and sixty-two, which means that they were born in the period from 1935 to 1961 and were part of an aging teaching cohort in Germany. Over ninety percent were born between 1942 and 1958, and over ninety percent within ten years either side of the end of the Second World War. I observed the classes of ten of the school's teachers, five women and five men, and interviewed them and a few others at length.

My subjects have lived in a Germany within which the negotiation of nationhood has been a recurrent theme. They grew up in the shadow and shame of National Socialism and the Holocaust. The Germany of their childhood and youth was occupied by the Americans, British, French and Russians. Many of the teachers were at university during the student unrest of the 1960s and some described themselves to me as "68ers". As young teachers in the 1960s and 1970s most taught the children of the first so-called *Gastarbeiter* ('guest workers') recruited to meet the labour demands of post-War reconstruction. More recently they have been teaching the grandchildren of these 'guest workers' and the many refugees who came to Germany under the liberal post-War asylum laws. They have also had the challenge of teaching *Aussiedler* (German 're-settlers' from Eastern Europe and the former Soviet Union: literally those who "settled out"). These immigrants are the descendants of German settlers in these regions over the centuries, and nearly all 'return' without any German language skills.

2. "We are the indigenous people of Germany"

My subjects were Germans. None of them would have disagreed with that, and they would have thought it rather strange had I queried it. Nonetheless, just what *deutsch* was assumed to mean varied with context. *Deutsch* was sometimes used to refer to those who held German passports: to be German was to be a citizen of the Federal Republic of Germany. In this civic understanding, a naturalised immigrant from Turkey was a German, and a German emigrant to Australia was not. On other occasions, being *deutsch* was constituted by virtue of being a member of a supposed ethnic community. This understanding was most often assumed or implied rather than explicitly stated. For obvious reasons my subjects did not call Austrians *Deutsche*, they were *Österreicher*, but they were nonetheless in some sense *deutsch*. Conversely, when it was known to my subjects, naturalised Germans of non-German ethnic heritage were frequently called *Deutsche*, but they were not seen to be unambiguously *deutsch*.

A conversation I had with Irma illustrates the ethnic German self-understanding which was, to a greater or lesser extent, taken-for-granted by my subjects. She and I were comparing the difficulties faced by various groups in both Germany and Australia. One of the disadvantaged groups I identified was indigenous Australians. Irma's response was to say, "Yes, but we are the indigenous people (*Ureinwohner*) of Germany." Irma was alluding to the politics of indigeneity the world over but at the same time was betraying a rather naive view of central European history and the nation-building process. The "We" she was assuming, modern 'ethnic' Germans, cannot unproblematically be traced back to an indigenous

'German' community.

Also of interest is what Irma's claim reveals about how she conceived of Germany and its people, both 'indigenous' and 'immigrant'. The assumption of an indigenous ethnic community implies that it has a particular political legitimacy for it is in Germany by historical or primordial right, and hence is host to the various immigrant groups. This conception of the nation is not specific to Germany but is a feature of the nation-state itself. All modern nation-states construct their nation as a unitary people with a particular legitimacy. For example, France, although founded on the republican idea of citizenship, was very soon constructed and imagined as a unitary super-ethnic community, 'the French'.[2] Even the 'settler' countries of the New World such as Australia, Canada and the United States of America tend to imagine themselves as a people of common heritage.

It is interesting to reflect that Irma made her remark about the indigenous people of Germany in response to my comparison of issues in Germany and in Australia. Irma did not regard her and my relationships to our respective states to be comparable, for I was not indigenous to my land in the way that she was to hers. The Australian nation is obviously not the continuation of a primordial community of the Australian continent. Indigenous Australians were struggling to survive the European invasion and settlement during the period of modern state-formation and hence nation-building. Their ways had limited impact on the formation of the founding idea of the Australian nation. It is far easier to imagine continuity between the ways of those who were incorporated into Bismark's *Reich* in 1871 (or, even more so, into the Weimar Republic) and what is generally understood as the German nation today. The fact that the nation is a recent construct is much less obvious for Germany than for a classical country of immigration like Australia. Indeed, Germans make a distinction between *ein Einwanderungsland* (a country of immigration), and a country which is not seen to be built on immigration but rather on an historical or primordial nation.

3. "Not a country of immigration"

In the light of mass immigration to the Federal Republic of Germany since the Second World War, the distinction Germans made between countries of immigration (*Einwanderungsländer*), and countries such as Germany which were seen to be nation-states, not countries of immigration, appeared rather incongruous to my Australian ear. I soon learned that the oft repeated claim, „*Wir sind kein Einwanderungsland*" (We are not a country of immigration) had to be understood as an expression of normative self-understanding not as a claim about actual experience or prohibition. „*Wir sind kein Einwanderungsland*" might be better translated as "We do not *understand ourselves to be* a country of immigration". For, clearly, the *Gastarbeiter* ('guest worker') recruitment programme was not conceived as a programme of permanent settlement. Preoccupied with the task of rebuilding a war-ravaged country the long-term realities of labour recruitment were, naively, not given a great deal of consideration, nor introduced with public consultation.[3] Similarly, neither asylum policy nor the resettlement of *Aussiedler* were prompted by the desire to build a multi-ethnic society. The multi-ethnic nature of post-War Germany was not something which was planned, even if many Germans have subsequently embraced it.

For many of those who were supportive or at least tolerant of immigration to Germany, such as my subjects, "not a country of immigration" was a means of distinguishing Germany and German policy from the *Einwanderungsländer* (immigration countries) of the New World such as Australia, Canada and the United States of America, and their various policies of multiculturalism. Given the stark reality of post-War immigration, some German academics during the period of my research were talking of Germany as an example of a new type of *Einwanderungsland*,[4] and were agitating for a distinct migration policy.[5] For many Germans, however, *Deutschland* continued to be understood in terms of a marriage of an historical or primordial nation and a modern state. This national self-understanding was not particular to Germany. All European countries understood themselves as classical nation-states, not as countries of immigration in the way that the United States of America, Canada and Australia are countries of immigration. Germany, however, was one of the most consistent in placing "not a country of immigration" at the centre of public policy.[6] Indeed, since 1977 the claim had been explicit in German government policy[7] and was only officially dismantled with the moves to introduce a distinct immigration policy in the first years of the twenty-first century.[8]

4. The nation-state

The dual ethnic-political implications of "nation" are now commonplace; it has come to appear the natural state of affairs. Following Gellner, in discussing nation-states I use the term 'state' to refer to the political unit which is also commonly called a nation in English, and reserve 'nation' to refer to the people associated with it.[9] The intimate connection of nation and state is reinforced in the English-speaking world by the use of 'nationality' to refer both to membership of cultural entities called nations and to the citizenship of states. The distinction is made rather more precisely in German. State membership (*Staatsangehörigkeit*) and participatory citizenship (*Staatsbürgershaft*) are clearly distinguished in the German lexicon from membership of the cultural entity commonly called a nation (*Nationalität*) or a people (*Volkszugehörigkeit*). Notwithstanding the clarity of this distinction, in Germany as elsewhere, the age of nationalism in the late nineteenth century gave credence to the idea that the nation and state should coincide. To follow Gellner further, I shall understand nationalism to be the political programme which assumes that the political unit (the state) and the national unit should be "congruent".[10]

Historically, 'nation' (including the German *Nation* and *Volk*) did not have political connotations but referred to a non-political linguistic and cultural group; a group, incidentally, which was important to a very limited number of people. The *Holy Roman Empire of the German Nation* was not the primary political structure nor an important identity category for most subjects of the *Reich*. Indeed, early in the twentieth century the shift to political understandings of 'nation' was the context within which Meinecke distinguished *Kulturnation* (a non-political cultural community) from *Staatsnation* (a civic community seeking self-determination).[11] Prior to the rise of the nation-state, political arrangements in Europe were typically quite independent of ethnic-linguistic groups (nations, in the older sense of the term).

As modern states arose they usually reached across pre-existing regional, ethnic and religious divides. Over time certain of these linguistic, religious, symbolic and, particularly, ethnic conceptions of 'groupness' transformed into the modern idea of the nation and came to dominate the cultural meanings of the new state. Nationalists emphasised the pre-existing elements of the national idea and often presented the new state as the inevitable outcome of national sentiment. However, whilst the nation had to have some "resonance" with its potential members to be successful,[12] nations as we understand them today are relatively recent constructs. Whilst this is not difficult for an Australian to accept of the Australian nation, Germans found the proposition that the German nation was a modern construct much more counter-intuitive.

The fact that Irma and other intelligent and educated Germans (and other nationals), understand the nation as an indigenous ethnic community illustrates the centrality and apparent self-evidence of these ideas. On other occasions the teachers, including Irma herself, employed much more fluid ideas of the nation and even critiqued national identities as such. However, these were occasions of intellectual reflection. The instincts and assumptions, the default position of day-to-day interaction, was more commonly constituted in terms of historical or primordial ethnic-national groups.

For whatever combination of factors, in a relatively short period nation-states came to be imagined as super-ethnic communities, complete with historical continuity, a sense of place, cultural tradition and even, with the nineteenth century discovery of the genetic heritability of traits, biological relatedness. This shift in understanding of the nation was quite dramatic. The liberal, bourgeois national consciousness of 1830-1880 gave way to the ethnic-linguistic national consciousness characteristic of 1880-1914.[13]

5. Nationhood, national identity and nationalism

Being a member of a cultural entity called a nation has become almost universal. I shall label this embeddedness in such a cultural complex 'nationhood', to distinguish it from membership of a state (commonly called nationality in English), and the ideological connotations of nationalism. It is useful to distinguish this taken-for-granted (if ambiguous) nationhood from one's national identity, where identity implies a greater degree of reflection and volition. I shall reserve national identity for the opinions, attitudes and practices which an individual layers on his or her nationhood. The distinction is somewhat artificial but it serves to distinguish that which the subject feels is given and that which he or she feels has been chosen. Understood in this way, national identity varies much more than does nationhood. What one feels about the nation in which one is embedded, one's national identity, is relatively more idiosyncratic and hence variable. During the period of my research, many Germans were highly ambivalent about being German and looked either to more localised identifications (e.g. region[14], city, dialect) or to supra-national identifications (e.g. Europe, the West, cosmopolitanism, a religious tradition). Others were more comfortable with their nationhood and constructed a positive national identity.

It is important to distinguish a positive national identity from nationalism (the political programme which assumes that the political unit and the national unit should be congruent). Nationalists hold that members of a state's (supposed) historical or primordial community, the nation, are the only legitimate members of this state. My subjects were far from German nationalists in this sense. They worked in a state school, one of the principal aims of which was to integrate students of varying backgrounds.[15] None with whom I spoke thought that only German 'nationals', by which I mean members of the cultural entity (not citizens of the state), should be able to live in the Federal Republic or hold German citizenship.

The nation is still important for our story, however. The teachers' construction and contestation of cultural difference was influenced by their ingrained nationhood and by their rather more moderate national identities. For my subjects, the sense that "we are the indigenous people of Germany" may not have been seen as a reason that migrants should not be in Germany but it certainly had implications for what was expected of them if they did in fact live in Germany.

6. Employing ethnic-national categories

Even though ethnicity is of recent vintage in English social science lexicons,[16] ethnicity has already found its way into popular usage in much of the English-speaking world. It was my experience that the word ethnicity had not found its way into popular usage in Germany. The adjective *ethnisch* is recognised[17] but was not widely used. I found it most commonly used in the expression "ethnic minorities" (*ethnische Minderheiten*). Notwithstanding the issues being discussed, in all of my interview material only one teacher used the word ethnicity, in the phrase "children with an ethnic identity," (*Kinder mit einer ethnischen Identität*) but this might be explained by the fact that she had spent many years in the United States of America. The noun *Ethnizität* was in use in academic circles in Germany but was yet to filter into general usage at the school. I used *Ethnizität*, rather inadvisedly in retrospect, in a set of printed questions I gave to teachers a few days before meeting for an interview. They knew what I meant but did not use the word in response. *Herkunft* (origin, background), *Abstammung* (descent) or, more generally, *Nationalität* (nationality) tended to be used to refer to what an English speaker might label ethnicity. As we have seen, *Nationalität* did not mean membership of a state as nationality can in English. Their reticence to use *Volk* (people, also nation) or the adjective *völkisch* has a long and complicated history: in some circumstances these words suggest 'race' or have been used as such, notably by the National Socialists.[18]

In English, 'ethnicity' is both vague and polysemous and hence I concur with Just that it is "a somewhat retrograde step that ethnicity should ever have entered into the *analytic* vocabulary of the social sciences".[19] However, as Just notes, in the European context ethnicity does evoke that conglomeration of historical continuity, geographical circumscription, state membership or incorporation, cultural tradition and supposed biological relatedness which characterises so much classification of groups of people.[20] There is something going on in the real world here, even if our analytical tools are rather blunt. There is now a vast literature on ethnicity, of which there are a number of helpful surveys.[21] I shall be employing ethnicity to label the sort of 'groupness' which is ascribed by members or outsiders in terms of putative collective 'origins'. What makes it useful to distinguish ethnic classification is that people consistently group themselves and others in terms of some such combination of their historical, geographical, state, cultural and biological origins.

The ethnic understanding of national categories and the employment of such categories by my subjects is illustrated by a conversation I had with Andreas concerning a student exchange between the *Gesamtschule* in Osnabrück and a school in Çanakkale in Turkey. I asked Andreas whether many *Gesamtschule* students of Turkish heritage had participated in the exchange. Andreas was rather surprised by my question and responded with passion:

> Absolutely none. No. This is a German-Turkish exchange. I made that clear to all at the outset. Turks can travel in Turkey when they want. But not on this occasion because it's a trip for Germans. Also - so that Turks don't visit a Turkish household here. That wouldn't be interesting. The point is that the Turks get to know Germans. Lot of Turks have wanted to go, but we said, no, only Germans - and in return only Turks. See what I mean? Because it's meant to be a German-Turkish exchange, not a Turkish-Turkish exchange.[22]

Andreas conceived of the school exchange as one between the primary communities of two modern states, what we have called nations. Andreas understood these national categories in terms of shared historical or primordial origins, that is in ethnic terms. He did not regard *Gesamtschule* students with a Turkish heritage to qualify for the exchange because they were not 'ethnic' Germans. The fact that virtually all 'Turks' at the school were born in and had lived all of their lives in Germany, spoke German, some monolingually, and would most likely spend the bulk of their futures in Germany did not make them Germans for the purpose of Andreas' classification.

Given the breadth of ethnicity as I have defined it, we need to consider just what combination of historical, geographical, state, cultural and biological origins that Andreas was assuming. I shall start with state membership. It is true that the 'Turks' precluded from the exchange would be unlikely to have been German citizens. I'm not sure, however, that citizenship was at issue. Had the year 8 students participating in the school exchange been old enough to naturalise and, indeed, become German citizens they would still have been from 'Turkish' households in Andreas' sense. They would still have shared too much with their potential Turkish hosts in Çanakkale to make the school exchange a substantive exchange. The point of the school exchange for Andreas was the experience of *cultural* difference. This meant that the *Gesamtschule* exchange students must come from, and Çanakkale exchange students must visit, 'German' households not 'Turkish' ones.

Andreas was well aware of what anthropologists have been telling us for decades, that there are vast cultural differences between Turks in Turkey and those in Germany.[23] During the very same conversation Andreas had suggested to me that 'Turks' in Germany were more religiously (*gläubig*) and politically fundamentalist than in Turkey. However, such cultural differences were not what Andreas had in mind for the school exchange. The cultural differences which were important, and this is what makes his classification an ethnic one, were those which were cultural 'traditions', that is those which had some veneer of historical continuity and association with a primordial people.

A. The traditions of ethnic nations

By associating his students with the particular traditions of discrete historical or primordial groups, Andreas was operating with a model of culture which Boddy and Lambek call the "contents and container model" of culture.[24] This model is of limited analytical value. As the teachers themselves implied on other occasions, groups of people are not characterised by fixed and finished traditions, but their collective attitudes and practices are constantly evolving. Indeed, the teachers' association of their students with fixed traditions they assumed to characterise putative historical or primordial groups, was constitutive of culture as I define it for my own analytical purposes: the evolving systems of shared meaning which are emergent in social action.

This dialectical or processual understanding of culture is difficult to reconcile with the popular assumption that the world is home to a multitude of reified and opposed cultures, each with their own fixed cultural content. Nonetheless, most social actors, including my subjects, assume that cultures are made up of fixed and finished traditions fashioned by the particular history of groups. The processes of culture change tend to be obscured or seen as a loss or destruction of culture. The principal limitation of essentialist understandings of culture is that they are unable to account for the fact that social groups are in a constant state of change.

Nonetheless, to dismiss essentialist understandings of culture as misguided is to ignore much of the social reality we wish to understand. All of us, on occasions, essentialise groups and associate them with reified cultures. We ascribe reified cultures to ourselves and to others because the assumption of a world made up of ethnic nations, religions, and other social groupings is reinforced in the course of our day-to-day interactions, and is consistent with the fact that groups do share and negotiate meanings with each other which are not typically accessible to outsiders. The idea of fixed and finished cultures serves a number of existential, political and predictive ends. As Baumann has argued, the assumption of distinct and contained cultures, whilst analytically flawed, facilitates strong group identity, provides boundaries for members and would-be dissenters, and is a powerful tool for predicting the behaviour of others.[25]

The assumption of distinct and contained cultures was certainly a part of my subjects' interpretive repertoire. This is, in part, because while our social action generates and changes culture we often experience culture as something fixed and external to us. Culture existed before we were born and will continue long after we are dead. "I know that I am a German but I don't feel particularly German," said Anna during a class discussion recounted in the following pages. That which she served to constitute felt alien and constraining of her. Notwithstanding the force of Anna's experience, it is we who constrain society. Not only what we do but also the way we think about culture is a part of the human action which constitutes it.[26] The observer is a participant, a part of the observed.[27] This is of fundamental significance for my purposes. My subjects were not simply experts on the negotiation of nationhood in multi-ethnic Germany, their actions and words constituted the subject matter itself. However, Anna's sense that culture is constraining of us should not be dismissed too readily. Embedded in a shared semantic context, people's actions are conditioned by the meanings they share. This is not to say that culture has any causal efficacy, just that people usually act in ways that make cultural sense.

B. Ethnic-nations and phenotypes

'Ethnic' Germans look more physically distinguishable from 'ethnic' Turks than from, say, 'ethnic' Dutchmen and women. As such, ethnic classification of Germans and Turks can more easily utilise these phenotypical differences than the distinction of Germans and the Dutch. Physical differences are less plausibly employed to distinguish Turkish ethnicity from, say, Greek ethnicity, for 'ethnic' Turks and 'ethnic' Greeks look more similar than do 'ethnic' Germans and 'ethnic' Turks. Where phenotypical difference is more distinct, it is more easily utilised in ethnic classification. The degree to which Andreas, or any of us, takes account of phenotypical appearance in the classification of groups of people is beyond the scope of this paper. What I do want to stress, however, is that to consciously or unconsciously make distinctions in these terms is not the same thing as racism. Racists believe that there are certain distinct races (human subspecies) which have distinctive characteristics which determine their respective cultures and intrinsic value. I wish to stress that

I hold this to be a scientific nonsense and a moral outrage. We cannot, however, avoid the fact that there is variation in population genetics and that such difference is taken into account in people's classification of each other.

Nor is this to argue that phenotypical difference was the criterion for Andreas' exclusion of 'Turks' from the school exchange. The fact that 'Turks' at the *Gesamtschule* looked different was simply one of the components of their 'Turkish' ethnicity, which, following the logic of ethnic classification, meant that they would not have had the 'German' cultural stuff necessary for a meaningful exchange. I should suggest that it is this cultural component which is central to Andreas' ethnic-national classification. If one conceives of the exchange as one between national cultures, what is the point of visiting a household in Germany if one speaks Turkish, eats 'Turkish' food and watches cable television from Turkey? As fascinating as the differences might be, this was not seen to be an *ethnic-national* cultural exchange.

I argue that it was culture, understood to be the traditions of a supposed historical or primordial group, which was central to my subjects' ethnic-national classifications. That is, for them, what defined a nation was its historical continuity and cultural traditions more than state membership, geographical circumscription or biological relatedness. Geographical, state and biological factors were present but they were nothing like as important as cultural tradition and assumed historical continuity in the teachers' ethnic-national classifications.

This is confirmed by the teachers' reluctance to regard *Aussiedler* ('German' re-settlers from eastern Europe and the former Soviet Union) as 'real' Germans. *Aussiedler* were generally regarded as nationals of their countries of birth. The fact that they had been permitted to 'return' to Germany because they had German ancestors (assumed biological relatedness), had been granted German citizenship and lived in Germany were marginal to the teachers' ethnic-national classifications of them. The fact that they did not speak German and were more accustomed to 'cultural' life in their countries of birth rather than 'cultural' life in Germany were the decisive factors. A comment by Irma, if in unusually strong terms, captures the sense of my subjects' ethnic classification of *Aussiedler* well:

> One can't identify *Aussiedler* as Germans unproblematically, absolutely not... because they are different culturally, but also in terms of civilization have lived differently. Some come from Kazakhstan - I have one from Alma Ata. As far as I can tell Alma Ata is

almost in Siberia. That is, they're not acquainted with certain technological developments here. The students were really differently formed... Some couldn't even read or write.[28]

The fact that an identifiable set of 'German' or 'Turkish' or 'Russian' cultural stuff is an idea rather than a reality is neither here nor there. It was sufficient that those who organised the school exchange, or imagined Alma Ata in frozen Siberia assumed a German national culture, a Turkish national culture and a Russian, or Soviet or Kazakh national culture. The problem for students of 'Turkish' or 'Russian' heritage living in Germany is that they do not fit into the reified stereotypes which Andreas and Irma employed. For the purposes of the school exchange, 'Turks' at the *Gesamtschule* were not regarded as German nationals and could not very well visit their own school, representative of an assumed Turkish nation. *Aussiedler* were in a similar dilemma. They had been accepted by the German state because of their German heritage but the Germans amongst whom they lived regarded them principally as nationals of their countries of birth.

C. On being German

The cultural traditions which are seen to constitute an ethnic-nation are both fluid and elusive. As a window onto the contestation of German national identity I shall recount a circumstance which took place not amongst teachers at the *Gesamtschule* but amongst my colleagues in the graduate research group (*Graduiertenkolleg*) at the Institute for Migration Research and Intercultural Studies (IMIS) of the University of Osnabrück.[29] Over a few drinks at the end of my research stay they presented me with a certificate:

> Herewith the doctoral students of the *IMIS-Graduiertenkolleg* attest that the Australian citizen and cosmopolitan gent, Nicholas White, has acquired and successfully employed the following 'German virtues': diligence, cleanliness, reliability, discipline, politeness, order, punctuality, thrift and linguistic correctness and exactitude. With this certificate Mr Nicholas White holds the right to present himself throughout the world as a German without German citizenship.[30]

The joke was that it was their Australian guest who was more characterised by these stereotyped German characteristics than many of them were. A combination of both personality and circumstance had made for this eventuality. Conducting research as a guest of the *Gesamtschule* and participation in doctoral seminars at the University soon after learning the German language, and all on a stipend paid in a weakening Australian dollar, made for a rather diligent, disciplined, polite, orderly, punctual and thrifty researcher who was constantly aware of the correctness and exactitude (or lack of them) of his German usage. In contrast, some of my German colleagues were laconic, larrikin, easy-going 'Australian' types.

The desire of my colleagues to deconstruct 'Germanness' has to be seen in the context of the German nationhood in which they were enmeshed. German nationhood has not been the most comfortable cultural complex for much of this century. It is not surprising that many Germans have been attracted to post-national identities. In both the Federal Republic of Germany and the German Democratic Republic, German identity and unity were subordinated to integration into the two blocs of the emerging Cold War. In the West this took the form of repressing any nationalism, and a commitment to the processes of European unity (as enshrined in the preamble to the Federal Republic's constitution).[31]

One's nationhood is not so easily forgotten, however, nor the evil to which it was so recently mobilised quickly forgiven. The relationship of my subjects and their generation to the Holocaust is extremely complicated and can only be alluded to here. What I wish to stress is that even though they were not personally involved, my subjects, together with all post-War Germans, have been associated with the Holocaust by others, non-Germans and Germans alike. This association, and for many its entanglement with questions of moral responsibility, has greatly complicated Germans' national identities.

7. **"Is it different for us as Germans to visit Auschwitz?"**

Poised with pencil and paper in the back corner of Jürgen's year 11 German class, I found myself scribbling furiously during a discussion prompted by his simple question, "Is it in some way different for us as Germans to visit Auschwitz?"[32] The class was preparing for an excursion to Poland which was to include a visit to the Auschwitz concentration camp.

The proposition that such a visit would be different for them as Germans was something which these students were reluctant to concede or, when sympathetic, found very difficult to articulate. The instinct of a number (of young men) in the class was to rail against the idea. For them, the Second World War was ancient history. Even though they were well informed about the history of this period,[33] they felt little personal ownership of the events or the national identity in terms of which the War was fought. David's immediate reaction was to insist that "one's nationality is irrelevant" and that "other peoples have committed atrocities too." The impulse to compare the Holocaust with other acts of genocide was shared by Matthäus. "There was genocide in Cambodia but it isn't treated in the same way as the Holocaust." Clearly these objections are not inconsistent with the proposition that it is substantively different for a German, as opposed to a non-German, to visit a Nazi concentration camp. It was only after some time and passion had been spent that the students began to narrow in on the specific question posed by their teacher.

Cordula was one of the few who addressed the question directly. She held in tension her insistence that "this generation bears no guilt" with an appreciation that, "It is recent past. I think that we should feel differently but I'm not sure why." Others continued to circle the issue at hand. "All people, not just Germans, need to appreciate the horrors of the Holocaust," demanded David. Stefan made a distinction between "guilt" (*Schuld*), which he was not willing to concede, and a "responsibility" (*Verantwortung*) to ensure that it doesn't happen again, which he felt he shared with all people, non-Germans included.

For many students to admit that their visit to Auschwitz would in fact be different for them as Germans was to admit some sort of connection with the horror. As he did frequently during the discussion, Jürgen repeated his initial question. "Yes, but is it primarily a need that Germans have? Is there something qualitatively different for a German to visit a Nazi concentration camp? Most of you have relatives who lived in Germany during the Nazi period. Can you imagine that the experience of going to Auschwitz as a foreigner or someone more recently settled in Germany would be different?"

Matthäus suggested that if, as a German born after the War, he shared in some sort of collective guilt (*kollektive Schuld*) then so too should those who had migrated to Germany and become naturalised German citizens since the War. It was clear that Jürgen had in mind an ethno-cultural 'Germanness' rather than simply a legal inclusion in the German state, and so he narrowed his question. "Is there a particular emotional response that is unique to Germans who have families which were involved in the Nazi period?" Cordula came closest to the kernel of Jürgen's question when she revealed that she had felt intense shame when she had visited the remains of the Dachau concentration camp on the outskirts of Munich.

The invitation to associate themselves with the Holocaust was something these students were very reticent to accept, perhaps in part because as Germans they find themselves associated with Nazism anyway. Anna was one to express this tension: "Regardless of what we feel we are associated with Nazism. Americans don't know where Germany is on the map but they know that we are Nazis. The problem is those who still have Nazi views, the Neo-Nazis. I don't feel any nationalism. In Holland I never say that I'm from Germany. I know that I am a German but I don't feel particularly German."

If one has to concede that it is in some way different for Germans to visit Auschwitz, then another avenue of escape from connection with the horror is to deny one's 'Germanness'. This distancing of oneself from the nation was expressed by a number of students, most starkly and forcefully by David who insisted that he was "a European" and didn't "feel a real connection with Germany." Whilst reiterating his primary question, Jürgen took the opportunity to interpret this shift in the discussion. "I agree that people feel more cosmopolitan, more European today than they did in earlier generations but is it that easy? What if someone in your family was a murderer? A murderer in the family, murderers in the national family; What is the difference?" For Stefan amongst others the difference had to be considerable. He was insistent that one's connection with family was nothing like connection with the nation. "Well if you can be that limited about it good luck to you," replied Jürgen.

8. Contesting national identities

Jürgen felt the draw of his nationhood more strongly than did many of his students or was more willing than they to acknowledge the connection. Intellectually Jürgen was attracted to European, cosmopolitan and other post-national identifications, but in spite of their appeal, the hold of a national identity was not quite as disposable as he might have liked. The realisation that national identities are relatively modern constructs is not sufficient to free oneself from the social complex in which one is embedded.

Nationhood and National identities are constructions both from within and from without. One's 'Germanness' is acquired by means of being so regarded, both by other Germans and by the members of other nations. A 'German' who constructs himself or herself as a Berliner or a European cannot avoid the fact that many others, both within Germany and without, will regard him or her as a German nonetheless. One's nationhood is constituted in conversation with others, it is not something which can be discarded at will.

Wars between nation-states reinforce *nation* as a fundamental category. Like the First World War, the Second World War was an inter*national* conflict. Whatever they themselves felt, the rest of the world was making it abundantly clear that they were Germans. If the rest of the world is calling you a German and international trade, sport and migration are conducted in national terms one cannot simply decide to be a cosmopolitan or European instead.

In addition, the rest of the world was making it abundantly clear that being German was not a good thing to be. Outside Germany, after the establishment of the Second Empire in 1870-1871, the mid-nineteenth century stereotype of romantic, emotional beer-drinking Germans whose rich cultural and religious heritage had made a major contribution to Europe were largely superseded by the stereotype of German preference for militarism. This image of Prussia was subsequently projected onto Germany more generally and later events (the World Wars, the Holocaust, subservience to the strong leadership of occupying forces, the German economic miracle and the successes of the *Deutschmark*) seen as a manifestation of this essential character.[34] Further, in light of the Second World War many nationals made little distinction between an anti-Semite, a fascist and a German. Even though the Allies had not fought a war against anti-Semitism, the national conflict gave anti-Semitism a national face, and the face was German. The distinction was blurred for many within Germany itself.

In this context it is not surprising that many Germans have sought post-national identities. However, whilst this shift from national categories was in evidence in their national identities, I'm not sure how much impact this concern with post-national identities has had on their taken-for-granted *nationhood*, the cultural complex in which they are embedded regardless of what they, individually, think. It appeared to me that such a shift from national categories was only just beginning to show up (if faintly) in the nationhood of their students. Jürgen took great heart from the fact that his students seemed to be less defined by their 'Germanness' than his generation was:

> An example which I think you witnessed yourself during discussion in the year 11 class. It concerned the question, Is it in some way different for us as Germans to visit Auschwitz? And a student said... "It is not an issue whether I'm a German or not. I regard myself as a person and as a European and as such it is an issue which concerns everyone". I think that things will tend more and more strongly in this direction. In Germany, at least, we have this opportunity because there is a national vacuum in German consciousness . [...] It was frowned upon in Germany to utter the words nation or national, because they were stigmatised by the Nazis. Now after the reunification (*Wende*), one is permitted to

> utter them again. [...] But there is actually no longer a national identity, such as the French for example are able to localise in Paris. [...] In Germany there are several centres, such as Hamburg, Munich, Cologne, Stuttgart, Frankfurt. [...] And these centres, these cultural centres, are not national centres but rather they all have a European orientation. [...] This centralisation, this pointing to one metropolis, as it was with Berlin prior to the War, doesn't exist anymore. Because of this de-centralisation Germany had a great opportunity to think European. Beyond borders. Also somewhat inter culturally, even if this is limited to the European context. I think this is a prerequisite for such a mentality to be able to develop amongst the young. Not in the first instance to think as a national but increasingly to think as a European.[35]

Whilst my subjects sometimes operated with reified ethnic-national stereotypes, such as those which Andreas employed in his organisation of the school exchange, on other occasions, such as in Jürgen's discussion above, my subjects contested the necessity of such categories.

The irony is that the very contestation of the nation as a category is a testament to its enduring importance. Indeed, Jürgen's question, "Is it in some way different for us as Germans to visit Auschwitz?" was predicated upon a shared nationhood and the implication that what had been done in its name demanded a common response, even from those not personally involved.

9. Conclusion

Embedded in the cultural complex I have called nationhood, the day-to-day activities of teachers at the *Gesamtschule* in Osnabrück assumed that the world was made up of ethnic-national groups and that they were members of the putative indigenous group in Germany. They saw historically continuous cultural traditions to be the primary markers of ethnic-national groups and these assumptions were so entrenched that they survived even the most sophisticated attempts to contest the necessity of nationhood. The ways in which I perceived these processes were shaped by the fact that I was Australian. Had I been seen to be indigenous to Australia, Irma might not have felt the need to claim her own indigeneity and had I felt indigenous to my land in the way that she did to hers I might not have been so intrigued by the claim that „*Wir sind kein Einwanderungsland*" (We are not a country of immigration) from those who lived in multi-ethnic Germany. In spite of cosmopolitan celebrations of selves constructed from a smorgasbord of cultural diversity, nationhood still had a significant hold in the multi-ethnic Germany of the late twentieth century.

Notes

1. See Davies 1999 and Okley 1992.
2. Weber 1976.
3. Chapin 1997, 10.
4. Bade 1994b, 12.
5. Bade 1994a.
6. Joppke 1999.
7. Joppke 1999, 63.
8. Reißlandt 2002.
9. Gellner 1983, 3-7.
10. Ibid, 1.
11. Meinecke 1919.
12. Smith 1988, 11.
13. Hobsbawm 1990.
14. Regional identity is strong in many parts of Germany. The historical usage of *Nation* is still in evidence here. Regions of Germany celebrate local specialities as their 'national drink' or 'national dish'.
15. Niedersächsisches Kultusministerium 1991, 8.
16. The word ethnicity appears in the 1950s and is increasingly used in the 1960s. Chapman 1993, 15.
17. *Wahrig Deutsches Wörterbuch* 1997 [1966], 448.
18. The English 'ethnicity', too, sometimes functions as a substitute for 'race' in popular usage.
19. Just 1989, 76.
20. Ibid, 75-77.
21. Banks 1996; Chapman 1993; Eriksen 1993; Jenkins 1997.
22. „Überhaupt keine. Nein. Das ist hier ein deutsch-türkischer Austausch. Und da habe ich von vornherein gesagt. Die Türken, die können in die Türkei fahren, wenn sie wollen. Aber nicht, weil wir jetzt gerade Deutsche mitnehmen. Dass sie auch, die Türken, nicht hier in ein türkisches Haus kommen. Das ist uninteressant, sondern die Türken sollen hier Deutsche kennenlernen. Also von daher haben wir - sie wollten immer mitfahren, viele - na. Und wir haben gesagt, ne, nur Deutsche, und dann nur Türken. Es ist klar, na? Denn es sollte ein Deutsch-Türkisch Austausch, nicht ein Türkisch-Türkisch Austausch sein."

23. For an excellent example see Schiffauer 1988.
24. Lambek and Boddy 1997.
25. Baumann 1999 84-87, 91.
26. This is not to say that society is a product of the ways we think about it. For a comprehensive rebuttal of radical social constructivist theses (ethnomethodology, and cultural and linguistic relativity arguments) see Collin 1997.
27. Post-structuralist theorists have made a great deal of this complication. Research strategies such as hermeneutics and analytic philosophy, which posit a mythical detached observer, have come in for intense criticism; for there is no view from nowhere. Curiously, however, many of these theorists seem to have concluded that the fact that there is no view from nowhere implies that nothing exists or at least that nothing can be said about that which does.
28. „Man kann Aussiedler nicht ohne Probleme als Deutsche identifizieren, überhaupt nicht, weil sie ... von der Kultur her anders sind, aber auch von der Zivilisation her anders gelebt haben. Manche kommen einfach aus Kasachstan und ich habe jemanden aus Alma Ata. Alma Ata ist so weit ich weiss ziemlich in Sibirien. Das heisst, die haben von ihrem technischen Fortschritt her manches hier noch gar nicht kennengelernt. Die Schüler war ganz anders geschaffen ... Manche haben noch nicht mal Lesen und Schreiben gekonnt."
29 Institut für Migrationsforschung und Interkulturelle Studien der Universität Osnabrück.
30 „Hiermit beglaubigt das IMIS-Graduiertenkolleg Sektion Doktorandengruppe, dem Australischen Staatsbürger und kosmopoliten Herrn, Nicholas White, den Erwerb und die erfolgreiche Anwendung folgender „Deutscher Tugenden": Fleiss, Sauberkeit, Zuverlässigkeit, Disziplin, Höflichkeit, Ordnung, Pünktlichkeit, Sparsamkeit, sprachliche Korrektheit und Genauigkeit. Herr Nicholas White erhält mit dieser Urkunde das Recht, sich as Deutscher ohne deutsche Staatsangehörigkeit in der ganzen Welt auszuweisen."
31. Fulbrook 1992, 178-180.
32. „Ist es was besonderes, dass wir als Deutsche Auschwitz besuchen?"
33. For example, during my sojourn in their class they were studying Peter Weiss' *Die Ermittlung* 1969 [1965], a play concerning the Frankfurt Nazi trials.
34. Gruner 1992, 210-216.
35. „Ein Beispiel, das hast du, glaube ich, selbst in der Diskussion in der Klasse 11 mitbekommen. Also, es ist um die Frage gegangen, „Ist es

was besonderes, dass wir als Deutsche Auschwitz besuchen?" Da sagte der Schüler... „Es ist für mich auch keine Frage, ob ich Deutscher bin, oder nicht. Ich betrachte mich eigentlich als Mensch und als Europäer, und das ist eine Frage, die dann, alle angeht." Und ich glaube, dass die Tendenz immer stärker in diese Richtung geht. Zumindest in Deutschland haben wir die Chance, also weil Deutschland hier eigentlich sowieso ein nationales Vakuum im Bewusstsein hat. [...] Es war ja, verpönt in Deutschland den Begriff Nation oder national in der Mund zu nehmen, weil er durch die Nazis [diese] stigmatisiert wurde. Und jetzt nach der Wende, darf man es wieder sagen. [...] Aber, es gibt hier eigentlich nicht mehr - diese Nationalidentität, die auch die Franzosen zum Beispiel lokalisieren können, in Paris, nicht? [...] Es gibt in Deutschland mehrere Zentren, also, Hamburg, München, Köln, Stuttgart, Frankfurt. [...] Und diese Zentren, diese kulturellen Zentren sind keine nationalen Zentren sondern sie haben immer eine europäische Orientierung. [...] Und diese Zentralisierung, diese Zuspitzung auf eine Metropole, wie es Berlin vor dem Krieg war, gibt es nicht mehr. Und durch diese Dezentralisierung hat Deutschland viel ja die Chance gehabt, europäisch zu denken. Also, über die Grenzen hinweg. Von daher auf eine gewisse Weise interkulturelle, auch wenn es in europäischen Rahmen bleibt. Und ich glaube, dass das eine Voraussetzung dafür ist, dass sich diese Mentalität insgesamt bei den jungen Leuten entwickeln konnte. Nicht in erster Linie national zu denken, sondern so nach und nach europäisch zu denken."

References

Bade, Klaus J. Ed. *Das Manifest der 60. Deutschland und die Einwanderung.* München: Verlag C.H.Beck, 1994a.
Bade, Klaus J. „Einführung." In *Ausländer, Aussiedler, Asyl in der Bundesrepublik Deutschland*, edited by Klaus J. Bade: 9-74. Hannover: Niedersächsische Landeszentrale für politische Bildung, 1994b.
Banks, Marcus. *Ethnicity: Anthropological Constructions.* London and New York: Routledge, 1996.
Baumann, Gerd. *The Multicultural Riddle: Rethinking National, Ethnic and Religious Identities.* New York and London: Routledge, 1999.
Chapin, Wesley D. *Germany for the Germans? The Political Effects of International Migration.* Westport: Greenwood Press, 1997.
Chapman, Malcolm. "Social and Biological Aspects of Ethnicity." In *Social and Biological Aspects of Ethnicity*, edited by Malcom Chapman.

Oxford and New York: Oxford University Press, 1993.
Collin, Finn. *Social Reality: The Problems of Philosophy*. London and New York: Routledge, 1993.
Davies, Charlotte A. *Reflexive Ethnography: a Guide to Researching Selves and Others* [ASA research methods in social anthropology]. London and New York: Routledge, 1999.
Eriksen, Thomas H. *Ethnicity and Nationalism: Anthropological Perspectives: Anthropology, Culture and Society*. London and Boulder: Pluto Press, 1993.
Fulbrook, Mary. "Nation, State and Political Culture in Divided Germany 1945-90." In *The State of Germany: the National Idea in the Making, Unmaking, and Remaking of a Modern Nation-State*, edited by John Breuilly, 177-200. London and New York: Longman, 1992.
Gellner, Ernest. *Nations and Nationalism*. Oxford and Ithaca: Blackwell and Cornell University Press, 1983.
Gruner, Wolf D. "Germany in Europe: the German Question as Burden and as Opportunity." In *The State of Germany: the National Idea in the Making, Unmaking, and Remaking of a Modern Nation-State*, edited by John Breuilly, 201-223. London and New York: Longman, 1992.
Hobsbawm, Eric J. *Nations and Nationalism since 1780: Programme, Myth, Reality*. Cambridge and New York: Cambridge University Press, 1990.
Jenkins, Richard. *Rethinking Ethnicity: Arguments and Explorations*. London and Thousand Oaks: Sage, 1997.
Joppke, Christian. *Immigration and the Nation-State: The United States, Germany, and Great Britain*. Oxford: Oxford University Press, 1999.
Just, Roger. "History and Ethnicity." In *Triumph of the Ethnos* [ASA Monographs 27], edited by Elizabeth Tonkin, Maryon McDonald, and Malcolm Chapman, 71-88. London and New York: Routledge, 1989.
Lambek, Michael and Janice Boddy. "Introduction: Culture in Question." In *Culture at the End of the Boasian Century* 41(3), edited by Janice Boddy and Michael Lambek, 3-23. Adelaide: Social Analysis, 1997.
Meinecke, Friedrich. *Weltbürgertum und Nationalstaat*. München: R. Oldenbourg, 1919.
Niedersächsisches Kultusministerium. Ed. *Gesamtschule in Niedersachsen: Was heißt Gesamtschule, und wie kann sie errichtet werden?* Hannover: Niedersächsisches Kultusministerium, Referat Presse- und Öffentlichkeitsarbeit, 1991.
Okely, Judith. "Anthropology and Autobiography: Participatory Experience and Embodied Knowledge." In *Anthropology and Autobiography* [ASA Monographs 29], edited by Judith Okely and Helen Callaway, 1-28. London and New York: Routledge, 1992.

Reißlandt, Carolin. "Kontroversen über Zuwanderung: Migrations- und Integrationspolitik unter neuen Vorzeichen?" In *Themen der Rechten - Themen der Mitte: Zuwanderung, demographischer Wandel und Nationalbewusstsein*, edited by Christoph Butterwegge, 11-42. Opladen: Leske + Budrich, 2002.

Schiffauer, Werner. "Migration and Religiousness." In *The New Islamic Presence in Western Europe*, edited by Thomas Gerholm and Yngve G. Lithman, 146-158. London and New York: Mansell Publishing Limited, 1988.

Smith, Anthony D. "The Myth of the 'Modern Nation' and the Myths of Nations." *Ethnic and Racial Studies* 11 (1988): 1-26.

Weber, Eugen. *Peasants into Frenchmen: The Modernization of Rural France, 1870-1914*. Stanford: Stanford University Press, 1976.

Weiss, Peter. *Die Ermittlung. Oratorium in 11 Gesängen*. Frankfurt am Main: Rowohlt Taschenbuch Verlag, 1969 [1965].

The Pacific Solution meets Fortress Europe: Emerging Parallels in Transnational Refugee Regimes

Justine Lloyd and Anja Schwarz

1.   **Introduction**
The concept of sovereignty is today practiced through the management of flows of people, rather than of capital, in first-world nations. This growing symbolic importance of migration control lies in its capacity to define 'insiders' and 'outsiders' in terms of categories of national identity, population planning, labour market demands, as well as humanitarian values. The contemporary increase of visibility and tensions around the figure of the refugee is closely linked to this development since refugees represent a new kind of subject in relation to the binary of belonging put in place by immigration regimes. As 'inside' outsiders they are, on the one hand, guests within the sovereign nation on the basis of a discourse on human rights. On the other, they are simultaneously subjected to a contingent geo-politics of admission and residency which aim to keep them from reaching this insider status.

In Australia, official attitudes towards refugees have historically been bound up with on the project of post-war reconstruction which, although remaining deeply implicated in the White Australia policy, emerged from broadly liberal humanitarian discourses. Refugees seeking settlement in Germany during the Cold War were admitted to the Federal Republic on similar humanitarian grounds codified in the country's constitution. The last 20 years however, have seen a literal and figurative 'sea-change' in attitudes towards refugees in both countries. Formerly only marginal to debates on immigration and national identity, the figure of the refugee has increasingly taken centre stage in public discourse. Now evoked as criminalised subjects threatening to pollute national space, refugees have since been increasingly kept from entering Australian and German territory both by intensified and extended border controls and the designation of non-national spaces within both countries. It appears that these newly fortified and discursively sustained spaces deliver western welfare states such as Germany and Australia from the paradox of globalisation: the desire for an increasing openness of national economies to worldwide flows of capital in opposition to increasingly selective and restrictive immigration policies in times of equally globalised migration flows.

The Italian philosopher and social theorist, Giorgio Agamben, has argued that the figure of the refugee constitutes the starting point from which to disentangle the effects of globalisation on the nation state, arguing that "[i]nasmuch as the refugee, an apparently marginal figure, unhinges the old trinity of state-nation-territory, it deserves instead to be regarded as the central figure of our political history."[1] Following Agamben's suggestion, our examination of changing discourses on asylum migration in Australia and Germany in this article therefore aims to shed light on the impact of globalisation on both countries' immigration regimes. In doing so, our analysis brings insights from cultural geography and discourse analysis to bear on a human rights problem. We link notions of space and discourse to show how, firstly, the spatiality of the new border regimes relates to the forging of new border-identities which, for instance, can be tracked in specific discursive formations such as 'queue jumpers' and 'Asylanten' (a term for asylum seekers with highly derogative connotations)[2]. Our analysis goes on to attend to the current fortifications of national space. Rather than a simple closure of borders in response to the incursion of 'illegal' and 'dangerous' people into the nation, Australia's and Germany's new border regimes produce a new, asymmetrical mobility order. This chapter, then, examines the geographical as well as discursive sites at which this new mobility order is instated and contested in Germany and Australia. Here, relationships between stable, national selves and mobile, foreign others, between legitimate border-crossers and unruly, undocumented, improper subjects are constructed. This construction of bodies and identities is bound up with a similarly binarised institution of sovereign national spaces and indeterminate border zones: in-between places which might be outside the state's borders but still within its realm of sovereign control or, conversely, within the nation's boundaries but without access to its welfare and legislative system.

In order to acquire a specific understanding of the fracturing of the nation state's territory into different geopolitical landscapes and the diverse identities that these new power geographies produce, the next section reviews useful theoretical approaches to these contemporary developments in Australia and Germany.

2. The fraying seams of the nation-state

In spite of the global nature of these developments, the new centrality of the border in popular discourses of the nation has often been linked to *internal* insecurities triggered by a loosening of the bond between capital and national economies and the resulting decline of the welfare state.[3] However, such an approach, while appealing, ignores the extent to which these internal changes are themselves put into train by large-scale processes. The predominately national, rather than global, focus of migration research and socio-political studies might be one reason why the close interconnections between Australian and German migration regimes have often been overlooked. While there has been a considerable amount of comparative work on questions of immigration in Australia and Germany[4], this has tended to treat developments in both countries separately. By taking one country as the foil against which the specific nature of immigration discourses in the other can be contrasted and analysed more clearly, such studies predominately emphasise difference. Seldom however, have comparative projects taken on a perspective which regards Australia and Germany as embedded in the same global processes. From this point of view, recent shifts in one country's border regime such as Germany's 'Polish Solution' might indeed be regarded as being motivated by the same global processes which induced Australia's 'Pacific Solution'.[5] An analysis of the new *transnational* nature of both countries' borders thus becomes crucial for an understanding of the complex 'mobility orders' (by which we mean a regime of structures, procedures and practices regulating the movement of subjects in space) invoked by the economic and geopolitical aspirations of contemporary nation-states.[6] We use the term 'transnational' here to suggest the way in which this new border is linked to national sovereignty, but attempts to reach far beyond the traditional domains of migration control and legislation both geographically and structurally to affect the networks of labour, capital and political repression that draw and propel migration.

Marxist geographer Doreen Massey's concept of the 'power-geometries of time-space'[7] is helpful in providing us with the theoretical grounding for this development of transnational border regimes. Globalisation, Massey argues "calls up a vision of total unfettered mobility; of free unbounded space"[8], a vision that conceals its limited validity only for the domain of capital. "[C]ome a debate on immigration and, [neo-liberal proponents of globalisation] have recourse to another geographical imagination altogether". Related to this first vision is a second imagination of "defensible places", of the rights of "local people" to their own "local places", of a world divided by difference, a geographical imagination of nationalisms.[9] Massey suggests that boundaries around communities, such as those around the nation state, gain augmented importance in the context of these two interrelated imaginations of space in the age of globalisation. National borders become "envelopes of space-time" functioning as "a way of domesticating space-time, of fixing and stabilising, or trying to fix and stabilise – for the task is an impossible one – meanings and identities in relation to time/space."[10]

To take this idea further, the introduction of a transnational dimension to the idea of the border suggests that it may mediate times and spaces that are beyond the grasp of the simple triad of the local-national-global relationship. A closer description provided below of the kind of spaces produced by this development constitutes a first point from which to embark on comparative work on Australia and Germany's current immigration regimes. In a second step, Massey's suggestion to 'think space relationally' and to inquire into how identities are formed in these spaces by "mutable ongoing productions,"[11] will be taken up in our analysis of the identities produced at both nations' increasingly transnational borders.

A. Border Spaces – Buffer Zones

The multidimensional development of First-World borders outlined by Massey is not restricted to the complex of asylum migration alone. As noted by Ruth Wasem of the US Library of Congress, increasingly close links between the country's economic and migration policies have resulted in a 'pushing out' of US-American borders. The mobility order thus produced keeps some migrants from entering the country through visa restrictions, whereas others gain free access on the basis of socio-economic class. "In one instance we (i.e., the United States) are pushing the border out to our consulates overseas in terms of visa issuances. We are [also] pushing our borders out by including immigration provision in free trade agreements".[12] The situation can thus be described as one in which, as Australian sociologist Michael Humphrey has suggested, first-world nations seek to control their borders 'at a distance', via this new transnational border. Instead of the line drawn around the nation state, as borders are habitually imagined and visualised on maps, this instalment of 'buffers' prompts an understanding of frontiers not as lines, but as zones.[13]

In the European context and, more specifically concerned with asylum migration, British geographer Sarah Collinson has commented on a similar emergence of transnational spaces around the nation state which she labels 'buffer zones'. Collinson argues that restrictive immigration policies of nations such as Germany force their neighbouring states "into a 'buffer role', obliging them to absorb asylum-seekers who fail to gain entry into western Europe and/or restrict asylum-seekers' access to the borders of potential 'receiving states'."[14] She takes the term 'buffer zone' to

> denote an identifiable geographical zone 'protecting', by non-military means, a group of powerful and essentially stable states from a perceived non-military security threat deriving from a proximate region of economic and political instability. It thus denotes the age-old idea of seeking to rescue borders by extending their depth ... providing an additional control zone controlling or distancing western [nations] from actual or potential refugee movements.[15]

Whereas such 'buffers' turn the area surrounding the nation into an extended border zone, a country's internal territory undergoes similar transformations when faced with refugees. This two-directional – internal and external – loosening of the link between the nation state and territory is exemplified most clearly by the 'special procedures' Australia and Germany have established in relation to air travel. On the one hand, steps taken by each country to extend and displace migration checks and controls along the trajectories of refugee movements have contributed to the transnational expansion of buffer zones. Firstly, changes to migration law, introduced by numerous European countries in 1987 and Australia in the early 1990s, made airlines, rather than officials, liable for carrying improperly documented migrants. Secondly, the placement of Airport Liaison Officers in refugees' countries of origin or transit ensured greater scrutiny of incoming air passengers, thus enlarging the area over which both states can exercise some form of control. On the other hand, special airport procedures for asylum seekers introduced by Germany in 1993 have resulted in the creation of non-national spaces *within* the national territory. The detainment of refugees in these so-called 'international zones' serves to uphold the fiction that these migrants have not entered German territory by declaring these spaces to be outside the nation's legal territory.[16] Refugees arriving there undergo an 'accelerated procedure' without full access to the German legal system which prevents them from fighting more effectively for their right to asylum.[17] Over the past decade, this programme has been subject to harsh criticism after asylum seekers died in transit during deportation from Frankfurt airport.[18] While no comparable legislation exists in Australia to include such camps within airports, the tensions between local, state and federal governments have been long-felt in the legal status of Sydney airport, which is placed out of reach of comment and criticism by local residents and politicians because of its tenure of Commonwealth land. Following several governments' push to privatise state-owned infrastructure, the airport's freight and passenger operations were sold in 1998 and are now managed by Macquarie Bank in partnership with 'border control agencies'. The 'buffer zone' is therefore a complex response to the international and domestic aspects of neo-liberal economic policy and the new relationship it forges between the state and its citizens.

B. Border-Identities

Massey alludes to the forms of identity produced by means of defining and controlling mobility in border regions. These identity formations are closely connected to what Pieterse has called integration and hierarchy: the increasing networking of capital markets and investment, at the same time as an intense stratification of access and privilege to first world economies.[19] This 'solution' of differentiated border configuration and access, depending on the nature of exchange, can be seen as arising from a sharp disjuncture between what Arjun Appadurai calls the 'financescape' and the 'ethnoscape' of the contemporary transnational situation. In a widely cited essay first published in 1990, Appadurai suggested different categories of flows, which when taken together offer a framework of examining the "new global cultural economy ... as a complex overlapping, disjunctive order that cannot any longer be understood in terms of existing centre-periphery models".[20] Appadurai's 'scapes' suggest that our contemporary spatial framework is not 'fixed' as a geographical landscape might be, but rather amorphous and flowing, made up of networks and boundaries of various sizes. He regards these as the 'building blocks' of contemporary imagined worlds. Referring to the identities produced by these 'scapes' Appadurai considers "the individual actor [as] the last locus of this perspectivial set of landscapes".[21] Following these provocative formulations of the new dimensions of the relationship between the individual and the space of the global, we are interested in the new kind of 'border identities' created by the transnational 'scapes' of migration flow and control.

Whereas the traditional model of the nation state allowed 'international' engagement and recognition at the border in terms of subjects meeting the nation state on equal terms, such a transnational model would have to account for far more layered and multitudinous notions of alterity. Faced with the figure of a border guard who is no longer the neutral arbiter of access to national territory but now the militarised and hostile agent of a new refugee regime, many of the subjects intertwined with the transnational border do not possess the kind of identity desired by the new immigration schemes (rich, highly skilled, young). This problem is compounded by the fact that often such refugees come from areas that might be seen to 'lack' sovereignty such as ethnically defined regions within a larger nation. These migrants are often forced to conceal their nationality and are thus are kept from engaging with the nation state 'behind the border' on meaningful, legal terms.

In a Foucauldian sense, we might therefore regard mobility in this zone as "the set of effects produced in bodies, behaviours, and social relations by a certain deployment deriving from a complex political technology". Together with the social categories of class, gender and race, this technology produces discursively specific identity-effects at the border.[22] More specifically, the creation of buffer zones at the border determines the subjectivity of asylum seekers as 'dangerous', 'polluting' or 'criminal', since their only modes of access have become limited to hard-to-come-by visitor visas, expensive forged entry permits or people smuggling. "Whichever option is chosen," British immigration lawyer Frances Webber states laconically, "the result of success is illegal entry."[23] An international newspaper report on the Ukrainian-Polish border from 2003 exemplifies this impact of transnational border spaces on identity formations in an extreme way. In the article, Krzystof Dyl, commander at the Huwniki border station reported that he had identified "suspected terrorists", when his unit caught "two Pakistanis with scorpion tattoos" that suggested their membership in a fundamentalist Islamic group: "They were sent directly from Huwniki to Guantanamo Bay."[24]

The new border regime does however not produce this criminalising effect in all the bodies that transgress its zone. One highly prized figure of global economy, the highly mobile, multi-lingual and culturally savvy transnational corporate entrepreneur materialises in one dimension, in global trade centres, tax-free and special economic zones and airport cities. Other bodies experience more precarious transformations of their selves. As Saskia Sassen's work has shown, the stateless person, the undocumented worker, and the economic (guest) worker are part and parcel of the same fluidity of global capital, and have appeared alongside the global entrepreneur as flashpoints for discourses of exclusion and marginalisation.[25] Some travellers are obviously facilitated and made hyper-mobile, while others are patently slowed down and fixed in space. The border in this discourse is no longer a uniform entity delineating a bounded community, but a kind of differentiated mobility machine, which determines different modes of access for the different groups made mobile by the processes of globalisation. In the next section of the paper, we examine the Australian situation in detail, and provide an account of how this transnational development of border-spaces and identities has arisen in a national context, before going on to cast a similar gaze on the German situation.

3. **Australia: a parable of borders**
   If the Tampa had not happened, John Howard would have invented it.[26]

Since its election in 1996, the Australian Federal government, a conservative coalition of Liberal/National parties, has reinforced the pattern established under previous Labor governments and attempted to prevent access to Australia's borders to flows of would-be refugees. The Asia/Pacific regional focus which characterised the prior Keating government has been re-oriented towards a stronger relationship with the USA, and a distancing from Australia's 'Asian' neighbours to the north of the continent. This detachment from the nation's geographical and political proximity to Asia has occurred while the Federal government has expounded neo-liberal philosophies of increased and deregulated trade flows, culminating in 2004, when Australia signed a Free Trade Agreement with the USA. This retreat from the imaginary of an Australia within the Asia/Pacific region established by governments since the 1980s has transformed the border between Australia and its northern 'others', particularly Indonesia, into a 'hyper-real' space in Australian public discourse, which is defined as always-already vulnerable and in need of constant surveillance and monitoring.[27]

The most striking example of this shift in the nation's geopolitical imaginary emerged in 2001, when the now firmly entrenched 'border protection' model became the corner-stone of the Government's migration framework during the *Tampa* affair of August and September. The Tampa, a Norwegian vessel, had been refused permission to land on Australian territory after it had picked up about 250 asylum seekers from a sinking ship in international waters and turned around intending to take them for processing at Christmas Island. The 'border protection' legislation passed in concert with lengthy debates on the Tampa incident in Parliament introduced a new distinction into the imaginary of Australia's national territory, calling the Australian mainland and its territorial waters 'the Australian migration zone', and the islands on its northern coastline 'excised off-shore places' in which the country's refugee and asylum laws do not apply (see figure 1).[28] Ostensibly designated to controlling flows of asylum-seekers brought by organised criminal networks to Australian territory, this border excision figured as part of a wider suite of policies dubbed the 'Pacific solution'. The 'solution' has involved a new protection, humanitarian and refugee visa regime for asylum applications. It also entailed the involvement of Australia's Navy in border patrol activities, most explicitly in Operation Relex, first touted at the National Security Committee on August 28, 2001. The committee instructed the Navy to implement a "Maritime control and response plan to detect and intercept and warn vessels carrying unauthorised arrivals for the purpose of deterring SIEVs (Suspected Illegal Entry Vehicles) from entering Australian waters".[29] Once apprehended, these undocumented arrivals were to be taken to sites across the Pacific run by the International Organisation for Migration and protected by the Australian Federal Police (these practices continue to be implemented today). In the months following the passing of Australia's new asylum legislation, camps designated for 'offshore' processing were established in Nauru, Manus and Christmas Island where asylum seekers are eligible only for Temporary Protection Visas which limit residence, deny refugees family reunion, full social security and equal treatment under the law.[30]

These policies were fully revealed to the electorate in September 2001 by the incumbent Prime Minister, John Howard, during a seemingly un-winnable election campaign. Together with the discussed changes to the nation's borders, Howard introduced a set of policies that prevent access to the automatic protections and rights normally held to apply to all people under Australian sovereignty for 'unauthorised arrivals', that is, the predominately Afghani and Iraqi people who had reached Australia by sea during the late 1990s.[31] After being returned to power in 2001, partly on the strength of these policies and their popularity after the September 11 attacks in the USA, the Howard government persisted with its mission to redefine Australia's borders and thereby repel would-be refugees.

By mid-December, the some of the most surreal aspects of this policy were highlighted when the Government secretly excised four islands close to the Western Australian mainland from the nation's territory in an attempt to thwart a boat load of suspected asylum seekers. *The Age* newspaper reported on 17 December 2001 that the excision came as a surprise to the two Western Australian councils responsible for the four islands which were excised, both based in the mainland coastal towns of Carnarvon and Geraldton. The first two of the islands, Bernier Island and Dorre Island, are about 200 metres apart and are uninhabited, providing sanctuary to five of the 26 most threatened mammal species in Australia, including the Shark Bay mouse and banded hare wallaby. Dirk Hartog Island, the third island, is the only permanently inhabited island and only within a couple of kilometres of the mainland it is occupied by only two people, Kieran Wardle and his partner, who run 6500 sheep and provide accommodation for surfers and divers. The fourth island, Faure Island, is tucked behind a peninsula and, Mr Wardle was reported in the *Age* as saying, it is so far from the open ocean "you would run into the mainland before you found it". It is run as a private nature reserve. Unlike Christmas Island, which at 600 kilometres from Jakarta, is actually closer to Indonesia than it is the Australian mainland, and located on traditional Indian Ocean sea trading routes, the islands on the West Australian coast had never before been a target of asylum-seeking boats. The now-you-see-it, now-you-don't phenomenon of the 2001 excisions was widely reported and commented on. The status of the islands in the wake of the legislation brought home to Australians on the mainland what is distinctly odd about the whole notion of territory constructed by the Pacific solution: these places are both part of Australian national space and outside it. They had entered what novelist Bernard Cohen has called 'not-Australia'[32], the system of detention camps and migration centres that physically and discursively releases the nation-state from its responsibilities towards refugees and forecloses the 'non-citizen' (in the non-nation) from any recourse to the framework of international human rights. Although the suspected 'illegal entrants' turned out to be a fisherman from Sri Lanka operating illegally in Australian waters, with no intention of claiming asylum, this move and the nature of the space it created epitomises the international phenomenon of the selective application of rights in border zones as a new strategy of migration control our study is interested in.

By enforcing limited suspensions of territorial sovereignty in response to specific instances of transgression by sea, the Australian Government has literally moved the border so that entry to Australia as a refugee has become almost impossible other than by air. Until 2005, this legislation, which attempted to excise more than 4000 islands on the nation's northern coastline had been blocked by the opposition-controlled Senate. The ability to pass this legislation permanent finally came into effect in July 2005, when power in the Senate shifted to the Government's

Coalition. The Labor party, should it ever be returned to power, has already stated that it would change some aspects of the policy, but maintain the excision zone for Christmas Island as 'the prime asylum seeker processing and detention facility'.[33]

The short-term costs of this policy have been high, and have been unfavourably contrasted with previous policy by the Senate Select Committee investigating the legislation. It noted concern about the cost of managing offshore the processing facilities at Nauru and Manus Island, as well as Christmas Island. It concluded that the so-called 'Pacific Solution' was not a cost-effective way to deal with this issue.[34]

Advocates such as Human Rights Watch were also greatly disturbed by Australia's new immigration regime and protested against the post-election decision on October 19, 2001 to return an Indonesian fishing vessel containing asylum seekers to international waters, after the vessel reached the "excised" Australian territory of Ashmore Reef. The most serious concern was that the new legislation, by permitting "offshore entry persons" to be excluded from Australia without access to asylum determinations, undermines Australia's international obligation of *non-refoulement* as codified in Article 33 of the 1951 Convention relating to the status of refugees[35]. A letter from Human Rights Watch to the PM of Australia on 31 October 2001 argued that

> The obligation of nonrefoulement must be upheld in all of Australia's territories, regardless of whether such actions take place within or outside of the "migration zone." Until the law is amended to conform to international standards, ministerial discretion must be exercised to ensure that each refugee arriving in Australia (whether inside or outside the "migration zone") is protected from direct or indirect return to a place where his or her life or freedom would be threatened.[36]

In the Australian case, the granting of such protection when returning refugees is particularly problematic because many of the boats which arrive in this zone travel through or depart from Indonesia, which is not a party to the 1951 Refugee Convention and lacks laws and procedures for determining refugee status.

Historically, the beach has been an important trope of a vulnerable limit space for national sovereignty in Australia (and the place of arrival of eighteenth century colonial explorers and settlers). The excision of the nation's northern sea boundaries from the country's migration zone, and the designation of 'boat people' as exceptional, illegal, unwanted non-citizens is also clearly iniquitous when compared with the far higher numbers of tourists and travellers on temporary work permits who overstay visas or work illegally.[37] In spite of such historical, financial and legal concerns, the policy has been regarded as highly successful in managing the tensions between global flows of people and sovereignty discussed above. Clearly, there are far-reaching implications of this withdrawal from borders and concomitant redirections of mobility. This uneven distribution of mobility depends not on the intentions of those entering the territory of Australia, but rather upon their mode of transport and thus socio-economic and legal status.

The introduction of these kinds of policies has not been limited just to Australia. In the next section we shift our attention from the case of Australia's wandering borders to show how efforts to control mobility via the control of border zones are also common to European migration regimes.

4. Germany: safely 'buffered'?

It has often been observed that the creation of a seamless European space as envisioned by the EU member states is predicated upon the construction of an external boundary. The realisation of the European Union therefore entails the removal of technical, physical and fiscal barriers to the freedom of intra-European travel of goods, persons, services and capital. However, this abolition of internal barriers goes hand in hand with more stringent control of the individuals seeking entry to a European country. This process has in the past has been complicated and further accelerated by the dismantlement of the Eastern Block states and civil war in former Yugoslavia setting in motion large numbers of migrants and refugees seeking entry to EU member states. More than exemplifying this process of EU border formation, the transformation of Germany's immigration regime in a number of instances prefigured or even instigated these changes on a broader European level. In what follows we provide an analysis of the changes to Germany's border regime over the past two decades. It offers insights not only on the national level but also helps to delineate the changing nature of border spaces and identities in the greater European region.

One might describe the history of the German nation state, as Jost Halfmann has done somewhat euphemistically, as one of "insecurity about the borders of the state territory and about the institutions and rules of inclusion in the state".[38] The reverberations of the end of what Mirjaana Morokvasic has called the 'bi-polar world' in 1989 have been felt most keenly in the dissolution of Germany's internal boundary and rapid ratification of the 'Oder-Neisse line', the border between Germany's territories and its eastern neighbours, which was a prerequisite to political reunification.[39] Simultaneously, this latter border became the site of anxious re-inscriptions of national sovereignty. In the years following the country's reunification, the influx of civil war refugees from Yugoslavia and ethnic Germans from the east led to an increase of net migration which placed Germany for several years at the top of immigration countries both in absolute and relative figures.[40] It went hand-in-hand with an increase of the number of asylum seekers, peaking at 438,191 in 1992.[41] Reacting to this development, the Federal Republic sought both discursively and physically to assert control over its eastern border, a boundary which was perceived as increasingly unstable. Public and political debates of the time often gave expression to this sense of uncertainty regarding the Eastern border, if not voicing an outright rejection of those who arrived from beyond that line. As Klaus Bade and Jochen Oltmer argue, it seems that the confusion of binaries of self/other and foreign/native which thus far had determined German identity formation further destabilised a national identity already thoroughly unsettled by the process of unification itself.[42]

In this climate of insecurity and heated political debate, the Federal Republic began to advocate the 'non-arrival policies' which currently characterise Europe's stance on immigration. These policies grow out of a particular geopolitical imaginary, as will be argued below. As Morten Kjaerum, director of the Danish Centre for Human Rights, argues, the formation of this European immigration regime took place in several stages:

> In the first period starting in the 1980s, these policies developed with a multi-faceted approach: visa requirements combined with carrier sanctions [ratified in the Schengen convention] ...; the creation of international zones in airports...; and safety zones within the home country where individuals received international assistance and protection (Kurdish refugees in Iraq and Bosnian refugees in Bosnia-Herzegovina). ... The next step in implementing these policies has been the posting of immigration officers of Airline Liaison Officers (ALO) in either countries of origin of asylum seekers or important transit countries such as Pakistan and Turkey.[43]

In a third step, EU member states ratified what came to be called the 'safe-third country' rule. Initially drafted in the 1970s as the concept of the 'first country of asylum' to prevent multiple applications for asylum in several states simultaneously or successively, the notion of safe third countries is now a standard feature. In spite of growing evidence for the dangers involved in deportation, it argues that refugees entering EU member states from 'non-persecuting' countries are not entitled to asylum and can therefore be sent back across the border.

In the German context, the legislation only became possible with a much-debated change of the country's constitution passed as part of the so-called 'asylum compromise' of 1993. Previously, the right to political asylum had been enshrined in Article 16 of the country's post-WWII constitution. The generous acceptance of people fleeing in small numbers from Eastern European Communist countries had often served to "embarrass and discredit adversary nations".[44] The new legislation which replaced it was accompanied by the drawing up of a list of countries considered 'safe' in the sense implied by the legislation. In 1993, the list already included Austria, the Czech Republic, Finland, Norway, Poland, Sweden, and Switzerland together with those countries which were party to the Schengen agreement.[45] With the enlargement of the EU in May 2004, this 'secure' status has been further consolidated, since all of Germany's Eastern neighbours are now EU member states. Related to the notion of 'safe-third-countries', and ratified simultaneously, was the notion of 'safe countries of origin' which is based upon a list of countries considered as 'non-persecuting'. Unless refugees from these countries are able to provide special evidence, they are prohibited from filing a claim to asylum. While refugee advocates argue that such practices run counter to the principle of *non-refoulement*, Germany as well as other EU member states claim that the asylum seeker is only returned to a country that has signed or ratified several human rights agreements and should therefore be relied upon to uphold civil liberties.[46]

Lists of 'safe-third-countries' and 'safe countries of origin' depend on the concurrent ratification of re-admission agreements which pave the way to a 'smooth' return of unwanted migrants to either their country of origin or those territories from which they entered the country. Sarah Collinson points out that Germany has been actively promoting this development since the 1990s, signing bilateral agreements with Romania (September 1992), Bulgaria (November 1992), Poland (May 1993) and the Czech Republic in November 1994.[47] In these treaties, the Federal Republic promised financial compensation to its eastern neighbours for accommodating much greater numbers of refugees than before and for the re-enforcement of their own eastern borders.[48] Interestingly, this process of creating what Collinson calls 'buffer states' did not stop on the level of the first concentric circle around Germany. Instead, these agreements were to a large degree dependent on one another:

> [T]he Czech Republic was unwilling to take back deportees from Germany until agreements had been secured with Romania, Bulgaria and Slovakia ... and the Slovak Republic was unwilling to implement an agreement with the Czech Republic until it had reached agreements with Hungary, Ukraine and Romania.[49]

By 2005, Germany had ratified 28 bilateral readmission agreements with European and non-European states that provide for a fast return of migrants from these regions, among them Vietnam, Hong Kong, China, Morocco, Algeria, Serbia and Montenegro, Macedonia, and Albania. The Federal Republic is currently in the process of drafting further agreements with Armenia, Georgia, Lebanon, Egypt and Afghanistan.[50] With the progressive synchronisation of the EU's refugee and asylum legislation the drawing up of such lists and the ratification of readmission agreements, formerly only practiced on a bilateral level, is now being pursued at a supranational level by the European Union itself. Endorsed by a decision by the Council of the European Union in November 2002, the EU Commission has since ratified readmission agreements with Hong Kong, Macao, Sri Lanka and Albania and is seeking further agreements with Morocco, Algeria, Ukraine, Russia, Pakistan, China, and Turkey.[51]

In spite of critical voices among human rights advocates, the combined measures of 'safe third countries', 'readmission agreements', as well as the 'international zones' mentioned at the outset of this paper, have proven highly effective from the perspective of the German state. The total number of people claiming political asylum has dropped continuously with the implementation of this catalogue of measures. With only 50.563 applications in 2003, the number fell to the levels of the early 1980s[52] and reached another low with 28.914 in 2005.[53]

In the context of the main argument of this paper, the changes to Germany's asylum legislation outlined here have resulted in a paradoxical enforcement as well as blurring of the nation's borders. Refugees seeking to engage with the nation state are prevented from reaching Germany's boundaries, turning the parachute into the only means by which they can reach the Federal Republic legally, as one commentator has sarcastically pointed out.[54] At the same time, the line at which the state's sphere of influence ceases has been extended, to now encompass a 'buffer zone' from the Ukraine to the Mediterranean. Taking up Appadurai's notion of the differentiated 'scapes' that contribute to shifting, amorphous landscapes, one could argue that the line which formerly defined Germany's boundary has been expanded to cover a zone outside the nation space within which the state continues to exert power over migrant and racialised bodies. This expansion of the state's 'ethnoscape' coincides with a shrinking of the state's 'ideoscape' of human rights, that zone within which the state acknowledges its responsibility for refugees. One might argue that Germany's illegal immigrants – figures for this group vary between 800 000 and 1.2 million,[55] embody the epitome of this development: although occupying the same geographical spaces as German citizens and fulfilling vital functions for the nation's economy, they have no or very limited means of accessing the state's legislative, educational and health systems while simultaneously living in constant fear of the state's power over their bodies.[56]

The following final remarks on Europe's most recent refugee crisis, the influx of African migrants on its southern borders, will further illustrate this disjunction between the 'scapes' of state control and those of refugee rights in Europe's contemporary immigration regime. It will, finally, also reveal the mechanisms behind the disappearance of the figure of the refugee from Germany's contemporary discourse on asylum migration, a disappearance which results from the paradoxical expansion and shrinking of nation space which characterises Europe's current immigration regime.

A. Ceuta. Grounding the transnational border

In recent years, Europe's southern border has become the new focus of struggles over refugee migration. In the summer months of 2004 and 2005, this boundary figured almost daily in the European media as numerous vessels carrying undocumented, predominately black African migrants were intercepted in their attempt to cross the Mediterranean between Morocco and Spain or Algeria/Libya and Italy. At the same time other abandoned boats were washed ashore carrying either no passengers or corpses. The Mediterranean has since acquired the label of 'Europe's biggest mass grave', for thousands of migrants die of thirst, sunstroke or simply drown there every year. This 'death zone' is most tangibly materialised in form of the fences protecting Ceuta, a Spanish enclave on Moroccan territory. Ceuta has been a favourite destination for migrants bound for Europe since 1999, when they first started to enter the enclave illegally, making their way over or through the border fences or swimming along the Moroccan coast until reaching Ceuta's beaches.[57]

Ceuta's border fortifications already exceed the historical inner-European Cold War constructions. In order to engage successfully with the EU territory behind the border, migrant have to penetrate a double line of barbed-wire fences four metres high between which Spain's Guardia Civil patrols a small stretch of bitumen. Infra-red and video cameras as well as sensors further enforce this construction.[58] However, the 60 million Euros already spent by the European Union on these fortifications do not appear to suffice. After the death of eight migrants during a number of spectacular break-ins in August 2005, the EU has agreed to spend another 26 million on a third fence and a form of ground cover euphemistically labelled the 'barbed-wire cushion'.[59]

Coinciding with these border reinforcements, the EU is currently attempting to introduce the concept of the 'buffer zone' in Northern Africa. Until now, the EU's legal and ethical space, extended to Ceuta's borderline, delimiting a line along which refugees could engage with the EU and lay claim to political asylum once they managed to get through the border fortifications. Currently, these 'scapes' are being detached from the EU's geographical territory in a process similar to that described above for

Germany's eastern borders. In a first attempt at establishing this North African 'buffer', 40 million Euros were granted to Morocco for the guarding of its southern borders. Further funding has been promised to the governments of Algeria, Tunisia and Libya to facilitate the training of border guards and civil personnel in asylum procedures.[60] Although unsuccessful, the suggestion made by Otto Schily, Germany's Minister of the Interior, in October 2004 to establish camps for the processing of asylum claims in Northern Africa has to be regarded as a further step in disrupting the linkage between nation state and the legal sphere of asylum. The re-admission agreement signed between Italy and Libya, which entitles Italy to return to its southern neighbour all undocumented migrants found in Italian waters furthers this agenda.[61] Spain and Morocco signed a similar document in December 2005.[62] These combined efforts, it seems, are already proving successful from a European perspective. Whereas 55000 people were recorded as having made the transition from Africa to Europe in 2004, only 12000 did so in 2005. However, rather than reading this as a positive indication of a decrease in illegal immigrants, Michael Schwelien remarks laconically: "Where the new tragedies take place, we no longer know".[63]

The EU's fortified external border in the Mediterranean turns Europe's southern shorelines into the tombs of innumerable refugees who die on the passage between Africa and the EU. Spain's beaches, the preferred holiday destination of many German tourists, have become a 'costa de muerte' patrolled every morning to clear the beach of bodies before the sunbathers arrive and take their place.[64] None of the visiting tourists would regard these shores as demarcating the boundary of the German nation state. The migrants arriving here figure merely as 'Spain's refugee problem' or 'Italy's asylum seeker crisis' in Germany's public discourse. In fact, these are the spaces in which the German state now engages with refugees as part of a greater European immigration regime. Quite apart from keeping asylum seekers from reaching the nation's border, the successful transformation of Germany's boundaries into flexible extended buffer zones has also resulted in the complete disappearance of asylum seekers from national discourse.

5. Conclusion

This chapter surveys a current trend in two wealthy nations, Germany and Australia, to 'push out their borders' and thereby transnationalise the once clearly-delineated boundaries between nation states and their others. In times of increasingly globalised flows of capital, both countries invoke powerful tropes of hypermobility (tourism, migration and the circulation of commodities), while endorsing immigration procedures which place at a distance the sites at which unwanted migrants arrive. We have explored the ways in which these procedures have produced a new kind of space which is neither of the nation nor excluded from it, but rather, flexibly and strategically networked within it. Far from being a place of firm and fixed identities and clear negotiations between self and other, the border is increasingly being vacated and positioned outside the 'ideoscapes' of human rights and citizenship. This new non-border space – legally defined and controlled by the state, yet strangely 'a-national' and deterritorialised for those located within it – thus offers a 'solution' to the conflicting demands of global flows of capital on the one hand and of national sovereignty on the other.

This global phenomenon, in the local cases of both Australia and Germany, has produced the precarious identity of the detainee. Whether located in the 'international zone' of Germany's airports, in Australia's notorious detention centres or in offshore camps on Nauru or, in the possible future, in Northern Africa, the detainee embodies the dialectical tensions inherent in the uneven distribution of contemporary mobility. Giorgio Agamben, whose argument for the centrality of the figure of the refugee in western political history has informed this paper, shifts our perspective on such developments. For Agamben, an acknowledgement of the refugee's situation is not simply an act of charity or altruism. Rather, "in a world in which the spaces of states have thus been perforated and topologically deformed" such an acknowledgement becomes necessary for the "political survival of humankind" altogether.[65]

The challenge therefore remains to formulate ways of imagining the nation that do not delegate refugees to the margins of both discourse and territorial imagination. An alternative imaginary would instead stress the interrelatedness of, on the one hand, stable notions of Germanness or Australianness and, on the other, those unstable subjectivities located in the perforated transnational geographies at the nation's boundary.

Notes

1. Agamben 2000, 21.
2. An analysis of the uses of these terms is provided in Gelber 2003 for the Australian and Mattson 1995 and Koopmans and Statham 1999 for the German context.
3. See, for instance, Halfmann 1997, 267.
4. Becker et. al. 2001; Bade 1993, 1996; Bommes et. al. 1999; Cica 1998; Luchtenberg 1997; Luchtenberg and McLelland 1998; Nier and Böke 2000; Thomas 2001.
5. Hoadley 2003, 13.
6. Rogers 2004, 164.
7. Massey 1999, 27-28.
8. Ibid, 33.
9. Ibid, 38-39.
10. Ibid, 1999, 42.

11. Massey 2004, 5.
12. Wasem 2003, 1.
13. Humphrey 2002; 2003.
14. Collinson 1996, 76. The example of Native American trackers from the Navajo and Tohono O'odham peoples, usually based on the US-Mexican border, who in May 2004 visited the Eastern End of the EU along the heavy forested and unfenced Polish-Ukrainian border might indicate the extend to which these processes are part of a greater global process that even transcends the transnational developments we focus on in this paper.
15. Collinson 1996, 78.
16. See Boswick 2000, 51.
17. Zimmermann 2000.
18. According to an Amnesty International report, a Nigerian national died of heart failure in 1994 during his forced deportation after having been "restrained, sedated and gagged with a device made by one of the police officers at home from socks and a belt from a window blind." (Amnesty International 1999). In 1999, another asylum-seeker from Sudan died after being restrained in a similar manner during his forced expulsion.
19. Pieterse 2002.
20. Appadurai 1990, 32.
21. Ibid, 33.
22. Foucault 1978, 127.
23. Webber 1996, 2-3.
24. Quoted in Nolte 2004, 31.
25. Sassen 2000.
26. MacCallum 2002, 47.
27. Khoo 2001, 39.
28. The Migration Amendment (Excision from Migration Zone) Act 2001 designates Christmas Island, Ashmore Reef and Cartier Islands, the Cocos (Keeling) Islands, and Australian sea and resources installations as "excised offshore place[s]" deemed outside the country's "migration zone." All laws relating to Australia's sovereignty over its Exclusive Economic Zone are still upheld. See Crock and Saul 2002, 99-116.
29. Marr and Wilkinson 2003, 66.
30. Browning 2004.
31. A very high percentage of these arrivals before 2001 were recognised as refugees. In the year ending 30 June 1999, 97 per cent and 92 per cent of Iraqis and Afghanis were recognised as refugees respectively. See Crock and Saul 2002, 33.
32. Cohen cited in Perera 2002, 25.
33. Senate 16 June 2003, 11347.

34. Senate Committee Report 2002, 88.
35. Article 33 states that "No Contracting State shall expel or return a refugee in any manner whatsoever to the frontiers of territories where his life or freedom would be threatened on accounts of his race, religion, nationality, membership of a particular social group or political opinion."
36. Senate Committee Report 2002, Chapter 4.
37. 1999-2000 and 2000-2002 were the only years since 1995 in which unauthorised arrivals by sea exceeded those by air. (DIMIA website).
38. Halfmann 1997, 267.
39. Morokvasic 2004.
40. Bosswick 2000, 48.
41. For background information on Germany's recent immigration history see Bade and Oltmer 2004.
42. Ibid.
43. Kjaerum 2002, 515-516.
44. Teitelbaum 1984, 430.
45. Abell 1997, 573.
46. See ibid, 573.
47. Collinson 1996, 85.
48. See Abell 1997, 583.
49. Collinson 1996, 86-87.
50. BMI 2005, 64.
51. Ibid, 64.
52. Ibid, 47.
53. Tagesschau 2005.
54. Klingst 2004.
55. Tendbrock and Uchatius 2002.
56. Anderson 2003.
57. Schwelien 2001.
58. Ibid; Idem, 2005b.
59. Schwelien 2005a.
60. Tagesschau 2004.
61. Klingst 2004.
62. A first attempt at treating Morocco as a 'safe-third-country' in returning undocumented migrants failed in November 2005 when the Moroccan officials simply dumped refugees returned from Spain in the desert at the country's southern borders.
63. Schwelien 2005b.
64. Bade 2001, 35; Schwelien 2003.
65. Agamben 2000, 25.

Parts of the Australian sections of this chapter have been presented to the

Activating Human Rights and Diversity Conference: Local and Global Voices, Southern Cross University, Byron Bay, July 2003 and at Crossing Borders: Culture, Media, Economy, University of Erlangen, Germany, November 2004. Justine wishes to thank the session participants and organisers for their useful comments and questions on those occasions.

References

Abell, Nazare Albuquerque. "Safe Country Provisions in Canada and in the European Union: A critical Assessment." *International Migration Review*, 31(3) (1997): 569-590.

Agamben, Giorgio. *Means Without End: Notes on Politics*. Minneapolis: University of Minnesota Press, 2000.

Albrecht, Hans-Jörg. "Fortress Europe? Controlling Illegal Immigration." *European Journal of Crime, Criminal Law and Criminal Justice* 10(1) (2002): 1-22.

Amnesty International. "Death of Sudanese Asylum-seeker." 3 June 1999. <http://www.web.amnesty.org/ai.nsf/print/EUR230011999?OpenDocument> (May 2002).

Anderson, Philip. *'Dass Sie uns nicht vergessen ...'. Menschen in der Illegalität in München. Eine empirische Studie im Auftrag der Landeshauptstadt München*. München: Landeshauptstadt München, 2003.

Appadurai, Arjun. "Disjuncture and Difference in the Global Cultural Economy." *Public Culture*, 2(2) (1990): 1-24.

Appadurai, A. *Modernity at Large: Cultural Dimensions of Globalisation*. Minneapolis & London: University of Minnesota Press, 1996.

Bade, Klaus J. "Die neue Einwanderungssituation im vereinigten Deutschland: Geschichtserfahrung und Zukunftsangst." *Europa gegen den Rest der Welt. Flüchtlingsbewegungen – Einwanderung – Asylpolitik*, edited by Christoph Butterwegge and Siegfried Jäger, 87-95. Köln: Bund Verlag, 1993.

Bade, Klaus J. "Einwanderungskontinent Europa. Migration und Integration am Ende des 20. Jahrhundert." *Zuwanderung und Asyl. Schriftenreihe des Bundesamtes für die Anerkennung ausländischer Flüchtlinge* 8 (2001): 13-54.

Bade, Klaus J. and Jochen Oltmer. *Normalfall Migration*. Bonn: Bundeszentrale für politische Bildung, 2004.

Becker, Jens, Dorothea M. Hartmann, Susanne Huth and Marion Möhle. "Gesellschaftliches Handlungsfeld Migration." In *Diffusion und Globalisierung. Migration, Klimawandel und Aids – Empirische Befunde*, edited by Jens Becker, Dorothea M. Hartmann, Susanne Huth and Marion Möhle, 46-139. Wiesbaden: Westdeutscher Verlag, 2001.

Bommes, Michael, Stephen Castles and Catherine Wihtol de Wenden.

"Migration and Social Change in Australia, France and Germany." *IMIS Beiträge* (13) 1999.
Bosswick, Wolfgang. "Development of Asylum Policy in Germany." *Journal of Refugee Studies* 13(1) 2000: 43-60.
Browning, Julie. "Negotiating Purpose and Place at Topside Camp, Nauru." *Paper delivered to Transforming Cultures Seminar.* University of Technology Sydney, August 2004.
BMI. Bundesministerium des Innern. *Zuwanderungsrecht und Zuwanderungspolitik.* Berlin, 2005.
Cica, Natasha. "Silence on Race Issues in Recent Elections." *Alternative Law Journal* 23(5) (1998): 256-257.
Collinson, Sarah. "Visa Requirements, Carrier Sanctions, 'Safe Third Countries' and 'Readmission'. The Development of an Asylum 'Buffer Zone' in Europe." *Transactions of the Insititute of British Geographers* (1996): 76-90.
Crock, Mary and Ben Saul. *Future Seekers: Refugees and the Law in Australia.* Sydney: Federation Press, 2002.
DIMIA. Department of Immigration and Multicultural and Indigenous Affairs. "Fact Sheet 81: Australia's Excised Offshore Places." 10 September 2002. <http://www.immi.gov.au/facts/81excised.htm> (July 2002).
Foucault, Michel, *The History of Sexuality* (Volume 1). New York: Vintage Books, 1978.
Gelber, Katherine. "A Fair Queue? Australian Public Discourse on Refugees and Immigration." *Journal of Australian Studies* 77 (2003): 23-30.
Halfmann, Jost. "Immigration and Citizenship in Germany. Contemporary Dilemmas." *Political Studies* XLV (1997): 260-274.
Human Rights Watch. "World Report." 2002.
<http://hrw.org/wr2k2/refugees.html> (November 2005).
Hoadley, Stephen. "Immigration, Refugee, Asylum, and Settlement Policies as Political Issues in Germany and Australia." *National Europe Centre Paper* 81 (2003).
Humphrey, Michael. "Humanitarianism, Terrorism and the Transnational Border." *Social Analysis* 46(1) (2002): 118-124.
Humphrey, Michael. "Refugees: An Endangered Species?" *Journal of Sociology* 9(1) (2003): 31-43.
Khoo, Tseen. "Penal Posturing: Australia's Patriotic Muscularity and the Myth of a 'Fair Go'." *Overland* (2001): 36-39.
Kjaerum, Morten. "Refugee Protection Between State Interests and Human Rights. Where is Europe Heading." *Human Rights Quarterly* 24 (2002): 513-536.
Klingst, Martin. "Schillys Lagerkoller. Asylcamps in Afrika? Der Innenminister provoziert mit seiner Flüchtlingspolitik." *Die Zeit* (33)

2004.
Koopmans, Ruud and Paul Statham. "Challenging the Liberal Nation-State? Postnationalism, Multiculturalism and the Collective Claims Making of Migrants and Ethnic Minorities in Britain and Germany." *The American Journal of Sociology* 105(3) (1999): 652-696.
Luchtenberg, Sigrid and Nicola McLelland. "Multiculturalism and the Role of the Media. A Comparative Study of Australian and German Print Media." *Journal of Intercultural Studies* 19 (1998): 187-206.
Luchtenberg, Sigrid. "Worüber berichten die Printmedien? Eine vergleichende Analyse deutscher und Australischer Zeitungen." *Medien und Fremdenfeindlichkeit. Alltägliche Paradoxien, Dilemata, Absurditäten und Zynismen.* Opladen: Leske & Budrich (1997): 255-276.
MacCallum, Mungo. "Girt by Sea." *Quarterly Essay* 5 (2002): 61-73.
Mares, Peter. *Borderline: Australia's Response to Refugees and Asylum Seekers in the Wake of the Tampa.* Sydney: UNSW Press, 2002.
Marr, David and Marion Wilkinson. *Dark Victory.* Crows Nest: Allen & Unwin, 2003.
Massey, Doreen. "Imagining Globalisation: Power-Geometries of Time-Space." *Global Futures: Migration, Environment and Globalisation*, edited by Avtar Brah, Mary J. Hickman and Mairtin Mac an Ghaill, 27-44. London and New York: MacMillan & St Martins, 1999.
Massey, Doreen. "Geographies of Responsibility." *Geografiska Annaler* 86 B(1) (2004): 5-18.
Mattson, Michelle. "Refugees in Germany. Invasion or Invention?" *New German Critique* 64 (1995): 61-85.
McMaster, Don, *Asylum Seekers: Australia's Response to Refugees.* Melbourne Uni Press, Carlton South, 2001.
Mintzel, Alf. *Multikulturelle Gesellschaft in Europa und Nordamerika. Konzepte, Streitfragen, Analysen und Befunde.* Passau: Wissenschaftsverlag Rothe, 1997.
Morokvasic, Mirjana. "Settled in Mobility': Engendering Post-Wall Migration in Europe." *Feminist Review* 77 (2004): 7-25.
Nederveen Pieterse, Jan. "Faultlines of Transnationalism: Borders Matter." *Bulletin of the Royal Institute for Interfaith Studies* 4(2) (2002): 33-48.
Nicholson, Frances. "Implementation of the Immigration (Carriers' Liability) Act 1987. Privatising Immigration Functions at the Expense of International Obligations?" *The International and Comparative Law Quarterly* 46(3) (1997): 586-634.
Nier, Thomas and Karin Böke. Ed. *Einwanderungsdiskurse. Vergleichende diskurslinguistische Studien.* Wiesbaden: Westdeutscher Verlag, 2000.
N.N. "Ruddock secretly excises islands." *The Age*, 18 December 2002.
N.N. *Tagesschau*, October 2004.
N.N. *Tagesschau*, 9 January 2005.
Nolte, Astrid. "Navajo Indian Trackers Trail Illegal Immigrants on

Europe's Wild Frontier." *The Sunday Telegraph*, 30 May 2004.
Perera, Suvendrini. "A Line in the Sea: the Tampa, Boat Stories and the Border." *Cultural Studies Review* 8(1) (2002): 11-27.
Rogers, Alisdair. "A European Space for Transnationalism." In *Transnational Spaces*, edited by Peter Jackson, Philip Crang and Claire Dwyer, 164-182. Routledge, London, 2004.
Sassen, Saskia. *The Global City: New York, London, Tokyo*. Princeton: Princeton University Press, 2000.
Schwelien, Michael. "Tod in der Straße von Gibraltar." *Die Zeit* 46 (2001).
Schwelien, Michael. "Wenn Grenzschützer Leichen am Traumstrand bergen." *Die Zeit* 45 (2003).
Schwelien, Michael. "Die Todessprünge von Ceuta." *Die Zeit* 41 (2005a).
Schwelien, Michael. "Die Einfalltore." *Die Zeit* 42 (2005b).
Senate Legal and Constitutional References Committee. *Migration Zone Excision: an Examination of the Migration Legislation Amendment (Further Border Protection Measures) Bill 2002 and Related Matters*, Canberra: AGPS, October 2002.
<www.aph.gov.au/senate/committee/legcon_ctte/mig_BP/Report/report.pdf> (November 2005).
Teitelbaum, Michael S. "Immigration, Refugees, and Foreign Policy." *International Organisation* 38(3) (1984): 429-450.
Tendbrock, Christian and Wolfgang Uchatius. "Geschlossene Gesellschaft." *Die Zeit* 13 (2002).
Thomas, Brook. "Civic Multiculturalism and the Myth of Liberal Consent. A Comparative Analysis." *The New Centennial Review* 1(3) (2001): 1-35.
Thouez, Colleen. "Towards a Common European Migration and Asylum Policy?" *The Journal of Humanitarian Assistance* Working Paper 27 August 2000. <http://www.jha.ac/articles/u027.htm> (November 2005).
UNHCR. "Preliminary Observations by UNHCR on the Austrian Presidency. Strategy Paper on Immigration and Asylum Policy." 9 September 1998. <http://www.proasyl.de/texte/europe/eu-a-unh.htm> (November 2005).
Wasem, Ruth Ellen. "U.S. Immigration Policy after September 11: Pushing Out the Borders." *Discussion paper given at Transnational Seminar Series, Sociology, University of Illinois Urbana Champaign*. 31 October 2003.
<http://www.soc.uiuc.edu/people/papers/Illinois_lecture.pdf> (November 2005).
Webber, Frances. *Crimes of Arrival: Immigrants and Asylum-Seekers in the New Europe*. London: Statewatch Publications, 1996.
Zimmermann, Elizabeth. "Algerian Refugee Commits Suicide in Frankfurt Airport's Asylum Zone." *World Socialist Web Site*. 24 May 2000. <http://www.wsws.org/articles/2000/may2000/asyl-m24_prn.shtml>

(March 2002).

Figure 1: map of excision zones (Senate Committee Report 2002, 9)

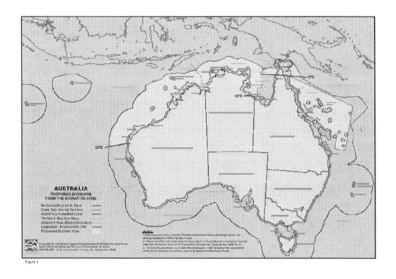

Index

Aboriginal English xiii, 31-2, 51-59
Agamben, Giorgio 247-8, 263
Althusser, Louis 125
Anti-Semitism 114, 240
Appadurai, Arjun 178, 251-2, 260
Appiah, Anthony 8
Assmann, Jan 3, 7
Assimilation xiv, 11, 13, 15-6, 47, 54, 67-9, 74-6, 140, 144, 177, 182-4, 190
Asylum 186, 189, 226, 228, 248, 250-2, 254-62
ATSIC 16
Auschwitz 7, 18, 237-241, 244
'Aussiedler' (German 're-settlers' from Eastern Europe and the Soviet Union) 77, 226, 228, 235-6
Austin, John xii, 41
(Australian) Aborigines 9-19, 32, 52-8, 103, 183, 218
Authenticity / Authentizität 33, 58, 128, 197
Autobiography 128, 130, 134-6
- transcultural 137-53
- and nation 135-6
Bade, Klaus 81, 258
Balibar, Etienne 2, 180, 182
Barry, Brian 161, 173
Barthes, Roland 127
- *Roland Barthes par Roland Barthes* 145
Beliefs 73, 94-5, 115
Belonging 133-4, 137, 139, 144, 178-9, 189, 193, 198-9, 247
Benjamin, Walter 18
Bitburg Affair 7
'Bodenlosigkeit' (having 'no ground under one's feet') 141-143
Border ix, xv, xvi, xviii, 128, 137, 145, 147-52, 178-9, 182, 186-7, 241, 247-63
Borges, Jorge Luis 121
Bourdieu, Pierre 2-3, 82, 127
Braidotti, Rosi 129-30, 137, 153
Bringing them Home Report 1, 11-4, 96
Brunton, Keith 11-2, 100, 104
Büchner, Georg 163
Buffer zone xviii, 250-3, 259-62
Butler, Judith xiii, 31, 36-7, 41-5, 50
- *Excitable Speech* x, 39-40
Caldwell, Arthur 69

Cantonese 131
Castro, Brian
- *Birds of Passage* 130
- *Looking for Estrellita* xv, 130-1
Christian Democratic Union (CDU) ix, 83-4
Censorship / Zensur xi, 33, 40, 50, 59
Ceuta 161-2
Citizenship 177-9, 184, 187
- dual citizenship 187, 193
Clark, Geoff 16
Clark, Manning 9
Clendinnen, Inga 17
Cohn-Bendit, Daniel 77-8
Collective memory 1
Colonial expansion 181-2, 204-11
Colonialism / Kolonialismus xvii, 203, 205
Colonial science / Koloniale Wissenschaft 210
Cosmo-multiculturalism 197
Counter-discourse 132, 135-6
Cultural diversity ix, xiv, 67-8, 74-84, 178-9, 184-5, 188, 190-1, 193-4, 197-9, 242
Devine, Frank 18
Green Party (Germany) / Die Grünen 84, 190, 193
'Diffusionsmodell' (model of diffusion) 211-217
Discrimination / Diskriminierung xiv-xv, 92, 103, 116
Duffy, Michael 18
Dürrenmatt, Friedrich
- *Der Tunnel* 165, 168
'Einwanderungsland' (country of immigration) 74, 187, 227-8, 242
Enlightenment xv, 161-5, 168, 188
Esser, Hartmut 75-76
Ethnicity xii, xvi, 70-1, 177, 185, 190, 192, 197, 198, 231-2, 234-5
- fictive ethnicity 180
Excision 254-6
Exclusion xvi, 164, 179, 183-4, 189-90, 193-4, 235, 253
Fassbinder, Rainer Werner
- *Lola* 163
- *Die Ehe der Maria Braun* 163, 166
- *Angst essen Seele auf* xv, 162, 166-8
- *Die Sehnsucht der Veronika Voss* 163
Faul, Erwin 80-1
fictionality / Fiktionalität xiii, 31, 32, 58
Flusser, Vilèm
- *Bodenlos* xv, 131-2, 141-4
Forced removal 1, 12, 14, 91, 96-101

Foucault, Michel x, 31, 95, 121, 123, 127-8, 134, 136, 143, 180-1
- *L'Archéologie du savoir* 125-6,
- *Les Mots et les choses* 123
- *La Volonté du savoir (Histoire de la sexualité 1)* /
    Der Wille zum Wissen (Sexualität und Wahrheit I) 33-44, 125
- *'Qu'est-ce qu'un auteur?'* 126
Franklin, Benjamin 165, xii-xiii
Freud, Sigmund
- *Moses and Monotheism* 3
Gaita, Raimond 13-4, 16
Geißler, Heiner 76-7, 82
Genocide xiii, 1-2, 11-3, 17-8, 96, 238
'Germanness' 16, 192-3, 225, 237-40, 263
Germany's Immigration Act 82-4
'Gesamtschule' (integrated high school) 225, 232-3, 235-7, 241
Globalisation 174, 177-9, 184-5, 190, 193, 247-9, 253
Goldhagen Debate 6, 107
Grasby, Al 70-1, 74
Guest worker / Gastarbeiter xv, 46-7, 133, 162, 165-68, 187, 226, 228, 253
Gwynne, Phillip
- *Deadly, Unna?* / *Wir Goonyas, ihr Nungas* 31, 53, 56-8
Habermas, Jürgen 5, 7, 95, 113
Hage, Ghassan 10, 67, 189, 193, 197
Hanson, Pauline 10, 13-4
- *The Truth* 14
'Heimat' (homeland) 47, 49, 128, 131-4, 138-9, 143, 149
Herron, John xiv, 91, 96-102, 111, 112, 115
Herzog, Werner
- *Where the Green Ants Dream* xv, 162, 164, 166-9
- *Das Enigma des Kaspar Hauser* 163
- *Woyzeck* 163
- *Aguirre, die Rache Gottes* 163
'Historikerstreit' (historian's debate) 113-4
Hohmann, Martin xiv, 91, 104-15,
Holocaust xiii, xiv, 5-8, 10-4, 17-8, 91, 95-116, 226, 237-40
Howard, John xvi, 10-1, 72-3, 102, 184-7, 254
Hybridity 132, 144-9
Ideology 71, 80, 93, 125, 190
Immigration xvi, xviii, 10, 15, 46, 67-84
Inclusion 179, 184, 193-4, 198, 238, 257
Indigeneity / Indigenous ix, xiii-xv, xii, 14-9, 91, 95-104, 166, 169, 183, 203, 208, 231, 241
Indigenous knowledge xvii, 203, 208, 217-8

Injury / Verletzung 32, 39-42, 45-6, 51
Integration ix, xiv, xvi, 15-6, 47, 67-8, 70, 74-5, 82-4
International zones xviii, 251, 258-260
Interpellation /Anrufung 32-33, 39, 46, 53, 57-9
Jay, Martin 17
Jews xiv, 1, 6, 7, 12, 15-8, 105-13, 132-3, 146, 150, 196
Johnson, Carol 93, 95
Jupp, James 69, 72
Keating, Paul 10, 184, 253
- Redfern Speech 10
Koelbl, Herlinde
- *Familie Deutschland* 190-3
Kohl, Helmut 6, 10-1
Contextualisation / Kontextualisierung 38, 40-2, 46-9, 216
Kühn Memorandum 74
Labor Party 9-10, 256
'Leitkultur' (leading, or hegemonic culture) xvi, 133, 188, 204
Localisation / Lokalisierung 37, 212-6
Luhrmann, Baz
- *Strictly Ballroom* xv, 163, 171-4
Mabo 10, 13-4, 168-9
Manne, Robert 13-4, 17-8
Mainstream ix, xv, xvi, 52, 70, 75, 77, 103, 133, 163-4, 168, 171, 173-4, 185, 187, 190
Massey, Doreen 249
McGuinness, Padraic 12-3, 16
Merkel, Angela ix
Migrancy 144, 146,
Mitscherlich, Alexander and Margarethe 5, 7, 12
- *The Inability to Mourn* 5
Morgan, Patrick 12
Mudrooroo
- *Wild Cat Falling* 53-55
- *Doin' Wildcat* 53-55
Multiculturalism xi, xiv, xvi, 16, 67-84, 161-3, 168, 173-4, 177-9, 184-5, 187-8, 190-1, 194, 197-99, 228
Multilingualism 151-2
Nation
- nationalism 15, 17, 132, 135, 139-41, 183, 190-1, 198, 229, 230, 237, 239, 249
- national imaginary 179, 187, 192, 197,
- national space xviii, 128, 178, 189, 193, 247-8, 250-1, 255
National Socialism 6, 12, 15, 18-9, 105, 112-113, 191, 226
Native title 103, 164, 168-169
'Naturgemälde' (image of nature) 215

New Australians 69-70
Nomadism 128-30
Non-refoulement 259
Offshore processing 254, 256, 263
One Nation Party 19, 177, 187
Osnabrück xvii, 225, 232, 236, 241
Pacific solution 249, 254-7
Parliament 83-4, 91-5, 103-4, 114-6, 254-6
Parody / Parodie 41-2
Performativity / Performativität x, 40-1, 144, 149, 182
Political discourse ix, 70, 72, 77, 93
Portuguese 131, 149-52
Postema, Gerald 9
Power-knowledge constellations / Macht-Wissen Konstellationen 35, 212, 217-8
Psycho-geography 181-2
Race 10, 12-3, 17, 68, 80, 103, 177, 183, 185-7, 189, 190-3, 198, 231
Racism 11, 13, 15, 18, 81, 234
Readmission agreements 260
Refugees xviii, 143-4, 178, 186-8, 190, 226, 247-64
Resignification / Resignifikation xiii, 31-3, 36, 38, 40-2, 45-6, 51-9
Reynolds, Henry 169
Rhetoric xii, xv, 12, 15, 72, 80, 99-102, 133, 140, 185
Romanticism xv, 134, 162-3
Rootedness / Seßhaftigkeit 128-33
Roussel, Raymond 123
Safe third country 159
Schmidt, Thomas 77
Science / Wissenschaft 203-18
Self-critical community 8, 19
Shakespeare
- *Coriolanus* 124
Simonis, Heide 49-51
Situatedness / Situierung 148
South Africa xi, 1
Spivak, Gayatri Chakravorty 127
Statistics xv, 97, 103, 110, 112, 114
Stolen generation xiv, 11, 17, 91, 95-102, 115-6
Strehlow, Carl 165
Subversion 32, 43, 130
Tampa 186, 253-4
'Tätervolk' (nation of perpetrators) 106-7, 113-4
Tatz, Colin 13
Teacher 225-42

Terra nullius 169
Thomas, Steve
- *The Hillmen* xv, 163, 169, 171, 173-4
- *Harold* 169
- *Black Man's Houses* 169
Tibi, Bassam 80
Traditional knowledge / Wissenstraditionen 207, 213, 217
Translation xii, 151-3
Transnationality xvi, xviii, 68, 132, 177-8, 189, 198-9, 204, 249-53, 262-3
'Trauerarbeit' (work of mourning) 7
Trauma xii, 1, 32, 42, 45-6, 51, 98, 139
- 'perpetrator trauma' 3-4, 6-9, 11, 17, 18-9
Truth 7, 18, 94-6, 100-2, 111-113, 115, 134, 181
Türkische Gemeinde Deutschland (Turkish Community in Germany) 83-4
UNESCO 68
Validity claims 95
Van Gogh, Theo ix
'Vergangenheitsbewältigung' (coming to terms with the past) 1-3, 15
Walzer, Michael 8
Watson, Don 10
'Weltwissenschaft' (world science) 216-7
White Australia Policy 15, 67, 69, 183-4, 247
Windschuttle, Keith 12, 15
Zahalka, Anna
- *Welcome to Sydney* 194-196
Zaimoglu, Feridun 33, 46-51, 58-9
- *Kanak Sprak* xiii, 31-2, 47-50

Notes on Contributors

Dr Fiona Allon is a Research Fellow at the Centre for Cultural Research, University of Western Sydney. Her research explores issues of mobility, place, and belonging, with particular emphasis on everyday life and the spatial transformations associated with globalisation. She is currently working on a number of projects that explore the city, urban culture and contested spaces. One recent project, *Open Cities*, focuses on experiences of 'urban citizenship' in Sydney and Berlin, and brings together her joint research interests in Germany and Australia. She has taught at universities in Australia and the UK, and was a Lecturer in the *Euroculture* program at the Georg-August Universität, Göttingen, in 2002. She has published widely in books and journals, including most recently chapters in *Media/Space: Place, Scale and Culture in a Media Age* (Routledge, 2004), and *Who's Australia – Whose Australia?: Politics, Society and Culture in Contemporary Australia* (WVT, 2005).

Dr Katharine Gelber is a Senior Lecturer in Politics and International Relations at the University of New South Wales. Her research interest are in human rights, free speech and hate speech. She has published *Speaking Back: the free speech versus hate speech debate*, (John Benjamins Ltd 2002), and has published articles in *Review of International Studies*, the *Australian Journal of Politics and History*, the *Australian Journal of Political Science* and the *Australian Journal of Human Rights*. She is currently engaged in an ARC-funded large research project into freedom of political speech in Australia.

Dr. Steffi Hobuss ist wissenschaftliche Mitarbeiterin am Institut für Kulturtheorie und lehrt Philosophie an der Universität Lüneburg. Studium der Philosophie, Germanistik, Sozialpsychologie und Geschichte an der Universität Hannover, Promotion in Bielefeld mit einer Arbeit zu Wittgenstein. Zur Zeit ist eine Studie zur Theorie des Sehens in Vorbereitung.
Dr Steffi Hobuß is a Lecturer at the Institut fur Kulturtheorie and teaches philosophy at the Universitiy of Lüneburg. She has published *Wittgenstein über Expressivität: Der Ausdruck in Körpersprache und Kunst* (Internationalismus Verlag 1998); *Konversionen. Fremderfahrungen in ethnologischer und interkultureller Perspektive* (together with Iris Därmann and Ulrich Lölke, Rodopi 2004) sowie *Erinnern verhandeln. Kolonialismus im kollektiven Gedächtnis Afrikas und Europas* (together with Ulrich Lölke, Westfälisches Dampfboot 2006).

Dr Justine Lloyd is an Australian Research Council Postdoctoral Fellow at the University of Technology, Sydney, working on comparative media history. She has taught Australian, cultural and media studies in Australia and Poland. She is also a board member of the Octapod Association, a community arts and new media organisation based in Newcastle, Australia (www.octapod.org).

Dr. Ulrich Lölke studierte Philosophie, Kunstgeschichte, Theologie und Freie Kunst in Berlin, Frankfurt a.M., Hamburg und in den USA. 1999 promovierte er an der Universität Düsseldorf mit einer Dissertation über die Philosophie im postkolonialen Afrika (2001 erschienen). Ulrich Lölke war Gastwissenschaftler an der University of Ghana, Legon und an der Zentralen Einrichtung für Wissenschaftstheorie und Wissenschaftsethik (ZEWW) der Universität Hannover. Er lehrt Philosophie und Kulturtheorie an der Universität Lüneburg. Er publizierte u.a. *Zur Lokalität von Wissen. Die Kritik der* local-knowledge-*Debatte in Anthropologie und internationaler Zusammenarbeit* (Reihe *Focus Afrika* 2002); *Konversionen. Fremderfahrungen in ethnologischer und interkultureller Perspektive* (zusammen mit Iris Därmann und Steffi Hobuß, Rodopi 2004) sowie *Erinnern verhandeln. Kolonialismus im kollektiven Gedächtnis Afrikas und Europas* (zusammen mit Steffi Hobuß, Westfälisches Dampfboot 2006).
Dr Ulrich Lölke teaches philosophy and cultural theory at the University of Lüneburg, and ist he author of Kritisch Traditionen – Afrika: Philosophie als Ort der Dekolonisation (2001) and *Zur Lokalität von Wissen. Die Kritik der* local-knowledge-*Debatte in Anthropologie und internationaler Zusammenarbeit* (2002).

Professor Tim Mehigan, formerly at the University of Melbourne, has been Foundation Chair of Languages and Head of Department of Languages and Cultures at the University of Otago in Dunedin, New Zealand since 2004. He is widely published in German literature and philosophy from the 18th century to the present. He is the author of two monographs on Robert Musil (*The Critical Response to Musil's 'Man without Qualities'*, Camden House 2003; *Robert Musil*, Reclam 2001) and one on Heinrich von Kleist (*Text as Contract. The Nature and Function of Narrative Discourse in the 'Erzählungen' of Heinrich von Kleist*, Lang 1988) and has edited several essay collections on literature, aesthetics and foreign language pedagogy (most notably: *Heinrich von Kleist und die Aufklärung*, Camden House 2000). He is the author of numerous articles and essays on writers ranging from Lessing, Goethe and Eichendorff to Brecht, Hemingway, Musil and Thomas Bernhard. In 1996 he initiated and directed an international festival of student drama in Leverkusen, Germany. Tim is the current president of the German Studies Association of Australia, was a Humboldt Fellow at the LMU in 1994 and 1995 and was elected Fellow of the Australian Academy of the Humanities in 2003.

Dr A. Dirk Moses studied in Australia, Scotland, the USA, and Germany, and has taught in the Department of History at the University of Sydney since 2000. He is the author of *German Intellectuals and the Nazi Past* (Cambridge, 2007), and editor of *Genocide and Settler Society: Frontier Violence and Stolen Indigenous Children in Australian History* (Berghahn Books, 2004); *Colonialism and Genocide* (Routledge, 2007), with Dan Stone; and *Colony, Empire, Genocide* (Berghahn Books, 2008).

Russell West-Pavlov is Professor of English at the Free University of Berlin. Among his recent publications are *Representations of Space on the Jacobean Stage: From Shakespeare to Webster* (Palgrave 2002), *Transcultural Graffiti: Diasporic Writing and Teaching of Literary Studies* (Rodopi 2005), and *Bodies and their Spaces: System, Crisis and Transformation in Early Modern Drama* (Rodopi 2006).

Anja Schwarz is a junior lecturer and PhD candidate at the Free University of Berlin. Her MA thesis examined multicultural discourse in Australia and Germany and her current PhD project undertakes an analysis of the beach as a (post)colonial paradigm.

Dr Nicholas White is a social policy advisor with the state public service in Victoria, Australia. He holds a PhD from the University of Melbourne, awarded for an ethnographic study of German national identity based upon 18 months of participant observation in Germany. During this period he was a guest of the Institute for Migration Research and Intercultural Studies of the University of Osnabrück.

Printed in the United States
By Bookmasters